MONTY'S MEN

MONTY'S MEN

The British Army and the Liberation of Europe, 1944–5

John Buckley

YALE UNIVERSITY PRESS
NEW HAVEN AND LONDON

For information about this and other Yale University Press publications, please contact:
U.S. Office: sales.press@yale.edu   www.yalebooks.com
Europe Office: sales@yaleup.co.uk   www.yalebooks.co.uk

Set in Sabon MT by IDSUK (DataConnection) Ltd
Printed in Great Britain by TJ International Ltd, Padstow, Cornwall

Library of Congress Cataloging-in-Publication Data

Buckley, John (John D.)
Monty's men : the British Army and the liberation of Europe / John Buckley.
pages cm
Includes bibliographical references and index
ISBN 978–0–300–13449–0 (hardback)
1. World War, 1939–1945—Campaigns—Western Front. 2. Allied Forces. Army Group, 21st. 3. Montgomery of Alamein, Bernard Law Montgomery, Viscount, 18871976. I. Title.
D756.3.B83 2013
940.54'1241—dc23

2013023139

A catalogue record for this book is available from the British Library.

10 9 8 7 6 5 4 3 2 1

Contents

Illustrations and Maps

Plates

Photo credits: IWM are courtesy of the Imperial War Museum; Challis are courtesy of the estate of Ernest Harwood; Lucas are courtesy of Matthew Lucas; Henderson are courtesy of Mrs Marylou Henderson.

Maps pages

Acknowledgements

As ever with a project of this nature, I owe a huge debt of gratitude to many institutions and individuals who aided and supported my research and writing over a long and protracted period. The staff at the Imperial War Museum, London; the UK National Archives, Kew, London; The National Army Museum, London; Churchill College Archives, Cambridge; the Laurier Centre for Military Strategic and Disarmament Studies, Wilfrid Laurier University, Waterloo, Ontario; the US National Archives, Maryland; and the Liddell Hart Centre, King's College, London, were all, as ever, helpful and efficient. The Arts and Humanities Research Council funded a period of leave for me to complete the manuscript, and my colleagues in the Department of History, Politics and War Studies at the University of Wolverhampton saw fit to free me from arduous duties and provide financial support for research trips on many occasions. I drew on the archives and libraries of many museums but I am most indebted to the staff at the King's Shropshire Light Infantry Museum, Shrewsbury and the Staffordshire Regiment Museum, Lichfield.

Colleagues and friends also offered insight and guidance over many years and I am grateful to Professor Mike Dennis, Professor Dieter Steinert, Professor John Benson, Professor Malcolm Wanklyn, Dr Howard Fuller, Dr Spencer Jones, Dr Peter Preston Hough, Professor Stephen Badsey, Dr Peter Caddick Adams, Phil McCarty, Iain McFarlane, Ian Daglish, Toby McLeod, Professor Terry Copp, Dr Michael Bechthold and Professor Gary Sheffield. I have presented various papers at conferences and seminars in the UK, USA and Canada and received useful comments and feedback from them all, most notably the British Commission for Military History and the Society for Military History. Tom Almond scrutinised the entire manuscript and eliminated many failings and weaknesses, whilst Paul Ruewell's discursive ruminations in Normandy were always illuminating. I am, in particular, grateful to Matthew Lucas whose dedication to our oral history project produced a rich source of testimony that I have been able to tap into for this book.

My greatest thanks are to my family – Julia, Annabel and Edward – who put up with my absences at archives, on fieldtrips or whilst simply hidden away in front of a computer. And finally to my late dad, whose war stories, however tall and imagined, nevertheless inspired me to want to know more.

John Buckley – Bridgnorth, Shropshire, February 2013

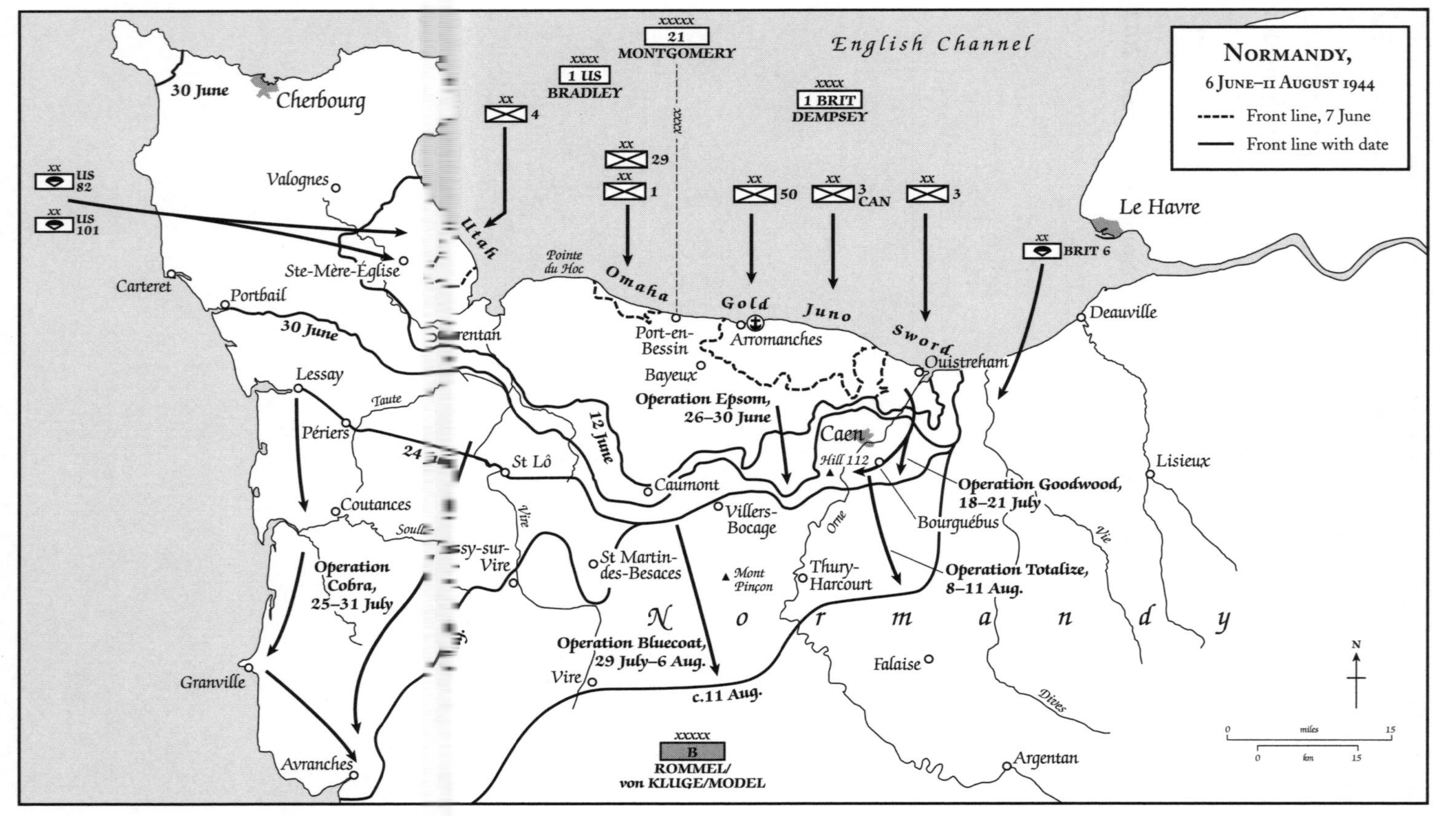
NORMANDY,
6 JUNE–11 AUGUST 1944
Front line, 7 June
Front line with date
English Channel
21
MONTGOMERY
1 US
BRADLEY
1 BRIT
DEMPSEY
4
29
1
50
3 CAN
3
US 82
US 101
BRIT 6
Cherbourg
30 June
Valognes
Ste-Mère-Église
Carteret
Portbail
Utah
Pointe du Hoc
Omaha
Gold
Juno
Sword
Le Havre
Deauville
Port-en-Bessin
Arromanches
Bayeux
Ouistreham
Lessay
Taute
Périers
St Lô
12 June
Operation Epsom, 26–30 June
Caen
Hill 112
Caumont
Villers-Bocage
Operation Goodwood, 18–21 July
Bourguébus
Lisieux
Vie
Orne
Coutances
Soulle
Vire
Operation Cobra, 25–31 July
St Martin-des-Besaces
Mont Pinçon
Thury-Harcourt
Operation Totalize, 8–11 Aug.
Normandy
Operation Bluecoat, 29 July–6 Aug.
Falaise
Granville
Vire
c.11 Aug.
Dives
B
ROMMEL/
von KLUGE/MODEL
Avranches
Argentan
N
miles
km
0
15

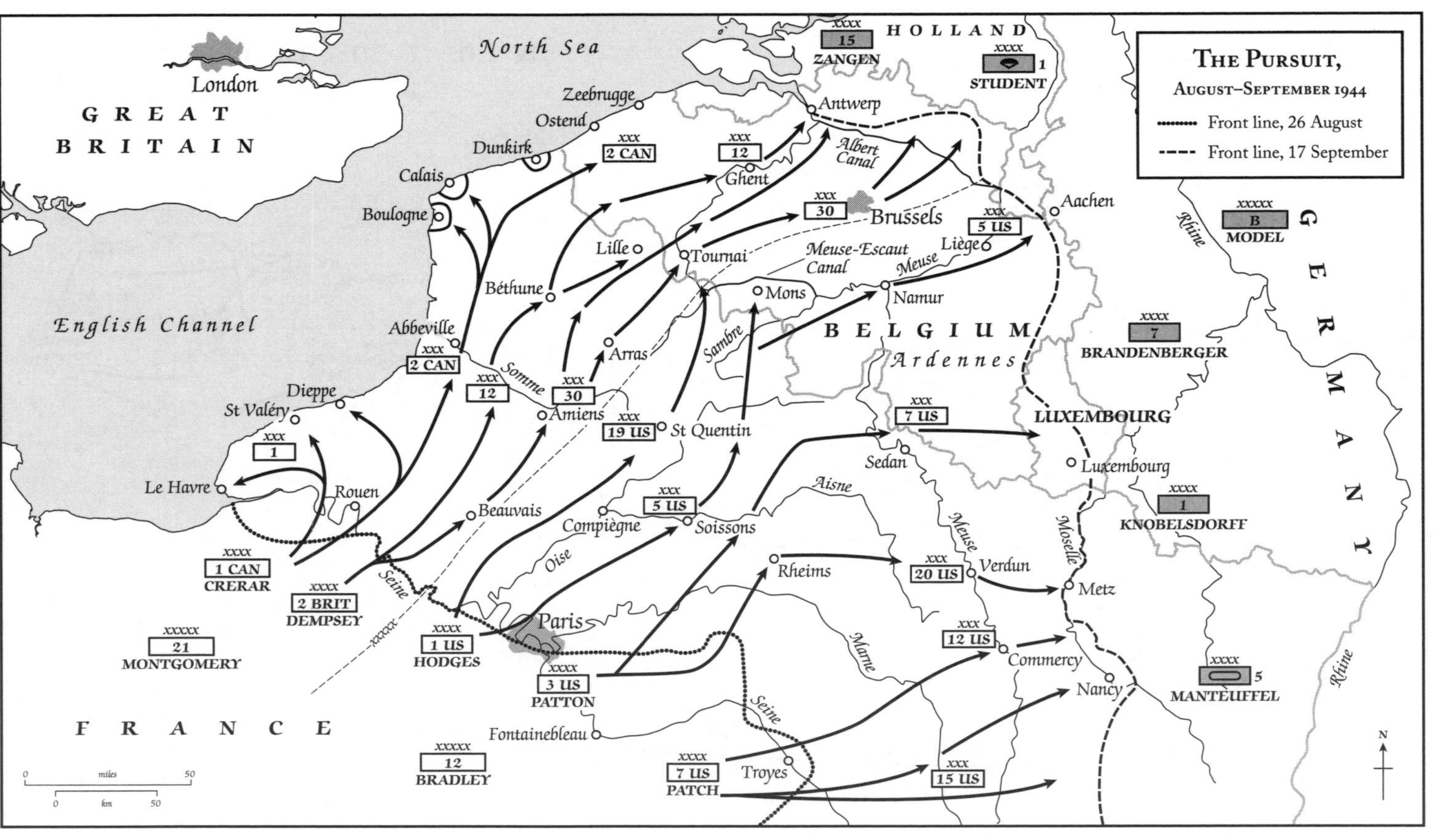
THE PURSUIT,
AUGUST–SEPTEMBER 1944
Front line, 26 August
Front line, 17 September
GREAT BRITAIN
London
North Sea
English Channel
HOLLAND
BELGIUM
Ardennes
LUXEMBOURG
GERMANY
FRANCE
Zeebrugge
Ostend
Dunkirk
Calais
Boulogne
Abbeville
St Valéry
Dieppe
Le Havre
Rouen
Béthune
Lille
Tournai
Ghent
Antwerp
Albert Canal
Brussels
Meuse-Escaut Canal
Mons
Namur
Liège
Aachen
Arras
Amiens
St Quentin
Beauvais
Compiègne
Soissons
Paris
Rheims
Sedan
Verdun
Metz
Commercy
Nancy
Luxembourg
Fontainebleau
Troyes
Somme
Sambre
Meuse
Aisne
Oise
Seine
Marne
Moselle
Rhine
xxxxx 21 MONTGOMERY
xxxx 1 CAN CRERAR
xxxx 2 BRIT DEMPSEY
xxx 1
xxx 2 CAN
xxx 12
xxx 30
xxx 19 US
xxx 5 US
xxx 7 US
xxx 20 US
xxx 12 US
xxx 15 US
xxxxx 12 BRADLEY
xxxx 1 US HODGES
xxxx 3 US PATTON
xxxx 7 US PATCH
xxxxx
xxxx 15 ZANGEN
xxxx 1 STUDENT
xxxxx B MODEL
xxxx 7 BRANDENBERGER
xxxx 1 KNOBELSDORFF
xxxx 5 MANTEUFFEL
0 miles 50
0 km 50
N

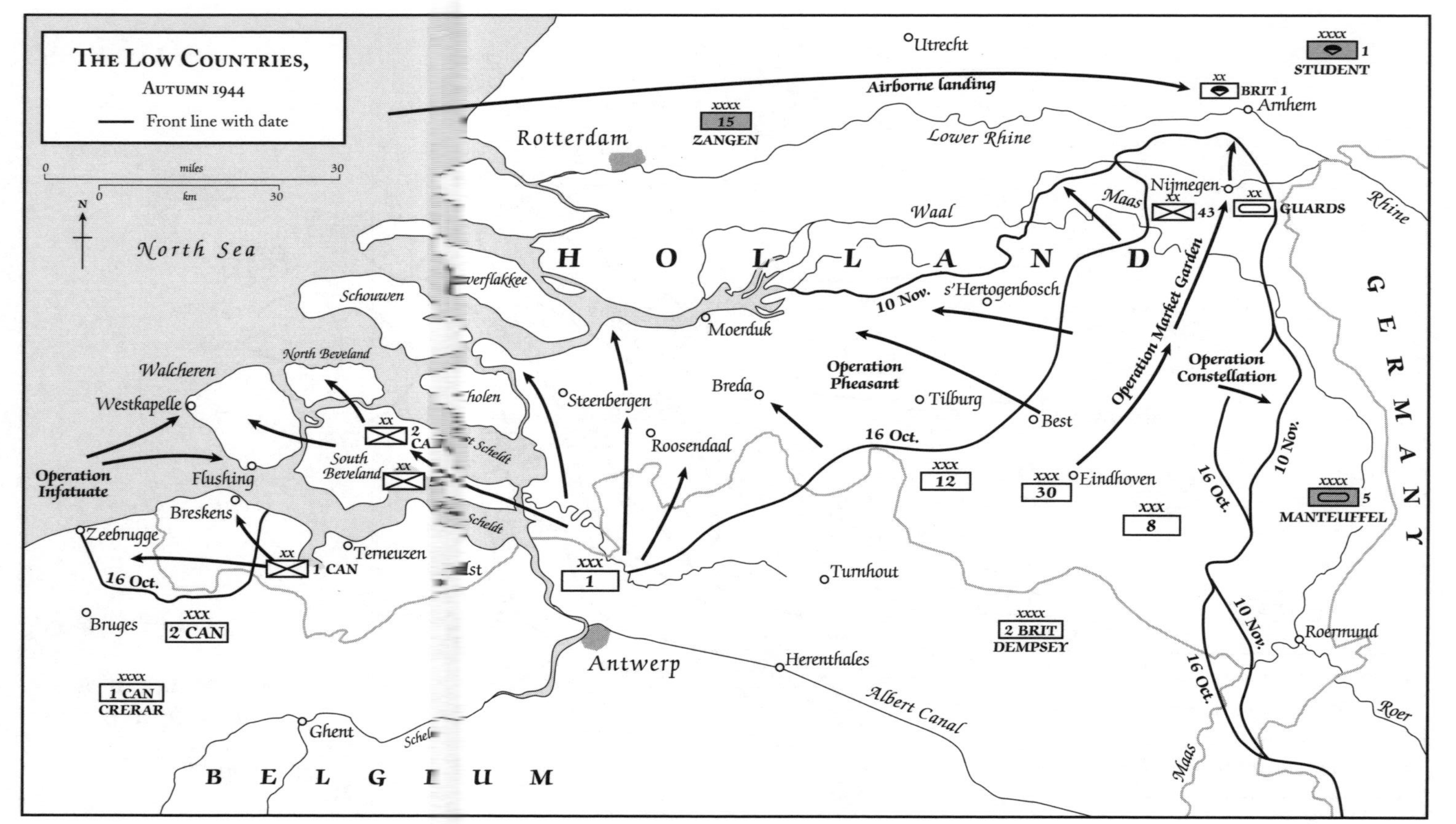
THE LOW COUNTRIES,
AUTUMN 1944
Front line with date
miles
km
0
30
0
30
N
North Sea
Utrecht
Airborne landing
XX BRIT 1
XXXX 1 STUDENT
Arnhem
Rotterdam
XXXX 15 ZANGEN
Lower Rhine
Nijmegen
XX 43
XX GUARDS
Maas
Waal
Rhine
H O L L A N D
G E R M A N Y
Schouwen
verflakkee
Moerduk
s'Hertogenbosch
10 Nov.
Operation Market Garden
North Beveland
Walcheren
Westkapelle
Operation Pheasant
Breda
Tilburg
Best
Operation Constellation
Steenbergen
Roosendaal
16 Oct.
XX 2 CA
South Beveland
XX
Operation Infatuate
Flushing
XXX 12
XXX 30
Eindhoven
XXX 8
XXXX 5 MANTEUFFEL
Breskens
Zeebrugge
XX 1 CAN
Terneuzen
Scheldt
XXX 1
Turnhout
Bruges
XXX 2 CAN
XXXX 2 BRIT DEMPSEY
Roermund
Antwerp
Herenthales
Albert Canal
XXXX 1 CAN CRERAR
Ghent
Roer
B E L G I U M

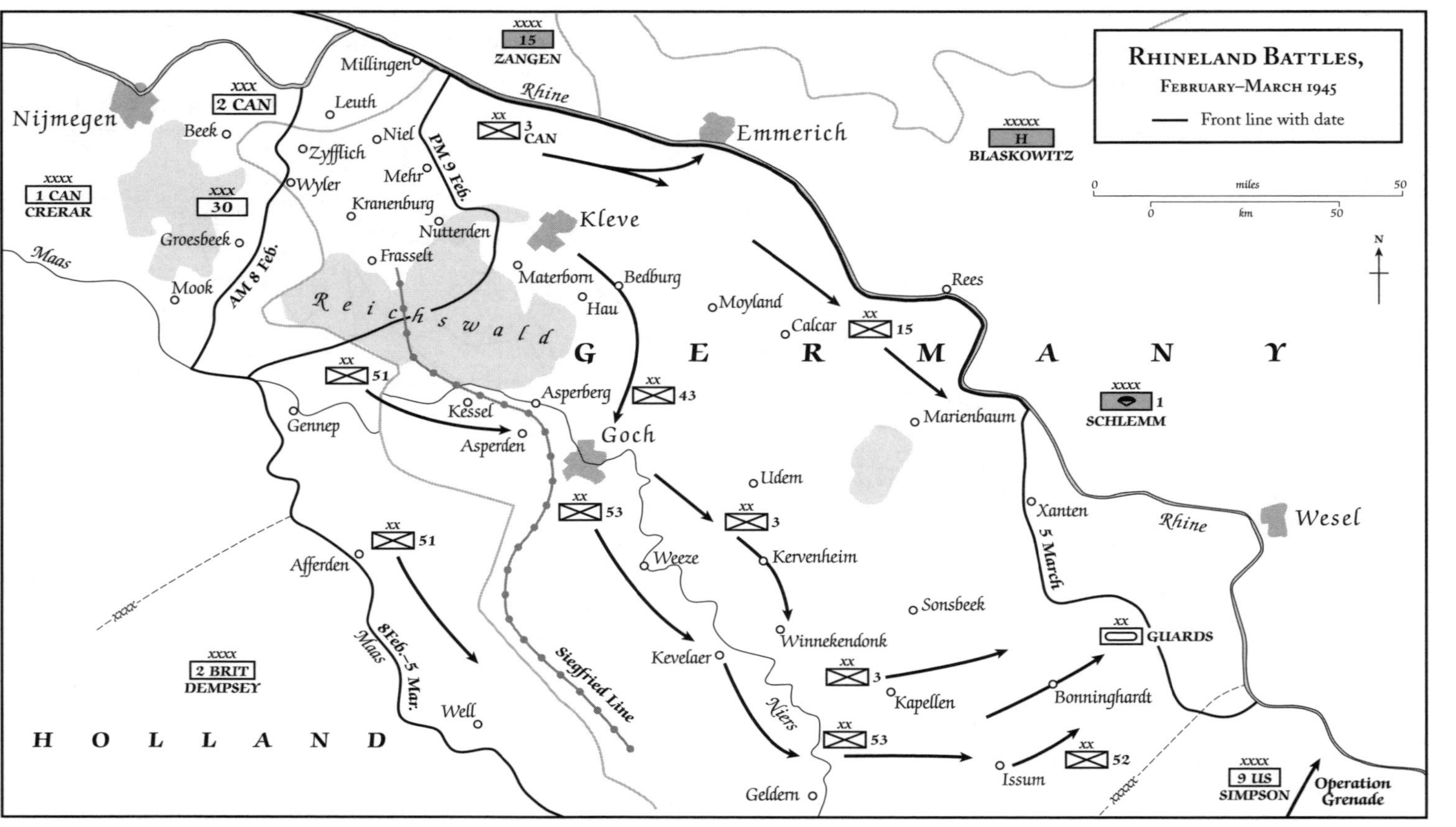

Rhineland Battles,
February–March 1945
Front line with date
0 miles 50
0 km 50
N
Nijmegen
xxxx 1 CAN CRERAR
xxx 2 CAN
xxx 30
Beek
Groesbeek
Mook
Maas
AM 8 Feb.
Millingen
Leuth
Zyfflich
Wyler
Niel
Mehr
Kranenburg
Nutterden
Frasselt
PM 9 Feb.
Reichswald
xxxx 15 ZANGEN
Rhine
xx 3 CAN
Emmerich
Kleve
Materborn
Bedburg
Hau
xx 51
Gennep
Kessel
Asperden
Asperberg
xx 43
Goch
Moyland
Calcar
xx 15
Rees
xxxxx H BLASKOWITZ
G E R M A N Y
xxxx 1 SCHLEMM
Marienbaum
Udem
xx 53
xx 3
Weeze
Kervenheim
Afferden
xx 51
Siegfried Line
Maas
8Feb.–5 Mar.
Well
xxxx 2 BRIT DEMPSEY
HOLLAND
Kevelaer
Niers
Winnekendonk
Sonsbeek
Kapellen
xx 3
xx 53
Geldern
Issum
xx 52
Bonninghardt
xx GUARDS
Xanten
5 March
Rhine
Wesel
xxxx 9 US SIMPSON
Operation Grenade

The Rhine to the Baltic, February–May 1945

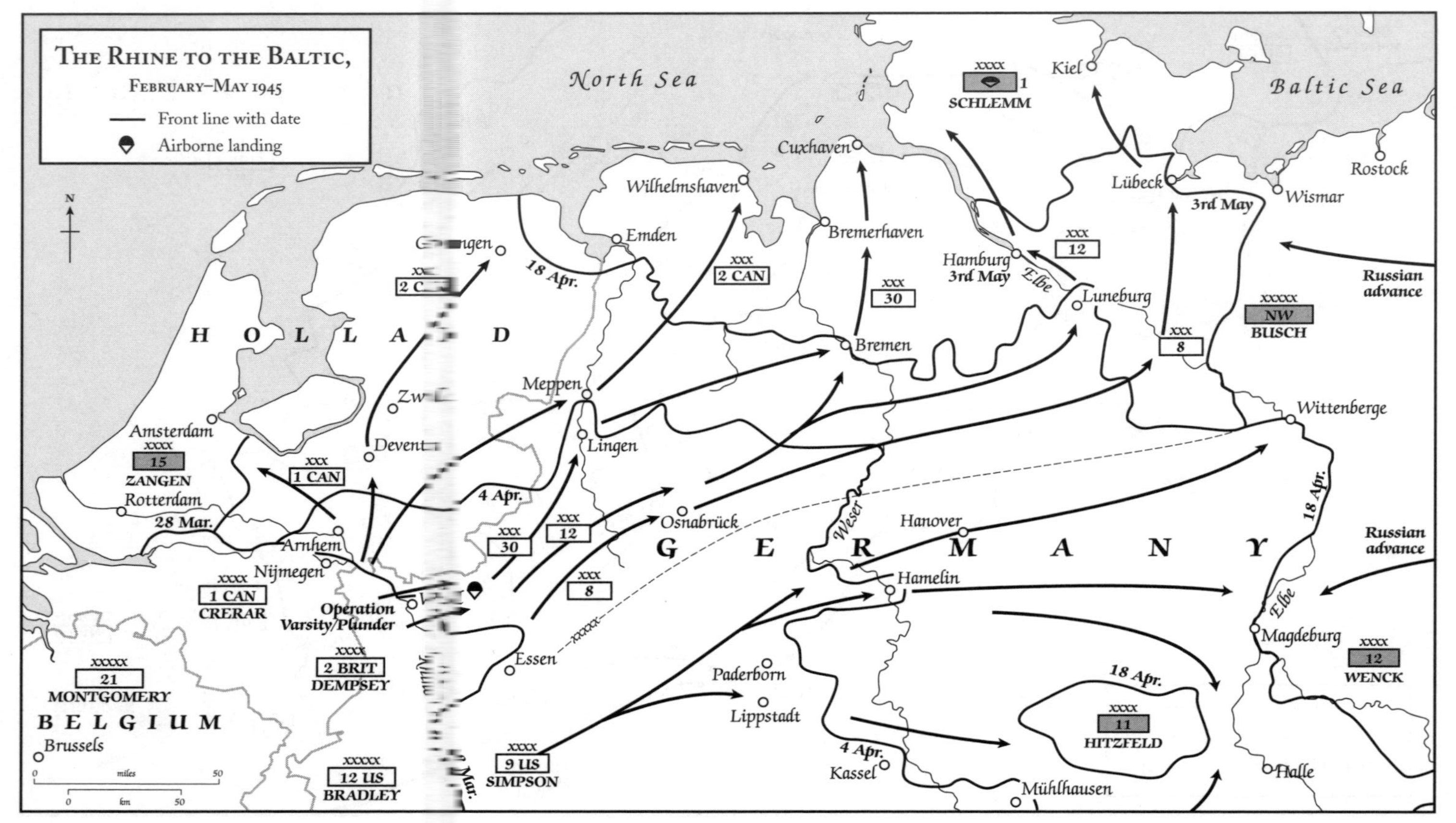

1

INTRODUCTION
The Test of Time

At 8 A.M. ON Saturday 5 May 1945 the British Army won its greatest victory of the Second World War, for on that day all the forces of the Third Reich confronting it in Northern Germany, the Netherlands and Denmark surrendered. In the space of a little less than a year, since 6 June 1944, the British and their Allies had driven the much feared and lauded German Army back from the beaches of Normandy, across France, through the Low Countries and into Germany itself. By May 1945 the British had reached the Baltic and captured Hamburg, the largest port in the disintegrating Third Reich, while American armies had struck deep into Central Germany and Austria and linked up with Soviet troops advancing from the east. Hitler was dead, the German government was in hapless disarray and the destruction of the Third Reich was all but complete.

For Field Marshal Sir Bernard Law Montgomery, commander-in-chief of 21st Army Group to which British troops in Northwest Europe had been allotted, this was the finest moment of his career, the validation of his philosophy and approach to command and leadership. Over the previous few days he had driven the one-sided negotiations with the Germans completely in the direction he desired, and was now intent on maximising the impact of the signing of the document of surrender in front of the press and cameras at 6 p.m. on 4 May. Monty was never a man to miss an opportunity to self-publicise, and certainly not the moment when the German Army was going to surrender, particularly as that capitulation would be to him and not to his rival American colleagues, Eisenhower, Bradley or Patton. Now firmly established in Northern Germany, Montgomery had set up his HQ on Lüneburg Heath, within sight of the town's two church spires and nestled against the nearby forest. When the German delegation first arrived on 3 May, led by Admiral Hans-Georg von Friedeburg and General Hans Kinzel, they received a frosty reception from Montgomery.

After initially keeping them waiting, when he did emerge from his caravan he had changed from his usual sweater and cords into a battledress and beret. One officer on the 21st Army Group staff recorded that Monty spoke to them as if they were vacuum-cleaner salesmen and snapped, 'What do you want?'[1] He became terser still when it emerged that the delegation was merely attempting to buy more time for German civilians and troops to flee westwards from the advancing Red Army. Montgomery made a big show of their desperate state and demanded that unconditional surrender of all German forces facing 21st Army Group was the only realistic option: 'No alternative . . . Finish!' he barked at them.[2] For Montgomery there was nothing to negotiate about and therefore he made little use of his intelligence officer and translator, Colonel Joe Ewart.[3] Such a demonstration reduced Friedeburg, head of the German Navy, to tears and he left Lüneburg Heath later that day to consult with his seniors. He returned the following afternoon on 4 May to sign the document prepared by the British, the terms and conditions of which had been broadly cleared by General Eisenhower, Monty's superior at Supreme Headquarters Allied Expeditionary Force (SHAEF).

Montgomery relished every moment of this denouement and few had seen the Field Marshal so upbeat and jocular.[4] Bristling with confidence that the deal would be done, he held an unusually lively press conference at 5 p.m. to update the media representatives, during which he was informed that the Germans had returned as expected.[5] Montgomery finished his briefing and then, standing outside his tent with the Union flag fluttering above, met the German delegation. First he received Friedeburg in his caravan to ensure that the Germans were willing to comply with the conditions demanded, after which, and with RAF fighters roaring overhead to emphasise Allied supremacy to the subdued Germans, he and the signatories moved to a prepared tent for the *coup de grâce*. Montgomery peremptorily instructed the Germans what to do and where to sit, glowering at one who took out a cigarette; the man in question quickly put the offending article away. Then, in front of the press and the BBC microphones, and with the rain pattering against the canvas roofing above, Monty, wearing his tortoiseshell-rimmed glasses, read out the Instrument of Surrender, prompted the Germans to sign it, and then did likewise on behalf of Eisenhower. Curiously, Montgomery initially dated the document incorrectly and had to scribble out the date and amend it; he nevertheless retained that version and sent only photostats to Eisenhower, despite being asked to send the original. Someone looking for a souvenir snaffled the pen used to sign the surrender.

After the ceremony Montgomery sighed, relaxed, took off his glasses, and said: 'That concludes the surrender.' This was met by an eruption of cheers from the British troops outside the tent, surreptitiously alerted by a confidant inside.[6] The war for the British Army and its Allies in 21st Army Group would come to an end at 0800 on 5 May. For the German officers tasked with signing the document there was little to cheer about, and within weeks three of them were dead: von Friedeburg took poison, Kinzel shot himself along with his mistress, whilst another was killed in a car crash.[7]

Though the moment of the German armed forces' humiliation arguably belonged to Montgomery, it was also a poignant time for all his soldiers, officers and men alike. He issued messages of congratulations and thanks to his senior commanders, troops and the other services:

> It has been a privilege and an honour to command this great British Empire team in Western Europe. Few commanders can have had such loyal service as you have given me . . . We have won the German war. Let us now win the peace.[8]

It was their triumph as much as his, and the manner in which the victory had been achieved was testimony to their resolve, determination and character. Meanwhile, as Monty was lapping up the act of surrender and the media attention, his men were experiencing and enjoying those days in their own memorable ways. Warrant Officer Arnold Johnson was at Second Army cipher HQ in Lüneburg itself when the message came through about the surrender. Just as the team was decoding it, the power supply failed and the most important message of the war had to be completed by candlelight. 'I was flabbergasted when I saw what it said. "This is it!" I shouted to the other men on the shift.'[9] Eddie Slater was on *Griselle*, one of Hitler's recently captured luxury yachts:

> Everything that could be screwed off the boat we unscrewed as a souvenir. I still have a few spoons with swastikas on the handle. My eldest sister's toilet has a beautiful enamel doorknob from Hitler's yacht. We celebrated by letting off the ship's emergency rockets.[10]

Albert Ricketts was attached to Monty's HQ and flew staff officers to various locations for meetings and conferences. Far from being able to relax and enjoy himself on 8 May, designated as Victory in Europe day, he was ordered to collect Major General Templar from First Canadian Army HQ, who sardonically quipped, 'We must be the only silly buggers working today!' Ricketts recalled, 'I found myself warming to a man of his understanding.'[11] Peter Hall, 1st Worcesters, recalled of VE day:

> It was a memorable moment and, I'm afraid, I got very drunk. I was not the only one in 21st Army Group to overindulge on this occasion. The next two weeks were wonderful. No more wondering if we would survive to see the sun come up another day.[12]

For the great majority of Montgomery's charges the cessation of hostilities in Europe was greeted with a mixture of relief and pride in a job being successfully completed. Many would continue to play a key role in controlling and administering Germany for some time to come, an essential and crucial role for a modern army to carry off effectively. For most the German surrender brought the welcome likelihood of a return home to Civvy Street and the prospect of a normal life once again. As an army constituted predominantly of citizen conscripts (around 75 per cent) rather than volunteers and professional military men, and unimbued with extreme political or racial ideologies, the priority had always been to get the job done as quickly and efficiently as possible, preferably with limited and tolerable casualties, and return home.[13]

The achievement of the British Army in 1945 was something the troops and commanders were suitably proud of. Albeit as a junior member of a grand alliance, and supported by American finance and resources, the British Army had delivered a complete victory in the final campaign against Germany. Losses had still been heavy, particularly by our twenty-first-century standards, with 141,646 British soldiers becoming casualties, of which 30,276 paid the ultimate price. The bitter fighting in Normandy in the summer of 1944 had exacted the highest toll in lives with casualty rates in excess of those endured even in the Passchendaele battles of 1917, regarded as the nastiest campaign the British Army had fought in the Great War. Each of the seven British infantry divisions in Normandy in 1944 suffered the loss of almost three-quarters of their initial strength by the end of August, and throughout the entire campaign the life of a rifleman remained the most dangerous of all. Although constituting less than 15 per cent of the entire army, the humble front-line soldier endured 70 per cent of the losses, and a junior infantry officer had only a one-in-ten chance of making it from June 1944 to May 1945 unscathed. It was no wonder that Lieutenant Sydney Jary's detachment was informed on arriving in Normandy in June 1944: 'Gentlemen, your life expectancy from the day you join your battalion will be precisely three weeks.' Yet, although stark and discomforting as these figures appear, the losses were well within expectations and were considered by the War Office in London to be entirely acceptable, particularly as the final victory had been won ahead of schedule. Most importantly of all, by May 1945 the German forces had been soundly beaten and given little or no opportunity to determine or impose any meaningful strategic influence over the campaign.[14]

The British Army had played a crucial role in the fighting, particularly in the summer of 1944, and yet Montgomery and his staff had delivered victory without recourse to the sustained and deep bloodletting of the First World War, or that of the Eastern Front where the Germans and Soviets had locked horns in the bitterest of campaigns between 1941 and 1945. Consequently, in July 1945 Britain was able to sit confidently at the conference table in Potsdam alongside its more senior partners, backed by having made a meaningful contribution to the defeat of Germany's armies, whilst still retaining a battle-hardened, functioning and capable army. The dark days of the ignominious Dunkirk evacuation in 1940 through to Lüneburg Heath may have been littered with mistakes, errors and blunders, but the British Army had rebuilt and reinvented itself. Though the campaign in Northwest Europe had been hard fought, the Allies had won their victory against what many then regarded, and indeed still regard very questionably, as the greatest army ever.[15]

Yet, by the twenty first century, the reputation of the British Army in the Second World War, including the victorious forces that contributed so much to the overthrow of Hitler's Third Reich in the campaign waged across Northwest Europe in 1944–5, has been severely tarnished by the passage of time and the ebb and flow of history. Despite the victory, many popular writers, historians and military professionals have been increasingly, openly and often stringently critical of the conduct and prosecution of the campaign by commanders and soldiers alike. Such was the weight of this criticism that, by the 1980s, an orthodoxy had emerged, one that identified the British Army as ponderous, predictable and heavily reliant on the Americans, and one which compared most unfavourably to the dynamic, *blitzkrieging* Germans. A cursory glance at contemporary military history writing offers a flavour of modern thinking. Max Hastings, for example, is deeply critical of the British Army's performance in the Second World War:

> The British had fought workmanlike campaigns in North Africa, Italy and France since their victory at El Alamein in November 1942. But their generals had nowhere shown the genius displayed by Germany's commanders in France in 1940, and in many battles since.[16]

Hastings also castigated British soldiers for their 'lack of aggression' and for their overt caution, a by-product and 'a price for the privilege of the profoundly anti-militaristic ethos' of the nation.[17] But of the enemy, he referred to the 'glory of German arms in Normandy' (albeit in an evil cause), and of the German Army's 'extraordinary fighting performance in the last year of the Second World War'.[18]

More recently, Antony Beevor concluded that the British Army had lacked ruthlessness, whilst academic studies have questioned the operational and tactical abilities of the British Amy.[19] In 2004, Robert Citino, the noted American military historian, offered a severe indictment of British effectiveness in Normandy:

> The real link between D-Day, Villers-Bocage, Epsom and Goodwood [Normandy operations] is that none of them was carried out within the spirit of mobile warfare . . . What the British army lacked were officers who could recognize such momentary opportunities when they arose and a military culture that encouraged them to seize those golden moments.[20]

Critics have also focused closely on high-profile failures in the British Army's conduct of the campaign, to illustrate crucial weaknesses and deficiencies. As early as the first few hours after landing on the beaches in Normandy on 6 June 1944, the British Army was supposedly fluffing its lines as it failed to capture the crucial city of Caen and make the most of the surprise and confusion caused by D-Day. The lightning strike on Caen ended up as a plodding advance by just a few hundred riflemen, as Alexander McKee described it. The lack of drive and dynamism shown that morning and early afternoon on 6 June brought about the stalemate that followed, forcing the British into fighting a series of attritional and costly battles around Caen for many weeks afterwards.[21]

Just a week after D-Day the British bungled matters again, suffering a bloody nose at Villers-Bocage when the veteran 7th Armoured Division (the Desert Rats) was stopped dead in its tracks, apparently by the action of a single Tiger tank. In the following weeks, and despite holding a considerable advantage in resources, the British battered away at the Germans defending the Caen sector in Normandy, but seemingly made little headway. Further west, American troops also struggled but nevertheless captured the crucial port of Cherbourg and the Cotentin peninsula, and manoeuvred their way southwards prior to the launch of Operation COBRA on 25 July, which broke the front wide open and threw the Germans into headlong retreat. The British attempt to blast their way through a week earlier with Operation GOODWOOD resulted in humiliating failure, with 400 tanks being knocked out, leading one historian to describe it as the death ride of the armoured divisions.[22]

Even when the Germans were driven back from Normandy all the way to the Low Countries, the British apparently made a hash of the pursuit.

Though they seized the vital port of Antwerp intact, they did not press on to trap the German Fifteenth Army north of the River Scheldt or secure the use of the port for many weeks afterwards. The supply headaches created by this failure afforded the Germans enough time to recover and fight on into 1945.[23] Most infamously of all, the British-led attempt to secure a crossing over the Rhine at Arnhem in the eastern Netherlands in September 1944 resulted in disaster, with almost an entire airborne division being written off the order of battle. Despite all the supporting resources the operation, MARKET GARDEN, was badly botched and much of the blame was directed at British commanders such as Frederick 'Boy' Browning, Brian Horrocks, Roy Urquhart, Allan Adair and Montgomery himself. American airborne troops who had carried out a desperate and courageous opposed river crossing over the Waal were excoriating about the subsequent limp British effort to push out of Nijmegen and rescue the beleaguered troops hanging on at Arnhem.[24] Even when the Rhine was crossed in March 1945, the moment when the knockout blow was delivered to Germany, the British made a hash of things. The operation was unnecessarily complicated, slow and ponderous, while the use of airborne forces was castigated as 'a spectacular shambles' and 'a folly for which more than a thousand men paid with their lives'.[25]

All these criticisms have been levelled squarely at the British Army, rising to a crescendo in the 1980s onwards, reinforced since in popular culture through films, television dramas, documentaries, and even board and computer games. The modern popular image of Montgomery's army in Northwest Europe in 1944–5 is without doubt then less than flattering. But why? How has the passage of history since 1945 turned the perception of a triumphant and successful army into one that is now of an unimaginative and plodding force which only prevailed against a dynamic and resourceful foe through sheer weight of resources and recourse to outmoded attritional methods?

It is an obvious point, though still worth noting, that history, like many other aspects of life, is shaped both by personalities and by trends, and the process by which the positive image of the British Army of 1944–5 began to unravel in the post-war years was no different. In the afterglow of victory and in the ensuing peace, few wanted to begin an in-depth process of evaluation and soul-searching over the army's performance, as most were simply relieved that the fighting was over. It was in this post-war atmosphere that the key players of the period, such as Churchill and Montgomery, soon began to stake out their place in history by publishing self-serving and hubristic memoirs. Monty's account of the campaign published in 1947, and both his memoirs and those of his Chief of Staff, Francis 'Freddie' de Guingand, published in 1958 and 1947 respectively, recounted a campaign in which next to nothing had gone awry, the army had performed superbly well, and Montgomery himself had barely put a foot wrong. Even for those who considered the campaign to have been a success, this was hardly helpful or realistic and ultimately contributed to the reaction of later historians who endeavoured to pick apart such simplistic analyses. Scepticism was not helped by the publication in the 1960s of the officially sanctioned two-volume history of the campaign, *Victory in the West*, written by Major Lionel F. Ellis. These official studies proved to be anodyne and unquestioning 'factual' accounts which did little to open any debate or discussion about what had not gone well and what had proven troublesome. Ellis underscored Monty's smug self-assessment: 'The conduct of the Twenty-First Army Group's operations during the battle of Normandy gives little occasion for adverse criticism. Its troops had been consistently well led.'[26] Controversies were lightly passed over or skirted around and served to fuel the opinion that Montgomery and the army were unwilling to countenance any serious criticism.[27]

Even in this period there were still, nonetheless, voices of dissent. The first and perhaps most important player in this process was the famous military historian Sir Basil Liddell Hart. He was a pivotal character in shaping and determining the military history of the twentieth century through his prolific writing and correspondence, and via the influence he exercised over the development of both academic and popular military history. Now considered to be a deeply controversial character, Liddell Hart's impact on post-1945 interpretations of the conduct of the war was profound. Keen to demonstrate that his pre-1939 writing on the importance of fast-paced technologically defined manoeuvre was the inspiration behind Germany's *blitzkrieg*, Liddell Hart obtained access to many of the surviving German generals after the war and proceeded to interview them. In the book that emerged from these studies, *The Other Side of the Hill*, Liddell Hart argued that the German Army had performed so well against superior numbers for so long because their commanders had grasped the basic principles of modern mobile warfare, as he had outlined prior to 1939. He claimed that the Germans had absorbed his ideas and that this was a key factor in the speed and dynamism of German operations in the war. Conversely, Allied commanders had not similarly appreciated his arguments and had consigned themselves to repeating the ponderous, attritional warfare of the Great War. When the two methods clashed, Liddell Hart argued, the Allies only won through the application of superior resources and because the German generals were hampered by Hitler's lunacy.[28]

According to Liddell Hart another root cause of the Allies' backward-looking methods was the lack of drive on the part of the front-line troops;

he claimed that they failed to display the determination and the capability to grapple with German soldiers in close combat unless lavishly supported by firepower from artillery and air forces. He even wrote that the statement 'lions led by donkeys', as used to describe the soldiers and generals of the Great War, could in fact be inverted when referring to the Second World War; the lions had now become the donkeys.[29] In some ways, Liddell Hart argued, Allied generals of 1939–45 worked with the materials they had, and this in part explained their inability to match the Germans in operational flair and dynamism.

Liddell Hart's interpretation was shaped by his desire to find what he was looking for, whilst the German generals, desperate to curry favour with anyone from the West, told him what he wanted to hear; Liddell Hart then embellished their testimony to underpin his thesis still further. Naturally, German generals were also keen to apportion blame for their defeat to factors other than themselves, and highlighting Allied weight of numbers and Hitler's insanity at the strategic level clearly suited their personal and professional purposes.

German influence was also at play in shaping the Australian journalist Chester Wilmot's very widely read account of the 1944–5 campaign, *The Struggle for Europe*, published in 1952.[30] Wilmot's credibility was reinforced by his being present during the campaign and being able to witness at close hand the ebb and flow of the fighting. Whilst working for the BBC he noted the concern that began to set in within Montgomery's senior team in late June and July 1944, when the Normandy campaign appeared to stagnate and the British commanders' frustration with their troops' inability to make headway despite the heavy support afforded them. Wilmot reinforced this view by using translations of documents issued by the German Army to its soldiers in 1944, which appeared to state that British forces, the infantry in particular, lacked drive and elan. German interpretation claimed that this was a product of the poor morale of British troops and that they had to fall back on artillery and air support to balance this deficiency. Rather than German shortcomings it was this materiel superiority that was carrying the Allies to victory.[31]

In reality, such documents reflected a desire on the part of German commanders to bolster their own troops' morale by criticising the enemy, and also illustrated the overemphasis placed on close combat in the German Army to the detriment of other arms. The Germans mistook the liberal use of firepower by the Anglo-Canadians as a sign of weakness, when in reality it was a deliberately chosen method that reflected Allied strengths, was intended to limit Allied casualties, and was designed to expose German shortcomings.

Wilmot's immensely readable assessment sold widely and helped to create the vision of German quality being swamped by Allied quantity.

The view that Allied soldiers had not shown enough gumption also dates back to the work conducted by the American military analyst S. L. A. Marshall in the 1950s, the notorious 'ratio of fire' research. Marshall's conclusions, since discredited, claimed that in American units only some 15 per cent of riflemen ever fired a shot at the enemy.[32] This was underscored by statistics which demonstrated that a large proportion of Allied troops in 1944–5 did not actually fight, being given over to the 'tail' of the army – logistics, administration and transport.[33] In contrast German soldiers were all able to double-up in difficult situations, with cooks and mechanics fighting in the front line as and when required; Allied soldiers were supposedly unable to display such flexibility. What was set aside was that German soldiers mostly resorted to such desperate measures on account of the parlous state of the German Army in the last two years of the war, and that the Allied armies clearly placed greater weight on logistics, intelligence and engineering in order to shape battles to their advantage. Although these tales of German flexibility were in any case often apocryphal, much stock has been placed in them to underpin the thesis that Germans were simply better soldiers, tougher, more determined and thoroughly 'professional'.[34]

Professional military interpretations of the Northwest European campaign in 1944–5 have not been kind to the British Army either. In the aftermath of victory in 1945 the army quite rightly basked in the glow of success, but soon afterwards, when confronted with the challenge of potentially facing down the Soviets in central Europe, re-evaluations of operational techniques, doctrines and tactics began to change opinions.[35] Initially, thinking in the British Army accepted that the methods employed against the Germans might have been successful in the Second World War but they were simply inappropriate against the Soviets; in fact the likely pattern to be used by NATO against the Warsaw Pact mirrored more closely the German experience in facing the massed Allies in 1943–5. Therefore a key question to be addressed by the British and American armies in the post-war era was how had the German Army resisted for so long when so heavily outnumbered and how might this capability be replicated? What lessons were to be gleaned from the Germans about the Soviets? The professional interest in the performance of the German Army rested on assumptions drawn from perceptions of the huge battles that shook the Eastern Front between 1941 and 1945, as well as the so-called *blitzkrieg* years. On the face of it German forces had won spectacular victories, often when outnumbered, and even when forced into drawn-out attritional and defensive battles they had still inflicted heavy casualties on their enemies.

Studying the German Army from a purely military perspective, and leaving aside the grim realities of the appalling atrocities perpetrated between 1939 and 1945, Western analysts identified the doctrine and training of the German Army as the key to their success.[36] It was contended that German commanders had employed a 'mission-based' approach to fighting (*auftragstaktik*), in which decision making was devolved to the officers on the spot, who could best judge the way to achieve their objective or complete their mission. Consequently, German forces were better led and much more flexible, both in defence and attack. This had been the cornerstone of their success and should be replicated in NATO armies facing the Red Army in the Cold War.

Such an interpretation too easily passes over the realities of the German Army in the Second World War: the brutality, the fear, the overtly poisonous racist ideology underpinning many troops' attitudes, the criminalisation of young soldiers, the extreme coercion and finally the desperation of the last year of the war. The front-line close-combat effectiveness of German soldiers was founded on these traits as well as training and doctrine, and this greatly complicates defining what made the German Army so dynamic up to 1942 and so obdurate afterwards.[37]

In contrast, according to this interpretation, Allied armies, and particularly the British and Canadian, had relied on 'orders-based' command (*befehlstaktik*), in which units and officers were issued with specific plans to which they were supposed to adhere. Montgomery especially wanted his commanders to conform to orders, and not deviate from the prescribed plan. In this way he could retain control of the battle as he believed only he could see the big picture, and thus eliminate the chance of gross mistakes being perpetrated by a raw, largely conscript-based army.[38] According to post-war analysts, the weakness of this system was that it stifled initiative and resulted in emerging battlefield opportunities being squandered, something that could prove disastrous against a mass enemy army such as the Soviets. A good deal of the evidence available to support the superiority of German methods was in fact drawn from Eastern Front battles between 1941 and 1945 for which, until the 1990s at least, the West was obliged to rely on German testimony for substantiation, as the Soviet Union's perspective was regarded as untrustworthy and in any case largely inaccessible to Western historians. Somewhat ironically, considerable reliance was therefore placed on the opinions of German commanders who all too often complained that the reason they had been defeated in the East was due to the masses of Soviet troops confronting them, and the inadequacies of Hitler's regime at home. When attention turned to the western battles of 1944–5, German commanders, even convicted SS generals such as Kurt Meyer, were again employed to offer their views on their defeat, which usually focused on the Allies' plentiful resources, the absent Luftwaffe and the madness of the Führer or his political acolytes.[39] Whilst the adoption of new doctrine, perhaps in some ways drawn from the tactical and operational methods of the German Army during the Second World War, may have been appropriate for NATO's Cold War armies, it nevertheless also soon began to reflect badly on the British Army in 1939–45. Fixation on fast manoeuvre, mobility, strategic level breakthroughs, all akin on paper at least to *blitzkrieg*, resulted in retrospective reinterpretations of how the Allied armies functioned in the Second World War. Why hadn't the British employed modern manoeuvre warfare methods to confront the Germans? By the 1980s, battlefield study tours of Normandy for British officers were intended by the army's senior commanders to demonstrate the superiority of German tactical and operational methods over British approaches, even when the army's own historians based at Sandhurst disagreed with this interpretation.[40] The British and indeed American armies were indulging in cherry-picking certain aspects of the Second World War to reinforce their views on how to fight contemporary battles.

Cornelius Ryan's *A Bridge Too Far* (1974), an accessible and fast-moving account of the disastrous Operation MARKET GARDEN of September 1944, inflicted severe damage on the reputation of the British Army in the 1970s, exposing it to ridicule and criticism, even more so when the similarly titled blockbuster film was released in 1977. The film offered a searing indictment of British planning and leadership that bordered on a character assassination of Lieutenant General Frederick Browning, who was portrayed as oily and self-serving by Dirk Bogarde. Equally, the British forces were caricatured as hidebound, timid and too interested in drinking tea.[41]

The 1980s proved to be pivotal in shaping our modern perceptions because of the publication of two books that coincided with the fortieth anniversary of D-Day. Max Hastings, the journalist and sometime editor of the *Daily Telegraph*, published *Overlord: The Battle for Normandy* (1984) in which he portrayed a ponderous, hesitant and cautious British Army, lacking drive and dynamism and one too heavily reliant on battles of attrition to win through. He also raised the positive image of the German Army to new heights, detaching almost completely its pure close-combat capabilities from the rest of the German Army's brutalised nature and wider inadequacies. Hastings castigated much British equipment, which, although plentiful, compared badly with German weaponry. British tanks such as the Cromwell and the American-built Sherman were criticised for their shortcomings, and compared most unfavourably to German tanks such as the Tiger and the Panther. Hastings sweepingly asserted that if only the British had had German tanks in Northwest Europe, then operations would have been carried through to rapid success rather than all too often foundering, having failed to achieve their desired objectives. Leaving aside the realities of armoured warfare in 1944–5, which impinge little upon such interpretations, the overly technocentric vision of success and failure on the battlefield tells us more about the approach of many male military historians who seek to explain complex issues through easily measurable technical performance.[42]

Hastings was not alone in his criticism of the British Army's approach to combat. Colonel Carlo D'Este's popular account of the fighting in the summer of 1944, *Decision in Normandy* (1983), devoted a whole chapter – 'The Price of Caution' – to the British tendency to evade close-quarter fighting where possible and rely heavily on firepower. This approach precipitated cumbersome operations which the Germans were able to stymie time and time again with limited resources, resulting in sluggish Allied progress. Montgomery was squarely implicated in this failing and was further criticised for over-controlling his commanders, which smothered battlefield initiative. He was also censured for later attempting to rewrite the history of the campaign in his favour. Ultimately, the price, as D'Este put it, was a prolonged campaign with increased casualties, when greater drive would probably have yielded a more rapid victory.[43]

D'Este's argument was in part shaped by the comments and criticisms levelled at Montgomery by Air Chief Marshal Arthur Tedder, Eisenhower's deputy, and General Frederick Morgan, who had devised the first OVERLORD plan, and who acted during the campaign as Deputy Chief of Staff at SHAEF. Tedder was never a fan of Montgomery's cautious operational approach, and also harboured considerable personal animosity; Morgan was always likely to be hostile once Monty had made his stinging criticism of Morgan's original plan on taking command of 21st Army Group. Both Tedder and Morgan briefed against Montgomery to the Americans at SHAEF during the 1944–5 campaign and served to fuel still further the already vexed question of Montgomery's disagreeable personality.[44] Monty's unerring ability to annoy many of those he worked with, particularly the Americans, certainly acted against the image of the British Army in the post-war world, especially when memoirs began to appear in the 1950s; his criticisms of Eisenhower published in his memoirs in 1958 in particular won him few friends in the US.[45] Personal antipathy towards Montgomery resulted in increased scrutiny of his methods and those of his forces, especially when they were apparently at odds with American approaches.[46] Certainly when Colonel D'Este came to write *Decision in Normandy*, his interpretation would have been formed in an atmosphere coloured by the lingering animosity to Montgomery and his methods felt in the US Army, in turn caused by Montgomery's arrogance and condescension, and his clumsy and tactless commentary on the conduct of the campaign.

From the time of the fortieth anniversaries onwards, Hastings and D'Este have done more than any other writers to popularise the image of the British Army as a slow-moving behemoth lacking wit and flair, whilst simultaneously extolling the virtues of the German Army. But this image has also been reinforced in other forms of popular culture such as Steven Spielberg's film *Saving Private Ryan* (1998), television series such as *Band of Brothers* (2001), and in computer games where the younger generation increasingly gains its first contact with the military history of the Second World War. The process of denigrating Allied armies was not only confined to Britain, as a similar movement in the USA emerged which similarly praised the combat prowess of the Germans, particularly when fighting the communist hordes of the Red Army.[47]

The reputation of the British Army has without doubt suffered due to unflattering comparison with its German counterpart. The fascination of the popular military enthusiast for all things pertaining to the German military machine of the Second World War has been the real driving force behind the enduring image of the *Wehrmacht* and the SS. The output of easily consumable published material on the German Army has been and continues to be vast, and though much of it relates to the banalities of camouflage patterns, kit and equipment, it takes as its starting point the inherent superiority of the German soldier and his flamboyant commanders.[48]

It is both disturbing and baffling that the marketability of German military ephemera of the Second World War is so much greater than that of other forces and armies, as any visit to a re-enactment fair will demonstrate. In the [illegible] to be members of German units, and of those some 75 per cent want to join SS units, an obvious indication of the enduring lurid fascination and dubious respect for the martial capabilities of the German Army. To many, despite the ultimate disaster that consumed the Third Reich in 1945, it is the German Army of the Second World War that remains held in high esteem, much more than the forces that defeated it.[49]

Yet the image is one based on a fairly narrow definition of what constitutes effectiveness, one that focuses solely on close-combat capability. At this German soldiers often proved adept, for a variety of reasons ranging across ideological motivation, tactical doctrine and, most importantly, greater experience. The ability of soldiers and units to engage the enemy in direct combat is obviously the most crucial element in defining fighting power, but it is not the only criterion by which it can and should be measured. An army's effectiveness is defined by a range of capabilities incorporating intelligence, logistics, planning, firepower, medical support, liaison, communications and engineering, in addition to close-combat tactics, and all such elements have to be brought together in a modern army in order to achieve battlefield objectives.

Although the German Army may have attained considerable capability in close-combat tactics, it proved much less capable in these wider aspects of military activity. In the Second World War artillery again proved to be the most lethal weapon on the battlefield, as it had been in the Great War, but it was *Allied* artillery, particularly British artillery, that gained a fearsome reputation in the second half of the war. German troops complained bitterly that they were unable to operate properly because British artillery held the battlefield in its grip, strangled manoeuvre and prevented concentration. The British Army paid much greater attention to all the elements supporting the infantry and armour, and considered that maintaining plentiful supplies of equipment and ordnance in the field was pivotal to success in battle. In contrast, German forces lived a hand-to-mouth existence, often because planners failed to accept logistical realities.[50]

Above the level of tactics lies the realm of operational warfare, that is how units are organised into larger formations, issued with orders and properly supported in order to achieve a series of larger objectives, all ultimately leading to victory in a campaign. Operations are the building blocks of victory and are the link between small-scale tactics and achieving politico-strategic aims. The German Army emerged from the Second World War with a reputation for operational excellence, as epitomised by *blitzkrieg*, though the term was never used to define its operational practices, nor did the army regard what it was doing as being anything particularly new.[51] But the Germans did focus heavily on manoeuvre as being the key to battlefield success, and panzers, mechanised infantry and mobile artillery, when deployed appropriately, even if in small numbers, defined this approach. Referred to as *bewegungskrieg*, or manoeuvre warfare, the method evolved during the first few years of the war and achieved startling success.

This operational approach, though much lauded then and since, concealed many shortcomings and deficiencies. German operational methods relied upon fast manoeuvre and the rapid application of limited but shock-based force to overwhelm an enemy quickly in order to conceal the army's weaknesses in logistics and long-term planning. Prior to the invasion of the USSR in 1941 this worked well enough as opponents collapsed before the initial German attack ran out of steam, but in the wide expanses of Russia and through the extreme weather conditions the weaknesses in German methods became all too apparent. Operations against the Red Army were often mounted without proper preparation, lacking good intelligence on the enemy and where an attack would deliver the best results, and without a realistic grip on what could be sustainably achieved with available resources. By repeatedly mounting major operations which lacked proper support and that all too often did not contribute sufficiently to an overall strategy designed to deliver victory with sustainable losses, the German Army soon began to haemorrhage. Front-line troops were forced into ad hoc fire, fighting to hold positions when support was lacking, supplies ran low or they were surprised by enemy action. German armies, far from being the doyens of operational art, in reality had solved only the problem of how to manoeuvre quickly and effectively; without the many other crucial aspects of operational planning and thinking, they could only deliver short-term success and were forced to live under the spectre of potential near disaster.

Any army has to undertake military operations of varying scale in pursuit of strategic aims, underpinned at the political level by a clear appreciation of achievable goals and aims, informed by a realistic understanding of capabilities. An army obviously does not function in a political vacuum and must fulfil the political and strategic objectives set down for it. It must also be capable of managing its assets sufficiently well for long enough to achieve its aims without destroying itself in so doing, or indeed beforehand. The army must additionally be in a position at the end of hostilities – both physically and psychologically – to deliver the circumstances by which peace or stability can be delivered. Such attributes are fundamental in defining a successful modern army, and they were startlingly lacking in the German Army of the Second World War.

Much military history focuses too heavily on close combat and equipment and ignores the wider perspective, when in reality armed forces exist in a real environment, in which political, social and economic, as well as technological, influences shape the conduct of great campaigns. The effectiveness of the British Army can, therefore, only really be understood by appreciating the context in which Montgomery's forces were expected to fight, the resources they had available, and the success with which the objectives set out for them were achieved; appreciation of close-combat tactics alone is simply not enough, important though that was. The British Army in 1944 existed in an era in which dwindling national military and economic power had to be balanced against the requirements of defeating the Third Reich. But the British Army also had to be seen to be playing a fully committed and active role in fighting the Germans in order to maintain the status of a great power. To complicate matters still further, the British had limited human resources to devote to the army's war in Northwest Europe in 1944, with so many personnel deployed in the bomber offensive, maintaining the Atlantic shipping lanes, fighting in Italy and combating the Japanese in Asia, as well as retaining a grip on the rest of the empire. Such troops as were available were mostly untested in battle, and though they would be well equipped and supported, they would be confronting an enemy with great depths of bitter and brutal combat experience. The British Army would also have to win without too many casualties in order to be in a position to deliver the conditions for a sustainable peace. It was not simply a matter of winning battles: the army had to deliver victory both in the war and the ensuing peace.

Finding a method of fighting the Germans that reflected these imperatives was fundamental to Montgomery and the leadership of the army, but it is also the yardstick by which their relative success or failure must be measured. In recent years there have been moves to evaluate the army more holistically, examining its place in the grand strategy of the British state in the Second World War, and how it developed and adapted to the needs of the United Kingdom after the disasters of 1940–41. Montgomery's methods and techniques have similarly been viewed in a more realistic light, with his peculiar and difficult personality having been set aside in order to understand his impact, whilst other studies have shown that particular arms and elements of the British Army functioned far more effectively than has previously been thought. The reputation of the Canadian forces in Northwest Europe has also been salvaged through accounts based on original documents, reports and operational analyses rather than dated journalistic volumes, self-serving memoirs and personal testimony alone.[52] The fundamental purpose of this book is similarly to assess the fighting power of the British Army in its campaign against the Germans from D-Day to the end of the war in Europe. By understanding why the British Army fought in the manner it did, and by examining its supporting arms as well as the front-line troops, a much clearer and balanced appreciation is possible, an appreciation of how the British Army won its war and achieved all that was asked of it.

But it is also crucial to begin to understand the men who fought in Montgomery's army, their attitudes to battle, the war and their place in it – this was after all a citizen-based army, one which drew upon all walks of life, albeit in an uneven manner. It was not imbued with great ideological fervour, or brutal military determination. But the army was still an effective tool that reflected the state from which it was drawn, which eschewed extremism and favoured functionality over desire. Colin Hall, a veteran of Arnhem, encapsulates that ethos:

> It was a grim time. We were just young men who would much rather be back at home, drinking, dating and living normal lives. We had been thrust into the defence of Europe which, although an honourable and worthy activity, was not our choice. Neither I nor any of my mates wanted to be there. I saw no cowardice, but I saw no heroics either.[53]

For the great majority of men in 1944–5 such attitudes rang all too true; but this was their army and their victory.

2

PREPARATION
The Road to D-Day

In Southern England in early June 1944 the British Army finalised its preparations for the greatest challenge it would face in The Second World War, a direct face-to-face confrontation with its nemesis of 1940, the *Wehrmacht*. Four years before as the *blitzkrieg* swept across Europe, the British Army had been unceremoniously driven from the continent, shorn of its equipment and confidence. Now rebuilt and underpinned by two years of successful campaigning in the Mediterranean, the British Army, in conjunction with powerful Allies and backed with vast resources, was ready. Although many soldiers had not seen actual combat, most had received considerable levels of training, and many units had a sprinkling of seasoned soldiers who had fought in 1940 or in some cases were veterans of the Mediterranean Campaign. Senior commanders at army, corps and in most cases divisional level had all seen action, whilst middle-ranking officers leading battalions or equivalents were now on average ten years younger than the older officers moved on after the disaster of 1940. Great play had also been made of the regimental system in an effort to boost morale, and soldiers were to wear badges and insignia to underpin unit identity, even if these might, on occasion, afford the enemy useful intelligence.[1]

Not that the army was without weakness or unafflicted with doubt. Field Marshal Alan Brooke, Chief of the Imperial General Staff, confided his deep unease over the Normandy invasion in his diary, and many other soldiers naturally did not relish the thought of a long and deadly campaign in Northwest Europe. Commanders worried about the determination and fighting spirit of their troops and the degree to which they could be pushed, while the senior officers themselves, often products of the Western Front in the Great War, were driven by concerns over needless casualties.[2]

Soldiers dealt with the stresses and pressures of war in many ways, but traditional British self-deprecation and sardonic wit were endemic. The army intended for action in Northwest Europe had originally been titled the British Western European Force, though the acronym of BWEF was regularly redefined by world-weary and impish soldiers as 'Burma When Europe Finished'. The replacement name, British Liberation Army or BLA, fared little better, being recast as 'Burma Looms Ahead'.

Black humour and a hint of cynicism pervaded the army. Austin Baker of 4/7 Royal Dragoons recalled 5 June:

> Major B read out messages from Eisenhower and Montgomery and told us that he personally thought we should all be very honoured to be in this affair. I think most of us felt we could have stood the disgrace of being left out of it.[3]

Similarly, Geoffrey Picot of 1st Hampshires recalled:

> One day an extremely young-looking commanding officer, still in his twenties, announced: 'We are going to be an assault battalion in the invasion of Europe.' To my surprise nobody cheered.
>
> [The experienced and decorated soldiers] were as solemn and nervous and sad as I was. So they were not a special breed! They were rather like me.[4]

Some soldiers were simply greatly relieved not to be entering the fray at the sharp end. Captain Trevor Jenks, tasked with waterproofing vehicles for D-Day:

> I was quite happy not to be part of the invasion forces. What those chaps achieved was incredible and I'm not sure I could have coped at all with what they had to endure.[5]

Soldiers were also a little sceptical about glib media comments. 'The men generally are in good heart,' noted Jack Swaab in his diary entry of 3 June 1944:

> . . . but I don't mean it in the newspapers' way. I just mean they are putting up with the bloodiness of everything with proportionately little grumbling.[6]

Yet many young and inexperienced men, and particularly junior officers, viewed the prospect of the campaign on the continent with excitement. Bill

Bellamy, then a young twenty-year-old troop commander in 8th King's Royal Irish Hussars, wrote:

> I tried to conceal my excitement with a veneer of sophistication . . . To me, it seemed like a sort of game . . . It didn't reduce my awareness of the dangers . . . but I decided that if I had to take risks in order to carry out my allocated task, then right was on our side, and they would be well worth taking.[7]

Many veterans who had spent years battling against the wily Field Marshal Rommel in North Africa were not looking forward to locking horns with their old adversaries once again and viewed their role in the vanguard of the forthcoming invasion with suspicion and disgruntlement. Peter Roach, 1st Royal Tank Regiment, commented:

> There was a feeling that because we had done well in the past this was no reason that we should be expected to carry the burden now. There were too many men who had done enough to warrant an easier passage.[8]

For many reflecting back after the war, this lack of spirit in veteran units impacted directly on their battlefield effectiveness, though in reality there is little hard evidence to support this contention.[9]

Yet this was an army in much better shape than its 1940 predecessor: better trained, better equipped, and infused with a clear and understandable approach to achieving victory. The British contributed nine infantry and four armoured divisions to the campaign in Northwest Europe, along with seven independent armoured and tank brigades, two airborne divisions, six large army group-level artillery formations, and a variety of special forces and other supporting elements. All units were at maximum strength on 6 June, complete with a near full inventory of equipment and supplies. All Allied land forces, including the Americans, initially fell under the command of Montgomery's 21st Army Group. However, as the US contingent was planned to grow in size and strength dramatically, it would by the end of August constitute its own army group, though still loosely under the strategic direction of Monty until 1 September. Most British forces in Northwest Europe would fight under the aegis of Second British Army as part of 21st Army Group, though some would operate with First Canadian Army when it became operational in late July, and others as part of the First Allied Airborne Army, the force which would later be blooded during Operation MARKET GARDEN, the ill-fated assault that resulted in the fighting for the bridge at Arnhem, infamously described as 'a bridge too far'.

The Second British and First Canadian Armies were principally made up of a number of corps – I, VIII, XII, XXX British and I and II Canadian – each with commander, staff, attached units and supporting troops. Corps could be moved around between armies as and when required, depending on operational needs and requirements. They were constituted from the pool of divisions and independent brigades, and again the allocation of units would be varied in number and type depending on the nature of the forthcoming action. Infantry divisions comprised some 18,350 men and 3,347 vehicles, split into three brigades, whilst armoured divisions were equipped with around 300 tanks but had fewer men, 15,000 or so. In the armoured divisions the tanks were initially intended to fight largely separately from the slower-moving infantry. All divisions also had a plethora of smaller formations of engineers, logistical troops, medical support, artillery and other pieces of equipment, which together made them fully functioning units.[10]

But despite this great strength in resources and equipment, there have been many critics of the British Army's approach to warfare in 1944, claiming that in action it proved to be slow, ponderous and predictable, and that this was a consequence of poor operational technique, inadequate doctrine or tactics, and an undue reliance on brute force. They would have preferred the British to have adopted more aggressive methods founded upon fluid manoeuvre, more akin to the German *blitzkrieg* era and later post-war NATO philosophy. Some post-war historians have even regarded British combat methods as a product of weakness and an unsatisfactory and muddled compromise.[11]

Yet it is clear that Montgomery and his staff *did* have a carefully considered idea of the best way to tackle the Germans and that these methods dovetailed neatly and closely with the prevailing political, economic and grand strategic pressures at play in 1944–5. Like all armies the British Army of 1944 had deficiencies, but the methods it planned to use to engage the enemy were intended to minimise the impact of such weaknesses, play to its own strengths, and exploit the failings of the Germans. Montgomery's operational methods were shaped directly by a number of factors and these in turn defined the manner in which the British Army fought in 1944–5. Clearly the army did not function in a vacuum and Montgomery and his superiors, most importantly Field Marshal Alan Brooke and Adjutant General Ronald 'Bill' Adam, had to devise methods for meeting their broader political objectives that best suited the situation in which Britain found herself by 1944. Most importantly, a policy of heavy attritional fighting against the Germans was politically, economically and strategically unacceptable; Britain simply did not have the manpower and resources to sustain the bloodletting that had accompanied the military effort of the First World War and had epitomised the war on the Eastern Front between the Germans and the Soviets since 1941. British efforts for much of the war had been directed towards large-scale strategic and tactical air forces, the Battle of the Atlantic, the Far East, and to maximising production in key areas. As the bulk of the British Army had spent the years after Dunkirk in training and preparation in the UK, priority had naturally been given to those areas where action had been both immediate and imperative. Until December 1941 Britain had had to confront the prospect of defeating Germany by means other than direct sustained land operations, as the British Army alone could never be big enough to deliver a victory against the much larger German Army in this way. After the fall of France in the early summer of 1940, this meant taking the war to Germany through bombing, blockade and subversion as the only potential route to success. In this scenario the army's role would be to act as a small, technically proficient, well-equipped force ready to spring into action and deliver a knock-out blow against an already collapsing and reeling Third Reich, undermined by economic and psychological warfare.[12] When the USA was drawn into the war fully by 1942, the grand strategy of the Allies obviously shifted to a more direct approach, but by then the British were faced with fighting a global war with dwindling resources, particularly in personnel terms. It was just as well that the British Army was fighting alongside powerful and plentiful Allies.

Ultimately the army for the liberation of Northwest Europe had to be relatively small, certainly compared to the mass armies of the Great War and the vast forces of the Third Reich, and even the relatively smaller proportion of German forces that occupied the West in 1944. It was also apparent to those planning OVERLORD that the small pool of available soldiers would barely be enough to meet the needs of maintaining even a modest-sized army. As early as October 1943 the War Office noted that it would have to transfer large numbers of troops from those units designated purely for home defence into 21st Army Group to sustain the expected effort in Normandy, and that some units might have to be disbanded to provide replacements for others as the campaign unfolded. The difficulty would be manageable, it was claimed, so long as losses did not exceed predicted levels. Across the campaign overall casualties remained within expectations, but concern grew in July 1944 when short-term losses did exceed predicted levels for a time, quite specifically in the infantry.[13]

Montgomery and his team were well aware of the constraints within which they were operating. Lieutenant General Gerald Bucknall, commanding

XXX Corps, was informed just five days before D-Day that the 'manpower and reinforcement situ [was] very touchy', while in April 1944 discussions over infantry training had focused specifically on how aggressive operations could be prosecuted against a background of needing to keep casualties down to a minimum.[14] Monty himself confided in March 1944 to Lieutenant General Ronald Weeks, Deputy Chief of the General Staff, that the liberation of Northwest Europe had to be accomplished 'with the smallest of casualties' and that the situation with regards to reinforcements was 'not good'. He still considered that if the British Army employed the correct approach in the forthcoming campaign, they 'could do it fairly cheaply'. After the war Montgomery told the journalist Chester Wilmot that by 1944 'the British Army was a wasting asset' and that the War Office had instructed him that a regular supply of replacement troops would only be available in the opening phase of Operation OVERLORD. It came as no major surprise to him when units later had to be broken up to provide replacements.[15]

Where the British erred was in estimating the losses to front-line infantry units. This became acute in the static phase of the Normandy campaign, from mid-June to late July 1944, and again in February and March 1945. This misjudgement was due to the expectation that the rates of losses to the various arms would remain at the same levels as in the Mediterranean, and, more importantly, because the Germans chose to dig in across Normandy and later in the Rhineland, consigning those battles to an attritional phase which made heavier than expected demands on infantry personnel. Paradoxically, despite surprising Allied planners and throwing Anglo-Canadian projections into some confusion, this strategy worked decidedly against German interests in the long term by bleeding their ground forces at unsustainable rates.[16]

Montgomery and his 21st Army Group staff were also driven by concerns about the determination and capabilities of their frontline soldiers, particularly those at the sharp end: the infantry, armour and sections of the artillery and engineers. Monty did not consider his charges to be bad or poor soldiers, but recognised that they were less proficient than their opponents at the tactical level due to lower levels of experience and their limited exposure to the harsh brutalities of warfare.

Senior commanders in the British Army claimed in the Second World War that the British soldier simply would not countenance the levels of obedience and sacrifice that had marked the generation of the Great War. In 1942 General Archibald Wavell argued that 'we are nothing like as tough as we were in the last war' and that British troops would not 'stand up to the same punishment and casualties as they did in the last war'. Field Marshal Alan Brooke concurred with Wavell: 'Our one idea is to look after our comforts and avoid being hurt in any way.' Even Montgomery in the aftermath of Alamein recorded that: 'The trouble with our lads is that they are not killers by nature', whilst in the Italian campaign in 1943 it was still being noted that British soldiers needed to be 'taught the desire to kill'.[17] Part of this lack of martial instinct was attributed by some commanders to the rise of socialism and the growing lack of deference. Wavell commented that 'it is softness in education and living and bad training, and can be overcome but it will take a big effort'.[18] For other commanders it was related to the collective experience of the army in the First World War, now passed on to the next generation across the interwar period.[19] It is also true that ageing officers often regard their own experiences as young men as being harsher and tougher than those facing the new generation of soldiers, particularly conscripted men; the expression that 'things were tougher in my day' can go some way in explaining the attitudes of senior officers to the morale and fighting spirit of their young troops in 1944.

For Montgomery, whether his views on the elan and drive in his troops were accurate or not, it was certainly a concern on his part in determining how he would prepare for and fight the campaign in Europe in 1944. He regarded good morale as pivotal to success in war, even modern machine-age war such as the forthcoming campaign in Northwest Europe. He later wrote in 1946 that the soldier was still the most important factor in war:

> His training is the most important consideration in the fashioning of a fighting army. All modern science is directed towards his assistance but on his efforts depends the outcome of the battle. The *morale* of the soldier is the most important single factor in war.[20]
>
> Without high morale no success can be achieved in battle; however good the strategic or tactical plan, or anything else.[21]

In his speeches to troops and civilians alike in the months before D-Day, Montgomery emphasised the vital importance of morale, referring to it as 'one of the chief factors for success'. He considered it important that commanders should bolster morale by visiting units and engaging in what others, including some of his troops, often saw as cheap publicity stunts. Monty certainly enjoyed the high-profile aspects of these events, but he also recognised that the soldiers needed to believe that he was confident, in control, and could be relied upon to do a professional job. Whether troops liked him or not was not really the point; it mattered much more whether they respected his ability and trusted him. Captain Andrew Burn, 5th Royal Horse Artillery, commenting on Monty, said that: 'He just seemed to know what he was doing, even if it was just a show at times. He exuded confidence and that mattered to the chaps.'[22]

Even those soldiers who blanched at his apparent attention-seeking, forced idiosyncrasies and gimmicks still grudgingly accepted that Montgomery had a firm grip on command in battle, and that was the key. For Montgomery it was imperative that soldiers believed in their commanders' ability to lead professionally and retained confidence in the army's ability to deliver success at a low cost in lives. He claimed in 1943 that 'soldiers will always follow a successful general', whilst in his memoirs Monty again stressed his firm views.[23] A commander:

> . . . must know his soldiers, and be recognised by them. I do not believe the leadership displayed on the Western Front in World War I would have succeeded in World War II. I would remind the reader that in World War I although I served in France, I never once saw French or Haig.[24]

Such thinking fused with Montgomery's concerns over the real abilities of his army in 1944. In public he made bold statements about the capabilities of his troops, referring to them as 'the finest in the world' though adding, 'if properly led', but his efforts to bolster morale and confidence belied his more realistic appreciation of the army he was to lead.[25] It was imperative to Montgomery that he inculcate a sense of confidence and self-belief into his forces, because he fully realised that their reserves of confidence might quickly drain away when his charges entered sustained battle against their German adversaries.

Although the manner in which the British Army planned to fight the Germans was shaped by the two overarching concerns of troop shortages and [illegible] resources. Although personnel were in short supply, equipment was not; indeed, it was generally plentiful and reliable, and backed by great investment in logistical support. Though Britain had, by design and circumstance, found itself with a relatively small army in 1944, it had always been intended that the army be fully equipped and supported with all the advantages that might be conferred by a machine-based and technologically driven approach to the conduct of war. While the German Army had made decisive use of its mechanised units in the early stages of the war, it remained essentially horse drawn, with only a few elite mobile forces, and throughout the war the Germans had been short of essential equipment, often living a hand-to-mouth existence. With a large army with many infantry divisions and a large pool of personnel to call upon, this approach was viable, at least in the short term, but the British were not afforded those benefits.

In contrast, though, the British had a more efficient economy, greater access to the world's resources, and an alliance with the USA, the so-called arsenal of democracy. These factors fused with Western perspectives on faith in technology to solve problems, greater emphasis on individualism, and the desperate desire to avoid the bloodletting of the Great War, to generate an approach to the conduct of the war against the Germans that placed equipment and machinery at its very heart. Senior British commanders were well aware of the philosophy. Brigadier Edgar 'Bill' Williams, 21st Army Group's chief intelligence officer, commented that: 'We were always very aware of the doctrine, "Let metal do it rather than flesh." We always said: "Waste all the ammunition you like, but not lives." '[26] Lieutenant General Charles Allfrey, a corps commander in Italy, always insisted on the 'maximum use of artillery and minimum use of bodies' in his battles. Such thinking was applied to armour too, and after-action reports pointed out that when under fire at close range, crews often bailed out of their tanks when hit, even if not knocked out, but that this was both understandable and acceptable as tanks could easily be replaced whereas crews could not.[27]

By 1944 the British Army was replete with artillery, tanks, trucks, munitions, small arms and all the other associated accoutrements of war, and was determined to maximise this superiority, in part to compensate for the limited numbers of personnel and the lack of battle experience of its soldiers. The approach was the antithesis of German military culture which placed battlefield craft and close combat at the heart of its philosophy, at the expense of other arms. For many German soldiers it was already apparent that the Allies intended to win by means of *Materielschlacht*, that is, great reliance on machinery and equipment. For disgruntled senior and sometimes unrepentant German commanders after the war, the cornerstone of Allied victory had not been fighting ability, prowess or operational techniques, but materiel superiority; in essence, the Germans had been overwhelmed by brute force and numbers.[28] At the very least, and however myopic, such sentiments tell us something of the British Army's approach to and conduct of the war in 1944–5.

Montgomery and his staff, along with Brooke and the War Office, were also operating under political pressure from Churchill, pressure which created further problems for the British Army in 1944. The Prime Minister delivered to Brooke and Montgomery a teasing political and strategic conundrum for the campaign to liberate Northwest Europe in 1944, one which demanded considerable military dexterity. While the first and obvious priority for the British Army was to deliver victory at some point in 1945, it was also essential that the victory achieved two other objectives.

First, for grand strategic reasons the British had to be seen as key players in the forthcoming campaign, as real contributors to the victory. It would be a politically untenable position for Churchill if victory over the German armed forces was achieved predominantly by the Americans and Soviets, with the British reduced to playing a peripheral role. In order for him to stand alongside Roosevelt and Stalin at the end of the war to oversee the reconfiguration and reconstruction of Europe, it was essential that the British Army play a full and decisive role from D-Day onwards; the army might be short of men but this could not allow Montgomery to eschew playing a full role in tackling the Germans. Churchill had already pressured the War Office in late 1943 into finding more divisions to boost 21st Army Group's role in OVERLORD to a position of initial parity with the US contribution, as he '. . . should like to be able to tell [the Americans that] we will match you man for man and gun for gun [in Normandy and this would] maintain our right to be effectively consulted in operations which are of such capital consequence'.[29]

Yet, by the end of 1944 the shrinking size of the British Army led the Prime Minister to record: 'I greatly fear the dwindling of the British army as a factor in France as it will affect our right to impress our opinion upon strategic and other matters.'[30]

This might have been construed as carte blanche for a direct and aggressive approach to battle, were it not for the second political driver: that the British Army still be in a fit state at the end of the war to play a full role in the occupation, administration and governance of the defeated Germany. If the army, whilst defeating the Germans in the field, was itself also crippled, it would not be able to play a major part in the post-war European situation, let alone provide reinforcements and resources for the myriad responsibilities [illegible] by Britain across the globe. It was essential that the British Army survive the war intact and be ready to play a future role as required; Britain not only had to win the war, it had to win the peace as well. According to Major General Kenneth Strong, SHAEF's chief intelligence officer, Churchill even attempted to persuade Eisenhower to ease the pressure on the British Army in Northwest Europe. Eisenhower apparently replied, 'if Britain wished to be in the van of the battle, as Montgomery had suggested, British casualties could not be avoided'.[31] Monty himself fully recognised the political dimension to his task: 'It was of no avail to win the war strategically if we lost it politically.'[32]

Both in the preparation and prosecution of the campaign, Montgomery was directly confronted with the task of balancing these political imperatives – the army making a decisive contribution whilst avoiding becoming compromised – alongside concerns over morale and dwindling manpower. But how was this balance to be achieved?

The manner in which he approached the puzzle was to develop still further the methods he had been employing against Axis forces since he took command of Eighth Army in the desert in 1942. Long before D-Day, Montgomery and his staff and commanders had begun to adopt a more materiel-based approach to operations against the Axis powers, an approach which limited risk, eschewed manoeuvre, emphasised firepower and which sought to impose the superiority in resources held by Eighth Army upon Rommel's Afrika Korps. By fighting a series of carefully planned and thoroughly organised 'set-piece' battles, heavily reliant on superiority in resources and particularly firepower, Eighth Army methodically wore the enemy down and broke them without themselves suffering intolerable casualties. The methods were repeated in Tunisia and then employed in Sicily and Italy to considerable effect. Montgomery delivered results because he identified the most appropriate way of fighting the Germans given the nature and capability of the forces under his command. His greatest achievement as a commander was in correctly adopting an operational approach that emphasised British strengths (firepower, planning, logistics and intelligence) and avoided weaknesses (close-combat tactics and manoeuvre). Equally, the approach of imposing well-organised attritional battles on the enemy minimised the impact of the Germans' superiority in battlefield craft and prevented them from using their skills in manoeuvre and close combat to any great effect. Only when the enemy had suffered severe casualties and losses did Montgomery allow or expect an operation to develop into a fully fledged breakout. To do so prematurely might expose his troops to combating the enemy without sufficient firepower support to tilt the balance far enough in favour of the British so as to minimise the risk of heavy casualties and morale-sapping setbacks. For Montgomery's armies, backed by superiority in material resources, it made perfect sense to fight in this manner, and in 1944 the growing concern over manpower shortages further justified the methods and reinforced the reasoning behind their adoption.

The set-piece battle favoured by Montgomery and his staff on all but a few passing occasions followed a simple plan, one later criticised for being unimaginative, yet considered by the enemy to be remorselessly efficient.[33] Operations had to be properly planned, with careful allocation of artillery and air support and with great consideration given to the logistical requirements necessary to ensure the plan's viability. Orders were often simple and direct and tended to be verbal to keep things straightforward. Officers and units were expected to stick to the plan in order that senior commanders could maintain a sound grip and overview of the operation; in this way the army was much less likely to get caught off balance by the enemy and would usually be in an excellent position to respond quickly and effectively to enemy initiatives.[34]

For the forthcoming Northwest European campaign it was intended that offensives would nearly always begin with a heavy concentration of firepower in order to inflict some casualties but more usually in the expectation of suppressing the enemy and preventing them from reacting effectively to the British advance. Firepower plans for artillery were to be nearly always focused on a small area in order to maximise the effects of the bombardment; assaults were therefore to be concentrated over narrow fronts, in stark contrast to American methods which emphasised broader assaults to impose greater pressure on the enemy, though at the expense of higher casualties, at least in the short term.

Troops leading the advance were to be further supported by rolling artillery barrages advancing ahead of the leading elements, again in a bid to keep the enemy suppressed until British troops were on top of them and in a position to seize the initiative. Leading forces would also be further supported by heavy tanks, engineers and other units in order to ease the passage forward of the infantry. The assault phase was always considered to be the most dangerous and likely to incur casualties, in spite of the support afforded it. Assuming the assault had been effective, British troops would then seek to consolidate their position on the objective as quickly as possible by bringing up reinforcements, anti-tank artillery, supplies and fresh units. This phase was considered fundamental to success as it would provide the means with which to defeat the expected enemy counter-attack.

German defensive thinking emphasised that the enemy was at their [illegible] ised, having lost some equipment and troops in the advance. An immediate counter-attack was considered the most effective way of retaking a position, whilst the enemy was in some disarray and before they had consolidated their positions. However, the longer the time spent preparing and planning the counter-attack, the less the chance of success as the enemy would derive even greater benefit for the defence from any delays.[35] Immediate counter-attack also made sense given the more devolved nature of command and initiative encouraged in the German Army, but it was flawed in two respects, certainly by 1944. First, and rather ironically given German criticism of unimaginative and predictable Allied methods in the war, the British and Canadians knew that the Germans would counter-attack after an Allied offensive and planned specifically to exploit it. Being able to predict how an enemy will react to your moves is a huge advantage in battle, and the Allies readily planned to deploy their great firepower to pummel enemy counter-attacks.

Secondly, Montgomery and his staff were also fully aware that whilst artillery inflicted the heaviest casualties on troops when they were advancing or moving, it was much less effective at wounding, injuring and killing troops who were dug in or prone. Therefore, the moment at which the heaviest losses might be inflicted on the German Army would be when they started to move, particularly in the counter-attack, especially given the effectiveness and capability of British and Canadian artillery. Montgomery's concept for breaking the enemy was in part predicated on the assumption that crippling losses would be inflicted during this counter-attack phase. All the evidence from the Mediterranean theatre led the British and Canadians to conclude that the Germans would continue with this approach in Normandy.

Lieutenant General Guy Simonds, an up-and-coming Canadian commander well thought of by Montgomery and appointed to lead II Canadian Corps in Northwest Europe, set down in detail the essence of 21st Army Group's approach and circulated it in February 1944 to Montgomery and the British Second Army commander, Lieutenant General Miles Dempsey. The latter commented that Simonds had obviously developed the same appreciation of fighting the Germans from the Mediterranean as he had – 'I agree with everything you say,' Dempsey commented – whilst Montgomery read it 'with complete agreement'. Crucially, Simonds noted that the success of the offensive battle hinged on the defeat of the German counter-attack and that the key to victory for the Allies was the use of 'all available artillery'.[36]

Montgomery also endeavoured to ensure that his army remained balanced and in full control, retaining the initiative at all times, dictating the flow of the campaign. The Germans certainly had to be prevented from ever getting the chance to launch troublesome operations of their own. By dictating the pace and location of operations, Montgomery aimed to keep the enemy reacting to Allied thrusts at different points in the front, inflicting losses upon the Germans they could ill afford, before he would 'concentrate great strength at some selected place and hit the Germans a colossal crack' precipitating a strategic breakout.[37]

Montgomery had effectively imposed his view of how operations should be fought on the British Army since his appointment as commander of Eighth Army in 1942. The army had historically always been remarkably susceptible to the influence of senior theatre commanders, as they were always encouraged to think for themselves and devise their own methods for dealing with problems. This flexible approach to the formulation of doctrine was essential in a far-flung empire where reliance on a single method or doctrine was unsustainable; much better for commanders to work to a broad set of principles but in essence think for themselves. But few commanders had imposed their will quite as ruthlessly as Montgomery.

On being appointed to command of Eighth Army, Monty was determined to stamp his authority on his officers and build a team imbued with a similar approach and style to his own. Whilst previous commanders had theoretically been able to do this, Monty was the first actually to enforce it. Those officers who did not toe the line were replaced or moved on. One such casualty was Lieutenant General Herbert Lumsden who, upon returning to London, stated: 'I've just been sacked because there isn't room in the desert for two cads like Montgomery and me.'[38] Monty had no time for niceties and would not accept bellyaching. Commanders were supposed to do their jobs efficiently and within the overall plan; deviation and prevarication were simply not tolerated. Commanders were trained and indoctrinated in Montgomery's methods with regular pep talks and meetings, and the issuing of pamphlets and notes that he expected his officers to read carefully and utilise, in itself a quite revolutionary approach for an army in which officers used written guidance and doctrine as a starting point and little more. After taking command of 21st Army Group, Montgomery hammered home his style and approach to his new charges; there was no reason to tinker with a victorious formula.[39]

Montgomery also tightly imposed his will on officers further down the chain of command to make sure that they conformed to his methods. He maintained close personal contact with his corps commanders, and used a team of liaison officers to keep tabs on his divisional leaders. These officers acted as his eyes and ears throughout the army to ensure that he knew what was going on as much as possible. Monty also relied heavily on radio communications both to keep in touch with his commanders and find out quickly what was happening. He did not want to wait hours for commanders to provide situation reports that would be out of date by the time he received them; he wanted immediate feedback to allow him to intervene if he thought it necessary. Though such tight control was occasionally resented by commanders and sacrificed a degree of localised initiative, it maintained balance in the army and greatly limited risk. As Montgomery and his staff had a fair idea of what was unfolding in a battle, they could direct resources and firepower to support units at critical moments.

Yet Montgomery also freed up his commanders to spend more time thinking about the battle they were about to fight, rather than poring over paperwork. He freed them from the tyranny of complex written orders, preferring to issue verbal directives which would then be acted on with simple direct orders to front-line units. The paperless culture in Montgomery's army was welcomed and Major General Pip Roberts, the highly regarded commander of 11th Armoured Division, considered the clarity and responsiveness in Eighth Army and then 21st Army Group to be a great improvement on what had preceded it.[40]

Montgomery also sought to impose his will on 21st Army Group by appointing his own team from the Mediterranean to key positions, often at the expense of officers who had done little wrong. He believed that as he had little time to evaluate the strengths and weaknesses of the existing 21st Army Group staff or to properly inculcate them in his methods to the extent that he would trust them, the Northwest European campaign would be best served by their replacement with his own trusted officers and commanders. Never one to stand on niceties, Montgomery's peremptory approach to the replacement of officers in 21st Army Group with his favoured 'Monty Men' did not endear him to General Bernard Paget, his predecessor at 21st Army Group. However unfair on Paget and his staff, it was nevertheless entirely appropriate and in keeping with Monty's approach that he parachuted in the team he wanted wherever possible to maintain continuity. Montgomery might have done this with more grace and his manner and style earned him yet more enemies.[41] His earlier dismissive treatment of Lieutenant General Frederick Morgan, the officer largely responsible for devising the outline OVERLORD plan, did come back to haunt him, nonetheless, as Morgan was appointed to Eisenhower's staff at SHAEF and briefed against Montgomery in 1944–5, to the extent that Monty later referred to it as a vendetta.[42]

Senior command and staff positions in 21st Army Group soon had a strong sprinkling of Montgomery-backed appointments such as Major General Francis 'Freddie' de Guingand (chief of staff), Major General George Richards (Royal Armoured Corps advisor) and Brigadiers David Belchem, Bill Williams and Charles Richardson to lead Operations, Intelligence and Plans teams respectively. The popular Freddie de Guingand was to prove crucial in the campaign for it was he who repeatedly smoothed relations between his chief, SHAEF and the Americans. Unfortunately this was a heavy burden and de Guingand's health was not good. When he was sick and away from 21st Army Group, Montgomery's failings in diplomacy, dealing with the media and personal relations were exposed.

Field appointments were also significantly guided by Montgomery: Miles Dempsey became commander of Second British Army, while Guy Simonds, Gerald Bucknall and Brian Horrocks, all protégés from the Mediterranean and obvious Monty Men, became or were earmarked for corps-level command in Northwest Europe. Of the other corps commanders, John Crocker and Neil Ritchie were favoured by Brooke, and Montgomery had no objection to their appointments, and only Richard O'Connor could be considered even very loosely as someone about whom Monty had reservations. O'Connor had been the principal field commander in the Western Desert when the Italians had been routed in 1940–41. He was subsequently captured during Rommel's counter-offensive in the spring of 1941 and spent two years in a prisoner-of-war camp in Italy before escaping in 1943. Still very highly regarded, O'Connor was proposed by Montgomery as his replacement to command of Eighth Army in Italy in 1943, though perhaps in an attempt to keep him out of OVERLORD.

But Montgomery did not have it all his own way and was on occasion forced to compromise. He had originally wanted Oliver Leese, a corps commander from the Mediterranean campaign, to lead Second British Army in Northwest Europe, with Dempsey as commander of First Canadian Army, but this scheme had foundered on the likely political opposition from Ottawa to a Briton commanding the Canadian Army in Northwest Europe. In any case Leese was wanted to command Eighth Army to ensure some continuity from Montgomery's regime, so he remained in Italy, while Dempsey took command of Second British Army. Montgomery was also particularly irked by the appointment of Harry Crerar as commander of First Canadian Army. He considered Crerar to be a likeable and convivial colleague but one quite unsuited to army command.[43] Conversely, Miles 'Bimbo' Dempsey was a clear Montgomery choice as Second Army commander. Monty did recognise that Dempsey was inexperienced at the level of army command and would have to be watched and helped, but he also knew that Dempsey would toe the line and employ Montgomery's operational methods. The approaches of the two men differed most in their respective attitudes to profile and attention: Montgomery clearly loved being in the limelight and in cultivating a 'presence' or persona, however contrived, both for the troops' morale and public consumption. In sharp contrast, Dempsey generally shunned publicity and merely got on with his job in the shadow of his mentor, although according to Bill Williams, Montgomery's chief of intelligence, Dempsey did try to sit up as high as possible in his staff car so that the troops might recognise him.[44]

After the war Dempsey was one of the very few senior commanders not to write an autobiography. He rarely said or wrote anything that might be considered critical of Montgomery (even when he disagreed with his former leader), and he burned his private papers to avoid courting controversy. During the campaign itself he remained largely in the background, accepting Montgomery's hands-on approach, and was at times even bypassed in the chain of command by Montgomery who would occasionally talk directly to corps commanders. As Montgomery's and Dempsey's approaches and views on fighting the campaign so neatly aligned anyway, it is difficult to see this as a lack of faith in Dempsey, more that both men knew what was required and both simply got on with it. Although Miles Dempsey remains an enigmatic character, he nevertheless played an important role in the leadership of the British Army in Northwest Europe. Renowned for meticulous planning and attention to detail, he had an unerring ability to read and interpret landscapes from maps:

> Wherever he went he inspired confidence and was a most welcome visitor to any harassed commander of a subordinate formation. Time and again he realised the tactical opportunity and saw it was exploited . . . I have never known anyone get to the point quicker.[45]

Dempsey retained the faith and backing of Montgomery throughout the campaign, despite erring in Operation GOODWOOD and admitting that the calamitous MARKET GARDEN plan was his responsibility, even though he never wanted to try to go for Arnhem. He nevertheless proved to be an intelligent, dependable commander, and a safe pair of hands in 1944–5, who understood his more illustrious commander's methods and quirks and who ensured that operations conformed to the overarching plan for defeating the Germans. Faultless he was not, but effective he proved to be.[46]

Montgomery's corps commanders were a mixed group of characters both in ability and temperament. Gerald Bucknall (XXX Corps) had Montgomery's backing, despite Brooke's reservations, who considered him 'quite unfit to command a Corps', a point Montgomery was later to concede. Neil Ritchie (XII Corps) had much to prove after having been sacked as Eighth Army commander in 1942, whilst John Crocker (I Corps) was thought dependable but unimaginative. Richard O'Connor's appointment (VIII Corps) courted more controversy. Montgomery was ambivalent about his appointment and there is some anecdotal evidence of a whispering campaign against O'Connor, implying that he had lost his touch, was too old, or not 'on message' with the Montgomery approach. Yet O'Connor was still considered senior enough to command many of the major battles in 1944, and Montgomery publicly expressed his support. Guy Simonds (II Canadian Corps) was regarded very highly by Montgomery but would increasingly play his part with the Canadian forces as the campaign progressed. In reserve Monty also had Brian Horrocks, who was popular and dynamic, but was still recovering from injuries suffered in the Mediterranean and was prone to bouts of sickness. Not all thought so highly of him either – one post-war writer even regarded him as a 'rather stupid man, with an overdose of personality' – and there is no doubt that Horrocks skilfully evaded any responsibility for the failure of MARKET GARDEN and somehow avoided censure for blundering in the Rhineland battles in 1945 through a policy of earnest candour.[47]

Although Montgomery could significantly influence operational techniques and methods, he was less able to shape the tactics of his front-line forces, particularly as he had less than six months in charge prior to D-Day to impose himself at this lower level. It may seem remarkable that Montgomery could not do as he saw fit, but the culture of learning and tactical development in the British Army worked against him. The army's historical attitude to doctrine had always been laissez-faire, primarily because the army had to function in a great variety of imperial roles across the globe in many theatres, environments and situations, and the formulation and imposition of a single set of tactical procedures was considered constricting and unhelpful. Commanders were imbued with a sense of independence and a problem-solving attitude that worked effectively in practice, if commanders proved up to the task. Whilst this approach was understandable enough in imperial policing, it proved less suitable in a rapidly expanding army which had to focus on fighting a major war in a specific theatre, especially when confronted by an enemy trained and intending to fight in that environment. The British found it difficult in the Second World War to impose a clearly defined set of tactical doctrines across its forces because the independent attitude of commanders railed at such enforcement; it was not so easy to throw off decades of thinking and a deeply embedded military culture.

This type of indiscipline was potentially a serious weakness. One critic of the British Army lay the blame for its inadequacies squarely on poor doctrine: 'The real cause . . . lay in the failure of the army leadership to enunciate a clearly thought out doctrine and then institute a thorough training program to ensure its acceptance throughout the army.'[48] When Montgomery attempted to impose his views about tactics on the forces preparing to invade France in June 1944, he met with only limited success. Some units accepted the Eighth Army way of doing things, some did so to a degree, and others hardly at all, preferring to work things out for themselves.[49]

Yet the British Army's culture also proved to be a strength in Northwest Europe. First, the Eighth Army methods Montgomery attempted to transplant into 21st Army Group were not always appropriate to the terrain and environment, but when they proved flawed, British commanders, inculcated in a high degree of tactical independence, felt able to abandon or adapt them and seek alternative methods. Paradoxically, if Montgomery had been readily able to impose Eighth Army tactics on all his units in 1944, it would have been more damaging, as these tactics were soon to prove less than helpful in Northwest Europe. Secondly, the German response to the Allied invasion was to dig in close to the coast and force a protracted period of fighting in dense and difficult terrain for which the Allies had neither prepared nor expected. Flexible British approaches to tactical learning facilitated a problem-solving attitude that would equip them to overcome this unexpected development. And finally, the British Army's flexibility allowed a more responsive and imaginative attitude to the unfolding campaign in 1944–5, and as new equipment and methods emerged, British commanders were more often than not receptive to them. There is little doubt that, despite initial weaknesses and some unevenness in the suitability of early methods, the British Army grew into the campaign and proved increasingly proficient in combating the enemy at the tactical level.

The three key combat arms with which the British Army intended to tackle the Germans were infantry, armour and artillery. Despite the impression gleaned from television documentaries, films and computer games, the principal fighting weapon on the Second World War battlefield was the infantry; the other arms were in essence there to support the actions of the foot soldier. Not that this was, or is, widely understood, and many popular views reflected the notion that the Second World War was a modern machine war won with tanks and aeroplanes. The American comedian Bob Hope offered a more informed view to the troops in his routines during the war:

> Let's face it, the infantry is really getting old-fashioned. There's practically nothing left for them to do. After the planes get through their job, and the tanks get through their job, and the artillery has done its job, about the only thing left for the infantry is to step in and do all the fighting.[50]

Supporting arms could do much to help the foot soldier, especially in a firepower-based army such as the British, but the crucial final steps in battle still had to be performed by riflemen. The infantry division was the sledgehammer force in the army, with the tanks there to provide support and a weapon of exploitation should the opportunity arise. If the supporting weapons and firepower worked well, the task of the infantry was made easier, but theirs was still the most dangerous job on the Second World War battlefield, even in victorious armies, and casualties always ran at alarmingly high levels.

Infantry formations and structures had been radically altered in the months leading up to D-Day, partly driven by the belated arrival of new equipment. Infantry battalions of around 800 men now had a heavily equipped and armed support company to draw upon. Anti-tank strength rested on the 6-pdr (pounder) gun, boosted by new 'sabot' ammunition which dramatically enhanced hitting power, and the PIAT (projector infantry anti-tank), which was a smaller spring-loaded anti-tank weapon designed as an answer to the American bazooka and German *Panzerschreck*. The PIAT was not well thought of, being idiosyncratic, too short ranged and by 1944 lacking in punching power. High-explosive firepower support was provided by newly improved 3-inch mortars and batteries of 25-pdr guns, which could lay down considerable bombardments to support infantry assaults. Infantry divisions also had trucks and a small number of tracked and half-tracked vehicles to keep some troops mobile, though close-assault in vehicles was still considered very dangerous.[51]

Infantry tactics in the British Army were dependent on supporting artillery keeping the enemy's heads down until the last possible moment in an advance, such that when the infantry reached their objective the enemy would still be recovering from the bombardment and in some disarray. Timing was essential: if the advancing infantry were too slow or were delayed, German troops would have had sufficient time to recover their senses and offer stout and determined resistance, inflicting heavy losses on assaulting British soldiers. Conversely, if the British infantry got ahead of themselves they risked suffering adverse losses to friendly artillery fire. Supporting tanks, thickly clad in heavy armour, would also be available to offer immediate and direct fire support to infantry at crucial moments in assaults. Coordinating armour and artillery with the infantry was therefore the key to success in the advance. Of less importance were fire and movement tactics that were only vital when fire support failed to suppress opposing forces sufficiently. When on the defensive, it was essential that the infantry be protected by anti-tank guns and be well supported by artillery directed by specialist forward observation officers (FOOs).[52]

Concern was raised in pre-invasion planning meetings at the School of Infantry (Barnard Castle, England) over the tendency of infantry sections to operate largely around the firepower of the Bren machine gun, most notably in the attack. Ammunition was sprayed around liberally and soldiers often acted merely as ammunition carriers for the Bren gun, instead of using their own rifles. The heavy use of Bren gun ammunition, despite the extra supplies carried forward, caused shortages once the objective had been achieved, potentially weakening the defence against the anticipated German counter-attack. The reliance on the Bren gun also served to undermine the other combat skills of the infantryman, and in circumstances where firepower was likely to be less effective and infiltration tactics were required, British soldiers might be found wanting.[53]

Armoured forces for Northwest Europe would in the main be used for infantry support and it was still the case in 1944 that the tank's primary role was to attack 'soft' targets, such as enemy infantry, buildings and dug-in positions, with high-explosive ammunition and machine guns. How this was to be achieved at the tactical level was still far from clear and units therefore differed in their approaches to integrating infantry and tanks in the assault. Experience from the Mediterranean had been fused with home-grown ideas, all shaped by the availability of equipment and its capabilities. Some units stood off from their objectives and blazed away in the manner of static artillery, contravening usual tank tactics which placed great reliance on mobility.[54] To complicate matters further, veteran units from the Mediterranean campaign brought back their own methods that reflected their experiences in the desert, and they were unwilling for 'green' units or desk-bound tacticians in the War Office to instruct them in how to fight differently in Northwest Europe. Unfortunately, Mediterranean methods did not always transfer easily into the European theatre with its quite different terrain, and many veteran units were in for a rude awakening.[55]

By 1944 British tanks fought in 'troops' of three or four vehicles, depending on their combat role, with each tank usually having a crew of five. Tanks were not expected to fight independently and intimate cooperation with infantry was vital, though not easily achieved. Coordination between tanks and infantry in close combat would plague the British and indeed all armies in the Second World War, largely because transporting infantry safely alongside tanks was complicated and dangerous; the infantry, even when in armoured half-track vehicles, were both vulnerable to enemy artillery fire and too slow. Yet they were vital to support tanks in the assault, as tank crews were largely blind being encased in their armour plate. The infantry provided the eyes for the tanks and the tanks the supporting firepower to deal with enemy positions. No army had successfully achieved this balance and kept casualties down prior to D-Day – even German tactics were repeatedly found wanting when facing an enemy well stocked with heavy and responsive artillery as they were to be in the Northwest European campaign.[56]

British tanks also still offered up technical problems in 1944. In fact, no weapon in the British Army of the Second World War has provoked more controversy than the tank. The MP Richard Stokes was a fierce contemporary critic: 'Thousands of the boys who went to fight for us are not coming home again because our Ministry of Defence failed, through stupidity and weakness in the department of weapons.'[57] And there appeared to be much evidence to support his view. In the early part of the war British tanks had suffered from crippling unreliability and by 1941 inadequate weaponry too. When superior American tanks began to be imported that year the War Office and the British Army in the field were enthusiastic supporters – they wanted nothing more to do with British home-designed and built tanks. By the summer of 1944 American tanks constituted close on 70 per cent of the entire British armoured force, but they were themselves flawed and inadequate. The famous M4 Sherman, though reliable, easily maintained and spacious, sported a weak 75mm gun that was of little use against heavy German tanks, whilst its armour provided minimal protection against enemy gunfire. It also had a tendency to blow up spectacularly when knocked out, or 'brew-up' as it was widely known, incinerating its crew in the process if they were unable to bale out quickly enough. British-designed tanks had improved dramatically since the nadir of 1941, but there were still question marks against them. The latest cruiser tank, the Cromwell, was faster than the Sherman, but its armour protection and firepower were similar and therefore just as inadequate. It was also a smaller and more cramped vehicle. The British also deployed the Churchill tank which had sacrificed speed and mobility for improved armour protection. This, in theory, allowed it to close on enemy positions with a greater chance of survival than lightly armoured Shermans and Cromwells. But though the latest types of Churchill tank carried armour thicker even than the feared German Tiger tank, they were still vulnerable to heavy enemy anti-tank guns.

The British Army was well aware of these issues, and initiatives were in hand to solve the firepower problem. A crash programme to fit the much heavier 17-pdr anti-tank gun into the Sherman had proved a qualified success and these resulting Firefly tanks were allocated at the rate of one per troop by the summer of 1944, specifically to deal with heavy German tanks should they be encountered. Lieutenant Bob Boscawen, Coldstream Guards, was suitably impressed by the enhanced firepower. On first firing the 17-pdr gun:

> There was a blinding flash, my beret was whipped off and out through the open turret hatch above. As the hot air and fumes subsided I just caught a sight of the tracer hitting the target and pulling it right out of the ground. A cheer went up from outside the Officers' Mess and the staff sergeant put his head into the turret and called out, 'Are you alright in there?'! An answer to the enemy's superiority in armour had arrived.[58]

Although a last-minute solution, the Firefly would prove to be well liked while the Americans, denied such extra firepower, looked on enviously. Other efforts to fit 17-pdr guns into tanks and vehicles fared less well with one product, the Archer, even carrying the gun backwards into battle.

Tactics on how to integrate Fireflys into units and how to deploy lightly armoured Shermans in close support of infantry were still in a state of flux in the summer of 1944, partly a product of tactical indiscipline. It was as well for the British that the enemy also had many similar problems; despite modern popular perceptions, most German tanks were no better than British types, and many were unreliable or in some cases cobbled-together hybrids. The British were nonetheless fearful of the German Tiger tank with its hard-hitting 88mm gun, which they had previously encountered in North Africa, and the Panther, of which they had less experience but which also appeared to be equally fiercesome. Thankfully, as the Royal Armoured Corps estimated before D-Day, these heavy tanks, particularly the Tiger, would not be encountered in great numbers.[59]

Although great attention was placed on the front line combat arms – the infantry and armour – the most potent weapon in the British Army's inventory in 1944 was artillery, which remained the biggest killer of the Second World War battlefield, as it had been in the Great War. By the summer of 1944, 21st Army Group could call upon a great weight of artillery, the heaviest concentrations of which were contained in the six formidable AGRAs (Army Group Royal Artillery).[60] But it was equally the dramatic improvements that had been made to the flexibility of British artillery both in defence and in attack that, by 1944, made it a potentially devastating weapon. It was the responsiveness and speed with which concentrations of force could be deployed that marked the British Army's artillery of 1944 as both superior and different from that which preceded it, responsiveness underpinned by air observation, excellent intelligence work and sophisticated communications links. Artillery was able to lay down heavy, suppressing concentrations of firepower in preparation for attacks, rolling artillery barrages to lead the way forward, and very rapidly call in fire support against targets uncovered during advances. In defence, the responsiveness and intensity of artillery support was crucial; against enemy troops advancing in the open, British artillery was simply devastating.[61]

Yet artillery was no panacea, despite the post-war claims that the British simply blasted their way to victory. It was potent enough against a moving target but the lethal effects of artillery fell away markedly against a dug-in and static enemy. The standard British field gun, the 25-pdr, had sacrificed weight of shell for range and mobility, but these attributes were now of little value against an enemy determined to adopt a defensive posture. Heavier British guns (5.5-inch and 7.2-inch types) carried greater destructive power but they still could not crush a prepared defensive line, merely suppress it. Accuracy and targeting still needed to be refined and good as British techniques were, they still left room for improvement. British artillery could prepare the way for assaults, but crippling casualties would only be inflicted if the enemy could be provoked into activity, particularly counter-attacks.[62]

In spite of all the tactical and operational thinking that underpinned the British Army's approach to the forthcoming campaign, the essential raw material remained the soldier, men that reflected the society from which they were drawn, with all its shortcomings, strengths and underlying facets. Around 75 per cent of troops were conscripts, the rest being professional soldiers who had been in place in 1939, and volunteers. Professionals had joined for the usual variety of reasons that have caused people to enter military service for generations, whilst volunteers signed up once war had broken out for a range of reasons – from peer-group pressure to adventure to a general desire to stop the Nazis from doing to their own families what had been inflicted on those in Poland, Belgium, Norway and many other countries.

Bill Partridge, 4th Somerset Light Infantry, had always hankered after a military life, considered himself ridiculously loyal to king and country, and therefore joined up to stop Hitler, despite being in a reserved occupation – 'silly really when you think about it'.[63] Lance Corporal Denis Avey, 2nd Rifle Brigade, was from a farming background with no military connections, but was nevertheless also swept up by the times: 'War broke out and like a silly arse I joined up.'[64] Private Colin Hall, 1st Airborne Division, had joined the Territorial Army in the spring of 1939 having been tempted by colourful posters that offered additional excitement to working for the Post Office. When war broke out, however, he and a friend were quickly drafted into the army full time, 'which was something neither of us had seen in the ad. An impulsive decision . . . was to direct the next course of my life.'[65] Charles Hanaway, like many others, was unsettled in his home life and, aware in 1941 that many of his friends were joining up, signed on for the army at the age of seventeen: 'The days of my youth were about to end.'[66] For some the army, or where they ended up in the army, were second choices. Lieutenant Dickie Cox, 4th Somerset Light Infantry, was from a military family, but recognised his limitations: 'I was not technically minded so I thought I'd better join the infantry.' He was too short to join his father's regiment in the Guards, so was 'consigned' to the light infantry.[67] Lance Corporal Stan Proctor, 43rd Wessex Division, had held ambitions to be a Spitfire pilot, but having failed the medical was soon in the army: 'I had been in the Boys' Brigade and knew about Morse code and that, so ended up in the signals', which was logical.[68] But the army struggled at times to allocate new recruits to appropriate roles and as a result the men concerned were often baffled by their postings. Private Harry Askew had requested to join either the engineers or the infantry, but somehow, and for no reason he could discern or that was ever explained to him, ended up in the Royal Army Medical Corps.[69] Such occurrences were a by-product of a rapidly expanding army quickly attempting to absorb new personnel, often without thorough and wholly effective selection procedures for doing so.[70] Once men had been admitted, the army did not always fulfil their expectations. Its attitude in the early years of the war remained one of processing individuals to conform to directed team work, often employing traditional and much resented methods of drill and pointless duties, underscored with antiquarian attitudes and outmoded notions. The first six weeks or so of training consisted of what soldiers called 'bullshit': square bashing (marching up and down on the parade ground), crude indoctrination, futile white-washing of anything that did not move, and kit inspections. 'The silliness of our training amounted to sheer stupidity at times, with lots of physical practice and lectures which dated from the last war,' Leonard Watkins of the Royal Engineers recalled. Although he was later trained in constructing pontoon bridges, the famous Bailey Bridge was nowhere in evidence for much of his time training in the UK:

> It was rumoured to fit together like a Meccano set and was strong and very quick to erect. No lectures were given about it and no pictures, but eighteen months later we had to build one in the dark and under enemy fire![71]

Joe Ekins, Northants Yeomanry, agreed about the balance of 'bullshit' to practical learning:

> If you got your knife and fork a quarter of an inch out of place you were on a charge, but in tank recognition lectures and talks you could fall asleep at the back and no-one seemed to bother.[72]

New recruits also grumbled about the inadequacies of poorly trained instructors, usually older NCOs, hidebound and institutionalised by years of service. Bill Partridge, 4th Somerset Light Infantry, recalled:

> NCOS in training were often old school and didn't have a bloody clue what they were talking about. At first there were no manuals or anything. Fortunately we had a couple of officers who put something useful together for us.[73]

Later training, focused on chosen or allotted service arms, was better, and most troops were eventually well instructed in the basic mechanics of their trade by the time of D-Day. Officers who had been young and inexperienced in 1940 had matured into competent junior commanders by 1944, relatively well versed in a whole range of necessary skills. Training stepped up in the two years leading up to D-Day with the development of training schools aimed at refining particular skills. Exercises could be dangerous with a real need to make them worthwhile and realistic, as Lieutenant Colonel Trevor Hart Dyke, 49th Division, recorded:

> Like other units we had our toll of accidents, but, to make the training realistic, normal safety precautions had to be relaxed. This policy was well rewarded when we went into battle, as we were not then unduly perturbed by the noise and danger of war.[74]

But there were continuing limits to the quality of practical tactical training imposed by available space, suitable equipment and shortages of ammunition. Tank crews fired just a few rounds on a range per year and may well have only loosed off some 15 to 20 rounds prior to entering action in Normandy. Tactical training was shaped by the types of tanks available, and units preparing in Britain had to use obsolete equipment that required inappropriate tactics, a situation not really resolved until 1943, by which time it was too late to stamp them out completely for D-Day. Matters were not helped by the late introduction of equipment such as the Firefly, which allowed gunners only some five or so shots with their weapon prior to going into action.

Experienced troops were more limited in number, but those veterans from [illegible] often disgruntled, believing it was someone else's turn to take the war to the Germans. Though there is little evidence that such grumbling was a direct cause of later battlefield failings or poor morale, it nevertheless provoked dismay. To make matters worse, NCOs within such units were further frustrated at having new, very junior and untested officers foisted upon them. It was a difficult transition for the new officers in such circumstances too, as they were well aware that old sweat sergeants would not take too kindly to being bossed about by 'snotty little know-alls who didn't know their arse from their elbows', according to Major Johnny Langdon, 3rd Royal Tank Regiment.[75] 'We had to tread carefully and listen to the senior sergeants and learn from them. It was quite embarrassing really, at first', recalled Captain Robin Lemon of the same regiment.[76]

The British Army also faced a challenge in creating a suitable atmosphere which might foster a greater willingness amongst its soldiers to confront the evils of Nazism. By 1941 the army's hierarchy believed that the German soldier's fierce determination in battle was in part derived from the ideological fervour and martial attitudes of National Socialism. Attempts to instil similar resolve in British troops, however, failed miserably. Officers were instructed to organise fireside chats with soldiers to discuss the nature of the war against Nazism and the necessity of defending democracy and freedom. But this did not sit easily with British soldiers drawn from a society which viewed political extremism with great suspicion; at its heart liberal democracy was anti-ideological and tended to produce apathy towards politicians and causes. Private James Sims, 1st Airborne, recalled the nature of the attempts to educate the troops in the necessity of fighting:

> We were also shown propaganda films and given lectures which were designed to clarify what we were fighting for. Getting the English worked up enough to defend democracy was an uphill task, as the average soldier appeared to have only three basic interests: football, beer and crumpet.[77]

Overt and obvious pieces of political propaganda usually elicited amusement, hoots of derision or contempt.[78] The army also had to tread carefully as political indoctrination was forbidden by the army's rules, *King's Regulations*, though army life naturally caused a degree of politicisation.[79]

British soldiers, like 1940s British society, largely rejected fanaticism and extremism, and the army's attempts to match German indoctrination were always likely to fail, perhaps thankfully so. Though British soldiers generally lacked the fervour of many of their German counterparts, this was no bad thing considering where the ideology of Nazism had led the German state. Even so, the record of British soldiers was never free from controversy and they were to perpetrate many criminal acts in the 1944–5 campaign, but these were as nothing compared to the atrocities and barbarism of German forces, the army as well as the SS, in the Second World War.

Despite concern over the impending campaign, by the summer of 1944, after three or four years of limited activity, many British soldiers had become restless. An inactive army, awaiting introduction to action, can be prone to indiscipline born of frustration and tedium. 'We were bored stiff, officers included,' recalled Trooper Joe Ekins, and some laxness in units over leave, both official and unofficial, had to be tolerated.[80] Though few troops were looking forward to the fighting, by the summer of 1944 they just wanted to get it over with.

As Montgomery and his soldiers prepared for OVERLORD, it was clear that they had a plan for the forthcoming campaign, one intended to minimise casualties, maintain the cohesiveness of the army and get the job done. It served to maximise the impact of British strengths in firepower and resources, and to mitigate the perceived weaknesses in tactical know-how and experience. Most importantly it matched very closely the needs and requirements of the British state in 1944. The British did not intend to mirror the methods employed by the Germans in the 1939–42 period, not out of weakness, but because relying on their own capabilities, skills and attributes served their needs much better and minimised risk.

The key to all of this was sustainability. Montgomery and his staff, and Brooke and the War Office, viewed the forthcoming campaign holistically and planned to match available resources and capabilities with political and strategic requirements. Because the British Army was likely to run short of personnel, but had a plethora of equipment and resources, operations and tactics were devised accordingly. Most importantly of all, everything was underpinned by logistical limits: if an operation could not be properly supported and resourced, it was rarely if ever undertaken. In contrast, the Germans mounted bold and risky operations with minimal thought given to long-term sustainability; their penchant for operational manoeuvre meant they were able to achieve their objectives in the short term, but it was often just a matter of time before it all turned sour.

The British, believing themselves to be in winning position in 1944, saw no reason to change the successful formula that had crystallised in the Mediterranean, and fully intended to employ the same plan in Northwest Europe. That there were deficiencies in their methods is not in doubt, but then neither was there an alternative better suited to their needs and to the [illegible] in the army. As Montgomery remarked in his memoirs:

> I . . . had the mental unrest of seeing certain aspects of the tactical conduct of the Second World War mishandled, and the British people thereby made to endure its horrors longer than should have been the case, with the loss of life which that entailed.[81]

In June 1944 he was determined to ensure that in the forthcoming campaign that would not be repeated.

3

BRIDGEHEAD
The First Step to Liberation

IN THE HISTORY of the Second World War, indeed of all warfare, the D-Day landings of 6 June 1944 hold iconic status. The story, retold many times and immortalised in films such as *The Longest Day* and *Saving Private Ryan*, and in the television series *Band of Brothers*, stands as perhaps the greatest Allied endeavour of the war to liberate Europe from the Third Reich. There is no doubt that the scale and the enormity of the task confronting the Allies in 1944 was an immense challenge. It called upon great skills in cooperative planning across and within services, institutions and nationalities to a degree the Axis powers could not possibly match, and represented easily the hardest military hurdle the Allies would have to clear in order to win the war.

Operation OVERLORD was a vast undertaking unparalleled in military history. At five points along the Normandy coastline Allied troops would storm ashore on the morning of 6 June – the Americans in the west on the beaches codenamed UTAH and OMAHA, and the Anglo-Canadians in the east at GOLD, JUNO and SWORD. To protect the flanks of the landing beaches, airborne troops would be dropped on the night of 5–6 June to seize key strategic points and sow confusion in the minds of the Germans. As the armies headed to continental Europe they would be supported in their task by some 12,000 aircraft, 1,200 fighting ships and 5,500 landing and naval craft. The whole operation was aided by an intricate deception plan and the coordination of many supporting services and arms.[1]

For the British Army, D-Day in Normandy would also carry with it the burden of history, of past experiences both recent and distant, that shaped attitudes and defined levels of anxiety. Many recalled the disaster that was Gallipoli in 1915 and more recently Dieppe in August 1942, both amphibious assaults that had ended in failure and bitter recrimination. Even the more successful beach assaults in the Mediterranean such as Operation HUSKY, the invasion of Sicily in July 1943, at Salerno in Operation AVALANCHE in September of the same year, and at Anzio in Operation SHINGLE in January 1944 had revealed and emphasised the dangers and predicaments of amphibious operations. Even as late as 28 April 1944 at Slapton Sands in Devon, Exercise TIGER, a small-scale rehearsal for D-Day, had again highlighted the dangers of amphibious operations, when German E-boats had got in amongst Allied ships. Yet much had also been learned from the previous years' amphibious actions and subsequently incorporated into NEPTUNE, the assault phase of OVERLORD. It was of paramount importance that air supremacy be attained prior to the operation, and it was imperative that assaulting forces must not in any circumstances be pinned to the beaches.

JUBILEE, the failed Dieppe landings in 1942, had taught the Allies other important lessons. First, a direct assault on an urban area from the sea was too dangerous and, secondly, armour was required to be part of the initial assault to provide close direct-fire support on the beaches, offer rallying points for troops, and help overcome enemy obstacles and strongpoints. A range of specialised armour had been designed for D-Day, the AVREs (Armoured Vehicles, Royal Engineers), all equipped with small portable bridges, mine-clearance machinery and bunker-busting explosives. The British had also introduced amphibious swimming tanks (Duplex Drive Shermans) to allow them to land directly on to the beaches for immediate close support. Lance Corporal Patrick Hennessy, 13/18th Hussars commented:

> The notion that we would swim our tanks across the water was difficult for us to understand . . . 'Surely,' we said, 'it will sink like a stone?' 'Not so,' said the Boffins.
>
> Fine in theory, but we had grave doubts![2]

Private John Chalk, 1st Hampshires, noted that training exercises increased in scale in the weeks leading up to D-Day and involved air and navy personnel too, as well as many new sights:

> It was around this time that we were becoming acquainted with all the unusual armoured vehicles we would no doubt be working with – flail tanks for clearing mines, flame-throwing tanks, swimming tanks and tanks for all sorts of jobs.[3]

The scale of the build-up of forces in the south of England resulted in many compromises in accommodation and lingering problems of boredom, both sometimes sources of disgruntlement for the troops.[4] Many were billeted in tents set in damp woods and forests, and in between exercises there was little to do. Beer was in short supply and a pub with a stock was soon inundated with soldiers in search of fun and relaxation. By May many soldiers simply wanted to get on with the job of the 'second front' and bring an end to the waiting; they viewed the forthcoming campaign with trepidation, but if they had to do it they preferred to get on with it sooner rather than later.

Frustration mounted as in late May a series of test embarkation exercises took place causing excitement and alarm among soldiers and civilians alike along the south coast of England, only to turn to grumpiness when the orders came to return to barracks. Trooper Duce, 8th Hussars, 7th Armoured Division, recalled:

> We had one false alarm at the end of May when we were paraded in Battle Order and marched down to the seafront to our respective vehicles with the intention of moving off, but after having mounted up and kept hanging about for orders it was suddenly cancelled. So we went back to our billets.[5]

For the troops in the assault wave the pressure was even more acute. Lieutenant Colonel James Moulton, 48 Commando:

> We could certainly do with some more training but we could never recapture the old intensity; there is a limit to the time you can train the way we had been doing, and the tension would now be snapped – better to go and have it over.[6]

When the orders were eventually issued on 3 June to begin assembling for D-Day, planned for two days later, the mood shifted to one of tension born of anxiety, in many cases heightened by inexperience of battle. Many were already embarked and at sea when the orders came through the following day postponing the invasion by twenty-four hours due to the inclement weather. Reactions naturally ranged from relief to frustration. Lieutenant David Holbrook commented: 'There was nothing more the men could do. They felt a depressing sense of flop. They tried to rest, but were anxious and downcast.'[7]

The following day the invasion was back on, having received Eisenhower's go-ahead despite the still less than favourable weather forecasts. It had been a difficult decision and a calculated risk for Ike, the Supreme Commander, but with little likelihood of a dramatic improvement in the conditions before the tides forced a postponement of some weeks, he had few realistic options.

As troops headed out into the Channel or clambered into their transport aircraft ready for airborne assaults, they were experiencing a range of emotions. Captain Douglas Aitken, medical officer with 24th Lancers, noted in his diary:

> We are on our way.
>
> Try to write home but it seems a hopeless task and no certain knowledge of when any letters will reach home.[8]

Brigadier Lord Lovat, commanding the 1st Commando Brigade tasked with a series of crucial specialist roles in the first wave, noted the less than ideal weather conditions as he crossed the sea:

> There was a knifing wind in the Channel. Rupert Curtis described the sea as 'lumpy' when I joined him on the bridge.
>
> Waiting for the darkness, Derek [Mills-Roberts] clambered over from his motor launch to mine. Immediate worries were over, with time to unwind before touch down.[9]

Many soldiers suffered from sea-sickness, often exacerbated by the smell of diesel fumes and the still choppy sea. Lieutenant Ian Hammerton, a mine-clearing flail tank commander, suffered this fate and having caught a whiff of fumes, 'found it necessary to hang over the stem and get rid of my last meal. Since then I have never been able to stomach the smell of diesel'.[10]

As the 130,000 troops crossed the Channel on the night of 5–6 June and with airborne troops already beginning to land in Normandy, Montgomery waited in England just outside Portsmouth for the first indications of how the plan was unfolding. Naturally, he was keen to get to France himself before the day was out and liaise with his army commanders, Omar Bradley and Miles Dempsey.[11] Despite the weather, Monty had argued to go ahead with the invasion the night before, such was his desire to get on with it, and now there really was no turning back; the three divisions of airborne troops were en route to France and across the five designated Normandy landing beaches initial preparations and operations were underway. The plan for the campaign and the expectations for the first phase were based on a series of assumptions and strategic imperatives. These factors then impacted upon how the British Army planned to grapple with the German forces opposing them. Montgomery's basic plan called for the Americans in the west to capture Cherbourg as quickly as possible to open up a major port to supply the Allied forces for later operations in France. Once this was secured the US forces would then turn south and west to clear Brittany and its important Atlantic ports before turning east towards Paris. For the British and Canadians landing on the eastern flank the main task was to push south-east to capture the high ground between the city of Caen set just a few miles inland from the coast and the town of Falaise, some 20 miles further to the south. This would threaten the road to Paris, force the Germans to commit themselves in this sector, and allow the Americans to seize their objectives more readily. The drive south would also capture valuable territory suitable for airfields, essential for easing the work of the Allied air forces. Normandy lies some 100 miles from the south coast of England and the extra flying time travelling to and fro across the Channel therefore reduced the time aircraft could spend over France supporting operations; it was essential that airfields be established in Normandy to ease this problem as soon as possible. Montgomery broadly expected the Allies to push on and thereafter pause at the Seine to regroup. It was all to be achieved in some three months.[12]

For the British and Canadians the key objective in the opening stages of OVERLORD was to capture the city of Caen and its crossings over the River Orne which lay directly astride the route to the south and Falaise. This posed the possibility of intense urban fighting with all the heavy casualties in personnel this was likely to bring, but bypassing Caen was unlikely to yield much benefit. To the east of the city, where 6th Airborne Division was to land on D-Day, the terrain was unsuitable for a rapid envelopment, being overlooked by high ground to the east, whilst to the west of Caen the smaller but nevertheless still problematic barrier of the River Odon cut across any axis of advance. Further west still the terrain became more rugged and covered thickly with the so-called *bocage*, areas of small fields, generally some 100 metres across, surrounded by high-banked hedgerows, a considerable aid to defence and hindrance to movement.

The solution was simple enough: capture Caen quickly before the Germans could react and thus avoid any prolonged street fighting, and from there the push into the more open terrain on the road to Falaise might be achieved. Miles Dempsey, the Second British Army commander, certainly believed this was possible and like Montgomery realised the crucial role to be played by the British and Canadian forces in bearing down on the Germans around Caen to facilitate an American push to Cherbourg and Brittany.[13] On 14 April 1944 in OVERLORD planning notes Montgomery instructed Dempsey to advance armoured brigade groups inland from the beaches as soon as possible on D-Day to secure crucial objectives, most obviously Caen:

> Armoured units and Bdes [brigades] must be concentrated quickly as soon as ever the situation allows after the initial landing on D-day; this may not be too easy, but plans to effect such concentrations must be made and every effort made to carry them out; speed and boldness are then required, and the armoured thrusts must force their way inland.
>
> I am prepared to accept almost any risk in order to carry out these tactics. I would risk even the total loss of the armoured brigade groups . . .[14]

These directions reflected the necessity of securing Caen quickly, but also the fear of being too timid in the first few hours of D-Day and squandering opportunities to seize territory. In this way the tone, pace and initiative of the campaign could be imposed from the start. Montgomery pressed the point again in his address to senior commanders on 21 May:

> Every officer and man must have only one idea and that is to peg out claims inland and to penetrate quickly and deeply into enemy territory. To relax once ashore would be fatal . . . senior officers must prevent it at all costs on D-Day and on the following days. Great energy and drive will be required.[15]

Montgomery was also very keen to present his counterpart, Field Marshal Erwin Rommel, his old adversary from the desert and now commander of Army Group B based in Northwest Europe, with as many headaches as possible to prevent him from organising counter-attacks. He knew and respected Rommel's tactics and style well, and was determined to dictate the tempo and nature of the battle and force his opponent to dance to Monty's tune. Far from being cautious and overly careful, the D-Day plan demonstrated boldness and dash, much to the satisfaction of Churchill who wanted to see no repeat of the sluggish efforts of Lieutenant General Mark Clark's US Fifth Army at Anzio.[16] Paradoxically, Dempsey claimed post-war that the D-Day plan, far from being too ambitious, was not ambitious enough. He argued that it was imperative for the British to grab what they could in the confusion generated by the landings and before the Germans had recovered their wits. In his view there was every reason to give 'the troops plenty to go for'.[17]

Yet there were obvious factors that might well militate against success. Much would depend on the weather as this would dictate the pace of the landings and the speed with which the follow-up troops for the drive inland could be mustered and organised. The scale of the opposition encountered would also be pivotal in determining success, and preparations by the British would necessarily be driven by the quality of intelligence on who and what they were likely to meet. In the absence of immediately available artillery support, the armoured groups would also be dependent on naval gunfire and tactical air support, the latter itself conditioned by the weather. The British would have to overcome their own military culture and attitudes, cultivated in particular by Montgomery since 1942. As an army taught to rely on materiel support, firepower and risk aversion, it would not easily embrace ad hoc and underprepared assaults and manoeuvre. To be in Caen as quickly as was hoped for would take a temporary shift in attitude on the part of troops and commanders, plus fair weather and manageable opposition.

Much depended on the landing forces having a clear idea of what they were to confront after arriving in Normandy, and for this they relied on intelligence briefings and summaries. Allied intelligence broadly served the army well for OVERLORD, on the grand scale in identifying German intentions and estimations relatively accurately, and on the small scale in building a picture of coastal obstacles, strongpoints and gun positions. The British Joint Intelligence Committee and MI14 (the German branch at the Military Intelligence Division) had pieced together much of the puzzle and kept the armed forces up to date with summaries for senior commanders and staff officers down to divisional level. Montgomery's own intelligence chief at 21st Army Group, Edgar 'Bill' Williams, was also regarded very highly indeed, being described as 'most able and clear-headed'.[18]

Yet the picture was not complete, nor was the process of integrating gathered intelligence into planning seamless. Intelligence was gathered and often made available to commanders until the very last moment, but it did not necessarily directly and obviously influence plans and orders. Much of the detailed planning for OVERLORD had been completed by April 1944, based upon and informed by intelligence gathered until that time and driven by the original date set for the invasion, 1 May. Alas, in the few weeks leading up to D-Day changes had occurred that directly shaped the first few days of operations and in particular the attempted drive on Caen. By 6 June enemy strength in Normandy was stronger than any analysts had predicted prior to 25 May and in excess of the level that SHAEF (Supreme Headquarters Allied Expeditionary Force) believed safely manageable by the D-Day forces.

Intelligence had identified the locations of all but two of the major enemy formations, failing to pick up that 352nd Infantry had strengthened the OMAHA and GOLD beach areas (though Williams suspected as much) and that 21st Panzers had advanced its anti-tank artillery and half of its infantry into position between the coast and Caen, precisely the route British troops would have to take if they wanted to capture the city quickly. Latest intelligence reports considered 21st Panzers to be further south and assaulting formations believed that it would take some hours before the tanks of 21st Panzers would be in a position to attack them.[19] At 21st Army Group HQ, Bill Williams estimated correctly the likely level of enemy armour in the sector on D-Day to be 280 (it was actually 276) but was unable to identify precisely where it was and how quickly it might intervene. Curiously, Second Army intelligence painted a very bleak picture, informing commanders that they might encounter immediate localised counter-attacks by enemy armour, and that by twelve to twenty-four hours after the landings they could be grappling with 540 tanks (double the real figure) with up to 160 vehicles of 17th SS Panzer Grenadiers following on closely behind (they in fact had just 42 assault guns and were near Poitiers on D-Day, some 230 miles to the south).[20]

In truth such estimates mattered little, because if they had been correct, logically it would have resulted in the postponement of OVERLORD. As it was the German garrison in Normandy had increased by some 50 per cent since 1 May and by July would have reached potentially daunting proportions. Ultimately, despite growing concerns and Second Army's worst-case scenario pessimism, by early June it was now or never. The British always understood that the success of D-Day would be determined by how rapidly the German forces in situ would be able to react, and thereafter by how quickly the enemy could move troops and equipment to Normandy relative to the speed with which the Allies could build up their forces from England.

It is unlikely that much could have been done to improve the prospects of seizing Caen on the first day, even if the British had known that elements of 21st Panzers were now blocking their route, unless it had been recognised many weeks in advance. Ultimately, failing to capture Caen quickly did not consign the invasion to disaster, though it naturally would make things much harder and, depending on the German response, could force the British to fight in terrain not of their own choosing.

If capturing Caen quickly would ease the progress of the campaign, securing the eastern flank of the landing beaches against attack was fundamental to the success of the landings themselves. To the east of Caen, across the River Orne and the Caen Canal which linked the city to the sea and the port of Ouistreham, lay a region of territory across which the Germans might muster a counter-attacking force and drive hard into the flank of SWORD beach, just at the moment the British would be attempting to push inland. Clearly, it would be necessary to prevent this and the primary objective of 6th Airborne Division on D-Day and immediately after was to capture and hold the crossings over the Orne and Caen Canal, a task described as 'of the upmost importance to the smooth conduct of future operations'.[21] Furthermore, elements of 6th Airborne would suppress the battery at Merville, which threatened SWORD beach, and deny to the Germans use of the roads and the area between the Orne and the River Dives further to the southeast and east of Caen. The airborne elements would then be reinforced by the bulk of I SS (Special Services) Brigade on the morning of D-Day as it advanced from SWORD beach, and later by 6th Airlanding Brigade which would arrive in Normandy in the afternoon of D-Day to strengthen further the bridgehead over the Orne.

Much had been learned about airborne operations since the British had first started investigating their use seriously in 1941. They had been used in Sicily in 1943 to reasonable effect but key lessons had been noted that influenced the use of 6th Airborne in Normandy. It was considered essential that key targets be captured and seized quickly, which required coordinated and concentrated insertions of troops – delays would only alert the enemy, raise the level of force necessary to capture objectives and multiply likely problems.[22]

Detailed planning for D-Day had begun in February 1944 when Major General Richard 'Windy' Gale was allocated the task by Second Army, and it was such planning and preparations that would mark out this airborne operation from most others conducted by the Allies in the Second World War. An initial problem that could not be avoided, despite the Allies' supposedly overwhelming resources, was a lack of transport and towing aircraft which necessitated a two-stage drop, albeit on the same day, 6 June. This factor further drove the desire to drop or land troops as close to their targets as possible to maximise surprise and immediate impact, something that would contrast with MARKET GARDEN some three months later.

Gale and his team had moulded 6th Airborne into a well-honed force, well versed in their respective tasks, but equally they fully realised that contact with the enemy was certain to throw up problems. Brigadier Hill of 3rd Parachute Brigade announced to his troops just prior to D-Day: 'Gentlemen, in spite of your excellent training and orders, do not be daunted if chaos reigns. It undoubtedly will.'[23] For the troops themselves more specific concerns predominated. Captain Gerald Ritchie, 12 Para, noted:

> It was difficult to imagine that by dawn on the next day, we should have been tipped out of our aeroplane over France and should have landed in the place where there were quite a number of evil-minded Bosch, whose one object would be to liquidate us before we could do the same to them.[24]

Major Clarke of 13 Para recalled:

> Felt that lack of bumping which indicated our being airborne . . . and the clunk of the wheels as they were retracted into their flying position. We were off. We were coming over Lord.[25]

The British airborne landings on D-Day stand as testimony to good planning, excellent training, tactical flexibility, and resolute morale and determination, on behalf of both the army and the RAF. Although there were shortages of aircraft and gliders, a problem that would hinder Allied operations for the rest of the war, considerable investment had been made into aircraft development and pilot training. The seizure of the Orne and Caen Canal crossings – later named Pegasus and Horsa Bridges – demonstrated how careful planning, efficient execution and dynamic action could achieve great tactical results. Of the six gliders dropped at 0020 on 6 June, five landed with impressive accuracy in the narrow strip between the river and the canal and both bridges were captured intact. A number of the shocked and surprised German defenders panicked and ran. All went according to plan and these moments have been immortalised in the film *The Longest Day*.[26]

Elsewhere the parachute drops were more dispersed and concentration of force proved difficult, in most cases achieving only some 40 per cent of intended strength. It was in these moments that the British troops demonstrated flexibility and *élan*: most famously, 9th Para which, under the command of Lieutenant Colonel Terence Otway, was tasked with eliminating the threat from the Merville Battery as well as other secondary objectives. The paratroopers had been scattered during the drop over an area of some 130 square kilometres, and only 150 men out of 600, with little specialist equipment, were in place for the assault at 0430. Otway and his team quickly revised the plan. Only two of the three supporting *coup de main* gliders reached the target and both were disrupted as they arrived. The aerial bombardment intended to soften up the objective prior to the attack also missed the target. Despite all this, the four guns of the battery were put out of action for the invasion.[27]

As the night wore on, elements of 6th Airborne achieved all of their main objectives, despite the dispersal of strength. German reaction was mixed and confused – the scattered paratrooper and glider drops sowing bewilderment – and sporadic attempts to drive north towards the coast were blocked. Nevertheless, as they awaited reinforcement from the beaches, British troops were forced to hold on desperately and grimly against elements of 21st Panzers and 716th Infantry well into the morning of D-Day.[28]

As the troops of 6th Airborne made their assault in the early hours of 6 June, the amphibious landing forces were approaching the coast of Normandy. Overhead the Allied air forces were zeroing in to pound German positions in preparation for the actual assault. The bombardment was intended to soften up the enemy sufficiently to ease the pain of the landings; planners believed that the cost of the assault on D-Day could be as many as 10,000 dead and all must be done to keep losses to a minimum.[29] Progress inland would be seriously delayed if the landing forces were so badly disrupted that they could not pass on the follow-up forces towards their D-Day objectives, such as Caen, and support the airborne troops in their defence of the Orne bridgehead.

Lieutenant Douglas Reeman commented:

> The air seemed to cringe to the mounting roar of engines. There must have been hundreds and hundreds of them. It seemed to take no time at all for the bombers to reach their first objectives. You could faintly see the blur of land beneath the bombardment while the clouds overhead danced and reared up in vivid red and orange flashes.[30]

Between 0300 and 0500 over 1,000 British bombers deposited some 5,000 tons of bombs on the coast, rapidly followed by the guns of the Royal Navy's bombardment. A positive view of the bombardment was painted in the official history:

> Never has any coast suffered what a tortured strip of French coast suffered that morning.
>
> Through billowing smoke and falling debris defenders crouching in this scene of devastation would soon discern faintly hundreds of ships and assault craft ominously closing the shore. If the sight dismayed them, the soldiers borne forward to attack were thrilled by the spectacle of Allied power that was displayed around them on every hand.[31]

Yet although the power of the bombardment, both aerial and naval, was indeed considerable, it by no means achieved all that many hoped for at the time and have since believed. Intelligence had identified many enemy gun emplacements and targets but not all, particularly those guns placed to provide enfilading fire down the beaches rather than out to sea.[32] More importantly, the weather interfered with the bombing programmes, forcing reliance on radar equipment which caused a sharp fall-off in accuracy, with many bombs from the heavy and medium bombers dropping short of their targets. The rocket-firing Typhoon fighter-bombers of the RAF's 2nd Tactical Air Force also failed to hit their targets due to the weather: later analysis demonstrated that they contributed little in a physical sense to the landings. It was subsequently argued by air force assessors that even though the targets themselves had often been missed, the bombing still 'helped to demoralise enemy reserves', but this cannot be proved.[33] The real and tangible effects of air attack on enemy ground forces were to be a continuing bone of contention between the army and the air force.[34]

The naval bombardment and the fire from artillery placed on landing craft also proved to have mixed effectiveness. The British insisted on a bombardment of two hours, backed by the view that gunfire of this type was likely to be inaccurate and therefore increased density raised the chance of scoring some useful hits. In contrast the Americans settled on a thirty- to forty-minute bombardment, a poor choice indeed when it proved that even the British two-hour option failed to inflict the damage hoped for. The Royal Navy's OVERLORD report later claimed that a good deal of neutralisation had been achieved, but admitted that actual destruction was limited. The artillery approaching from the sea also suffered from the inclement weather and its fire was both disrupted and inaccurate.[35] Ultimately, although the bombardment would be of some assistance, the coastal strongpoints, guns and bunkers would have to be eliminated by the infantry and their supporting armour.

The landings began around 0700 when British and Canadian troops hit the shore on GOLD, JUNO and SWORD beaches. On GOLD Lieutenant General Gerald Bucknall's XXX Corps was supposed to press inland towards Bayeux, whilst Lieutenant General John Crocker's I Corps at JUNO was to head towards Carpiquet and on SWORD to drive on with the objective of seizing Caen and linking up with 6th Airborne across the Orne.[36]

On the Anglo-Canadian beaches a good deal of faith had been placed in the support that could be offered by assault armour, such as the Duplex Drive amphibious Sherman and the specially designed Royal Engineer tanks. Lieutenant H.M. Irwin observed the first mine-clearing flail tanks landing on GOLD, 'King' Sector:

> The first tank moved out. Amazing, unbelievable, not a shot fired! All was quiet for a minute or two – nobody on the beach but one tank. An explosion as the waterproofing was disposed of. Her flails started. The black smoke came from the tank as she was hit and it caught fire. This was H-1 minute.[37]

The specialised armour achieved good results. Seven out of twelve planned paths through the minefields and obstacles were cleared on GOLD and 33 out of 40 DD tanks got ashore on SWORD. In total, Major General Percy Hobart's 79th Armoured Division, which provided much of the assault armour, lost 12 out of 50 Crab mine-clearing vehicles and 22 out of 120 AVRE tanks.[38] Armour arrived in sufficient quantities to begin having the desired effect, demonstrating the worth of the specialist equipment. The Churchill AVRE tank fitted with the petard 290mm 40lb bunker-busting projectile certainly proved its worth:

> The petard fired and something like a small dustbin hit the house, just above the front door. It collapsed like a pack of cards, spilling the defenders, with their machine-guns, anti-tank weapons and an avalanche of bricks into the courtyard.[39]

Across the landing beaches matters were hindered by the weather, as stronger than expected winds caused the tide to rise faster than planned, concealing beach obstacles and preventing their neutralisation. By mid-morning there were only 10 metres of hard sand between the sea wall and the water.[40] In turn this slowed down follow-up forces, as only specific areas were deemed safe. Logjams and confusion followed and the beginnings of the friction that was to undo the drive on Caen began to emerge. The weather was poor enough to persuade commanders to land the DD tanks intended for GOLD directly on to the beach rather than releasing them off the coast to 'swim' ashore. Consequently the first wave of infantry landed without immediate armoured support.[41]

Progress was still good enough from GOLD and JUNO beaches. Opposition against 50th Division (part of XXX Corps) on GOLD beach was less than elsewhere and as D-Day progressed troops began to close in on Bayeux. Arromanches, soon to be the site of the British artificial harbour codenamed MULBERRY, was captured by 1st Hampshires, whilst 6th and 7th Green Howards and 5th East Yorks had pushed on to the east of Bayeux, coming closest to reaching their specified D-Day objectives.

But the follow-up troops, in particular 8th Armoured Brigade, who were supposed to press on quickly inland as per Montgomery's orders, found themselves snarled up in congestion and traffic on the coast. For this the weather and the tide were largely to blame, and many of the brigade's tanks and troops were only forming up by the end D-Day. Those who got into action were caught up in mopping-up operations and fell well short of the high ground around Villers-Bocage.[42]

On SWORD beach the troops of the East Yorkshire and South Lancashire battalions approached the shoreline shortly after 0700. Major A.R. Rouse of the South Lancs commented on the beach obstacles:

> We had studied them on air photographs and knew exactly what to expect but somehow we had never realised the vertical height of them, and as we weaved in between iron rails and ramps and pickets with Tellamines [or Teller Mines] on top like gigantic mushrooms we seemed to be groping through a grotesque petrified forest.[43]

Fierce fighting ensued as the beach defences were overcome, but the tide interfered with the work of the engineers and some routes off the beaches were blocked for up to two hours.

The principal objective in determining British success on D-Day remained the prize of Caen, and the Canadian push from JUNO beach to Carpiquet was in part to shield and protect the advance by British 3rd Division towards that target. The division's 8th Brigade was to assault SWORD beach as part of the first wave, and drive inland quickly to capture the Périers Ridge, some 3 miles from the coast. From the second wave of landings 2nd King's Shropshire Light Infantry (KSLI), mounted on the tanks of the Staffordshire Yeomanry, would then dash for Caen, supported by the Royal Artillery and flanked by the other two infantry battalions of the brigade. Deploying infantry as tank riders was considered highly dangerous and likely to increase casualties, but time was of the essence in this action.[44] Brigadier Kenneth Pearce Smith, commanding 185th Brigade, had been briefed not to expect too much opposition, he recalled much later, and certainly not the elements of 21st Panzers that had moved into his path in the days prior to D-Day.[45]

[illegible] the progress of the Staffordshire Yeomanry to the assembly points and Pearce Smith was forced to push the 2nd KSLI forwards on foot to Caen alone with the aim of pressing the tanks on in support when assembled. This was hardly ideal and would later be described as 'the lightning punch at Caen [having] been reduced to a few hundred plodding riflemen'.[46] Matters were made worse by the need to divert two squadrons of the Staffordshire Yeomanry to help suppress and capture the 'Hillman' bunker which lay close to the route to be taken by the 1st Norfolks who were supposed to be advancing on Caen in support of 2nd KSLI. The Norfolks suffered 150 casualties just attempting to bypass 'Hillman' and the neutralisation of the bunker therefore became essential. It had been intended in planning that the air and naval bombardment would have destroyed 'Hillman' but this had not been achieved, and it now proved to be a difficult and time-consuming process for the British infantry and armour to eliminate the bunker as the Germans held it in much greater strength than had been expected. It took until the evening to eliminate 'Hillman', by which time the advance on Caen had stalled.

The leading elements of 2nd KSLI, and parts of the Staffordshire Yeomanry once they had caught up, pressed on towards Caen in the afternoon of D-Day reaching Bieville, 4 to 5 miles short of their objective. An attempt to push on to Lebisey Wood failed and the British were soon under attack from some 40 Panzer IVs of 21st Panzers along with their supporting infantry. Even though the Germans were beaten off, further sustainable progress was not possible. The troops tasked with seizing Caen had battled hard, having been hindered by the weather and forced to change their plans at the last moment, but when units of 21st Panzers appeared in their path much earlier than anticipated the chance of capturing Caen quickly evaporated. The 2nd KSLI suffered some 113 casualties or around 14 per cent of its strength on D-Day, mostly around Lebisey Wood.[47]

Of greater concern than achieving ambitious objectives was the threat to the viability of the bridgehead posed by the presence of a panzer division, albeit somewhat dispersed, in and around Caen. The British were fortunate that the Germans' dysfunctional command structure caused any fleeting opportunity there might have been to inflict serious damage on the British and Canadians in and around JUNO and SWORD beaches to be frittered away. General Edgar Feuchtinger, commanding 21st Panzers, claimed that 6 June was the most frustrating day of his life as he had been constrained by very specific orders that would not allow him to deploy his armour without the agreement of his senior commanders General Hans Spiedel (standing in for Rommel who was absent from Normandy on D-Day) and Field Marshal Gerd von Rundstedt, commander of German Forces in Western Europe. They in turn were unwilling and unable to act without clearance from Berlin, and too many were fearful of disturbing Hitler so early in the morning without knowing for sure that this was the real invasion. Others have claimed that Feuchtinger was actually absent himself, being in Paris with his mistress, though he claimed that he was at his post as the battle began.[48] This delay resulted in the advantage of having 21st Panzers in almost the perfect position, being rendered worthless. Feuchtinger, unable to act quickly enough, found that the bridges on the route east of Caen to the beaches were now held in some strength by the British and was forced to strike to the west of Caen towards the coast. By the time he had mustered sufficient strength to do so the odds were stacked heavily against any significant success.

Planning for such a counter-attack by the Germans, the commander of the Staffordshire Yeomanry, Lieutenant Colonel Jim Eadie, deployed his Firefly tanks sporting their 17-pdr anti-tank guns in a concentrated gun line on Hermanville Ridge to deal with enemy armour.[49] The Panzer IVs of 21st Panzers came to grief here, and although one small force slipped through and reached the coast at Lion-sur-Mer they subsequently pulled back on sight of the second wave of airborne troops and gliders arriving to reinforce the position of 6th Airborne.

By nightfall on 6 June the Germans were attempting to reinforce their position in and around Caen. The remains of 716th Infantry Division, upon whom the weight of the British and Canadian attack had fallen on D-Day, was linking up with 21st Panzers, which itself had lost some 50 tanks. The 12th SS Panzer Division was also beginning to arrive in the sector, having eventually been released for action on the afternoon of 6 June.

Although Allied progress across the three Anglo-Canadian landing beaches had been less than had been hoped for, it was nevertheless impressive and casualties were well within expectations. Most importantly of all, the very dangerous first few hours of the landings had been negotiated without disaster. American forces, despite a near disaster at OMAHA beach and chaotic airborne landings, had also done well and it was clear that D-Day had been a tremendous success.

Many German commanders, including Rommel who was speeding back to Normandy on 6 June having been away visiting his wife, believed that their best chance of defeating the Allies would come in the first few hours of the invasion. The fortuitous positioning of 21st Panzers gave them a theoretical chance of some success. But this came to nothing as the German chain of command was hopelessly compromised and the defending forces were [illegible] Allied invasion. The following few days were still pivotal and offered the last chance for the Germans to compromise the invasion. German LXXXIV Corps commander Erich Marcks commented that 9 or 10 June was the last moment at which the invasion might have been defeated – after that point it became merely a case of damage limitation, a situation that troubled Marcks little as he himself was killed in an Allied air raid on 12 June.[50] The Germans also failed initially to appreciate Allied objectives; they were convinced that the Allies' absolute priority was the capture of the port of Cherbourg, in the west, to facilitate supply and reinforcement. On 9 June Rommel commented that 'everything must be used to defend Cherbourg' and on 11 June ordered the German 7th Army to replace the armour protecting Caen with infantry to allow the panzers to move west to defend Cherbourg.[51]

In reality the Allies had anticipated this port and supply problem and began construction of their two artificial MULBERRY harbours at Saint Laurent and Arromanches on 7 June, which released some of the pressure to capture a major port quickly. The Allies were also subsequently surprised by how efficient they proved to be at landing supplies and equipment directly on to the beaches, which lessened the importance of the MULBERRYS and reduced still further the immediate necessity of capturing Cherbourg; it was certainly by no means the make-or-break objective imagined by the Germans. The Germans were not ignorant of the presence of the MULBERRYS, however, having some photo-reconnaissance material and documents captured close to OMAHA beach on 7 June to work on. Yet this intelligence did not influence the manner in which Rommel and Friedrich Dollman (commanding the German Seventh Army in Normandy) developed their response to the invasion.[52]

For the Allies the days immediately after the landings were crucial; they were presented with the conundrum of pushing inland to maintain pressure on the Germans and retain the initiative, yet simultaneously having to link up the five beaches as soon as possible to build a continuous bridgehead. The priority proved to be the latter as Montgomery indicated on 7 June, and Allied efforts were focused on this objective for the next five days. German attempts to counter-attack the beaches were repeatedly repulsed with heavy losses, Allied firepower, and naval gunfire in particular, proving decisive.[53]

These counter-attacks proved extremely foolhardy and detrimental to the German position around Bayeux and caused the near collapse of the 352nd German Infantry Division. Allied troops were soon pushing through the resulting breach in the German lines into the valley of the River Seulles and towards Caumont, some 20 miles from the coast. Field Marshal von Rundstedt was forced to commit his only full-strength German division in Normandy, Panzer Lehr, to plug the gap. By 9 June Panzer Lehr was in contact with XXX Corps in and around Tilly-sur-Seulles and the British push southwards slowed. But the rapid insertion of Panzer Lehr was only achieved by moving it in broad daylight, which exposed it to the Allied air forces that inflicted considerable casualties, though these effects were considerably exaggerated. Even so, Panzer Lehr's front-line combat-ready armoured strength was reduced to a third by 18 June, indicating the severity of the fighting and the effectiveness of the pressure applied by the British.[54]

The fighting around Tilly was particularly intense for the 50th Northumbrian Division and 8th Armoured Brigade as they adapted to the new dense terrain. Trooper Arthur Reddish recounted:

> My mate, Ray 'Busty' Meek didn't think much of the bocage countryside. 'You'll get a shock after the desert,' he said, 'we could see the buggers in the desert and they could see us. Here, they could see us but I'll be buggered if we could see them. This country's ideal for defence but attacking through it gives you the bloody creeps.'[55]

Corporal Frederick Spencer, 8th Battalion, Durham Light Infantry, recalls the fighting around Saint Pierre in early June:

> At night it was standing patrols in the valley on our right flank to prevent infiltration by German patrols. The worst hazard was getting back to the safety of our slit trenches before first light. Our positions were on a forward facing slope and we were harassed each day by an 88mm SP gun which came forward to fire at us at very close range.[56]

Whilst progress in the west of the Anglo-Canadian sector was grinding to a halt, Montgomery's main aim in the east was still to push on towards Caen. In contrast to Rommel, he believed the German position hinged on holding back the British and Canadians in and around that city. British pressure here would draw the Germans into committing their reserves, so making the Americans' task in the west that much easier. As Montgomery put it to Bradley later, 'Caen is the key to Cherbourg.'[57]

The build-up of follow-on forces in the east was no better than that in the west and the units earmarked for offensive operations south from the Orne bridgehead, the 51st Highlanders and 4th Armoured Brigade, were still arriving on 8 June and any thrust towards Caen was consequently delayed. This allowed the 12th SS *Hitlerjugend* Division to take up strong positions to the west of the city whilst 21st Panzers held the city and the area to the east of the Orne. Feuchtinger's armour and troops continued to fling themselves against 6th Airborne and their supports, still occupying the ground east of the Orne, but no headway could be made.

Montgomery met with his army commanders, Miles Dempsey (Second British) and Omar Bradley (First US), on 10 June to discuss their next moves. Montgomery had already ruled out a direct assault on Caen on 8 June, stating so in a letter to his old friend Major General Frank 'Simbo' Simpson at the War Office: 'The Germans are doing everything they can to hold on to Caen. I have decided not to have a lot of casualties by butting up against the place.'[58]

At the 10 June meeting Montgomery outlined a complex and ambitious plan codenamed WILD OATS. This would involve a double envelopment of

Caen, with XXX Corps, spearheaded by the newly arrived 7th Armoured Division, striking through Villers-Bocage and then southeast towards the Orne, with 51st Highlanders and 4th Armoured Brigade of I Corps pushing south around the east of the city. They would all meet up with 1st British Airborne Division, which would be dropped to the south of Caen. It was certainly a bold plan, but not one simply plucked out of the air as it had been discussed before D-Day by Dempsey's staff.[59]

Unfortunately, Monty's bold concept quickly unravelled. Air Chief Marshal Sir Trafford Leigh-Mallory, OVERLORD's air force commander, blocked the airborne drop as it would put too many of his aircraft at risk. This objection drew from the normally polite Monty a damning response: 'Obviously he [Leigh-Mallory] is a gutless bugger who refuses to take a chance and plays for safety on all occasions. I have no use for him.'[60] Meanwhile the eastern arm of the pincer movement fell victim to the slow rate of delivery into Normandy of the 51st Highlanders and 4th Armoured Brigade, neither of which were ready to take part in any immediate offensive action. The Orne bridgehead was also placed under considerable pressure by 21st Panzers and 346th Infantry Division on 10–12 June, necessitating the use of some of the Highlander units in supporting 6th Airborne. A bold attack by Richard Gale's paratroopers on 12 June brought a halt to the German offensive, but at a cost of 141 casualties out of the 160 involved.[61] Attempts by 51st Highlanders to break out came to nothing. There would be no immediate strike out of the Orne Bridgehead to the east of Caen.[62]

The only part of WILD OATS now available was the XXX Corps element, but this also soon began to stall as 50th Division and 8th Armoured Brigade made little impression on Panzer Lehr just north of Tilly-sur-Seulles. Even the introduction on 10 June of the famous 7th Armoured Division, the Desert Rats, with their vast combat experience, made little difference. The Panzer Lehr Division, arguably the most powerful formation at the disposal of the Germans, was proving troublesome, but in fact there was nowhere near the required superiority in strength on the part of the British which would normally be required to launch such offensive operations as XXX Corps was attempting.

On 12 June Dempsey visited 7th Armoured Division HQ to meet the Desert Rats' commander, Major General George 'Bobby' Erskine, to explore options. It transpired that although Panzer Lehr was providing a severe obstacle, the collapse of 352nd Division to the west in the US sector had allowed American troops to penetrate southwards to Caumont, along with XXX Corps' reconnaissance troops, the 11th Hussars. Although the Americans could press on no further, Erskine wanted to divert 7th Armoured towards Caumont and then head towards Villers-Bocage deep behind Panzer Lehr's left flank. A subsequent push towards Caen and the Orne Valley by 7th Armoured's tanks would force the Germans to fall back and ideally suffer heavy casualties as their position collapsed. Erskine later argued that he had wanted to begin this operation the day before but had received little support from his corps HQ.[63] Gerald Bucknall, XXX Corps commander, confirmed that the idea had been circulating at his HQ since 10 June, but had not been acted upon. In reality the opportunity for earlier action was not as evident as was subsequently implied, because the Americans only pushed on to Caumont on 10–12 June and it was this move that demonstrated the weakness of the German position in the area.[64]

Dempsey was enthused by the prospect of the flanking manoeuvre and quickly ordered Bucknall to realign his forces to make what was now code-named Operation PERCH a reality, though the plan itself was still a XXX Corps-directed action.[65] Montgomery was also chipper about the prospects, noting that 'All this is very good and Pz Lehr may be in grave danger tomorrow.'[66] But the Allies were also aware, via *Ultra* intelligence (from Bletchley Park), that 2nd Panzer Division would soon arrive in the sector to shore up the German position: the window was closing fast and the realistic chances of success were receding quickly.

Belying the criticism that British formations were too static and conventional, Erskine, after just two days of fighting, had reorganised his division to meet the requirements of combat in the close terrain of Normandy. He had mixed his brigades to integrate, albeit temporarily, his armour and infantry more closely. By the end of 12 June the leading elements of the Desert Rats' 22nd Armoured Brigade were in Livry, where rather limited opposition nevertheless provoked the brigade's commander, Robert 'Loony' Hinde, to halt until the following morning, the first in a number of tactical errors.

At 0530 on 13 June, 22nd Armoured Brigade began the advance once again, with 4th County of London Yeomanry (CLY) together with the mechanised infantry of 1st Rifle Brigade leading the way. Inexplicably, the formation did not employ its reconnaissance assets to scout ahead, the light Stuart tanks of the reconnaissance troop being deployed behind the first squadron of tanks. Encountering little opposition, the first British forces entered the town of Villers-Bocage around 0800 to a warm welcome from the locals. 'A' Squadron, with troops of the Rifle Brigade in support, then hurried on to Point 213, a position one and a half miles east of the town that commanded dominating views of the Odon valley to the south and the direct road to Caen. Viscount Lord Cranley, commanding 4th CLY, would have preferred more time to reconnoitre, but Brigadier Hinde had continued to apply pressure to keep moving.[67] The British column halted at this point in order for the senior officers to confer as to their next move.

Unfortunately, the British were unaware that watching them from a track just to the south of Point 213 were Tiger tanks of 101st SS Heavy Tank Battalion which had been rushed to the area by General Sepp Dietrich, commanding I SS Panzer Corps. The heavy tank battalions were principally equipped with fearsome Tigers, clad in heavy armour on all sides and wielding 88mm guns. Though unreliable and notoriously difficult to maintain, they nevertheless constituted a considerable battlefield threat. The 2nd Company of four operable Tigers, commanded by the famous tank ace Michael Wittman, was positioned just a few hundred metres to the southwest of Point 213 by the morning of 13 June after a desperate rush from Beauvais via Falaise the previous day. Although his tanks were in need of maintenance and repair, Wittman decided to launch an immediate attack on the British forces on Point 213, thus precipitating one of the most famous and mythologised actions of the Northwest European campaign. Wittman despatched two of his Tigers to tackle the British forces on Point 213 itself, whilst he himself attacked from the rear knocking out two surprised British tanks, including a 17-pdr equipped Firefly (Wittman's fourth Tiger had broken down). He then cut on to the road descending down from Point 213 to Villers-Bocage and boldly headed straight into town scattering startled infantry, destroying half-tracks, reconnaissance tanks and other light elements. Wittman then promptly eliminated 4th CLY's command troop of Cromwells and the artillery-spotting tanks of 5th Royal Horse Artillery. He only withdrew from the town when a Firefly from B Squadron opened up on him from the other end of the high street. As he headed out back up to Point 213 his Tiger was disabled by a 6-pdr anti-tank gun at point-blank range, though Wittman and his crew were able to escape. The remaining British forces now isolated on Point 213 were whittled away throughout the morning as German strength increased with the arrival of Ralf Möbius's 1st Company of 101st Heavy Tank Battalion and elements of Panzer Lehr. By 1300 the British force on Point 213 had been snuffed out, and Cranley himself was captured shortly afterwards.[68]

British and German forces then clashed again in Villers-Bocage in the afternoon, though the troops of 7th Armoured performed much better driving out a foolhardy assault by Möbius's unsupported Tigers. German resistance in the area was hardening, nonetheless, and the British withdrew northeast from Villers-Bocage, much to Dempsey's annoyance, into a defensive 'brigade box' position. The Germans duly impetuously attacked, and suffered heavy casualties in so doing. Montgomery expressed his pleasure at the failure and casualties suffered by the Germans in and around Villers-Bocage and noted that: 'So long as Rommel has to use strategic reserves to plug holes, then we have done well.'[69] Yet there was now no likelihood of a British advance into the flank of Panzer Lehr or indeed on to Caen. With opposition clearly hardening and 7th Armoured somewhat exposed, Bucknall, supposedly with Dempsey's agreement, ordered Erskine to withdraw north on 14 June; the front was beginning to congeal as Dempsey had feared it might.[70]

However much the subsequent attacks by the Germans on 13 and 14 June proved costly, they did little to redress the balance of the disaster that had overcome 4th CLY on the morning of 13 June. Hinde attempted to blame the terrain, for which he and his troops were unprepared and which was a great hindrance to the mobile warfare preferred by the Desert Rats. He also blamed the failure on the pressure to maintain the rapid pace urged by Erskine, perhaps to make up for the time Erskine believed had been lost in the forty-eight hours prior to the launch of PERCH.[71] This urgency may well have prompted the error in judgement by Hinde in launching 4th CLY on to Villers-Bocage without properly reconnoitring the route ahead, though it hardly exonerates him. Cranley and his troops could also be censured for not remaining on full alert when they entered Villers-Bocage, especially as Cranley knew that the position had not been properly scouted. Many of the troops had stopped to brew up tea and smoke cigarettes when the advance halted. One of the Regimental HQ tanks was presented with a point-blank range flanking shot at Wittman's Tiger as it advanced through the town, but was unable to fire as its gunner had gone to urinate.[72] There was no immediate evidence of enemy activity in Villers-Bocage that morning, though there were some German administrative troops in the town, but again 7th Armoured had showed a slackness and a disregard for basic battlefield craft, perhaps born of the arrogance of success in the Mediterranean.[73]

It is also true that the strength of the British column as it advanced to and through Villers-Bocage was woefully short of what was required in order to embark upon the kind of operational manoeuvre imagined by Dempsey and Montgomery; for this Bucknall and Erskine must shoulder responsibility. Though the 7th Armoured was a veteran unit, the culture and past experience of the troops also defined their tactical approach: they were used to going 'swanning', making rapid advances into lightly defended areas, rather than tackling significant opposition. Limited though the German strength was in and around Villers-Bocage on 13 June, it appears to have been fierce and therefore British strength needed to be far greater to make progress. There were more troops available, particularly the infantry required to shore up the position in Villers-Bocage on 13–14 June, but Bucknall did not push more into the gap opened by 22nd Armoured Brigade. Erskine still believed that the situation was defendable on 14 June and much more might have been achieved if his corps had acted quickly. He was also culpable because elements of his own division were left uncommitted on 13–14 June when speed and support were of the essence.

The British also miscalculated the level and strength of the opposition forming around them on 13–14 June; few elements of 2nd Panzers were actually present and the Tigers of 101st Heavy Tank Battalion had suffered losses on the afternoon of 13 June. A forceful attack out of Villers-Bocage by a reinforced 22nd Armoured supported by artillery and air power may well have been able to drive Panzer Lehr back from Tilly in some disarray, though a major breakthrough to Caen, the Orne Valley and even Mont Pinçon to the south, the highest point in Normandy, was probably beyond them. The troops at the sharp end in Villers-Bocage had in truth suffered a bloody nose, having had 4th County of London Yeomanry decapitated. Hinde was apparently shattered by the losses suffered by 4th CLY and on 13 June 7th Armoured Division filed a report claiming that 40 Tigers tanks were in the vicinity of Villers-Bocage, hugely inflating the scale of the opposition.[74]

Dempsey was appalled by the manner in which PERCH had been prosecuted. He later stated that when he visited Erskine on 12 June he tried to chivvy him along and that Bucknall likewise needed prodding into more aggressive action:

> If he [Erskine] had carried out my orders he would never have been kicked out of Villers-Bocage but by this time 7th Armoured was living on its reputation and the whole handling of that battle was a disgrace. Their decision to withdraw [on 13 June, not that of a more general withdrawal northwards taken the following day] was made without consulting me; it was done by the corps commander and Erskine.[75]

Ultimately, Dempsey's confidence in both Bucknall and Erskine was badly dented as a result of the Villers-Bocage battle and this sowed the seeds for their dismissal in early August. The failure of the Desert Rats also raised questions about their suitability for operations in Northwest Europe.

Badly bungled though Operation PERCH was, it has been the aftermath rather than the reality that has served to tarnish the reputation of the British Army and elevate this relatively minor action to almost ludicrous levels. The German propaganda machine moved quickly into action in the days after the Villers-Bocage battle, emphasising the role played by Wittman to near superhuman levels. It was claimed in German newsreel and newspaper reports that Wittman and his Tiger tank alone had stopped and repulsed the advance of the entire 7th Armoured Division and that Wittman had eliminated the force on Point 213; it was even stated that the afternoon actions had been led by Wittman rather than Möbius. As the Germans were in possession of the battlefield it was difficult for the British to repudiate the German claims, and the British were in any case dismayed by the setback and unwilling to dwell openly on the failure of 7th Armoured.

Such reasons cannot excuse the casual manner with which many historians through to today continue to repackage unquestioningly Nazi propaganda to underscore the superiority of the Germans over the British.[76] Too often in the post-war world writers have referred to how one Tiger tank defeated the entire 7th Armoured Division when even cursory study demonstrates that this was far from the truth. There is no doubt that Wittman's bold and decisive actions helped to cause 4th CLY to stall their advance, but these were certainly not the actions of just one tank. Even when Wittman was charging into Villers-Bocage his colleagues were tackling 'A' Squadron on Point 213, and Wittman played no part in the afternoon fighting.

The effects on 7th Armoured Division were severely damaging. Attitudes in the division had been darkened by their 'elevation' to spearheading the advance from the bridgehead in the days after D-Day and tempers were not eased by the replacement of their trusted Shermans with the new untested Cromwell tanks.[77] Yet disgruntled though the troops of the division were, there is no contemporary evidence that this had damaged morale to the extent that it was a contributory factor to their failure in PERCH. Quite the reverse was true, as they pressed on recklessly on 13 June, and according to Erskine, they would have stuck to their guns around Villers-Bocage that night if Bucknall had afforded them sufficient support, though Bucknall refuted that allegation after the war.[78] It was in the aftermath of the Villers-Bocage [illegible] how the experience of the Mediterranean played out in Northwest Europe quickly followed, and that this was taking place once in theatre demonstrates how little rethinking in preparation for D-Day went on in veteran units when transferred back to the UK for OVERLORD. Bucknall was still happy with 7th Armoured Division's morale and stated as much just a few days after PERCH, claiming they were as cheerful as ever. However, he noted German perceptions that the division did not know how to handle its tanks and appeared to believe that it was still in the desert, perhaps underscoring the view that the Desert Rats' malaise was one of tactics and know-how rather than morale. Montgomery's policy of bringing back veteran units to fight in Northwest Europe was proving questionable, though based on tactical shortcomings rather than issues of morale.[79]

Yet the British were learning and adapting even within the first days of the campaign. It was quickly becoming apparent that the tank's primary role in combat in Northwest Europe, more so than the desert war, was supporting infantry, not firing at other tanks. Even tank crews in the armoured divisions were beginning to accept this reality and adapt their operating methods. At various times during the campaign, 7th Armoured employed a flexible force structure in which infantry and tanks were deployed in balanced formations to aid mutual support, whilst the newly arrived Guards Armoured Division soon noted the necessity of trying to improve infantry-tank tactics. But it would take the experience of their first major actions to prompt wholesale restructuring of the armoured divisions to meet the challenges of fighting in Northwest Europe. The difficulties in integrating armour and infantry in the assault remained throughout the entire campaign, and although considerable progress was made in developing appropriate tactics the problems were never entirely resolved. The early moves by the British Army to deal with these issues nevertheless demonstrate an ability to adapt and revise approaches; this was certainly no monolithic and unthinking institution.[80]

In the aftermath of Villers-Bocage, alongside the recriminations and dismay over the battle, it was clear that the opening phase of the campaign was coming to a close and that the front was beginning to firm up or congeal. The Germans were moving sufficient units into the line against the Allies to offer a continuous front, even if this was only being achieved at the cost of feeding in troops as soon as they arrived to plug gaps rather than as part of a concerted and coherent strategy to take the battle to the Allies.

For Montgomery and Dempsey it was now clear that any hope of a rapid encirclement of Caen had passed, underlined by the limited progress made by 3rd British and 3rd Canadian infantry divisions towards the city in the second week of the campaign. On paper it seemed as though across the sector the number of enemy divisions facing the British was reaching parity, but in reality the German formations were already badly battered and merely holding the line as best they could. The long-term prognosis required that the British and Canadians would now have to force the pace and draw newly arriving German units into battle before they could be organised for a serious counter-offensive; it was imperative that such a battle be on the terms and the terrain of Montgomery's choosing if he were to retain the initiative. On 18 June he therefore committed the British and Canadian forces to a major multi-corps offensive to be played out to the west of Caen, codenamed Operation EPSOM.

4

CAEN
The Cauldron

ON THE NIGHT of 18–19 June 1944 the so-called Great Storm swept through the English Channel, battering Allied forces at sea and on land; 30-knot winds peaked at gale force, causing six- to eight-foot waves. Poor weather in the English Channel had been lingering since before D-Day and it slowed the rate of Allied reinforcements and supplies arriving in Normandy, but the storm which whipped up on 19 June lasted three days and caused immense damage to the Allied landing facilities. The scenes were indeed disturbing for those in situ, as Squadron Leader A.E.L. Hill of Balloon Command recalled:

> On the beach just west of where I was at JUNO, there was utter chaos; literally hundreds of small craft were washed ashore by the gale at high tide and lay on the road which traversed the beach rather like a cargo of timber logs.[1]

The troops waiting inland viewed the poor weather with dismay. Jack Swaab, an artillery officer in 51st Highlanders, recorded in his diary on 19 June:

> God what a bloody miserable day . . . As dawn broke, rain, which has persisted all day varying in ferocity. The CP has done its best but, shell splinters have punctuated our covers . . . so it's been pretty wet at times.
>
> We have baled out water from the roof and sides and now seem temporarily on top.
>
> Still raining miserably. It patters unevenly on the covers, and flips about the grass behind us. Men stand about singly or in twos and threes, smoking dejectedly. If you walk 5 yards here, you pick up about 5 pounds

of mud and straw. In two days it will be the longest day of the year. Today I could believe it.[2]

The speed with which fresh troops and equipment were being landed in France fell further behind an already lagging schedule, adding to Allied planners' woes. Compared to the period 15–18 June, the storm reduced the numbers of troops landing in the Anglo-Canadian sector by three-quarters, vehicles and stores by half. Second British Army was already two brigades behind schedule, but by 22 June found itself three divisions short of the target set by planners.[3] The effects of the storm might have been much worse were it not for the contingency planning of the Allies, which mitigated some of the potential damage. The OVERLORD plan had incorporated the identification of sheltered areas for shipping and transport craft in the eventuality of bad weather; thus, although the storm was damaging, causing the destruction, loss or stranding of some 800 vessels, the impact was not as severe as it might have been. Nevertheless, the strategic implications of the storm were profound and had a direct impact on the conduct of subsequent operations. Thanks to the intelligence provided by the RAF and *Ultra* from Bletchley Park (where the British code-breaking work was conducted) Montgomery was well aware that Rommel was desperately trying to assemble a strong enough force to mount a counter-attack against the British and Canadians. How feasible this was depended on how quickly the Germans could extricate their armour from the front line and replace it with infantry in order to concentrate their mobile strength for the offensive. The speed with which new reinforcement panzer formations could be moved to Normandy was also fundamental to the potential mounting of a serious counter-attack, and therefore the storm gave Rommel more time to achieve this. In contrast, Montgomery was attempting to mass his strength preparatory to a series of new offensives intended to maintain the pressure on the Germans and retain the initiative. In order to do this the British needed to strike first, and the chances of that had now receded because of the delay caused by the storm. Although Montgomery retained an air of confidence, he was well aware that winning the battle of the build-up was now fundamental to the cause.

The Allies also knew that 1st SS Panzer Division had left Belgium on 17 June and that II SS Panzer Corps was en route from Poland.[4] Delays in Second British Army operations as a result of the storm might well surrender the initiative to the Germans, something Montgomery wished to avoid at all costs. He had already delayed the start date of his next major offensive to allow more troops and equipment to be shipped over from England, but to hesitate too long courted disaster. Montgomery would have to strike first despite not having everything in place.

He outlined his worries in a letter to Frank Simpson at the War Office on 20 June:

> This weather is still the very devil. A gale all day yesterday; the same today. Nothing can be unloaded. [An exaggeration as some unloading did indeed continue, though at a greatly reduced rate.] Lying in ships off the beaches is everything I need to resume the offensive with a bang.
>
> The real point is that the delay imposed on us by the weather is just what the enemy needs.[5]

At a senior staff conference on 22 June he outlined the situation, emphasising that the build-up was now five to six days behind schedule. Montgomery nevertheless emphasised his confidence in their position and that, barring some great error, which he would not allow to occur, the Allies would prevail. His intention was to commit the newly arrived VIII Corps under the command of Lieutenant General Richard O'Connor to a new offensive to the west of Caen. Dempsey's staff at Second Army HQ had rejected a tentative plan, codenamed DREADNOUGHT, to drive south out of the lodgement on the east side of the Orne, as being risky and impractical. Because a direct assault on Caen was ruled out as too likely to result in friendly casualties, an assault to the west of Caen became the only viable option.[6] The plan, codenamed EPSOM, would utilise one armoured and two infantry divisions, with two further brigades of tanks in support, and incorporate some 60,000 troops and over 600 tanks.[7] Montgomery's original hopes had been for an even more ambitious multi-corps offensive with strong supporting operations mounted by XXX Corps to the west of VIII Corps and I Corps to the east. Because of the weather, these secondary operations had been scaled back to focus available resources on the main thrust. Even so, XXX Corps actions would play a key supporting role in the forthcoming battle.

EPSOM was to launch from a starting point between Tilly-sur-Seulles and Norrey-en-Bessin, drive south through the village of Cheux, down into and across the River Odon valley, and up on to the high ground of Hill 112. This final first-stage position offered commanding views of the open ground to the south of Caen and would provide an ideal launching point for an armoured division, in this case the 11th, to push on and threaten the whole German position in and around the city. The opposition would initially consist of Panzer Lehr and 12th SS Panzer Divisions. These were formidable units, but they had taken a battering since the invasion, particularly their infantry formations.[8] EPSOM's start date had originally been 23 June, but the effects of the storm pushed the date back by three days to allow sufficient preparation and build-up to take place, though Montgomery and his staff were well aware that the operation was not going to receive the support for which they had originally hoped.

The EPSOM plan suited the British Army's, and indeed Monty's, temperament very well. It was to be a set-piece engagement in which the full weight of artillery support could be applied, in excess of 700 guns, providing a heavy initial bombardment followed by rolling artillery barrages moving ahead of advancing infantry supported by thickly armoured tanks. Formations would pass through each other as objectives were seized in order to maintain fresh units at the sharp end, and once an initial break-in had been forced, an armoured division would surge through and break out into the country beyond. The advance was to take place across a narrow front to maximise concentrated fire support ahead of the leading troops and to ensure a determined assault in depth to maintain pressure. The expected German counterattacks could then be crushed by Allied artillery, with air support applied when feasible.[9]

In many regards EPSOM appeared to conform to Montgomery's blueprint of how to engage and defeat the Germans. In reality there were a number of weaknesses that served to undermine the operation. First, the continuing low cloud and rain were hampering air support and a key element in the Allied inventory was consequently rendered much less potent. Second, the main thrust began over a frontage of some 2 miles and would produce an uncomfortably narrow salient with exposed flanks, a situation that deteriorated as the penetration deepened: all this was a result of the flanking attacks of I and XXX Corps being scaled back because of the effects of the storm, conflicting with the necessity of striking before the Germans. Third, the terrain, though a better alternative than trying to fight through the heavily wooded hills, valleys and *bocage* to the west or through Caen itself, was still not conducive to rapid operations, especially the push down, across and up the valley carved into the Norman countryside by the River Odon, all of which would be viewed with ease by dug-in German defenders.

The two limited preliminary flanking attacks intended to distract the enemy and draw reserves away from the area of VIII Corps' main thrust began on 23 June with an intelligently conceived attack by 152nd Brigade of 51st Highland Division against Sainte Honorine la Charndronette to the east of Caen.[10] Previous efforts to take the village had stalled, but on the night of 22–23 June and without a large artillery bombardment British troops caught the Germans by surprise, captured the village and over the ensuing hours beat off a series of fierce counter-attacks by 21st Panzers, who lost 13 tanks in the fighting. The British employed good infantry-tank cooperation tactics and made effective use of supporting artillery to inflict heavy casualties on the counter-attacking Germans. Considering the supposedly poor performance of 51st Highlanders over the following weeks, the innovative approach and success of this action was nonetheless remarkable.[11]

To the west of the forthcoming EPSOM battlefield, 49th West Riding Division, 'The Polar Bears', supported by 8th Armoured Brigade, began their diversionary attack codenamed Operation MARTLET at 0415 on 25 June in thick mist and darkness. The objective was the village of Fontenay and the Rauray Ridge further to the south, the capture of which would assist the progress of VIII Corps the following day by denying the vantage point over the EPSOM battlefield to the enemy. The plan had been carefully explained to the troops the night before the attack:

> Every man in the Bn had the whole scheme explained to him on a cloth model prepared in a barn. The Divisional Commander [Evelyn 'Bubbles' Barker] came up the evening before the attack and made us feel it was a dead cert and too easy: he inspired us all with great confidence. This was the division's first big attack and we were going to succeed.[12]

MARTLET began with two brigades of infantry leading the advance, supported by 250 guns. Because of the mist and the smoke, visibility was very poor, down to under five yards at times, but progress was good, particularly on the right flank. On the left, progress was slower but Fontenay was eventually captured, though it was not completely cleared of the enemy until the following day. After intense fighting, the objective of Tessel Wood was also seized by the 1/4th King's Own Yorkshire Light Infantry supported by Sherman tanks of the 24th Lancers. These formations demonstrated close, effective and intimate infantry-armour cooperation throughout the engagement, displaying skills unrecognised by later critics of the tactical acumen of the British Army.[13] A determined German counter-attack by 12th SS was beaten off after suffering heavy casualties. Private Rex Flower recalled:

> It was very, very hard labour to dig in under the hot sun. It was the hottest day up to now in more ways than one as it was to prove.
>
> The vicious crash, crash of shells spoilt my reverie. They were dropping all over the field and they were the enemy ones. The long awaited counter attack was on us . . . we kept firing and firing.

> In the baleful flickering light of burning tanks, amid the smoke and smell of battle, we spent the night. Just in case the enemy came again. But he didn't come.[14]

The German response to MARTLET had been poorly coordinated and the counter-attacks had been costly thanks to British firepower, a pattern that was to be repeated throughout the campaign. Panicked by a five-kilometre wide and two-kilometre deep penetration in the German front, Kurt Meyer, commanding 12th SS Panzer Division, arrived to coordinate the response, but as EPSOM began the following morning attention soon shifted away from the advance by 49th Division. It was clear that in MARTLET the British had achieved one of their objectives in providing a distraction for the Germans whilst imposing upon them yet more attrition they could ill-afford. Importantly, however, the high ground of the Rauray Ridge remained in German hands, and this was to prove to be a thorn in the side of the British during EPSOM. The troops of 12th SS Panzers fully recognised that holding the feature and its commanding position was vital. As Kurt Meyer recalled after the war: 'The view would make the Panzer men who have found their way painfully through the broken terrain up to here heave a sigh of relief.'[15]

Meanwhile, for the British soldiers of 15th Scottish Infantry Division moving into position over 24–25 June ready for the launch of EPSOM, a degree of trepidation, apprehension and excitement prevailed; this was, after all, their first taste of action. One junior officer commented: 'The troops in amazing spirits. For here was the Second Front. We were upon the rostrum of the world . . . These were wonderful moments.'[16] For others there was a more prosaic memory: 'We spent that night [25–26 June] huddled under some bushes in steady drizzle, cold, tired and feeling sorry for ourselves.'[17]

At 0730 the artillery bombardment began and the advance, initially led by less than one thousand troops, headed off. Soldiers were formed into sections of ten men: one carrying a Bren machine gun; a section commander and a sergeant, often armed with a semi-automatic weapon such as a Sten submachine gun; and the others with rifles. Troops would be spaced about five yards apart, and not in a cluster as this would make them highly susceptible to mortar or artillery fire. Three sections constituted a platoon and two sections of each platoon would lead the assault side by side, followed by the platoon commander, troops carrying equipment such as mortars, PIAT anti-tank weapons and radios, and the third section following in reserve. Three platoons, constituting a company, employed similar arrangements, with two platoons leading followed by the company HQ and the third platoon following on in reserve. A battalion was made up of four such companies, with a support company of heavier weapons such as mortars and 6-pdr anti-tank guns. Battalions would advance with two or three companies up, one or two in reserve, and the support company following, ready to act as and when required and directed by company HQ.

The infantry was further supported by the Churchill tanks of 31st Tank Brigade. The Churchills were for the most part armed with 75mm guns, quite capable of laying down considerable high-explosive firepower against soft targets but less effective against heavy armour. Tank troops, each consisting of three Churchills, were dotted across the front line to work with the infantry in the assault, but coordination of armour and men, already tactically demanding and difficult, was further threatened by 15th Scottish Infantry and 31st Tank Brigade not having worked together before. In an army where professional relationships between commanders as much as formal doctrine were critically important, this was a concern.

The sections advanced across wet fields of crops waist and even shoulder high, with heavy, dark clouds scudding overhead precluding air support. The artillery barrage, after an initial ten-minute blast, rolled forward ahead of the British infantry sections at the rate of one hundred yards every three minutes. It was crucial that the infantry maintained pace with the barrage; failure to do so could expose them to heavy casualties against an unsuppressed enemy.

Practical difficulties hindered the advance in a number of places, with tanks being held up by minefields and obstacles, and errors in map-reading causing troops to be caught in their own supporting bombardments. The greatest difficulty was caused when advancing British troops swept through areas but failed to locate dug-in and camouflaged German defenders who subsequently sprang to life and shot up the British troops from the rear. Locating the enemy in fields of high crops, clumps of trees, farm buildings and thick hedgerows proved challenging. Sergeant Jimmy Blair, 2nd Glasgow Highlanders, later recounted:

> We soon bumped into a burst of machine-gun fire. The enemy positions were well camouflaged. My friend Walker was killed . . . others were killed by snipers . . . they didn't attempt to take cover, walked on forward instead of dropping down and crawling.[18]

Communications between tanks and infantry also proved technically demanding as the No. 38 radio sets proved ill-suited to the task, and as the advance went on the leading elements of 15th Scottish Infantry began to lose contact with the protective rolling artillery barrage. Despite careful planning by VIII Corps staff, the friction of war was throwing up a range of problems and difficulties.[19]

The Germans were also suffering and were shocked by the intensity of the offensive. One prisoner captured on the first morning remarked: 'We were caught in the fury of the barrage, had gone to ground and emerged only to find ourselves surrounded by tanks or furious Scotsmen throwing grenades.'[20] Whatever the shortcomings of the British Army's operational methods, later described by critics as too predictable, they achieved a high degree of effectiveness, even when practised by troops as green as those in 15th Scottish Division and 31st Tank Brigade. Steady progress was made throughout the morning and by lunchtime elements of 15th Scottish were battling in the villages of Cheux and St Manvieu where bitter hand-to-hand fighting took place. Ernest Powdrill, 13th Royal Horse Artillery, recalled:

> There was a bloody battle where infantry, tanks and self-propelled guns, ours and the Germans', were at times inextricably mixed. At one point, in a rift in the ground midway between Norrey-en-Bessin and St Manvieu I brought my four guns into action in the midst of hand-to-hand bayonet fighting between a Scottish company and some panzer grenadiers, which I watched (and almost had to take part) as a horrified spectator.[21]

The British supported the attack on St Manvieu with flame-throwing Churchill Crocodile tanks which had been attached to 31st Tank Brigade. The flame-throwing Crocodiles soon came to be feared and loathed by German troops, especially when employed in groups rather than singly as they were in the early days of the campaign, and indeed in EPSOM. Analysis later demonstrated that they were between two and two and half times more effective in supporting infantry in an assault than other tanks, and that the morale of German troops faltered in their presence. Crocodiles were, however, in short supply.[22]

To add to the woes of the British infantry a German *Nebelwerfer* brigade began unleashing rocket-fired mortar rounds at them, a highly unnerving experience for green troops quite unused to the distinctive whining sound made by *werfer* fire. Troops of the 4th King's Shropshire Light Infantry, who were also blooded in EPSOM, initially had grave reservations about *werfers*, or Moaning Minnies as they were widely known. Lieutenant Dick Mullock remembered:

> [EPSOM] was the first time we experienced the Moaning Minnie. It was very scaring at first because you could never judge where the bloody things would land. With shells it was different. If you heard the whistle it had passed over.

Sergeant Rowley Tipton recalled:

> Then we had our first experience of heavy shelling and showers of 'Moaning Minnie' mortar bombs . . . With no slit trenches for cover we lay face down on the open ground . . . Although we did not enjoy this we suffered nothing worse than being showered with soil and debris thrown up by exploding shells and mortar bombs. During this blitz many and varied were the strange Scottish oaths uttered by the Cook Sergeant, Jock Murdock, who had come up with us.[23]

Lieutenant Colonel Jack Churcher, commanding 1st Herefords, recognised that *werfers* were not as bad as they sounded:

> As the days went by and with practice one discovered where they would fall and the interesting thing about that weapon was that it made a tremendous noise, it had a great explosion but its splinter effort was extremely poor, therefore its lethal effects were much reduced.[24]

Yet mortars, traditional and *Nebelwerfer*, accounted for some 75 per cent of British casualties in Northwest Europe, and these were most often inflicted when troops were advancing or caught in the open; soldiers were much less likely to become physical casualties if in slit trenches, hard cover or lying down. For Allied soldiers carrying the burden of the offensive this was a much greater problem than for German troops who, although often pinned down or suppressed, spent much less time moving in the open.

Steadily and surely the British cleared Cheux and St Manvieu against fierce and fervent opposition, but progress was slowing and the main objective of the first day, the bridges over the River Odon, were still some 2 miles away to the south. Opposition was hardening and the British were starting to believe that the German front line, which they had spent the morning breaking their way through, had in fact been held in only limited strength; stiffer opposition had been positioned further back and had been troubled little by the artillery bombardment. Intelligence summaries from the evening of 26 June stated as much: 'as yet only the fwd defences had been driven in and that [the enemy's] main defences had still to be tackled'.[25] The depth of

German defences and their disposition were concerns that would come back time and again to haunt British forces, but in truth German defences that afternoon were stretched to breaking point.

Time was now running out if EPSOM was to keep moving, so O'Connor at his VIII Corps tactical HQ decided to thrust 11th Armoured Division into the fray earlier than had been planned in order to maintain momentum. He hoped to reach the Odon quickly, and certainly before the Germans could move more troops into the line ahead of the British offensive.

Major General Philip 'Pip' Roberts, commander of 11th Armoured Division, and at thirty-seven the youngest general in the British Army, was not optimistic at the prospect of prematurely advancing his forces through the area currently being contested by the remaining stubborn elements of the 12th SS Panzer Division. Much of the terrain was unsuitable for armour and the road network, already rudimentary, had been blasted by Allied artillery, while the choke point of Cheux was littered with wrecked vehicles, burning buildings and scattered rubble. As 11th Armoured's reconnaissance regiment, the Northants Yeomanry, predominantly equipped with the new Cromwell fast cruiser tank, began their advance at 1230, Roberts noted: 'I never thought much of their luck if they had to make a fight of it.'[26] O'Connor's hope that the application of his armoured division at this stage would reignite the momentum of EPSOM was soon dashed as first the Northants Yeomanry and then the 11th Armoured's whole armoured brigade failed to break through, stymied by the terrain, confusion, and the newly arrived Panzer IVs of 12th SS Division, which had been rapidly redeployed from a planned counter-attack on the positions won by British troops in MARTLET the previous day. Lieutenant William Steel Brownlie commented:

> We had gone about three hundred yards when two armour piercing shots came through us from somewhere on the right, sending up showers of earth and killing a couple of infantrymen on the ground. We wheeled right and picked up the turrets of three Tigers at about 1,800 yards' range. [These were almost certainly Panzer IVs as there were no Tigers operating in this area at this time. Panzer IVs were often mistaken for Tigers as they had a similar, if smaller, silhouette.] After an exchange of shots for some minutes they disappeared.[27]

As the day came to a close the British were still over a mile short of the Odon bridges, though troops were now preparing to continue the assault again at first light. Because the Rauray Ridge to the west and Carpiquet to the east remained in enemy hands, EPSOM had created a salient into the

German lines which became known as the Scottish Corridor, a corridor overlooked from both flanks. The German position had held, but only just, and the price had been high; 12th SS Division suffered the loss of over 700 troops killed, wounded or missing, the most in any single day of action. British losses too had been heavy, with 15th Scottish Infantry suffering over 550 casualties.[28]

Fighting the next day followed a similar pattern; British troops hammered away and slowly but surely forced the Germans back, by nightfall at last opening up a passage across the River Odon. A German counter-attack spearheaded by 17 Panthers, which was intended to retake Cheux, was beaten off in large part by heavy Allied artillery. German tanks were able to survive the bombardment, but their mechanised infantry was stripped away, and denuded of such support the counter-attack failed. It was a scenario to be played out many times in the Northwest European campaign.

Over the night of 27–28 June infantry of 11th Armoured Division infiltrated their way into positions to the south of the Odon, preparing a base for a planned advance by armour the following morning on to Hill 112. For inexperienced troops to complete such a task in darkness was impressive, although it was not achieved without mishap. Brigadier J.G. Sandie had not impressed his battalion commanders thus far and as the troops passed through Cheux they found him, '. . . standing on the side of the road and his only orders to us were to wave his arms and say, "into battle, into battle!" '[29] When Sandie issued his orders for the night-time advance across the Odon, his battalion commanders clashed with him. Lieutenant Colonel 'Mossy' Miles (4th KSLI) pointed out that according to the maps there was no bridge for his troops to get across the Odon, whilst Lieutenant Colonel Jack Churcher (1st Herefords) argued that there simply was not enough time to form up and be in a position to follow the artillery barrage which kicked off at 2130. Churcher continued: 'I shall start when I am ready, and not before – it may be as late as 2300 hrs', to which Sandie replied, 'You will start at 2130, and that is an order. Carry it out or take the consequences!'[30] The KSLI made the start line in time after a confused briefing from Miles carried out in a ditch a few feet away from a Sherman tank duelling with the enemy, but the Herefords did not, though it is unlikely that Churcher was reprimanded as within two days Sandie had been sacked by 'Pip' Roberts, the division's commander. Churcher claimed that no guidance or orders had been forthcoming from brigade HQ in the battle that followed the crossing of the Odon, and that Sandie had been found drunk in a pew in a local chapel. Roberts had found Sandie to be in 'a sorry state, quite over-wrought' and mentally crumbling under artillery fire, even though there had not been any casualties in his brigade HQ. Roberts acted decisively, and replaced Sandie with Churcher. Roberts later claimed that Churcher was good at set-piece battles, less so in fluid operations; he was obviously a difficult personality, and after clashing with Sandie went on to quarrel with the armoured brigade commander in 11th Armoured, Roscoe Harvey. Miles, commanding officer of 4th KSLI, was also replaced as a result of the battalion's first action; he had cracked up under the pressure after just five days.[31] Soldiers and commanders who had performed well enough in training were often found out in battle conditions and soon replaced.

Despite the failings of two of its senior commanders, the troops of 11th Armoured's infantry brigade crossed the Odon and seized their objectives, and on the morning of 28 June the division's tanks and motorised infantry pushed on to the primary objective, Hill 112, with its dominating views of the Orne valley overlooking the southern approaches to Caen. Furious fighting ensued as the Germans desperately attempted to evict the British from their new position. The Germans' situation was also threatened by 43rd Wessex Division's advance on Marcelet and Mouen to the east of the Scottish Corridor, and the efforts of 49th Infantry Division and 4th Armoured Brigade in capturing the village of Rauray to the west.[32]

Although prospects of further British progress were diminishing rapidly, corollary aspects of Montgomery's operational approach were about to kick in. The Germans had been planning a major armour spearheaded counter-offensive against Second British Army, to be directed by the staff of Leo Geyr von Schweppenburg's Panzer Group West, now sufficiently recovered after being targeted and hit by Allied air forces guided by *Ultra* intelligence on 11 June. The offensive was principally to employ the newly arrived forces of II SS Panzer Corps. Montgomery and Dempsey were aware of the arrival of this new formation and that it was preparing to go into action, but they reckoned that by continuing with EPSOM they would retain the initiative and force the Germans to commit these units to action piecemeal in an essentially defensive battle at a time and on terrain of British choosing; they wanted to force Rommel's and Geyr's hand. By so doing Montgomery and Dempsey also calculated that reactive German counter-attacks against the salient formed by EPSOM could and would be more easily defeated by Allied firepower as the artillery was *in situ* and the naval guns were prepared and ready for action. Ultimately, EPSOM was about to deliver an opportunity to inflict heavy attrition on the remaining fresh front-line forces available to Rommel in the theatre.

This is largely what ensued. Because of the growing seriousness of the British penetration in EPSOM, Geyr von Schweppenburg cancelled the offensive he had planned and committed his forces to tackling the salient created by the British assault; there was no real alternative, especially as Seventh Army Commander Friedrich Dollman was pressing hard for this. O'Connor's troops knew they were about to be attacked and prepared accordingly. German prospects were diminished further by the absence of key commanders at this critical time: Rommel and von Rundstedt had been summoned to meet Hitler, and Dollman had cracked under the strain and committed suicide, prompting a reshuffling of senior leaders. Within days von Rundstedt himself had been dismissed after heatedly offering some home truths to Berlin in the wake of the futile meeting with Hitler, and on 3 July in the aftermath of EPSOM Geyr's practical assessment of the German position in Normandy prompted his dismissal by Hitler. With Dollman dead and others absent, responsibility for the counter-attacks fell to Paul Hausser who had moved from II SS Panzer Corps to command Seventh Army. Hausser had wanted to stick with the original plan rather than reacting to EPSOM but did not feel able to change the new directive. He was dismayed at beginning the attack prematurely and would have preferred more time to deploy properly, but he was prevailed upon to start quickly.[33] It was left to Hausser's replacement at II SS Panzer Corps, Wilhelm Bittrich, to prosecute the attacks against the Scottish Corridor, though further delays pushed back the start time into the afternoon. The early stages of the attack caused some British units to fall back or be overrun: 'Bullets streamed up every lane; the place was in flames; the wireless link with brigade had been knocked out; the telephone wires had been cut by shelling. . .'. At Cheux, the crucial chokepoint for British supplies and troops heading into and out of the Scottish Corridor, the German attack provoked desperate action:

> The Germans were less than a mile away to the west, hammering away with everything they had. Shells and mortar bombs were dropping, throwing up great fountains of earth and smoke. Vehicles were on fire . . . Men were digging in; drivers, cooks, and mechanics; anti-tank guns were being manhandled into position; Churchill tanks were everywhere, engines pulsating, moving off in groups.[34]

But the German attacks were stalling and suffering heavy losses due to air attack and Allied artillery fire. Hausser later claimed that the Allies' overwhelming artillery, naval gunfire and anti-tank defence were the key factors behind the attacks being repulsed. On 30 June Geyr's Panzer Group West diary noted that: 'The attack is halted . . . by the most intense artillery fire', whilst German Western Theatre command recorded that 'after several hours of fluctuating fighting the II Panzer Corps attack was smothered . . . Our forces suffered grievous losses.'[35]

The assault proved such a failure that VIII Corps staff believed that a more concerted effort must surely follow. On the main thrust of the attacks:

> . . . from prisoners' statements it would appear that they were intended to be on a much larger scale, but that concentration had been prevented by our bombing and artillery fire. As it was the enemy achieved nothing and suffered heavy casualties both in men and tanks.[36]

Dempsey had already switched to a defensive mentality over EPSOM once the array of German panzer formations were in the line ahead of his forces, and ordered the withdrawal of 11th Armoured's tanks from Hill 112 into a safer, more defensive position on the north bank of the Odon. For the troops who had fought to take and hold Hill 112 this seemed baffling, though the divisional commander, 'Pip' Roberts, had previously thought his troops were out on a limb with exposed flanks.[37] Bill Close, A Squadron commander in 3rd Royal Tank Regiment (RTR), was able to balance the disappointment of not being able to advance further with the relief at being able to withdraw from Hill 112, the scene of so much bitter fighting.[38] In reality the likelihood of a meaningful and low-risk breakthrough into the terrain to the south of Caen appeared small, and Montgomery and Dempsey had accepted that EPSOM had now become a means with which to impose further attrition on the enemy. With such a concentration of force arrayed against them, however ineffective II SS Panzer Corps' attack had been, it was considered prudent to dig in and absorb and defeat the counter-attacks. Further efforts on the night of 30 June by the SS to dislodge 11th Armoured's infantry still holding positions on the south bank of the Odon were again beaten off, with the Germans enduring yet more severe losses:

> An inspection of the ground in front of our positions revealed that the British DF fire had slaughtered the enemy in their hundreds. No less than 23 machine-guns were picked up amid the litter of abandoned equipment.
>
> It had indeed been a holocaust for the Germans. Their dead lay in piles among the wheat. It had been the type of battle which Montgomery planned and hoped for – drawing the Germans into attacking his own troops in a prepared position.[39]

A concerted effort by Kampfgruppe Weidinger and later by 9th SS Panzer Division to dislodge 49th Division from the Rauray position also floundered on 1 July and suffered heavy losses in so doing. Curiously the fighting performance of two battalions of 49th Division, which had fought on and around the Rauray Ridge since MARTLET began and had repulsed these assaults, has been called into question. The troops of 1st Tyneside Scottish were described as streaming back from their positions in disarray when in reality, although some sections did fall back under the weight of the attack, their primary objectives were held.[40] More famous is the case of 6th Duke of Wellington's Regiment (DWR) who, it was claimed, were simply not up to the quality of 15th Scottish or 6th Airborne soldiers and therefore folded under pressure. Much of this was based on a report filed by a replacement commanding officer of the battalion who argued that the unit was unfit at that time to stay in the line and should be withdrawn, retrained and reorganised, or failing that, disbanded. It is quite probable that the officer's pessimistic state of mind at that time was influenced by the desperate experience of 6th DWR thus far in the campaign. It had endured almost 50 per cent losses: all but 12 of the original officers had been lost, the commanding officer and every rank above corporal save two lieutenants had been lost from the battalion HQ, and all the company commanders had been lost.[41] Montgomery replaced the commanding officer for his candour and disbanded 6th DWR to create replacements for 7th DWR, still fighting as part of 49th Division. The breakdown of the unit is not in question, though the extremity of its losses in key roles is perhaps too easily passed over, but the inference drawn by some from the crumbling of this one unit is that there was a problem with British fighting troops. That the other eight battalions in 49th Division performed well, demonstrating some considerable skill in close-combat cooperation and tactics, and repulsed a heavy and determined attack by experienced German troops, is peculiarly ignored, as is the fact that this was the division's first serious action.[42]

By the end of 1 July the battle had reached stalemate. The British still held their positions on the south of the Odon, though they had given up Hill 112, which in hindsight was perhaps a premature decision. The German line had survived and the front maintained, though at the considerable expense of feeding in the reserves and sacrificing the chance of mounting Panzer Group West's counter-attack. Ultimately, EPSOM can be viewed as a considerable success if regarded as a building block in an Allied strategy intended to wrest control of France from the Germans through means of carefully planned operations likely to inflict casualties and impose attrition via concerted and applied firepower. If, however, the operation was viewed as a planned breakthrough to force the Germans from Caen, then it was unsuccessful. Clearly the intention was to achieve both objectives, but in light of Montgomery's overarching approach to the campaign and the manner in which the British Army intended and planned to engage the Germans, EPSOM was one step closer to victory and an important, if costly, one.

The German position in Normandy never fully recovered from the mauling it received in EPSOM; the initiative was surrendered for good, tactical methods for assaults had been exposed as hugely costly in the face of Allied firepower, and the German command structure and central strategy was dealt a mortal blow. But for the British the intensity of the fighting had been shocking indeed. The 15th Scottish Infantry Division, at the point of the offensive, had suffered close on 300 killed and a further 2,400 wounded or missing. In itself this would appear to be a little under a 15 per cent casualty rate for the division, but the vast majority of these losses were concentrated on the infantry battalions, and in particular the rifle companies which constituted only 20 per cent of the division's strength, yet suffered 80 per cent of the wounded, killed or missing. Of the division's total losses in the whole Northwest European campaign (June 1944 to May 1945), one quarter was endured in EPSOM.[43] The other units employed in the operation and MARTLET suffered an additional 2,500 casualties.

Despite the theoretical benefits of the operational techniques employed in EPSOM, some of the fighting demonstrated naivety. This was to be expected with fresh troops unused to combat, but the British had to learn and learn quickly. 'Pip' Roberts noted the poor infantry-armour cooperation between 15th Scottish Division and 31st Tank Brigade, but also recognised that the handling of his own infantry and armoured brigades had been less than exemplary.[44] British soldiers were now recognising that the German policy of digging in close to the coast of Normandy in difficult and dense terrain was placing a premium on small-scale tactical capability and intimate all-arms cooperation. EPSOM demonstrated that artillery and firepower could ease the way forward only so far in close terrain, and that armoured support was less helpful than in more open country; unless the Germans began conducting a fighting retreat, as the Allies had initially expected, British soldiers would have to reconcile themselves to a grim and bloody battle in which the infantry would bear a substantial burden.

Even as EPSOM was winding down a follow-up action began taking shape, conducted principally by Canadian troops and with the aim of capturing Carpiquet some 5 miles to the west of Caen and its adjoining airfield. Originally intended to work alongside EPSOM and MARTLET on 28 June, WINDSOR under the I Corps command of John Crocker, deployed a reinforced brigade, a regiment of tanks and units from 79th Armoured Division, supported by artillery, air units and naval gunnery. The offensive was launched on 4 July but the desperate and determined resistance by 12th SS Panzer Division thwarted the assault around the airfield, though Carpiquet itself was captured. The Canadians beat off furious counter-attacks, inflicting some 155 casualties on the 12th SS Panzers, and they held on to the village, but they could not prise the airfield from German control.[45] Canadian casualties were heavier at 377 men, many caused by the Germans' highly effective concentrated use of mortars, a factor that induced a modified approach to future operations where a broader front assault was employed to dissipate the effects of the enemy's fire.[46]

This broadening of assaults was included as part of Montgomery's next move to rid Caen of the Germans, this time by direct assault. The Allies had wanted to avoid urban fighting as much as possible, as this was a particularly casualty-intensive form of warfare that hindered the effective use of firepower. By early July, however, with little apparent progress being made, Monty was forced to resort to such a direct attack as he had run out of alternatives: an attack to the east of Caen was ruled out due to lack of manoeuvring space and the distribution of unhelpful terrain; the attack to the immediate west had ground to a halt; and the terrain further west still, around Caumont and adjacent to the US sector, was considered too rugged. In any case, the objective most desired by Montgomery and his staff was the Bourguébus Ridge and the more open ground to the south of Caen, on the road to Falaise. The only realistic way to get there was to drive the Germans out of Caen by direct assault. Monty had run out of options.

The task was allocated to Crocker's I Corps and the operation was to be codenamed CHARNWOOD. Three divisions of infantry, 3rd British, 3rd Canadian and 59th Division, supported by three armoured brigades, 33rd, 27th and 2nd Canadian, were to lead the assault, and considerable fire support was once again assembled to assist the operation. Medium and field artillery of five divisions totalling some 656 guns, and the naval guns of HMS *Rodney*, the monitor *Roberts* and two cruisers, were to provide the initial bombardment, whilst tactical air support was to be provided by the RAF's 2nd Tactical Air Force.

Additional firepower was added to CHARNWOOD at the last minute in the form of the heavy bombers of the Allied strategic air forces, a further attempt to ease the path of the ground forces into Caen. This last measure was not without controversy. The use of the heavy bombers in this type of tactical role had been suggested to 21st Army Group by Air Marshal Leigh-Mallory earlier in the campaign, but was not sought until CHARNWOOD. Eisenhower's deputy, Air Marshal Arthur Tedder, was highly sceptical about this use of strategic air assets, and believed, with some justification, that if successful the army would repeatedly request such support and draw the heavy bombers away from their main task of attacking Germany itself. There is also evidence that the Allies had become aware of the strengthened positions of the Germans in and to the north of Caen and that this provoked 21st Army Group staff, in conversation with Allied air force staff, to call for the support of Bomber Command.[47]

Unfortunately, the request was made so late in the day, at a meeting on 7 July and less twenty-four hours before CHARNWOOD was to begin, that the bombing plan was rushed, ill-considered and proved frustratingly unsuccessful. Still, the sight of the 450 RAF Lancaster and Halifax bombers filling the skies over Caen on the evening of 7 July, and unloading some 6,000 bombs, was undoubtedly a boost to the British and Canadian troops waiting for the off a few hours later:

> The psychological effect on the infantry brigade my regiment was supporting was electrifying – you must remember that we had been stopped for a month in front of Lebisey Wood – we had lost two commanding officers and a significant number of casualties from mortaring and shellings – consequently the sight of the bombardment was a tremendous morale boost. Officers and soldiers were jumping out of their slit trenches and cheering.[48]

The RAF, uneasy about the accuracy their forces would be able to maintain in this unusual role, had insisted on a wide safety margin to avoid friendly bombing incidents and the bombs were dropped some 3 kilometres ahead of the Anglo-Canadian lines. They were fused to explode six hours after the bombing to coincide with CHARNWOOD's start in the early hours of 8 July, but they were still too far behind German positions and served little purpose other than fully alerting the Germans to the imminent attack. The Germans claimed later that they only lost 2 tanks and fewer than 20 men in the bombing; they were further baffled by the six-hour delay between the bombing and the assault.[49]

An investigation conducted after CHARNWOOD found that little damage had indeed been done to the German positions and that any future use of heavy bombers would require an integrated fire plan and not the last-minute addition of 'icing on the cake'. Contrary to popular belief the damage done to the city itself did not cause all the advancing British troops undue concern. Some were hindered by the rubble ('It was like scrambling over the Giant's Causeway')[50] but others did not record any difficulties.[51]

For the assaulting Commonwealth troops on the morning of 8 July there was to be a rude awakening. The Germans fully expected an attack on Caen itself, having followed the same reasoning as Montgomery's team, and were desperate to get 12th SS Panzer Division out of the firing line and into reserve; alas for them their replacements in the dug-in positions around Caen, the 271st Division, had not yet arrived, and the 12th SS Hitler Youth Division remained in position when CHARNWOOD began. This intensified the opposition for Crocker's forces, but imposed yet further attrition on an elite unit wasted in such a reactive defensive role.[52]

The British and Canadians attacked across a wide frontage of some 14 kilometres in an attempt to dissipate the defensive mortaring of the Germans and to avoid being enfiladed as had occurred in EPSOM. The armoured brigades operating in support of the Allied infantry were equipped with Shermans and often adopted stand-off artillery tactics rather than advancing with the infantry on to the target, a reaction to the lighter armour of their tanks, and this may well have been a contributory factor to the Allied casualty rates. Allied armoured losses were still considerable with some 80 tanks written off. German losses were not insignificant with 10 Panthers and 22 Panzer IVs being destroyed, whilst 12th SS's foot soldiers, as expected, took yet another hit and had its strength reduced to the equivalent of just one battalion. Many of these losses were again suffered in localised counter-attacks, and in one case 17-pdr-equipped M10s of the Royal Artillery inflicted 13 losses on German panzers in one brief action.[53]

A typical action was recorded by Major Glyn Gilbert of the Lincolns, who had seen his company reduced to 40 fighting men in the assault on 8 July:

> . . . assumed a defensive position in an orchard on the southern edge of the village [Hérouville] and twice German tanks and infantry counter-attacked us. Fortunately we repelled both attacks and destroyed one tank . . . The remainder of the day was relatively quiet although the ever present mortars at Colombelles harassed us.[54]

For the inexperienced troops of 59th Division for whom CHARNWOOD was their baptism of fire, the grim and appalling realities of combat were a chastening experience. Lieutenant Brown of 6th North Staffordshire Regiment recalled:

> I came across a still smouldering Tiger tank; lying alongside was a boot with the foot and stump of a charred leg still attached. Over all hung a

most appalling smell, from the grotesque carcases of bloated cattle and horses lying in the fields.[55]

Despite the difficulties endured in the assault and the less than resounding success of the bombing, the Germans realised the game was up. Sixteenth Luftwaffe Field Division had ceased to exist as a functioning unit as a result of the Allied offensive and 12th SS Panzer Division was at breaking point. Even Kurt Meyer, the fanatical Commanding Officer of the *Hitlerjugend*, recognised the futility of remaining in northern Caen:

> The division's front is stretched to breaking, reserves are no longer available. I cannot stand this any more. We can hold out for a couple of hours longer, but there won't be any survivors from the division.[56]

Without waiting for official confirmation Meyer sanctioned the withdrawal of German troops to the south bank of the Orne and by 9 July the Allies were taking control of the city. Second Battalion Royal Ulster Rifles was first into the city in the late evening of 8 July and the following morning British units properly established themselves in Caen:

> At 0930hrs the Rifles advanced into the city with B Company leading the way. Progress was slow, a sharp lookout had to be kept for booby traps and the occasional sniper's bullet caused delay.[57]

Yet progress was made and once again an Allied operation, whilst not a resounding success, had brought considerable benefits. Germans losses were crippling, and indeed Meyer's elite 12th SS troops had been reduced to a shadow of their former selves, as its commander noted on 9 July:

> They went to war weeks ago with fresh blooming faces. Today, camouflaged, muddy steel helmets shade emaciated faces whose eyes have, all too often, looked into another world. The men present a picture of deep human misery.[58]

The surviving position in Caen was becoming untenable for the Germans. Just over a week later when the British began Operation GOODWOOD, a major armoured assault to the east of Caen in part made possible by the capture of the northern half of the city, the Canadians initiated ATLANTIC and drove the Germans completely out of the city.

For the hard-pressed Germans there was to be no respite. Just twenty-four hours after CHARNWOOD finished they were once again drawn into action around Hill 112 as the British launched yet another assault: Operation JUPITER. In the hope that the Germans would be forced by CHARNWOOD into a retreat from Caen, JUPITER had been planned to exploit this situation by seizing Hill 112 in the confusion. This operation was conducted by 43rd Wessex Division, under the command of the fearsome and humourless Major General Ivor Gwilyn 'Butcher' Thomas, reinforced by an extra infantry brigade and two brigades of armour. It also had the fire support of two AGRAs and the artillery of two further divisions in support. The targets were Maltot, Eterville and, of course, Hill 112, described by General Hans Eberbach, Geyr von Schweppenburg's replacement as commander of Panzer Group West, as 'pivotal to the whole position . . . in no circumstances may it be surrendered'.[59]

Operation JUPITER began in textbook fashion at 5 a.m. with a bombardment, followed by a rolling barrage leading the infantry and armour forward. As at EPSOM the heavy Churchill tanks of 31st Tank Brigade provided the support but suffered casualties from the 88mm guns of the Tigers in 102nd SS Heavy Tank Battalion. The Churchills' heavy armour proved insufficient protection at these battle ranges and they were forced to drop back into cover, leaving the infantry temporarily without close fire support.[60] Progress was nevertheless made by the British troops who secured Maltot and captured Eterville for a time. Hill 112 was fiercely contested and the northern slopes were seized, but further progress appeared unlikely. The fiery and foul-mouthed Thomas pressed Michael Carver (later Field Marshal Lord Carver), recently promoted to the command of 4th Armoured Brigade, to bring his Shermans forward to push on. Carver, conscious of the losses suffered by the Churchills and fully aware of the tactically disadvantageous situation for his armour, point blank refused, leading to a furious radio exchange. To Carver, advancing his thinly armoured Shermans over the crest of a hill against heavy anti-tank guns that were clearly unsuppressed, was tantamount to suicide.[61]

Although the British were forced to relinquish Eterville temporarily, JUPITER succeeded in once again provoking localised German counter-attacks that exposed them to casualties and largely proved ineffective other than diminishing their strength still further. British casualties were also heavy, some 2,000 in total for the two-day battle, whilst 31st Tank Brigade saw 25 per cent of its tanks knocked out. Overall progress was mixed, due to the Germans not actually withdrawing from Caen as expected following CHARNWOOD, and because of the tactical difficulties the British had encountered in attacking across open, downward-sloping ground in view of well-positioned enemy units.[62] Richard O'Connor, the VIII Corps commander directing JUPITER, noted some hard-learned lessons. Narrow front attacks were fraught with risk but the strategic situation and limited numbers of deployed and available units made them a necessity. O'Connor also pressed for a greater awareness of terrain in operations; he saw that simply attacking a target because it was a village name on a map was counter-productive, and argued that operational objectives in undulating terrain should be dictated by the occupation of high ground.[63]

Ultimately, although the British and Canadians had demonstrated increasing battle awareness and had made some progress in forcing the Germans into fighting on Allied terms in and around Caen, the hoped-for push into the more open countryside to the south of the city had not materialised. The Germans were stubbornly and determinedly hanging on, in spite of mounting casualties that they could ill-afford. From the Allied perspective, by the time JUPITER and CHARNWOOD fizzled out on 10–11 July, the campaign around Caen appeared to be faltering, whilst in the western sector the Americans had captured Cherbourg and secured the Cotentin Peninsula, progress that cartographically appeared much more impressive. The rivalry was not helped by the heavier casualties endured by the US forces as indicated in the American press.

With General Bradley's First American Army now shifting its attention southwards following the capture of Cherbourg achieved by 29 June, the prospects of a concerted series of offensives overwhelming the stretched German forces were promising. Initial American efforts to push south fizzled out, however, and though the Allies still retained the initiative, it was now imperative that they plan their future strategy ever more shrewdly. To that end Bradley, Dempsey and Montgomery met on 10 July to thrash out the next steps in the campaign. Montgomery's and Dempsey's thinking that day was in part shaped by a report filed by Brigadier Charles Richardson, 21st Army Group's chief planning officer, that pressed for the greater employment of British and Canadian armoured forces in an effort to ease the burden on the infantry. They were also governed by a meeting with Lieutenant General Ronald 'Bill' Adam, the adjutant general. Adam emphasised once again the growing problems in finding replacements for the casualties being endured in Normandy, a difficulty most apparent in the infantry. As Second Army enjoyed a superiority in armour over the Germans of four to one, and with concern over infantry losses mounting, an armour-heavy operation appeared the most likely and strategically appropriate use of resources.[64]

The opportunity to enact this thinking emerged during and after the meeting of 10 July. Bradley emphasised that his forces would require more time to manoeuvre their way into position before launching a major offensive, the offensive that would become COBRA. Consequently, the British and

Canadians would have to maintain or intensify the pressure around Caen to lock the elite German units and heavy armour currently situated there in place. Montgomery ordered that Second British Army prepare for strong offensives to the south of Caen and that it secure bridgeheads over the River Orne, and he made an armoured corps available to support this should the occasion arise. He wrote: 'I am not prepared to have *heavy* casualties during these actions . . . as we shall have plenty elsewhere.'[65] The Second British Army commander, Miles Dempsey, was tasked with maintaining this fine balancing act of low casualties and offensive operations.

Miles Dempsey is rather hidden away in the story of the British Army in Northwest Europe, but there is considerable evidence that he was a forceful and determined character. General Richard 'Windy' Gale later described Dempsey, shortly before the latter's death in 1969, as an enigma. 'He's as close as a dam' but was ' . . . one of the cleanest thinking generals' he had encountered. Brigadier Charles Richardson worked with Dempsey for a time in June 1944 and considered him to be akin to a highly intelligent headmaster and someone for whom he would have happily served.[66] Although Dempsey was happy to live in the shadow of his illustrious commander Montgomery, he nevertheless wanted to impose himself upon the campaign as and when necessary, and with the Americans needing more time to prepare COBRA he saw a crucial opportunity for the British and Canadian forces to play a more prominent role in the breakout from the Normandy lodgement.[67] After Bradley had departed the meeting on 10 July to continue the detailed planning of COBRA, Dempsey pressed Montgomery to allow him to take up the challenge of instigating the big showdown with the floundering Germans. Dempsey considered that the best way to deliver this would be to mount a major attack from Caen southwards that would present a direct threat to Falaise, a threat which the Germans simply could not ignore. He pushed for this to be a potential breakout that would change the dynamic of the campaign's strategy, but Montgomery demurred. He was unwilling to countenance such a drastic step, though he agreed that a dramatic operation in the Caen area, timed to hit the Germans just before COBRA, could yield great rewards. Dempsey later claimed that once Monty had ruled on the status of Dempsey's planned operation, the issue never arose again. 'There was no question of an attempted breakout,' Dempsey later claimed, but Montgomery was hopeful that the new operation to the east of Caen would fix the heavier German units firmly in place in the British sector in having to defend the road south from Caen, which potentially opened the route to Paris. 'That will draw them in,' he stated once he had seen the scale of Dempsey's alternative plan.[68]

Initially the operation, codenamed GOODWOOD, was still highly ambitious, calling for the use of all three British armoured divisions in the theatre to lead a sweeping southwards manoeuvre across fairly open country to the east of Caen, with the initial objective of reaching the high ground of the Bourguébus Ridge lying to the southeast of the city. Flanking actions would support this main thrust, most notably a Canadian operation, ATLANTIC, designed to clear the rest of Caen. Dempsey considered that the employment of the three armoured divisions in this punching role would ease the pressure on the infantry, though he knew that Montgomery was in principle opposed to the use of an all-armoured corps following some painful experiences in the desert; Montgomery had even stated in January 1944 that he would never employ such a formation.[69] But by mid-July 1944, circumstances dictated that the British Army embrace a more flexible approach.

Dempsey had been greatly impressed by the potential impact of employing heavy bombers of the strategic air forces alongside naval guns and artillery to blast a path through the Germans lines, having noted its potential, albeit unrealised, in CHARNWOOD. He hoped that the carpet-bombing ahead of the leading armoured forces in GOODWOOD would sufficiently suppress and disrupt the German defenders and result in them being quickly overwhelmed.[70]

Dempsey's ambitions for GOODWOOD were soon dampened down by Montgomery and Second Army intelligence reports during the planning stage. On 15 July, three days after being issued, the first plan's wings were clipped when mention of striking south from Bourguébus towards Falaise was altered to a more circumspect probing by armoured cars and reconnaissance elements which would 'spread alarm and despondency and discover . . . the form'. Only if prospects looked excellent would the possibility of pushing further south to 'crack about' become possible.[71] Montgomery clearly considered it crucial that Dempsey and those directly commanding GOODWOOD should fully realise what was being attempted and that they all sing from the same hymn sheet because, on 15 July, Montgomery issued what was the only formal written directive in advance of the detailed planning of an operation throughout the campaign in Northwest Europe. Dempsey later recalled that Montgomery stated unequivocally, 'let's be quite clear about this' when scaling back the stated aims of GOODWOOD.[72] Brigadier Harold 'Peter' Pyman, then Dempsey's chief of staff, considered that the principal reason for the change was a series of Second Army intelligence reports which strongly implied that the Germans had thickened up the defences to the east and south of Caen, making the prospects of GOODWOOD breaking open the front much less likely. Montgomery was also concerned that an over-ambitious plan might unbalance the Allied position ahead of the Americans' push timed for a few days after GOODWOOD. Montgomery had to consider the bigger picture and his vision of GOODWOOD was of an operation to fix the heavier German units and most of their armour in and around Caen and impose further attrition on them. In this way Bradley's Operation COBRA and the breakout into Brittany, then a primary concern, could more easily be effected. Ultimately, of course, Montgomery did not want his plan to be seen to fail and he considered that advertising grand objectives which were unlikely to be achieved would be bad both for morale and his reputation. Dempsey clearly was more ambitious for GOODWOOD, even after the 15 July meeting, and he intended to place his tactical HQ alongside O'Connor's corps HQ to direct a drive south towards Falaise, should the opportunity arise. He was also a believer in issuing bold objectives in order to inspire his troops to keep pushing forward rather than sit back.[73]

Montgomery's change of emphasis in the plan was to cause huge and lingering controversy, for this moderation was neither transmitted below the level of corps commander nor beyond the confines of Second Army's staff; indeed, not even all senior 21st Army Group staff were fully briefed.[74] This was to have two profound effects. First, Montgomery and his team had received enthusiastic backing for GOODWOOD from Eisenhower and SHAEF after the first operational plan had been issued, precisely because it appeared very ambitious and a turning point in the campaign away from remorseless attrition towards dynamic manoeuvre. Eisenhower informed Montgomery:

> We are enthusiastic on your plan.
>
> We are so pepped up concerning the promise of this plan that either Tedder, or myself or both will be glad to visit you if we can help in any way.[75]

This in turn had prompted the strategic air chiefs to offer their full support and had secured the scale of bombing Dempsey desired to ease the way forward for his armoured troops. Yet when the plan's intentions were scaled back on 15 July by Montgomery this was not communicated to SHAEF. Though this might be considered to be a breakdown in communication – Second Army's revised plan was supposedly forwarded to SHAEF on 17 July only for it not to be received – Brigadier Charles Richardson was still lobbying senior air staff in England on 16 July with the original plan as his pitch, not the scaled-back version.[76] It was little wonder that in the aftermath of GOODWOOD and its disappointing outcome, as measured against the high hopes of the original plan, military and political leaders in the UK felt seriously misled and vented their anger at Montgomery. Brigadier David Belchem, chief of operations at 21st Army Group, claimed after the war that Montgomery had deliberately withheld the newly limited objectives for GOODWOOD in order to maintain the highest level of support from SHAEF:

> The reason for the secrecy was to avoid disclosure above all to Tedder . . . and Eisenhower that GOODWOOD was intended to pin down the enemy armour in the British sector.
>
> GOODWOOD was to have very limited objectives in terms of distance.[77]

The limited objectives also explained the block on the use of the new Kangaroo armoured personnel carriers, freshly arrived in Normandy and theoretically available for GOODWOOD. These fully tracked armoured vehicles allowed the cross-country transportation of infantry at the pace of tanks and their rapid deployment into action, something that even half-tracks could not manage. O'Connor lobbied for their use in GOODWOOD, but Dempsey refused, probably on the grounds that no major breakout was expected. O'Connor still believed after the war that their use would have reduced casualties in the armoured brigades.[78]

Divisional commanders in VIII Corps tasked with commanding the armoured assault were also left in the dark about the more limited ambitions for GOODWOOD. Major General 'Pip' Roberts, commander of 11th Armoured Division who was to lead the attack, was seriously puzzled by O'Connor's orders and dispositions in the lead-up to GOODWOOD. Roberts' armour was to spearhead the advance but, due to the current structure of armoured divisions in the British Army, had only limited integral infantry support in the form of a single motorised battalion. Roberts foresaw that as his leading armoured troops pressed southwards to the Bourguébus Ridge and ideally beyond it, they would need more immediate infantry support to deal with emerging battlefield problems, yet his infantry brigade had been directed to secure two villages very close to the start line of GOODWOOD and would therefore be too far behind to offer support at the crucial moment. This seemed perplexing and Roberts badgered O'Connor to release his infantry from this task in order to keep it free to support his armour. O'Connor refused and this caused considerable friction between the two of them. Many years later Belchem attempted to clarify the reasoning to Roberts:

> While I fully understand your misgivings about Dick O'Connor's handling of the initial phase (in particular) of the operation, my purely personal reaction is that Monty imposed upon him the secrecy angle.[79]

Roberts later conceded that had he known of the more limited objectives of GOODWOOD, he would have more readily accepted O'Connor's decision as complying with Montgomery's aims from the 15 July meeting. It it is also possible that Dempsey wanted his divisional commanders to retain an ambitious perspective, but it is more likely that in the rush to put GOODWOOD together, the subtle though important differences that emerged between 12 July and 17 July were lost in translation further down the command chain. Whatever the cause, at the time Roberts believed he was being asked to lead the assault with a serious handicap.[80]

Dempsey claimed later that whilst the strategic impact and reasoning behind GOODWOOD had been sound, in other ways the plan was flawed, or as he put it 'not a very good operation of war tactically'.[81] There was little chance of surprising the enemy because the movement of three armoured divisions so close to Caen would be obvious and virtually impossible to conceal, especially as the Germans still held the factories at Colombelles with their high chimneys that afforded excellent viewing positions overlooking the area through which the GOODWOOD forces would pass as they assembled. An attempt to seize and destroy the factory chimneys on 11 July by a brigade of 51st Highland Division ended in failure and heaped further opprobrium on a formation already under pressure for a supposed lack of results in Normandy, despite its veteran status. In truth the Colombelles operation was far too limited in scope to stand much chance of success, and it was later to take two divisions to force the Germans to give up Colombelles.[82]

Despite this failure, Dempsey still attempted to conceal the intent and scale of GOODWOOD for as long as possible. To that end two minor diversionary operations, POMEGRANATE and GREENLINE, were mounted to the west of Caen by XII and XXX Corps in the days leading up to GOODWOOD; neither was a great success and they contributed little to deceiving the Germans. They were also a cause of disgruntlement to those involved as they were not well managed. As one officer said of GREENLINE:

> This operation was excused as a feint for ops EAST of the ORNE and CAEN. Even if this was the case there seems no reason for Operation GREENLINE to have been such a pointless muddle.[83]

As attention was focused elsewhere, there was little time to devote to serious planning and few resources were allocated to these operations. Troops were also aware of the diversionary nature of these actions and there was little stomach for a serious fight. When the British Army was afforded sufficient time to plan an operation, it was reasonably successful; it was less so when planning was rushed, though it would improve at this. At best some German resources were held in place by POMEGRANATE and GREENLINE, but no more.

In a further effort to conceal the intent of GOODWOOD Dempsey held his armoured divisions on the west of the River Orne and the Caen Canal, with the first of them, 11th Armoured, only advancing to the east side on the night of 17 July, prior to GOODWOOD beginning the following morning. The others were to follow on once 11th Armoured had started to move south. Even if this had confused the Germans, which is doubtful as they fully expected a major operation to the east of Caen, the difficulties in moving three armoured divisions across six small bridges, in a few hours at night, was fraught with danger and liable to cause confusion and delay.

Yet, in spite of the clouds of thick dust thrown up by the thundering mass of vehicles, the traffic-control personnel were able to cope with the initial movement of forces into the cramped areas of concentration east of the Orne:

> It was already crammed to bursting point with the leading regiments, with their tanks, attached guns and riflemen's vehicles, interspersed with enormous and weird looking objects which loomed blackly all around us. They proved to be derelict gliders, for we were in the open space in which 6th Airborne Division had made their landing on D-Day. We huddled up against the sides of the gliders, and, beating off continual mosquito assaults, we slept for what was left of the night.[84]

Much of the artillery required to support the tanks once they plunged into the German defences was still situated to the west of Caen, and it would take a herculean effort and considerable management to get them into a position to the east to maintain fire support once the British armour was deep into German territory. In recognition of this, Dempsey had ordered O'Connor to prioritise moving the armour and motor battalions across the bridges first, at the expense of their supporting elements.

Forward momentum was an obvious vital requirement of GOODWOOD and it was essential that the armour keep moving south as quickly as possible in order to exploit the effects of the heavy bombing that would pummel the

German positions ahead of the attack, and to maintain contact with the rolling artillery barrages that were to sweep the path ahead of the leading armoured elements. Critically, this meant not getting bogged down in winkling out small pockets of resistance, not getting embroiled in clearing out the villages dotting the landscape through which GOODWOOD would unfold, and avoiding delaying terrain features.

Much of this depended on the fire plan being effective in suppressing and neutralising the German forces between the start line and the Bourguébus Ridge long enough for the armour to seize their objectives. If it was not and the Germans were alerted and prepared in and around the Ridge and capable of mounting significant resistance, the leading elements of the British armoured forces would be forced to battle against them with insufficient infantry, dwindling artillery support as the guns had been left too far behind, and in tactical conditions that markedly favoured the German defenders.

Major Tony Sergeaunt of the British Army's No. 2 Operational Research Section attached to 21st Army Group was horrified by the GOODWOOD plan, for he foresaw a scenario in which largely unsupported armour with little opportunity for using cover and with few hull-down or concealed positions would be battling against dug-in and unsuppressed German anti-tank guns in and around the Bourguébus Ridge. He pointed out that such a tactical situation would favour the Germans enormously. The average range of effective anti-tank engagements in Normandy was under 700 yards, and Allied tanks would usually be afforded liberal artillery or air support in addition to the weight of their own guns. Yet the open terrain around the Bourguébus Ridge was likely to precipitate battles between British tanks and well-sited German anti-tank guns at ranges of 2,000 yards, distances that greatly benefited the Germans. British tanks mounting 75mm guns needed to be at ranges of no more than 800 yards to have a good chance of dealing with a dug-in gun before the gun could inflict crippling losses on them. But at 2,000 yards British tanks would need to use some 15 rounds to eliminate a dug-in German anti-tank gun, during which time they were likely to suffer the loss of some four to five of their own number. The primary reason why this was rarely, if ever, such a problem for the Allies was because they usually did not operate beyond the effective range of the great weight of artillery firepower that 21st Army Group could so rapidly and effectively deploy, and it was this arm that usually fixed the enemy in place, suppressing them and sometimes crushing resistance. Sergeaunt felt that the GOODWOOD plan actually worked against these crucial tactical imperatives; just when the British tanks might well need their artillery support the most would be the very moment they were least likely to get it.[85]

Operation GOODWOOD therefore broke the blueprint for how the Anglo-Canadian armies had previously planned to deal with the Germans; everything now depended on the aerial bombardment being effective in neutralising the German defences for long enough, right up to and on to the Bourguébus Ridge. It was a risky venture quite out of character for Montgomery and his army. Many other tactical problems emerged as GOODWOOD played out on 18 July, but essentially its primary and underlying weakness lay in that it did not play to British strengths – as other operations and actions generally had done and would do so in the future.

As the Allied air forces droned overhead on the morning of 18 July to begin their bombardment of German positions, few British soldiers or commanders were aware of the potential difficulties ahead caused by the inherent risks in GOODWOOD; those who were, for the most part anyway, considered that the risks were outweighed by the potential great success which might be delivered. There is little doubt that the scale and apparent effects of the bombing were intoxicating for the British troops afforded views of the spectacle. A little after 0500 some 1,000 RAF Bomber Command Lancasters and Halifaxes in their 'gaggle' formation began streaming overhead at around 3,000 feet, their dark silhouettes visible against the lightening sky. From the ground British artillery batteries targeted German anti-aircraft guns to the extent that only six bombers were lost to ground fire. Once the RAF bombers had deposited their payloads on the German positions around Colombelles, Cagny and 21st Panzer Division in the Touffréville and Émiéville areas, the ground fire, now supplemented by naval gunnery from the Channel, moved to targeting German artillery positions ahead of the advance. The German defenders were afforded no respite, however, for once RAF Bomber Command had departed, 318 B25 Mitchells and B26 Marauders of US 9th Air Force unloaded over 500 tons of bombs on positions held by 16th Luftwaffe Field Division, supplemented by 570 B24 Liberators and B17 Flying Fortresses of US 8th Air Force, which dropped 1,340 tons of fragmentation bombs on German positions around Troarn, and positions between Frénouville and Bourguébus. One British officer recalled:

> The bombers flew in majestically and with a dreadful unalterable dignity, unloaded and made for home.
>
> Everyone was out of their vehicles now, staring in awed wonder till the last wave dropped their bombs and turned away.[86]

For the defenders the Allies' use of heavy bombers to smash their way into and through German defences was mightily dispiriting, for they had no real answer to it. Nineteen-year-old Captain Freimark von Rosen of 503 Heavy Tank Battalion (equipped with Tigers) later commented:

> We were located in the very middle of this bombardment [not actually true as they were at the western area of the targeted zone], which was like hell, and I am still astonished to have survived it. I was unconscious for a while after a bomb had exploded just in front of my tank, almost burying me alive.[87]

Even 54-ton Tiger tanks were upturned in the bombardment, others covered in earth, engines full of sand, guns out of alignment. Soldiers went insane, committed suicide, or fled the bombing, never to be seen again by their comrades. The effects of the bombing, naval gunfire and artillery bombardment were savage, and if German positions had not been as unexpectedly deep as they proved to be, GOODWOOD would now be viewed differently.

Yet in reality all was not well with the plan from the start. The bombing had been very effective but targets were missed and some later aircraft abandoned their bombing runs due to poor visibility, a product of the dust and smoke thrown up by earlier bombing and artillery bombardments. Equally crucial was that the initial advance by 11th Armoured's tanks at 0745 started in some confusion. Owing to the pressures on space in which to form up, the first regiment into action, 3rd Royal Tank Regiment (3 RTR), had been pushed closer to the start line than was prudent. This, in conjunction with some inaccurate artillery fire caused by wear and tear on the guns after weeks in action in Normandy, resulted in some rounds from the rolling artillery barrage falling short and on to British units preparing to move out. Many tank crewmen waited until the last few moments before mounting up, in order to enjoy a last cigarette, mug of tea, or to enjoy some freedom of movement prior to being cooped up in a confined space, most probably for hours on end. This was dangerous and invited injury; some 20 per cent of tank crew casualties came as a result of being wounded or killed outside their vehicles. If this was caused by shortfalling or misdirected friendly fire, then it was all the more ironic.[88]

Consequently, 3 RTR's first-wave squadrons lost two troop commanders, whilst C Squadron lost its overall commander, Major Peter Burr, a desert veteran waiting to be promoted to brigade major. Overall, 3 RTR's initial advance began in a state of some disorder, owing to rapid reassignments of command, poor visibility due to the smoke and dust thrown up by the bombardment, and constrained avenues of advance out of British positions caused by poorly located defensive minefields sown by 51st Highland Division during its miserable occupation of the area east of the Orne.[89]

On the face of it, the ground ahead of 3 RTR and the other armoured regiments following in GOODWOOD was excellent tank country, being much more open than the terrain hitherto fought across. Such was the openness that, for once, the armour could deploy in squadron formation rather than in dispersed penny packets, as had been the norm since D-Day. Colonel David Silvertop, commanding 3 RTR, deployed two squadrons in front, A to the right (commanded by Bill Close), B to the left (commanded by Jock Balharrie), with C Squadron in reserve at the rear. In the middle of the grouping, behind A and B Squadrons, came the regimental HQ units with the carrier-borne infantry, specialised support tanks and other elements attached. At the rear of the whole formation followed the motorised infantry in half-tracks, and the 25-pdr self-propelled artillery.

The first forces into battle were to be A and B Squadrons, both deployed in square formations with one of their four troops of tanks at each corner and the squadron HQ troop in the centre. The troops were made up of four Shermans, three regular types with 75mm guns in arrowhead formation, each around 30 yards apart, and a fourth, the Firefly, sporting the 17-pdr, to the rear ready to be brought forward to duel with any heavy enemy armour uncovered.[90]

The 3 RTR formation headed off just before 0800 from the fields to the west of Escoville, attempting to keep pace with the rolling artillery barrage as it swept southwards at 5 mph. Ideally, the Shermans were to press as close to the barrage as possible to exploit its suppressing effects, but the murk created by the smoke and dust, along with craters caused by scattered bombs, hindered the advance. Major Bill Close, A Squadron commander, recalled:

> We roared on through boiling clouds of dirt and fumes, thirty-eight Shermans doing their best to keep up with the rolling curtain of fire. I could see tanks either side of me slowly picking their way through the ever increasing number of bigger and bigger bomb craters.
>
> I kept willing us on.[91]

The armour swept south, bypassing dazed German soldiers who merely endeavoured to surrender or who watched bemused and were rounded up and directed to the rear by the carrier platoons. There is no doubt that the immediate effects of the fire plan were as all-encompassing as could have been hoped for, and the initial opposition, even if still technically capable, was unable to offer much coordinated resistance. Robin Lemon captured the initial exhilaration of the British armoured troops as they plunged into the German positions:

> Rather enjoyed the first few minutes. There was little opposition and one had a wonderful feeling of superiority as many Germans, shaken by the preliminary bombing and shelling, gave themselves up.[92]

A defensive line of ten panzers around Cuverville and Démouville had escaped the bombardment but was quickly overwhelmed by the British armoured forces, and only one German tank escaped.[93] More problems were caused by physical obstacles such as the Caen-Troarn railway embankment, a feature that 11th Armoured's Aerial Photographic Interpretation Section had dismissed as insignificant, which, according to 'Pip' Roberts, proved to be their only mistake of the entire Northwest European campaign.[94] The railway embankment proved easily traversable by tanks but caused delays to the half-tracks and other soft-skin vehicles. The Churchill AVRE tanks and sappers eventually blew further gaps in the embankment, but contact with the rolling barrage was proving difficult to maintain. At 0845 the artillery barrage rolled on, this time heading southwest towards the Bourguébus Ridge. The 29th Armoured Brigade War Diary recorded: 'Barrage moves forward again on next phase. 3 RTks not all able to keep up with it, but try and catch it up.'[95] The armour and soft-skin vehicles were held up once again just 500 metres beyond the railway line by a thick hedgerow, and the leading tanks of A and B Squadrons were pressed to move on past pockets of resistance unsuppressed by the bombing and bombardment. The little hamlet of Le Mesnil Frémentel had been passed over by the Allied fire plan and the defenders were intact, but they had little in the way of anti-armour equipment to slow 3 RTR down and merely looked on, bemused by the passing parade of British tanks. They did, however, tie up for a time the motorised infantry elements following on behind the tanks.

[illegible] their ears, and with little infantry support to aid any attempts to clear built-up areas such as Le Mesnil or Grentheville anyway, 3 RTR shimmied by, merely 'brassing' up such targets with machine guns and high-explosive rounds fired on the move. They then pressed on towards the primary objective for the morning: the Bourguébus Ridge. They were fortunate that the defensive resistance now emerging from villages, trenches, foxholes and bunkers in and around them had carried little in the way of menace to armour. Not so for their sister regiment, the 2nd Fife and Forfar Yeomanry, which had thrust forwards to the left and east of 3 RTR. The Fife and Forfars suffered from having less time to deploy and organise due to constraints of time and space, and had been further weakened by an outbreak of dysentery caused by fouled water supplies. Employing a similar regimental deployment to 3 RTR they had, nevertheless, charged on between Le Mesnil and Cagny. The two leading squadrons swept by without significant incident, as did the second wave of regimental HQ troops and equipment.

In an incident now so much a part of the mythology of the battle that it has become iconic, Major Hans von Luck of 21st Panzers, who had rushed forward into the battle area upon returning hastily from Paris that morning, intervened at Cagny. Cagny, unlike Le Mesnil, had been targeted by the bombing but was only partially neutralised. On his arrival von Luck noted a battery of Luftwaffe 88mm guns pointing at the skies awaiting aircraft to shoot at whilst a stream of Allied tanks swept by to the west between Cagny and Le Mesnil Frémentel. Von Luck asked the Luftwaffe battery commander to move his guns and train them on the British tanks, but he refused, at which point von Luck later recalled, 'I drew my pistol levelled it at him and said: "Either you're a dead man or you can win yourself a medal." '[96] Unsurprisingly, according to the legend, the officer acquiesced and very soon C Squadron of the Fife and Forfars was under heavy and destructive fire from the now supposedly repositioned Luftwaffe 88s in Cagny.

Major von Luck's account of how the situation developed, colourful and enthralling though it may be, is largely unsubstantiated, however. There is in fact no evidence, either documentary or photographic, that there were any Luftwaffe guns in Cagny at that time; indeed their presence there would be extraordinary given the known dispositions of other Luftwaffe batteries that day. It may well be that von Luck's role was less important than he made out and his pivotal place in the battle was largely a product of his fanciful memoirs and of the publicity derived from the British Army's battlefield tours conducted from 1947 onwards, in which von Luck was a regular, popular and controversial feature.[97]

But there is no doubt that heavy anti-tank gunfire from in and around Cagny began to account for British tanks.[98] Most of C Squadron was knocked out in very short order. Jack Thorpe recalled:

> Along the column of tanks I see palls of smoke and tanks brewing up with flames belching forth from their turrets. I see men climbing out, on fire like torches, rolling on the ground to try and douse the flames.
>
> The tank twenty yards away from us is hit, flames shoot out of its turret, I see a member of its crew climbing out through the flames, he is almost out, putting one foot onto the rim to jump down, he seems to hesitate and he falls back inside. Oh Christ![99]

Soon C Squadron was effectively eliminated as a fighting force and Lieutenant Colonel Alec Scott, commanding 2nd Fife and Forfars, was forced to abandon his original plan of using A and B Squadrons to push forward and then have C Squadron exploit through the opening created and seize their regimental objectives on the Bourguébus Ridge. Still, by 1030 the leading elements of 3 RTR and 2nd Fife and Forfars were probing towards the villages in and around Bourguébus. The rolling artillery bombardment had ceased and the armour was now deploying in formations more appropriate to fire and manoeuvre tactics. By this time the British had expected to be through the main German positions and be driving largely unopposed deep into open country. Yet the villages around them, Soliers, Four and Bourguébus itself, appeared to be actively defended and resistance began to stiffen.

To the west 3 RTR, now straddling the north-south ore railway embankment at Grentheville, attempted to reconnoitre the apparently quiet village of Hubert Folie that lay directly ahead of them. Lieutenant Colonel David Silvertop commanding the regiment explained the requirement to nineteen-year-old Lieutenant David Stileman, as Stileman later recalled:

> . . . the gallant colonel . . . beckoned me over and said, 'Boy, we must find out if Hubert Folie is occupied.' 'Jolly good idea, sir,' I said or something equally fatuous. 'How do you propose to do it?' 'You're going to do it,' came the reply.[100]

Stileman and two carriers were dispatched towards the village under a brief barrage from the 25-pdrs attached to the battle group and returned unscathed. Unfortunately, the village was occupied and when 3 RTR advanced in strength all hell broke loose and the tanks were driven back with heavy losses. Sergeant Jim Caswell, B Squadron 3 RTR, had his tank knocked out and three of his crew killed. He pulled Stan Duckworth, who had been seriously wounded, from the still-reversing tank and after administering morphia he carried him back to safer ground:

> I was limping and the battle was still raging around us.
>
> Above the corn I could see the tall chimneystacks of the Colombelles ironworks so I decided to make for them.
>
> After an hour of carrying Duckworth for four miles I came across an Advanced Field Dressing Station where I collapsed and was sent back to a field hospital near Bayeux.[101]

Lieutenant Johnny Langdon in A Squadron reached the most southerly position of any tank in his regiment that day, but his Sherman was soon knocked out:

> I had a gunner very badly wounded, a shot came in where he was sitting and it went through his legs, right through the tank and out the other side. We got down by the side of the tank and then it really started; it really went up [the ammunition]. We had come through the corn, but the nearest corn was 150–200 yards down behind the hill. The only thing for it was to get away from this tank or be blown up by our own ammunition. We were absolutely exposed but not a shot was fired at us.[102]

With little in the way of artillery support the British armour could make scant headway against the defended built-up areas. The Fife and Forfars hit similar difficulties when advancing on Soliers, Four and Bourguébus, and the addition of 23rd Hussars in support did not significantly aid their efforts. Major John Gilmour commanding B Squadron of the Fife and Forfars recounted that as they swept between Soliers and Four:

> Quite suddenly we were hit by heavy fire first from Soliers, then from Four. Of course while the enemy were in concealed positions we were completely exposed in open ground.
>
> I could see German tanks and SP guns up ahead in the Bourguébus and La Hogue area. But they were way out of range and, as we had now outrun our artillery barrage, there was nothing I could do about them.[103]

Tony Sergeaunt's prognosis had come to pass: British tanks were battling dug-in enemy positions and guns without the aid of substantial artillery and infantry support, and their position was made more precarious because they were operating beyond the effective range of their artillery. Repeated attempts over the late morning and early afternoon achieved little, save the writing off of yet more tanks. Despite later claims that air support was absent due to the FAC (Forward Air Controller) with 29th Armoured Brigade being knocked out of action shortly after midday, the RAF was directed into action through alternative lines of communication and did excellent work, particularly in breaking up later German counter-attacks. But it cannot be denied that a more robust and closely integrated air-ground communications system would have yielded better results.

By early afternoon GOODWOOD had blown itself out. Heavy German units had been rushed into the line to contain the British thrust and no further headway was made that day. The Guards Armoured Division following on behind the 11th Armoured became embroiled in a battle to take Cagny and was threatened by German counter-attacks coming in from the east, including the Allies' first battle encounter with the very heavily armoured King Tiger tank. This turned into something of a damp squib as the King Tiger advance fizzled out near Banneville when the 70-ton tanks got stuck in craters or were knocked out by 17-pdrs.[104]

The 7th Armoured Division failed to deploy forward properly, much to the chagrin of the beleaguered 'Pip' Roberts. Brigadier Robert Hinde, commanding 7th Armoured's 22nd Armoured Brigade, appeared at Roberts's tactical HQ around noon. As Roberts later wrote:

> I thought 'this is good, we will soon have 7th Armoured Division to take over the area between us and Guards Armoured Division'. But not at all; when he reached me he said, 'There are far too many bloody tanks here already. I'm not going to bring my tanks down yet.' I was staggered and before I could explain that a lot of the tanks he had seen were knocked out, he had disappeared.
>
> I'm afraid to say that at that moment I cursed my old division and my old brigade.[105]

In reality Hinde and his divisional commanding officer, Bobby Erskine, were correct insofar as more armour was probably not the answer, but with the armoured divisional infantry either embroiled in clearing villages near the start line or held up much further to the rear along with the artillery there was little else that could be done. O'Connor met with Roberts and Erskine in the early afternoon to plan a new way forward, but with traffic jams, increasing German resistance and the leading elements of 11th Armoured in particular having suffered heavy losses of armour, the moment had passed.

The offensive made some headway the following day and with better balanced and coordinated attacks the British armoured divisions demonstrated what could be achieved by good infantry-armour-artillery cooperation, even against a prepared and alert enemy. The assault by 11th Armoured on Hubert Folie and Bras was carefully and skilfully managed. Major Bill Close recalled:

> Some 300 Panzer Grenadiers were killed, wounded or taken prisoner during the attack, with over twenty anti-tank guns of various sizes accounted for. It was said later in a history of the Division that this had been a model exhibition of an attack by armour and infantry.[106]

But it was already much too late to salvage GOODWOOD and the operation eventually spluttered to a halt in rain and mud on 20 July.

Dempsey was aware as early as the afternoon of 18 July that no great breakthrough was imminent. The equipment losses to the three armoured divisions were huge, with some 400 tanks knocked out, leading one historian to describe GOODWOOD as the 'death ride of the armoured divisions'. Another pointed out that although the Americans lost more tanks in Normandy, the British did it with more style, wonderfully capturing the essence of GOODWOOD. Many tanks would be recovered and reintroduced into battle, and by subsequent operations the divisions were recovered in numbers.

Morale was another issue. Three troop sergeants in A Squadron 3 RTR, only one of whom had been physically wounded, asked to be withdrawn from the front line for a while in the aftermath of GOODWOOD. Even though two soon returned, their commander noted that they had lost a little bit of confidence and enthusiasm. Actual personnel losses across the four corps that fought during the GOODWOOD-ATLANTIC period were significant but not crippling, numbering some 5,500, but rates of desertion and going AWOL increased in the armoured divisions proportionate to the amount of contact during GOODWOOD and the subsequent major operation, BLUECOAT.[107]

It would be misleading to assume that GOODWOOD was a disaster. Although there were many tactical errors that ultimately coalesced to undermine any real chance of a major breakthrough, it achieved many of its strategic aims, as Dempsey argued after the war. Operation ATLANTIC, launched by II Canadian Corps alongside GOODWOOD, drove the Germans from Caen completely, whilst I Corps had expanded the bridgehead to the east. And many tactical lessons were learnt by the British Army in the aftermath of the action. The armoured divisions were restructured to integrate armoured and infantry elements more closely, the future use of the strategic air forces was to be nuanced into a two-phase approach rather than single hit, and the need to embrace armoured personnel carriers to allow infantry to keep up with the armour and debus directly into the heart of the battle was finally accepted. O'Connor had lobbied for this final point prior to GOODWOOD but Dempsey, perhaps mindful of the limited aims of the operation, had held back, possibly preferring to wait for a more obvious breakthrough battle in which to unleash the nascent armoured personnel carriers.

There is no doubt that Montgomery's principal aim of fixing the Germans' heavier units in place around Caen had succeeded. In the days after GOODWOOD and by the time of COBRA (25 July), the British and

Canadians were confronted by over 600 tanks, including the heavy Tiger tank battalions, whilst the Americans faced just 100 tanks from one and a half panzer divisions. The repeated set-piece battles launched by the Anglo-Canadian forces around Caen drew in enemy units as they arrived in Normandy and wore them down to such a degree that German forces were stretched to breaking point by the last week of July. GOODWOOD itself had contributed only partially to this process, as material losses inflicted on the Germans were significant rather than shattering. More importantly, it seriously undermined the will of the German leadership in Normandy and their resolve crumbled. Already reeling from the loss of Rommel from air attack just before GOODWOOD and the failed Stauffenberg plot on Hitler's life of 20 July, the generals in Normandy had to confront a bleak reality. General Sepp Dietrich, whilst arguing that the position had been held around Caen, stated:

> The position has inevitably deteriorated, as we have lost a good deal of ground, and this can only be to the enemy's advantage. I see their next effort as being the most crucial for them and us.[108]

Field Marshal Hans von Kluge, newly appointed to the command of the west in the wake of von Rundstedt's dismissal, could only look on in dismay, his early optimism quickly evaporating. He wrote to Hitler on 21 July:

> The moment is fast approaching when this overtaxed front line is bound to break up.
>
> We must hold our ground, and if nothing happens to improve conditions, then we must die an honourable death on the battlefield.[109]

Meyer's 12th SS Panzer Division had been reduced to just 15 operational tanks, whilst 16th Luftwaffe Field Division had effectively ceased to exist as a fighting unit. Hans Eberbach, commanding Fifth Panzer Army now parincipally pinned to the Caen sector, warned:

> Daily losses by the divisions in a struggle which is terrible all the time are so great that in a short time their strength will be used up and it will be no longer possible to make good that strength.[110]

Eberbach and his fellow commanders realised that throwing everything at the front line to hold the Allies, mostly around Caen, was a doomed strategy, for once the Allies broke through, the game would be up.

Should GOODWOOD ultimately be seen as a success or a failure? It was both and neither. As an important step towards victory in Normandy there is no doubt that GOODWOOD was crucial, dramatically increasing the pressure upon the enemy and causing heavy casualties. The Anglo Canadian efforts in and around Caen were achieving their strategic aims and GOODWOOD was an integral part of the pattern that had been in place since mid-June. Yet there can be no denying that GOODWOOD was flawed, most obviously because it did not conform to the operational principles that had underpinned previous actions. Some tactical rethinking was required to capitalise on the ambitious drive to the Bourguébus Ridge, but this did not take place, and the plan fell between two stools, neither conforming to the prescribed method of operations nor working through the tactical implications necessary to break the mould, even though the first-phase objectives, including the limited 15 July aims, were ambitious and required units to operate beyond the comforting umbrella of heavy artillery support.

The view of GOODWOOD from beyond Normandy was less than positive. Led to believe that this was to be a major breakthrough operation, Eisenhower and his staff were deeply unimpressed by the advance; Ike was apoplectic. With 7,000 tons of bombs dropped to gain just 7 miles, Eisenhower sardonically fumed whether 1,000 tons per mile was a realistic strategy, even for the resource-rich Allies.[111] SHAEF had also been misled by the positive tone of Montgomery's ham-fisted press briefing on the evening of 18 July, which was later described by his senior intelligence officer, Bill Williams, as 'bloody stupid'.[112]

Though comments that Montgomery was close to the sack over GOODWOOD have been much exaggerated, there is no doubt that many, including Churchill, Bradley and George Marshall, the US Army's chief, were beginning to question whether he was the right man for the job. Arthur Tedder at SHAEF lobbied for Montgomery's replacement, though this was never a realistic option. Field Marshal Alan Brooke, Chief of the Imperial General staff, for one, remained a firm supporter and was undoubtedly correct in believing that there was no one better placed than Monty to lead 21st Army Group. Monty knew of Brooke's support and in an effort to curry favour in London at least, prevailed upon him to tell everyone that all was going well and according to plan.[113]

Curiously, little criticism was aimed at Dempsey who, as architect of the GOODWOOD plan and a vigorous prosecutor, should surely have been held partially responsible for its tactical shortcomings. But it was Montgomery who took the heat: as Dempsey later stated, whilst Monty took the acclaim when things went well, he also took responsibility rather than pass it on to others when they did not.

Montgomery was nevertheless under intense pressure. The Americans in particular were dismayed at the apparent lack of progress, and the press were on their tails in the US leading to serious questions and pressure being placed on Eisenhower, and through him on Montgomery who was not highly regarded in Washington. Eisenhower was prevailed upon to take control in Normandy, demonstrate that it was an American show, and stop Monty from claiming the credit.[114]

Once Montgomery had met Eisenhower on 20 July for an apparently frank exchange in which the latter had effectively rebuked the former, and had then mollified Churchill by agreeing to the Prime Minister visiting him in Normandy shortly after GOODWOOD, the pressure eased a little. Monty grumpily noted in his diary that he had had to put Ike right on the notion that the eastern sector of the front in Normandy was being closed down and the burden of the offensive being shifted to the Americans. Still, after his meeting with Eisenhower, Monty was minded to up the ante in his next directive in which he called for intensive pressure to be applied along the front, a policy that led to the bungled Canadian Operation SPRING on 25 July and the movement of the Second British Army to the west of the Anglo-Canadian sector, leaving the newly operational First Canadian Army to mount operations southeast from Caen.[115]

After six weeks of fierce, largely attritional battle the situation in Normandy appeared to be stagnating. The Americans had made only slow progress since capturing Cherbourg and Bradley's Operation COBRA had yet to be carried out. The British and Canadians, now committed to a strategy of drawing the Germans around Caen, had made only limited geographical impact, despite a series of large-scale set-piece operations, and personnel losses, precisely what they wanted to avoid, were mounting steadily. Allied intelligence was unable to offer a clear picture of the desperation of the Germans and that the breaking point was very close. It is ironic that just a week after the despair of GOODWOOD, the situation would change completely and the Normandy campaign would decisively and openly tilt in favour of the Allies.

5

STALEMATE? Frustration in Normandy

IN THE DAYS after Operation GOODWOOD, the realities of combat in Northwest Europe against a resourceful and obdurate foe were beginning to impact on the British Army in a forceful and uncompromising manner. The wave of optimism that had swept through the Allied troops after D-Day began to dissipate by the end of June and the experience of EPSOM, the brutal fighting for Caen and the dramatic actions to the east of the city from 18 July onwards further highlighted the harsh truths behind the British Army's experiences since the beginning of the campaign to liberate Europe. Frustration at their situation and the perceived lack of progress was telling on the troops. Geoffrey Picot, 1st Hampshires, recalled a discussion with an officer of the East Yorkshires in late July:

> 'Now,' said this East Yorks officer, 'look at General Alexander in Italy. He's getting a move on. They'll have to bring him over here to make a success of this invasion.' We parted thinking that the war, like the poor, would be with us forever.[1]

Others cursed that it was not like this in Sicily or Italy, though in truth the campaign there had bogged down through the winter of 1943–4. Trooper Joe Ekins, Northants Yeomanry, recalled:

> The six weeks in the bridgehead was the worst part of my entire war – terrible, absolutely terrible.
>
> During that time I realised it didn't matter whether you were a good soldier or a bad soldier, an officer or not, brave or not, getting killed was random.[2]

Many of the difficulties had come as a direct consequence of the German strategy of digging in close to the Normandy coast, a policy that considerably aided defence and simultaneously forced the Allies to adapt to fighting in terrain they had not expected the Germans to contest so fiercely; they thought the Germans would fall back into more open ground that suited manoeuvre. The long-term consequences of the German decision consigned them to slow, lingering but inevitable destruction, and in many ways played to Allied strengths in firepower and resources. The Allies were undoubtedly tactically caught out by Hitler's 'no retreat' policy, precisely because it made little sense to them; German strategy may have staved off retreat for a while, but it had nevertheless now made defeat in France inevitable. The problem for the Allies was that they had to adapt operating practices and techniques to the tactical situation that had been thrust upon them, and these difficulties were largely faced by troops at the front line, from middle-ranking leaders downwards, some time before senior leaders began to grapple with the problem. For those at the sharp end it mattered little to them that on the strategic level the Germans were being remorselessly chewed up by the Allied fighting machine, and that the 21st Army Group policy of imposing upon the Germans set-piece operations of the Allies' choosing and then pummelling the enemy's resulting counter-attacks with heavy firepower was working well. Much more immediate was the reality of engaging in brutal close combat with forces well versed in flexible, defensive tactics in terrain that suited defence and appeared to be restricting the impact that supporting Allied artillery, air power and armoured firepower could have in limiting their own infantry casualties. Without doubt it was the infantry who were suffering more than any other arm, with 70 per cent of all the British casualties falling on the 15 per cent of the army that constituted the rifle companies.[3]

What then of the notion that firepower would pave the way to victory and ease the burden of the infantry? The principal arm that British commanders expected to deliver success on the battlefield was the artillery, and its importance had grown still further in the first few weeks of the campaign as pressure on the infantry had increased. Certainly since the Villers-Bocage debacle, the British and Canadians had built their operations ever more around firepower support. The British, like their American Allies, had distributed their artillery between immediate organic support in the form of field artillery – both towed and, increasingly by 1944, self-propelled versions – and corps-level AGRAs (Army Group Royal Artillery) formations. They differed in their greater reliance on highly responsive communications systems, which allowed British units to draw quickly upon their reserves of firepower to deal with emerging situations. They also preferred to blast targets systematically one at a time rather than trying to hit everything in one go, as preferred by the Soviets, a resource-saving approach only made possible by advanced communications systems.

British artillery was used as a weapon of neutralisation and suppression in an attack in the form of preliminary bombardments and rolling barrages, and as a highly destructive and responsive weapon in defence when breaking up enemy counter-attacks. But debate still continued between advocates of predicted fire, wherein batteries would blast targets according to map references and often with a predetermined plan, and those who preferred observed or adjusted fire. The former generated surprise and could wreak havoc on enemy positions caught unawares but could be wasteful of resources and effort, whereas the latter was more accurate and capable of better results but was largely more responsive to situations rather than driving them.

In Normandy, in close terrain with poor visibility for advancing troops, the importance of predicted rather than observed fire became apparent, despite the use of aerial observation posts, often the only method of controlling and adjusting artillery. The Germans were well aware of the damage that an aerial observation post could impart and endeavoured to attack them with fighters flying at very low level to avoid radar detection. In spite of their air supremacy, such tactics required the British to devise defensive anti-aircraft gunnery practices to protect their air-based observers.[4] The effectiveness of rolling artillery barrages, still a favoured tactic of the British, remained questionable, with some arguing that they were costly in resources, too predictable and inflexible. Forces advancing behind them also often failed to maintain contact with the barrages – clearly an issue in GOODWOOD. Such was the necessity for attacking troops to reach their targets quickly after a barrage that artillery experts argued that: 'Unless the assaulting troops are sufficiently close behind the barrage to close with the enemy within two minutes of the barrage lifting, the barrage is wasted.'[5]

Critics of barrages favoured the 'stonc', or standard concentration on target, which hit harder and with more force, but due to its intensity could equally keep advancing troops away, for fear of friendly-fire incidents, to such an extent that the enemy was afforded too much recovery time. It was also still unclear how much time was available for attacking troops to get on target following a heavy concentration rather than a rolling barrage. Vitally important to the use of artillery was the degree to which terrain was devastated by the liberal amounts of heavy firepower used to support advances. Ironically, whilst heavier bombardments of artillery suppressed targets for longer, they could also churn up the ground, particularly roads, so much so that advancing troops were slowed down, thus negating the positive effects of the firepower. That such debates were continuing as the campaign was waged indicates that the jury was still out on how best to use the firepower assets available.[6]

Concerns began to emerge over the inappropriate use of artillery due to ignorance about realistic capabilities and a growing reliance on firepower to solve all battlefield problems. As early as June, Royal Artillery reports had indicated that officers were over-using and misusing artillery support to such an extent that the practice was described as an epidemic: 'Day after day one saw concentrations – regimental at least – being put down on targets which were only troop targets.'[7] This supposedly excessive use of artillery fire was producing considerable pressure on, and confusion over, ammunition stockpiles. One officer concluded: 'It is no exaggeration to say that a promising operation might have to be postponed unnecessarily for lack of information on whether enough ammunition was available.'[8]

Though the British had great strength in artillery, it was not a limitless asset. At corps level and above, after each operational briefing senior commanders would strive to get the ear and attention of the logistics staff to ensure that an adequate supply of ammunition and firepower would be available to support their forthcoming actions. Fatigue was also becoming a major issue for artillerymen in Normandy, particularly when they were required to fire or be on constant alert for hours and days on end. Guns firing regular bursts kept gunners awake for excessively long periods:

> All the while the guns have been firing constantly with only brief pauses between targets, seldom of sufficient duration . . . to allow you to grab a catnap. Infantrymen describe falling asleep while continuing to walk robot-fashion up a road. And you know from experience a man can fall [illegible] having done so on more than one occasion recently while leaning over the artillery board.[9]

Human error brought on by fatigue was supplemented by the wear and tear on the equipment. Repeated use wore out rifled barrels, causing them to become inaccurate, sometimes dropping shells short, and therefore liable to inflict casualties through friendly fire. The greatest issue confronting British artillery in Northwest Europe, and during the Normandy campaign in particular, was the lethality (or killing power) of the weapons and their real effectiveness against enemy targets; the blast and smoke may have appeared impressive to British soldiers looking on, but how effective were they proving against an enemy well versed in concealment and digging-in? Evidence and reports were hardly comforting for the troops at the sharp end. Operational research reports indicated that all was not as had been hoped for, with tactical shortcomings emerging that were being exacerbated by the Germans' chosen policy of static defence, and the basic truth that even in 1944 a soldier in a slit trench was much less vulnerable to artillery fire than one moving in the open.

The ubiquitous British 25-pdr provided the most responsive and immediate form of artillery support, being deployed directly in the field. But this weapon had sacrificed some weight of shell to facilitate range and manoeuvrability, and its explosive effects were limited. A 25-pdr shell had to fall within 3 feet 6 inches of a target in order to register an effective shock wave on a slit trench, and had to score a direct hit to inflict actual casualties, yet only 3 per cent of shells actually fell into a trench during a bombardment. AGRAs fired off heavier weights of shell such as 5.5-inch and 7.2-inch rounds, and these had more effect, but poor accuracy remained a significant issue, and in Normandy this was sufficient to limit the effects of artillery against a dug-in enemy.

In order to be truly suppressive a bombardment had to carry the threat of inflicting serious casualties, and experienced enemy troops knew how to sit out a barrage and emerge in its wake quickly enough to confound British forces advancing behind the bombardment. Increases in the weight of bombardment did show that it caused a reduction in British casualties suffered in an attack, though it was a diminishing return the larger the increase became. More effective still was the psychological effect of bombardment; experiments in the UK conducted prior to D-Day had indicated that after two to four hours' continuous bombardment, enemy troops would reach the limit of their endurance and begin to suffer debilitating drops in morale. What was crucial, and a lesson that slowly spread across the army in Northwest Europe in 1944, was that for this effect to work the weight of shell mattered less: the key factor was the number of shells delivered on to an area in a given time, and so units began firing every available weapon possible to produce what would be known as the 'pepperpot effect'. By 1945 these tactics would be widespread, but in Normandy in 1944 they were still being developed.[10]

With enemy forces dispersed over a wide area there simply were not the number of Allied guns available to saturate a target area sufficiently to achieve the desired effects in 1944. Concentrations were impressive but only rarely matched the levels of artillery saturation achieved in the closing stages of the First World War. Even highly concentrated barrages produced only limited results, particularly as methods of predicted fire often resulted in mean points of impact being awry by some 100–300 yards. Gunners knew that the so-called 50 per cent zone – the area in which half the shells would land – was much larger than they desired, but they did not know that their fire was further undermined by such variability in point-of-impact accuracy. Predicted fire, on which the British Army placed great faith, was simply not delivering the results necessary to ease the burden sufficiently on the infantry involved in an offensive.

It was, of course, a different matter if the enemy could be provoked into counter-attacking and therefore leaving their entrenchments. In such circumstances results could be dramatic, exemplified by the crushing losses meted out outside Villers-Bocage on 14 June and to the 12th SS Panzer Division as they attempted to force the British out of Baron on the night of 30 June–1 July. Yet initial advances had to be made in order to provoke such an enemy reaction, and with the effects of British artillery fire not all that had been hoped for, the consequences for advancing troops were significant. Artillery tactics did improve during the campaign, but many British infantry units slowly realised that pressing into the rolling barrage (or 'leaning into' as it was known), in effect staying as close as possible to the supporting barrage as it advanced towards its objective, was the best practice, or the least worst option available, even if some friendly fire casualties might ensue. As a result of experience in the Mediterranean, advancing troops were advised to keep to between 50 and 200 yards behind a barrage, but this was both dangerous and difficult. Highly effective though artillery was, more work had to be done to improve it, and the German response to the Allied invasion was exposing some deficiencies.[11]

For the Germans the weight of British artillery firepower was debilitating, stifling their ability to manoeuvre freely, and inflicting heavy casualties when they did. What marked out British artillery from American or Soviet was its responsiveness in action and the immediacy of concentrations when needed, derived from the great improvements in command, control and communications systems generated by the British over the course of the war and since the Great War. Density of guns to front line was generally lower in 1944–5 than it had been in the 1916–18 era, but this was more than counterbalanced by speed, flexibility and responsiveness.[12]

Artillery firepower was to be supplemented in Northwest Europe by air support, but the fighting in Normandy was also exposing shortcomings in the degree to which air-based firepower could deal with a recalcitrant and stubborn enemy who refused to move. Since the campaign became static by mid-June the ability of tactical air support, the fighter-bombers in particular to inflict actual damage, had markedly diminished, and the impact and effectiveness of heavy-bomber support were mixed. The cost to the RAF was also not insignificant and higher than might be expected, given the dominance of the Allied air forces by the summer of 1944. In June alone the RAF had lost over 700 aircraft and in total during the fighting in Normandy, 2nd Tactical Air Force and Air Defence Great Britain suffered the loss of 829 aircraft and over 1,000 aircrew, mostly to anti-aircraft guns. Air-to-ground actions meanwhile remained the most dangerous in any air force in the Second World War.

Much flying time and effort was also being expended in crossing the Channel, as there was still insufficient space in the beachhead to provide enough airfields. Additionally, with demand for air support growing, pilots and aircrew were experiencing increasing pressure and fatigue. Important though the support of air-based firepower was, there was a price to pay.[13]

Air-based firepower suffered from the same problems as artillery: accuracy and lethality. Locating a small, well-camouflaged target from a fast-moving aeroplane was difficult enough; hitting it with the weaponry of 1944 was an altogether more demanding task. The most famous weapon of 2nd RAF Tactical Air Force, the 3-inch rocket as launched from Hawker Typhoon fighter-bombers, was notoriously inaccurate as the RAF realised, though they refused to admit it openly. Training personnel had emphasised to pilots that it took considerable skill and practice to fire rockets with any realistic chance of hitting a target owing to the weight distribution of the weapon, the need to take into account wind speeds and direction, and dive angles. Despite three-week courses in rocket firing and refresher sessions at camps in the UK, accuracy was woeful. In order to establish a 50 per cent chance of hitting a target the size of a Panther tank, some 140 rockets (or 17–18 sorties by Typhoons) needed to be deployed, and this even before battlefield conditions were taken into account. A pilot loosing off all eight of the rockets carried by a Typhoon had a mere 4 per cent chance of hitting a target the size of a German tank, and only a direct hit would cripple the vehicle. Though German tank crews may not always have believed it to be true, feeling as though they were sitting ducks, there is little doubt that the safest place on the battlefield during an air attack was inside a tank as the armour would provide protection against all but a direct hit.[14]

Considerable debate broke out between the RAF and the army over the effectiveness of rockets against targets such as tanks, with the RAF later arguing that although the numbers of tanks actually destroyed by rockets were admittedly small, the psychological effects of the weapon were vital and it was this fear factor that prompted German tank crews, and indeed other troops, to flee. This may have been to some degree true, but it could not be proved.

Free-fall bombs were even more inaccurate than rockets, and the only effective way of hitting small targets from the air was with cannon and machine guns. These weapons increased the chance of securing hits, but they did not carry sufficient penetration power to knock out tanks. They were, however, highly effective against soft-skin and lightly armoured vehicles, so though the tanks themselves could survive air attacks, their support vehicles were much more vulnerable. This slowly weakened German armoured units as supplies, replacements and fuel, all carried by trucks and lightly armoured transports, were whittled away over the course of the first few weeks of the Normandy campaign. German armoured tactics were also shaped by the vulnerability of mechanised infantry to air attack; denuded of mobile infantry, German armour simply could not prosecute attacks into built-up areas and woods.[15]

Tactical air support was ideal when an enemy was manoeuvring, attacking over open areas, or when it could be weakened by attacks on supply lines, as accuracy was not so crucial. Against targets that were static in defensive positions and camouflaged or dug-in, as the Germans largely had been since mid-June, air strikes could do much less in terms of physical damage. Even the use of heavy bombing at CHARNWOOD and GOODWOOD had not delivered the anticipated results, because of poor accuracy, inadequate intelligence and fear of inflicting friendly fire casualties. The heavy-bomber fleets were neither trained nor well-equipped for tactical, or more accurately, operational-level support, though the effectiveness of this weapon would improve. The tactical situation in Normandy by mid to late July was demanding greater accuracy to winkle out stubborn German units, but air attack was simply too blunt a weapon to deliver the level of precision required.

Yet the effects of air attack could be crucial. The heavy bombing at GOODWOOD, despite missing some targets, generally achieved tremendous short-term results, with the enemy stunned into submission and in some cases brought to the point of mental breakdown. The constant pressure of air attacks, like artillery, acted as a great suppressing force on the ability of an enemy to react to situations, more so as the psychological impact of repeated bombing broke men's resolve faster than artillery. Reports concluded that:

> The greatest effect of attacks by rocket firing Typhoons in close support is [on] morale, both on the enemy and our own troops. The effect on the enemy is of short duration only and therefore needs to be closely co-ordinated with military operations.[16]

As with artillery bombardments, material impact was modest but suppressive effects were significant, resulting in it being imperative that advancing troops get forward on to their objective as quickly as possible to derive positive results from the air attacks; the longer the delay in prosecuting the ground-based attack after a bombing raid, the less likely it was to be achieved with minimal casualties. In GOODWOOD evidence strongly suggested that timing had been a key weakness in the bombing. One after-action analysis concluded:

> It is considered that if these areas [in and around the Bourguébus Ridge] including Cagny had been attacked one or two hours after the others, instead of at nearly the same time, enemy resistance would have been much less. The tactical development of the battle indicated the desirability of a bombing timetable which is progressive so that targets in depth are bombed just before the assault upon them.[17]

These lessons would be incorporated into future planning, though operation COBRA under General Bradley, which launched just five days after GOODWOOD, largely mirrored the methods used in the latter: the great difference was to be the much shallower depth of the defences confronting the Americans compared to those dug in around Caen.

Just as with artillery bombardment, soldiers, especially the many non-battle-hardened troops learning their trade in theatre, were struggling to hit their objectives quickly enough following air raids. In the tactical situation in Normandy this skill was fundamental to winning actions with tolerable casualties.

From the other side of the hill the picture appeared somewhat different. German troops loathed having to operate under the cloud of Allied air supremacy, because it suffocated them and constantly sapped their will. Rommel commented to Field Marshal Wilhelm Keitel in Berlin:

> Our own operations are rendered extraordinarily difficult and in part impossible to carry out [owing to] the exceptionally strong and, in some respects overwhelming, superiority of the enemy air force.
>
> Neither our flak nor the Luftwaffe seem capable of putting a stop to this crippling and destructive operation of the enemy's aircraft.[18]

At the front line views were equally bleak. Martin Pöppel wrote in his diary: 'It's become virtually impossible to travel the roads by day. Despite all precautionary measures, the pilots are always finding new victims.'[19] Rommel himself was to become such a casualty. Ewald Klapdor, 10th SS Panzer Division, wrote:

> There's no peace, even at night. The enemy has succeeded in paralysing the supplies for the frontline across hundreds of kilometres. What a change in conditions from the Eastern Front.
>
> In the invasion area there's only one air force – the Western Allies.[20]

Reports by Nazi political officers warned their superiors in Berlin that morale was strained and that the men were thoroughly dismayed by the absence of the Luftwaffe. German soldiers may have turned their ire on the virtually non-existent Luftwaffe for letting them down so badly, but this was testimony to the effect that Allied air power was having. Yet German Forces were suffering only a slow death at the hands of the RAF and USAAF, and the apparent effects to onlooking British soldiers during the grinding battles around Caen were much less stark.

Even though air power helped to break up German counter-attacks, and inflict withering long-term damage on the enemy's ability to sustain a high-intensity fight, the greatest demand on air power since shortly after D-Day – effective precision attacks on concealed, dug-in enemy forces – could not be adequately met. Thus, like artillery, air power provided only a partial solution to the pressure mounting on the British Army's armoured and infantry forces. Far from simply blasting their way to victory, the British were having to seek some alternative answers to solve the difficulties of prosecuting offensives.

With firepower having more of a long-term damaging effect on the fighting strength of the enemy, but with limited utility against a dug-in and obdurate opponent, the burden of engaging the enemy in direct action fell to the major front-line arms of the British Army: armour and infantry. The damaging effects of firepower could only be inflicted upon the Germans if they could be provoked into movement and counter attack. Only direct assault by tanks and fighting men could achieve this, even if the terrain and German strategy were making the task more difficult. Of the two main fighting arms, armour was struggling most to impose itself on the campaign, thus imposing a still greater burden on the infantry.

By July 1944 the British had deployed three standard armoured divisions to Normandy (the Canadians and Poles would add two more in August), but they had been unable to impose themselves on operations as they would have liked on account of the close, constricting terrain and the limits placed upon manoeuvre by Montgomery's tightly controlled operational methods. The seven independent brigades of armour deployed by the British, particularly the tank brigades operating Churchills, had encountered problems of their own, with tactical methods thrown into some confusion by the intense static fighting in Normandy in terrain that placed an even greater premium on infantry-armour cooperation, something the British were still working out. Though the armoured forces adapted their doctrine and demonstrated considerable flexibility in thinking, it was hard going. They had expected a more fluid campaign but since mid-June they were forced to slug it out with the Germans in close combat, and this highlighted two significant problems: inadequate firepower and difficult tactical positioning.

Although great weight was placed on all-round technological deficiencies compared to German armour, the reality was somewhat different. Though many British tank crews then and after the war complained bitterly that their tanks were weakly armoured compared to their German adversaries, evidence from after-action analyses demonstrated that increasing armour protection on British tanks sufficient to make them resistant to German anti-tank guns was simply not possible, for it would require such an increase in weight as to make the tanks nearly untransportable. In part this was because tank engagements in Normandy took place at such short ranges – two-thirds of tank firing took place at under 1,000 metres and the usual range at which tanks were likely to be hit and disabled was less than 600 metres – that tanks would have to be very heavily armoured on their sides as well as their front. Operational researchers referred to this as homogenous armour distribution, and it would increase weight enormously. No tank in Normandy had all these attributes, not even the Tiger, and certainly not the Panther, which was vulnerable to penetrations on the side, something far less likely when battling at longer ranges on the Eastern Front when frontal armour alone was paramount. It was concluded that up-armouring the fronts and sides of Allied tanks by 50 per cent would only reduce penetrations by 15 per cent. Thick frontal armour alone was not the answer, as even the new Churchill VII and VIII with six inches of frontal armour were still vulnerable to heavier German anti-tank gunfire.[21]

For those in the firing line it was a different reality. Lieutenant 'Steel' Brownlie, 2nd Fife and Forfar Yeomanry, recalled:

> My crews got almost obsessive about not having a thick sloping glacis plate in front like a Panther. I recall deliberately backing into a firing position so as to have the protection of the engine. There was the added advantage that if you had to get out in a hurry you had all the forward gears.[22]

Twins Steve and Tom Dyson, 34th Tank Brigade, noted:

> We also learned to our dismay of the devastating effects of the German 88mm high velocity guns, mounted SPs, anti-tank guns and Tiger tanks. The shells went through our Shermans like a knife through butter.[23]

Analysts accepted the perceptions of tank crews as being damaging to morale as much as the physical realities: 'It would seem that the tank crews expect protection from their armour and feel that they have been let down when they find by experience that it gives very little protection.'[24] But there was little that could be done; at standard battle ranges in Normandy the armour on Shermans and Cromwells, and even Churchills, offered very limited protection against even standard 75mm German guns. At 500 yards or less it was difficult not to be hit once engaged by the enemy, and after a minute of such combat the chance of a tank not being hit and knocked out was virtually nil. One report stated that in such circumstances the survival chances of a tank halved every six seconds. Almost all enemy 75mm and 88mm AP hits penetrated a Sherman's frontal armour, and in almost two-thirds of cases the tank was knocked out.[25]

As crews were all too frequently witnessing their tanks being ripped apart by German gunnery, they took whatever measures they saw fit when and wherever possible. From June 1944 onwards sandbags, track links, lumps of concrete and similar materials were all attached to the front of Shermans and Cromwells in an attempt to enhance protection. This was to little avail as such improvisations made no material difference, though analysts did point out that if crews believed such enhancements helped and bolstered morale they should not be discouraged, within reason.[26]

Sherman tank crews were also increasingly dismayed by the habit of their tanks of bursting into flames, or 'brewing-up' as it was known colloquially, seconds after being hit and penetrated by enemy gunfire. Reports demonstrated that around two-thirds to three-quarters of Shermans brewed-up when knocked out and that crews had some six seconds to bale out to avoid being incinerated inside their tank, a grisly and appalling death. Some tank units even went into battle with their hatches open to facilitate a speedier exit.[27] Such was the frequency with which tanks burst into flames that Shermans sardonically became known as Ronsons, after the cigarette lighter which, according to its advertising slogan, always lit first time. One commander noted that: 'A hit almost inevitably meant a "brew up" . . . you were in a Ronson and if you were hit it was best to bale out p.d.q.'[28] Even the Germans were aware of the problem and named Shermans 'Tommy cookers'.

Many British tank crews believed that the root of the problem lay in the Sherman's petrol fuel tanks igniting when the tank was hit and penetrated; this was particularly apparent to them because British-designed tanks they had been used to in the desert had been powered by diesel engines, and they believed that diesel was much less prone to explosion. Yet although explosions related to fuel tanks were not unknown, they were quite rare, and many burnt-out tanks were discovered that still had their fuel tanks intact. Assessment soon indicated that the cause of most 'brew-ups' was the Sherman's own ammunition, which exploded soon after the tank was knocked out.[29] Internal ammunition stowage bins in Shermans were poorly positioned, but worse still many tanks went into battle with extra ammunition to reduce the need to rearm, and this was left openly exposed in the tank's interior. In formations where illicit ammunition stowage was discouraged, casualties from brew-ups were far fewer.[30]

Dealing with the positioning of stowage bins was a greater issue. The application of extra 1-inch-thick appliqué armour plates on the exterior of the hull, where the ammunition bins were located, proved worthless; such extra protection was simply inadequate. One operational research report noted: 'It should be recognised that in no recorded case in our sample has the extra appliqué armour resisted any hit.'[31] Another concluded: 'There does not seem to be a very strong argument for these plates. It seems doubtful whether the fitting of these plates is justified.'[32] Worse still, the plates may have acted as aiming points for German gunners, and could well have increased the likelihood of enemy shells being deflected into the bins. The bins were better than having the ammunition lying around the tank, but it was not until under-floor and wet stowage bins were introduced that the problem was brought under control, reducing brew-ups to 15 per cent of penetrations.[33] However, for crews battling in Normandy in the summer of 1944 this was of no comfort; such measures lay in the future.

Allied tank crews had other issues to cope with – for example, Cromwells had a tendency to draw carbon-monoxide fumes into the fighting compartment when standing still with their engines running, a problem only later resolved in theatre by a quick engineering fix. Yet the two major recurring difficulties confronting armoured forces, as evidenced by the first two months of fighting, centred on the tactical positions in which they found themselves and inadequate firepower. Crews complained bitterly about the weakness of their main armament against German armour, particularly Panthers and Tigers. The standard 75mm gun sported by some 85 per cent of British tanks in Normandy simply was not up to the task of defeating (or penetrating) the armour protection on the heavier German tanks at standard battle ranges in Normandy; it even struggled to deal with Panzer IVs and Stugs, which constituted a much larger proportion of German armour than their more famous heavy cousins, the Panther and Tiger. The 75mm gun was an effective enough weapon against soft targets such as infantry and buildings, but against tanks it was by 1944 quite obsolescent. Bill Close, 3rd Royal Tank Regiment, recalled: 'Our ordinary 75mm gun could not knock out either a Tiger or Panther except at about 500 yards, and in the rear, and with a bit of luck in the flank.'[34] Sandy Saunders, 2nd Northants Yeomanry, agreed: 'The 75mm gun was only capable of knocking out German Mark IVs, and Panthers at point-blank range.'[35] Steve Dyson, 34th Tank Brigade, was informed by experienced crews that their 75mm guns were 'about as much good against the Jerry tanks as a pea shooter'. When attempting to discover the form, one inquisitive officer, newly arrived in Normandy, was told:

> Panthers can slice through a Churchill like a knife through butter from a mile away.
>
> And how does a Churchill get a Panther?
>
> It creeps up on it. When it reaches close quarters the gunner tries to bounce a shot off the underside of the Panther's gun mantlet. If he's lucky, it goes through a thin piece of armour above the driver's head.
>
> Has anyone ever done it?
>
> Yes. Davis in C Squadron. He's back with headquarters now, trying to recover his nerve.
>
> How does a Churchill get a Tiger?
>
> It's supposed to get within two hundred yards and put a shot through the periscope.
>
> Has anyone ever done it?
>
> No.[36]

The problem was underlined by operational research reports which examined the first few weeks of fighting. Even though almost 50 per cent of German armour was being accounted for by Allied anti-tank guns, the inferiority of the 75mm gun against heavy armour was clear to see. Whereas it took on average 1.6 hits to knock out a Sherman or 1.5 a Panzer IV, it required around 2.55 to account for a Panther and a dispiriting 4.2 to deal with a Tiger; it was as well that there were only some 120 Tigers involved in the Normandy campaign, though they were, alas, all in the front line against the British and Canadians. Only the 17-pdr-equipped Sherman Firefly offered equality in firepower, and these tanks had just recently been introduced; there were merely 84 available on 11 June, 149 by the end of the month and 235 by the end of July. There was also some continuing debate about their tactical deployment.[37]

The inadequacies of British tanks precipitated real concern in 21st Army Group for a number of weeks from D-Day until early August, with reports circulating that all British tanks were inadequate and that even the 17-pdr anti-tank gun was not up to the task. Much of this emanated from XXX Corps reports following the Villers-Bocage debacle, which were alarmist and served only to fuel the crisis further.[38] Brigadier Harold 'Peter' Pyman, XXX Corps chief of staff and an expert on armoured warfare, wrote to Major General Erskine at 7th Armoured Division on 16 June outlining the difficult situation British tank forces now faced. He claimed that recent operations had revealed 'that Tiger and Panther tanks now form a higher proportion of the equipment of German Armoured Regiments', and that these tanks were far superior to the Shermans and Cromwells of the British: 'The result is that while 75mm shot [of the Allies] has been failing to penetrate the front face of the Tigers and Panthers at ranges down to 30 yards, they can knock Shermans and Cromwells out at ranges up to 1500 yards with ease.'[39] Erskine added his own comments, claiming that even the 17-pdr anti-tank gun would 'not touch the German Panther or Tiger'. He continued '. . . it cannot be stressed too strongly that at the present time we are fighting with inadequate equipment'.[40] Lieutenant Colonel J.R. Bowring, XXX Corps' chief liaison officer, then issued a highly pessimistic report on British armour based on the material presented by Pyman and Erskine which then circulated through Second Army and 21st Army Group.

The contents were leaked to the War Office and beyond, forcing Montgomery to issue a statement arguing that in fact all was well, something he knew to be untrue. James Grigg, the Secretary of State for War, believed that William Anstruther-Gray, an MP serving in the Guards Armoured Division, had leaked information to the outside world, leading to questions being raised in the House of Commons by the maverick MP Richard Rapier Stokes. Stokes had raised the issue of poor British tanks before and was to do so again after the war, but his inquiries in 1944 were met with evasion and inaccuracy.[41]

Montgomery's major concern was bolstering morale and he was privately furious about Bowring's paper and its widespread circulation. He described Bowring to Brooke as an 'unbalanced officer and his views are of little value' whilst informing Dempsey that no further papers of such despondent tone were to be circulated without his say so.[42] Major General George Richards, 21st Army Group's armoured warfare advisor, was also livid at the tone of Bowring's paper, and pointed out that there were no more Panthers and Tigers in Normandy than had been predicted, and that the problems encountered in dealing with them had been highlighted in a Royal

Armoured Corps pamphlet circulated in April 1944: 'Therefore nobody should have been surprised when they found out that what had been said in theory was proved correct in practice.'[43] To assuage fears, Monty issued a public letter on 25 June to James Grigg, the Secretary of State for War, stating that:

> . . . we have had no difficulty in dealing with German armour, once we had grasped the problem.
>
> We have nothing to fear from the Panther or Tiger tanks; they are unreliable mechanically, and the Panther is very vulnerable from the flanks. Our 17-pdr gun will go right through them. Provided our tactics are good we can defeat them without difficulty.[44]

Yet he knew full well that his forces needed as many 17-pdrs as quickly as possible to close the firepower gap. But he also realised that there was little point in agonising over the point; his troops had to manage the issue as it existed, and undermining their morale with an open acknowledgement of weakness at the height of battle would serve no great purpose.

Montgomery's rebuttal of the criticism of the armoured corps' fighting equipment rather overegged the pudding when he claimed that the 17-pdr could deal with everything, and that with good tactics Tigers and Panthers presented no problem, particularly as they were mechanically unreliable. All such points were to a degree true, but the 17-pdr was only just capable of penetrating the armour on the front of the Panther, and there were simply not enough 17-pdr-equipped tanks available in June and July. Good tactics helped to some extent but operations against German armour were still very dangerous for British tank crews, and whereas the Tiger was mechanically unsound, the Panther was not and it was this weapon that confronted the British in greater numbers. Increasing numbers of 17-pdr-equipped tanks and self-propelled anti-tank guns such as the M10 tank destroyer were all arriving by July and into August. Coupled with the more widespread introduction of new discarding sabot ammunition, which dramatically increased the anti-armour effectiveness of 6-pdr and 17-pdr guns at standard battle ranges, the firepower issue subsided.

Yet in late July 1944 the greatest benefit to the British tank crews would come from the freeing up of the armoured forces from their confined spaces in Normandy. By this time British tanks were mechanically sound and reliable and backed by good logistical support networks; once the campaign became more fluid and mobile, British armour would enjoy a considerable advantage over the more unreliable German armour.

It was also still the case that the tactical situation in Normandy greatly favoured defence. Despite the shortcomings in British tank equipment, save possibly the firepower issue, the greatest problem lay in attacking a well-concealed enemy firing effective anti-tank weapons from initially static positions. Lieutenant General Gerald Bucknall, commanding XXX Corps, took a balanced view of the tactical situation facing British tank forces:

> The country is not good tank country but it has certain advantage from our point of view in that the enemy is not able to use to the best advantage the greater range at which he is capable of penetrating our tanks.
>
> Most tank encounters take place at comparatively short range . . . the chap who gets in the first good shot usually wins at this range.[45]

Locating the positions from where tanks were being fired upon was the greatest difficulty, and the advantage in these situations lay firmly with the Germans who were largely on the defensive in close, concealing terrain. Observation was fundamental to success and though official advice was for tank commanders to stay buttoned up with their hatches closed, practical experience showed that a commander had to see as much as possible around him to enhance situation awareness. Staying 'buttoned up' so restricted vision as to make effective command untenable. Some commanders also advised new arrivals to use only one half of their earphones so that they might 'hear' the battle around them and better locate where incoming fire might be coming from. The price for this greater awareness was high; tank commanders fighting with their heads exposed suffered the highest casualty rates of any tank crew member.[46]

Dealing with enemy forces that suddenly opened fire required intimate cooperation between British troops and tanks; the infantry were more likely to locate the enemy but required the tanks to offer them fire support to suppress and eliminate enemy infantry. Early encounters indicated the premium placed on intimate cooperation between infantry and tanks and the specific requirements. Erskine's 7th Armoured Division noted this around the time of Villers-Bocage:

> The need for more infantry was felt at once and the country, particularly in front of 5RTR, was unquestionably one for infantry supported by a few tanks and not for tanks with a small supporting component of infantry.[47]

On arriving in Normandy, Guards Armoured Division also began adapting their tactical methods to reflect the operating environment, whilst

Major General 'Pip' Roberts at 11th Armoured Division had already noted the deficiencies in his own formations' handling of infantry-armour cooperation in Operation EPSOM.[48]

Armoured units operating in close support of infantry soon recognised that during the assault, leading with tanks followed by infantry and then more tanks, the Eighth Army method brought back by Montgomery and his staff from the Mediterranean, was unworkable in the much closer terrain of Normandy. Major Stanley Christopherson, Sherwood Rangers Yeomanry, noted: 'On Sunday 11 June we had our first experience of the difficulty of supporting infantry in a village St Pierre and in very enclosed country.'[49] The 4/7th Royal Dragoon Guards, from 8th Armoured Brigade, acting in support of the infantry of 6th Green Howards in an attempt to capture Cristot on 10–11 June, used the Eighth Army tactics, but noted that the concealed German infantry let the first wave of tanks pass, then shot up the following wave of infantry, which left the leading tanks unsupported and near blind. Of nine tanks only two returned to safety. Trooper Austin Baker recalled:

> The attack on Cristot turned out to be a flop. Our first set piece attack with infantry planned just as in the text books, to have tanks 'B' Sqn leading, followed by infantry (Green Howards), followed by more tanks 'C' Sqn. This arrangement proved to be dismal failure. The Jerries lay low until the tanks had passed, then opened up on the infantry with Spandau [machine guns]. Then they set on the cut-off tanks.[50]

But in a subsequent attack in the Cristot area five days later 4/7th RDG used more integrated tactics, with infantry and armour supporting each other directly in the first wave. This proved much more effective.[51]

Some units equipped with Shermans rather than the more heavily armoured Churchills were concerned about providing close support and preferred to stay back from the target and use static fire in the style of self-propelled artillery. The tactic was not devoid of merit in that it kept tank losses down and maintained firepower throughout an assault, but when the infantry got close to the objective and when visibility was reduced by light, smoke or the weather, the effectiveness of the tanks' more distant fire support dwindled markedly, placing greater pressure on the infantry. More importantly still, the tanks would then not be in place to provide immediate anti-tank support against the likely German armoured counter-attack.[52]

Units began to adopt tactics that best suited the terrain in which they were now fighting, but mixing infantry and armour and getting them to cooperate closely was challenging. Often results were improved when units that had cooperated before or had trained together in the UK continued to work in tandem, but formations were rotated and relocated and this caused disgruntlement; each new partnership created difficulties in devising agreed operating procedures prior to going into action, and there was not always the time available to work them up properly. Major T.M. Lindsay, Sherwood Rangers Yeomanry, commented on this rotation:

> This was the horror of belonging to an independent armoured brigade – one changed hands from day to day like a library book. The Regiment would be flung into a battle at a moment's notice with infantry who had *never* had experience of co-operating with tanks. Then as soon as the infantry had been taught to work with us . . . we would be moved to support a different, strange formation.
>
> It was all very disheartening. One officer commented: 'All infantry brigadiers look the same; middle-aged, rather grim, slow thinkers and without any sense of humour.'[53]

Generally, such close cooperation was patchy within the British Army in June and July. The armoured divisions had expected to fight with their tanks and infantry largely separate as had been more usual in the desert, whilst independent brigades had a variety of differing approaches as how best to cooperate with infantry in battle. EPSOM had exposed some of these weaknesses, but by July units were nevertheless developing better systems and tactics for harnessing armour support for infantry in close-confining terrain.

Following the difficulties in integrating armour and infantry thrown up by the first six weeks' fighting, the armoured divisions moved to restructure their organisation to facilitate better understanding, particularly after GOODWOOD. Rather than fighting largely separately, 'Pip' Roberts (11th Armoured) and Major General Allan Adair (Guards Armoured Division) mixed their brigades such that each had two regiments of tanks and two battalions of infantry. This allowed armour and infantry to fight in a more balanced manner and be able to support each other more readily. Unfortunately, this rebalancing also created other problems. Only one battalion of infantry in each division was equipped with half-tracks and other lightly armoured vehicles to deliver troops into battle zones; the other infantry battalions were transported to the edge of the battle area in trucks and they then marched into action. Trucks were far too vulnerable to enemy fire to be allowed close to the fighting. But if the armour had to operate at the pace of the foot soldier, even in Normandy, this would restrict their ability to manoeuvre. A short-term fix was for soldiers to be carried into battle on the backs of tanks as tank riders, though this had been rejected in training in Britain as being too dangerous. In Normandy and in combat the advantages of infantry being able to debus straight into action whilst the tanks could maintain their speed outweighed possible increases in accidents and the vulnerability to enemy fire of infantry riding on the backs of tanks. Infantry commanders also rode on armoured formation commander's tanks in order to coordinate actions more effectively.[54] The long-term solution would be the nascent armoured personnel carriers such as the Kangaroos, but these were as yet untried and in limited supply, hence Dempsey's reluctance to unleash them until ready. It was indicative of prescient thinking on the part of the Anglo-Canadian armies that they had devised a modern solution to the problem of infantry transport in battle, an approach more advanced and workable than the half-track concept beloved of the Germans and also the Americans, and less casualty-intensive than the tank-riding approach of the Soviets.

The terrain and the depth of enemy defences also created problems for the British armoured forces. Mobility was hindered and with narrow and heavily focused operational plans the scope for armour to move freely was again limited. In the confined terrain of Normandy tank crews were forced to rethink their operating methods. Roy Dixon, 7th Royal Tank Regiment, recalled:

> When we first landed we were in these tiny, little fields with these great big banks, and it was difficult just physically getting from one field to another . . . Everything was at very close range . . . You were creeping around rather than rushing, and people were discouraged by that . . . We [illegible][55]

Commanders were forced to adapt methods to meet the conditions. Bill Close, 3rd RTR, noted:

> We had to treat things quite differently. We had to travel on roads, for instance, instead of being able to deploy and open up your squadron or regiment. In fact many times we operated on the divisional centre line and squadrons were put out on parallel roads, perhaps two to three miles to the right or left flanks, and travel in the same direction.[56]

British crews reported that the quality of German tank crews had declined since the Desert War and the enemy could be panicked into abandoning their vehicles through use of artillery bombardment and repeated firing, even if the likelihood of penetrations was low. Many German tanks were found abandoned in perfect working order.[57]

Though British armoured forces had many problems, their losses in personnel were small compared to those of the infantry; this was the arm that suffered most as a result of the German strategy of digging in and forcing the campaign into an attritional slogging match. The shortcomings of artillery and air support compounded the difficulties thrown up by the terrain and 21st Army Group's operational techniques, thus forcing a greater burden on to the infantry. Consequently, the infantry proportionally suffered the highest casualties of any arm. Although the army's overall casualties were well within pre-OVERLORD projections, by a third or so, conversely infantry losses were a third higher than had been planned for, estimates based on experience in the Mediterranean theatre. There was real concern over shortages in replacements and the threat of having to break up some units to maintain the numbers in others.[58]

Such losses were not unsustainable in the short term, nor were they wholly unexpected, but they could not be maintained indefinitely. The damage to morale, and an underlying and prevailing concern with senior British commanders, particularly Montgomery, might well have been debilitating, especially as the heavy price being paid did not appear to be matched in progress. Rates of advance were painfully slow in Normandy: in daylight an infantry battalion would advance around 380–525 yards per hour, at night 305–420 yards. Such low speeds allowed the Germans to slow advances with small numbers of troops long enough for reserves to move into position and stymie the advance.[59] Moreover, the problem still remained that troops had to learn to lean into or follow behind an artillery barrage as closely as possible in order to minimise the risk of the enemy recovering from the bombardment.[60]

This tactic could work well enough if the commander drove the soldiers forward hard, near mercilessly it might have seemed to some. Geoffrey Picot, by then with 7th Hampshires, remarked:

> I place a section of 10 men in front, in line abreast. I follow immediately behind, with the other 25 members of my platoon strung out behind me. For 10 minutes I do not stop shouting. 'Keep up the pace. Don't slacken. Keep up the pace. Don't stop. Keep up.'

Picot refused to allow his troops to react to enemy fire other than to keep up with the barrage; nor did he allow the wounded to be attended:

> 'It might be dangerous to leave them,' the soldier persists. 'Shut up,' I bellow. 'Don't stop. Keep up. Keep up!'[61]

The reward was the capture of a target with no casualties. Official pamphlets and advice repeated right until the end of the war argued that troops should lean into a barrage as much as possible, because the consequences of not doing so could be so much more calamitous. Reports from Italy in late 1943 indicated that even if lavish artillery support was possible, should infantry not keep up with the barrage it was the soldiers at the sharp end who would suffer. In May 1945 the War Office noted in a pamphlet that: 'Even now it is clear that some commanders do not seem to realise that neutralising fire on the immediate front of the assaulting troops is greatly reduced in value if those troops . . . do not keep as close as possible to it.'[62] As this message was continuously reiterated throughout the Northwest European campaign, it is clear that it was either not always heeded or, more likely, was simply difficult to enact under battle conditions. Of particular concern was the issue of faith on the part of the advancing infantry in the ability of artillery to deliver the effects suggested – as has been seen, British artillery fire was not the panacea that many then and since have claimed. Those with experience of the Mediterranean campaign believed that even if artillery support was afforded to an assault, it was 'not nearly so effective as one would have imagined'.[63]

Maintaining contact with artillery barrages or advancing quickly following a 'stonc' may not have been the whole solution but it was the most effective tactic available. If it failed and infantry units were forced to assault an enemy position which had not been suppressed, they were expected to employ fire and manoeuvre tactics, employing methods known as 'lane' or '[illegible]'. The [illegible] heat of battle and for lanes of attack for machine-gun fire to be identified and employed. But it was considered impractical in battle conditions and was possibly only employed successfully on one occasion in the whole campaign in Northwest Europe.[64] The latter entailed small groups of infantry using cover to advance but not offering themselves as targets long enough for the enemy to inflict heavy casualties upon them. 'Pepper-pot' was much easier than 'lane' to enact but it was clumsy and it effectively amounted to advancing in small, often uncoordinated groups. Generally, British troops still relied heavily on suppressive firepower at the section (ten men) and platoon (thirty men) level, and the Bren light-machine gun was the key weapon; it had been noted in one conference prior to D-Day that although rifles were used in defence, in the attacking phase of a battle most soldiers effectively became mere ammunition carriers for the Bren gunner; much less importance had been placed on fire and manoeuvre tactics.[65] Yet the Bren, though more accurate than German machine guns such as the MG34 and 42, could not lay down sufficient suppressing fire to match the effects of the enemy's weapons. For many British troops it was a chastening experience. As one officer noted: 'The machine-gun's chilling, unmistakeable sound – almost like a cloth being ripped – always sent a shiver through me, even when it was not firing in my general direction.'[66] Sydney Jary, the noted infantry commander whose memoir *18 Platoon* is required reading in modern-day British officer training, agreed that German machine guns could pin down a section or platoon much more easily than a British Bren gun. The effects of the fire may well have been psychological to a significant degree, but it had the required suppressive effect. He recognised, however, that the British Army's infantry was one part of a combined-arms team, and that examining its behaviour in isolation from artillery support was a fatuous exercise. The plan remained an integrated one and trying to ensure that it worked properly was more effective than seeking plan B alternatives; such flexibility would come with experience.[67]

Yet improved methods and thinking were emerging. The most significant additional factor in Normandy for infantry, as indeed it was for armour, was location of the enemy once under fire. The terrain militated against rapid identification of the enemy's position and this made the task for infantry immensely difficult. Some commanders began to deviate from usual practice in order to meet this challenge. It was common for an infantry company to advance behind a barrage with two platoons leading and one in support, but by leading with a smaller 'opening bid' as Lieutenant Colonel Douglas Taylor of 5th Duke of Cornwall's Light Infantry described it, the enemy could be triggered into action, thus exposing their positions to the rest of the British formation following on behind, at least 300 yards further back. Once the British commander had noted the enemy's position he could manoeuvre his second-phase troops much more effectively. Taylor's battalion only once failed to carry a target throughout the rest of the campaign following his appointment in July 1944. It would take time and painful learning for the British Army to grasp these points fully, though it is clear that by late July its infantry had learnt many lessons.

The pressure on the British Army in July 1944 was growing, nonetheless. Progress was cripplingly slow and infantry losses were worryingly high. For an army that had enjoyed the success of D-Day and the following period, the weeks of frustration from the middle of June, particularly after EPSOM, caused mounting concern.

Planners had expected a fluid campaign in which the burden of the fighting would be shared between the different arms; by late July, the burden on the infantry was intense. Both physical and mental casualties were mounting to sometimes alarming levels. As Geoffrey Picot, 1st Hants, noted: 'The only future we were expecting as July came to an end was more dour battles and advances measured in yards rather than miles.'[68]

Throughout the army the intensity of the campaign was beginning to tell. Lieutenant Stuart Hills, Sherwood Rangers, recalled:

> It's only before battle (or after it) that the turmoil takes place and one has to conquer that all-important emotion of fear, which every single man inevitably experiences. Battle is pretty grim, but it's the after-effects and the realisation of losses and dangers encountered that is the other half of it.[69]

Joe Ekins, Northants Yeomanry, noted: 'Most distressing was not the bodies for some reason but seeing bits of personal kit lying around in hedgerows, you know, photos, letters, mess tins.'[70] Tom Renouf, 51st Highland Division, recalled meeting an old friend, Tommy Layton of 5th Black Watch, who had experienced intense fighting since early June:

> This was not the same Tommy I had known . . . His eyes had shrunk into their sockets, he had lost all colour from his face, and his cheeks were hollow. He moved like a zombie. I found him sitting by his pal, Chugg, also from Northumberland. They both seemed to be in deep despair and had obviously been through hell.
>
> He had seen so many comrades perish that his own life had been shattered.[71]

Bill Close, 3rd RTR, and a veteran of campaigns since 1940, had long since decided that forming strong friendships was unwise: 'It did not pay to make special pals. Too many friendships were cut short.'[72]

The peculiarities of tank combat and its potential consequences posed gruesome realities in the pressure-cooker atmosphere of Normandy. Tank crew were repeatedly told not to peer into burned-out tanks, yet morbid curiosity got the better of some. Les Taylor, Northamptonshire Yeomanry, recalled:

> I climbed up to look inside the turret. The stench was indescribable. I saw the loader-operator, his hands frozen in the act of feeding a belt of ammo into his machine-gun, his head resting sideways on his arm.

> [T]he appalling thing was, the body was as black as coal. The gunner was just a shapeless mass of decomposition on the turret floor, but the most horrific sight of all was the crew commander . . . the projectile on entry had decapitated the poor man. I scrambled down from that chamber of death and corruption and lit a cigarette . . . and vowed never again to look inside a k.o.'d tank.[73]

By July the mounting pressure was forcing commanders and NCOs into occasionally employing strong measures to hold panicking and jittery troops in place. In addition to the occasional psychological tricks of claiming not to recognise battle exhaustion as a reality and labelling it as cowardice, officers sometimes were forced to draw weapons and threaten fleeing soldiers. In the intense fighting for Hill 112 in July, Lieutenant Colonel Lipscomb of the 4th Somerset Light Infantry used his pistol to rally retreating infantry of the 5th Duke of Cornwall's Light Infantry whilst bolstering his own troops. John Majendie later recalled:

> In the chaos I remember seeing he had got his pistol out and was waving it about and I wondered at the time what was going on. Because these chaps came back at the double it was a very dodgy moment, and I think if they had gone on I dare say a certain number of our chaps may have been tempted to go with them. Somebody I knew very well told me that he shot a chap . . . [who] was legging it, 'so I shot him'.[74]

Lieutenant Colonel Turner who took over the failing unit 6th Battalion, Duke of Wellington's Regiment, claimed on 30 June that he had twice been forced to draw his pistol to prevent soldiers from fleeing. The collapse of 6th DWR, following heavy losses and sustained engagement with the enemy, caused Montgomery to withdraw the unit, perhaps, as Field Marshal Lord Carver later considered, to set an example to the rest of his army. Their calamitous experience in Normandy, whilst not unique, was not usual and there is little evidence that other units' morale crumbled to the same degree.[75]

Though the intensity of infantry combat in Normandy had surprised the British, it did not cause any discernible crisis in morale as some later claimed, though it did throw up a series of problems around resources for the treatment of symptoms, and created severe pressure on rifle companies who bore the brunt of the fighting. Anecdotal evidence and the highlighting of one or two examples does not constitute proof of an overall problem, or that British troops were wavering to any problematic degree. Even if it can be accepted that initially solid morale dipped somewhat as the fighting bogged down in July, it does not mean that this had an important impact on the fighting or the conduct of the campaign.

Fundamentally, morale is a notoriously nebulous concept to measure and evaluate, and in the case of British soldiers fighting in Northwest Europe this proved to be no different. So-called 'battle exhaustion' cases, referred to as 'shell shock' in the Great War, offered one indicator. The British Army understandably wanted to avoid the term 'shell shock' with its overly negative overtones and eventually alighted upon 'battle exhaustion', which implied a temporary fatigue that could be more easily corrected rather than a worrying mental condition.[76] Despite levels of battle exhaustion peaking in July 1944 following a series of intensely hard-fought battles, they did not exceed predictions made in pre-OVERLORD planning by Lieutenant Colonel Tom Main, RAMC, the psychiatric advisor to 21st Army Group. Although battle exhaustion was a serious problem, it never became a major crisis in the British Army in the summer of 1944.[77]

Troops displaying symptoms of battle exhaustion would typically suffer from tremors, profound loss of confidence, odd behaviour patterns and withdrawal from everyday life. Lieutenant Stuart Hills recalled:

> Our gunner . . . was carried off in an ambulance. Nobody quite knew what had happened but for some reason he would not come out of the tank. He slept in it, ate in it, refused the opportunity even of a game of football, which he loved. Perhaps he had drawn too deeply on his own particular well of endurance, had seen too many terrible sights, suffered too many vivid nightmares.[78]

Trooper Joe Ekins noted one example: 'One bloke, every time he got within two yards of his tank was sick. He was carted off and we never saw him again. I didn't blame him though.'[79]

Despite such examples, the issue of battle exhaustion did not become a problem until the first serious heavy battles took place; there were no recorded instances of exhaustion on D-Day itself and instances were well below the levels reported on the Italian front. Battles such as EPSOM changed the picture and intensified the pressure, with a consequent increase in recorded battle-exhaustion rates. In early to mid-June 10 per cent of non-fatal battle casualties had been exhaustion cases, but infantry battalions started to report rates of over 20 per cent during intense periods of fighting from EPSOM onwards, peaking at round 30 per cent in some instances. The average for July was around 24 per cent. Rates subsided once the campaign became fluid again in late July and early August, but the numbers of cases threatened to overwhelm the structures put in place to deal with them. Both the British and Canadian armies lagged somewhat behind the Americans in identifying appropriate amounts of resources to deal with potential problems, and attitudes to battle exhaustion were, by today's standards, hardly subtle. Until cases began to increase dramatically in July, Major General Edward Phillips, Director of Medical Services, 21st Army Group, maintained the view that psychiatry was 'a new form of witchcraft', and some commanders resorted to using psychological pressure on their charges by announcing that there would be 'none of that sort of thing' in their unit.[80]

That some units showed higher incidences of exhaustion than others is undeniable, perhaps indicating problems and issues, but the figures do not always match the assumptions made about the fighting capabilities of units. The 51st Highland Division initially reported similar rates and levels to the highly regarded 6th Airborne, but saw a marked spike by the end of June, perhaps reflecting their deterioration and later labelling as temporarily unfit for action. Yet 3rd Division, a formation with a decent reputation, endured exhaustion levels around 33 per cent in July and some 1,000 were treated by the end of the month, figures in excess of 51st Highlanders. With such discrepancies the only clear inference that can be drawn from Second British Army's exhaustion figures is that, overall, infantry formations suffered much higher rates than armour.[81]

As a conclusive indicator of the prevailing morale in the British Army, the exhaustion rates offer up a series of problems. In June, for example, the number of cases steadily increased before they were brought down again by strongly worded instructions issued by senior RAMC commanders who reminded battalion and regimental medical officers to stick very closely to the guidance distributed prior to D-Day on diagnosing battle exhaustion. Phillips himself went to Normandy to investigate the cause of the problem with a view to tightening up procedures. Corps exhaustion centres had been set up by the end of the month and recorded exhaustion rates fell for a time in response to the new directives and measures. This, of course, does not conclusively prove that actual battle-exhaustion problems eased, no more than that there had been a problem in the first place.[82]

Figures are also open to question because individual medical officers throughout the campaign identified battle exhaustion in differing ways, some being draconian, others liberal, further distorting the data. Medical officers were also put under pressure by their commanding officers to limit battle-exhaustion rates so as not to make the regiment look bad in the eyes of others. Inquiries were instigated to explore why the figures were high in certain units with a view to bringing them down to acceptable levels, rather than discovering what the causes of battle exhaustion were.

Ultimately, whilst battle-exhaustion figures can offer a glimpse into the nature of morale, they are not wholly reliable. But, as figures increased in mid to late July in spite of the reissued guidance, it can be reasonably deduced that there was an increasing incidence of battle exhaustion at that time to a level that might well have been underestimated. By September the figures began to fall, reflecting the improvement in the total casualty figures being suffered and the troops' perceptions of how well the campaign was by then unfolding.

Self-inflicted wounds were also an indication of poor morale within units. In the British Army as a whole the fighting in 1944–5 saw a tenfold increase in court-martial convictions on the wartime figures up to that time. Troops would 'accidentally' shoot themselves or break their ankles jumping out of their tanks. Others could be more creative. Steve Dyson, 5th/RTR, recalled:

> We saw a troop sergeant . . . being carried away unconscious in a scout-car having deliberately inhaled the exhaust fumes of a petrol-driven portable battery charger.
>
> We never saw him again.[83]

Many soldiers regarded fellows willing to inflict actual serious harm upon themselves as being too far gone to be of use and wanted them out of their units.[84] But this was not always the case: 'We couldn't do the same for a corporal, and a tank commander at that, who suddenly rushed away from his tank and crouched in a ditch, trembling as though shell-shocked.'[85]

Actual figures of self-inflicted wounds cases are patchy for the British Army in Northwest Europe, but a study conducted in July 1944 noted that most suspected cases occurred in infantry formations, that there was no indication that [illegible] and that overall there probably was no serious threat to morale from a small increase in these cases.[86] Findings were complicated by the occasional lack of help from embarrassed commanding officers who preferred to hush up suspected cases and deal with them in-house, and from the difficulties in disaggregating real accidents caused by temperamental weapons such as Sten guns and captured Luger pistols from true cases of self-inflicted wounds. Ultimately, there appears to be little evidence from the incidence of self-inflicted wounds that the British Army's morale was faltering in July 1944.

Desertion, going absent without leave (AWOL), drunkenness and insubordination also offered insights into prevailing levels of morale in the army in Normandy. For a soldier to abandon his unit or friends was never a simple or clear-cut decision, and for most the act of desertion was not premeditated but one that suddenly emerged following an intense burst of action and a long period of remorseless pressure. Many troops became lost in the midst of battle, then just kept their heads down, and only returned to their units afterwards; if their nerve was too far gone at that point they tried to melt into the background. Many would return to their units to take their punishment later. What distinguished premeditated absenteeism from battle as opposed to panic caused by breakdown was difficult to pinpoint, as 21st Army Group medical records acknowledged:

> Some men went sick and were evacuated. Others in much the same state, ran away and were awarded penal servitude. The physical escape of the deserter and the psychological escape of the hysteric were expressions of the same mechanism but the former was severely punished and the latter treated with sympathy in hospital.[87]

The difference between going AWOL and desertion was also always unclear, and appreciating the true state of morale in the British Army in the summer of 1944 is further complicated by a crack-down in July by the Judge Advocate General's department. Commanders were told to enforce severe penalties to keep troops in line and were reminded of their responsibilities in charging deserters. There was even a lingering perception on the part of some senior commanders that the abolition of the death penalty in 1931 for desertion had removed a crucial level of enforcement for the army in pressured situations as were now developing in Normandy.[88]

Cases of drunkenness and insubordination were also indications of problems with morale, and as the pressure of battle increased some soldiers took to maximising opportunities for imbibing alcohol to damaging levels. Clearly this was a problem if troops were operating equipment or commanding others. Brigadier Sandie of 11th Armoured Division had already been replaced following accusations of being found drunk, and in early August a similar case befell a senior Canadian commander. Many other soldiers resorted to alcohol for Dutch courage, even though the army's official line was that it should be administered only in situations where hot drinks could not be provided in night-time conditions. The consensus among front-line troops was that the acquisition of local cider (which was rarely strong) and calvados (which varied from delightful to awful gut rot) was an occasional fillip but not a widespread problem.[89]

There had been a spike in AWOL levels in the weeks leading up to D-Day as soldiers took their chances prior to being committed to action, but overall levels of such acts, from which it might appear that the army was suffering from a dip in morale, do not show an alarming increase. Infantry formations suffered most, as ever, with 50th Northumberland Division showing the highest incidence, perhaps underlining views expressed as early as 23 June that the division was tired.[90] The much-criticised 51st Highlanders showed no significant increase in the levels of convictions, and sustained rates lower than 15th Scottish, a division with a much superior reputation in battle. Armoured formations had fewer convictions proportionally, though 22nd Armoured Brigade of 7th Armoured Division saw a sharp rise in the period of July–August, perhaps reflecting their sustained contact with the enemy and their deflating performances.[91]

Yet ultimately, although convictions for all of these offences increased in July and August 1944, they did not get out of hand, again indicating that although pressures increased the British Army coped well enough. There were only 978 cases of desertion and AWOL across the most intense period of fighting – June to September – out of a total establishment of around 420,000 troops.[92]

There remained the vexed question of the morale of veteran units in the British Army. To this day it is alleged that the units Montgomery brought back from the Mediterranean to add experience to his front-line forces underperformed and displayed signs of battle fatigue, exhaustion or unwillingness. Lieutenant-General Brian Horrocks, who was to replace Bucknall as XXX Corps commander in August, noted that:

> After a longish period of fighting, the soldiers [in veteran units], though capable of looking after themselves, begin to see all the difficulties and lack the *elan* of fresh troops.
>
> No doubt that this is what happened in Normandy to these veteran divisions from the Middle East.[93]

'Pip' Roberts, commanding 11th Armoured, thought similarly:

> I think there can be no doubt whatsoever that Monty's principle of including experienced formations and units in the invasion force was unsound . . . I noticed on . . . several occasions the differences in dash between formations which had been fighting a long time and those who were fresh.[94]

Yet many of the comments made about the lack of drive in veteran units came after the war's end and little was recorded before D-Day about potential problems. Many units afforded veteran status actually performed well in

Northwest Europe, for example, 4th Armoured Brigade, 3rd RTR and the Sherwood Rangers, and little has been stated about poor morale in these units. Veteran troops undoubtedly demonstrated canniness and knew how to limit their exposure to casualties when and where possible, but this did not prove poor morale – rather, greater battlefield awareness. It also does not mean that even if such units were dismayed at being thrust into the fray once again after their exigencies in the Mediterranean, that poor performance as a result of weak morale was the consequence. Poor battlefield performance in the case of 7th Armoured Division was founded upon inappropriate tactics being transplanted too unquestioningly from the desert into Northwest Europe and the severe reverse at Villers-Bocage in June, rather than poor morale, though it is, of course, likely that morale dipped following such setbacks.

The problems confronting veteran infantry battalions, both in infantry and armoured divisions, were more apparent. The 50th and 51st Infantry Divisions recorded significant rates in either battle exhaustion or convictions for acts of desertion, though interestingly rarely both. Montgomery infamously informed Brooke in mid-July that, in the opinion of Dempsey, Crocker and himself, the 51st Highlanders were not fit for front-line action; the divisional commander Charles Bullen-Smith was fired and Tom Rennie brought in. The division's fortunes improved throughout August, particularly when employed in Operation TOTALIZE under the tutelage of Guy Simonds' II Canadian Corps.[95] The battle-exhaustion rates of 50th Northumbrian Division were consistently high and a cause of concern, whilst the 131st Infantry Brigade in 7th Armoured Division suffered both high levels of exhaustion and convictions in July and August. Veteran infantry formations therefore demonstrated a higher propensity to indications of dipping levels of morale, but this only rarely provoked a marked falling-off in battlefield performance, even in the intense combat in Normandy.

Yet it was clear that by late July and with no apparent end in sight for the British soldiers mired in the heavy combat of Normandy, particularly in the aftermath of the failed GOODWOOD operation, pressure and concerns over morale were beginning to affect the spirits of the troops, and through them the commanders. Infantry units were most obviously suffering, but frustration and pessimism were emerging everywhere. However, although largely unbeknownst to the British, their mounting problems were as nothing compared to the Germans, whose forces were haemorrhaging to death and enduring quite appalling casualties far beyond those of the Allies. By 23 July German Army Group B had reported 116,863 casualties in Normandy, but only some 10,000 replacements had arrived to make good these losses.

By the time that Operation COBRA began on 25 July the Germans were outnumbered by some 3.8 to 1, whilst the *Wehrmacht*'s High Command War Diary recorded that 481 tanks and assault guns had been irretrievably lost by 31 July. With a further 470 in workshops, this constituted over 50 per cent of the entire German armoured forces in the theatre.[96] It seems remarkable that German soldiers continued to fight with such obduracy in this period, until we acknowledge the desperation and fear that underpinned their attitudes and outlook. Whereas troops suffering from battle exhaustion were treated reasonably well in the Allied armies, and those convicted of desertion and being AWOL were no longer confronted by the threat of execution, German troops were faced with something quite different. Though only 48 German soldiers had been executed in the whole of the Great War, by as early as March 1943 some 1,500 had already been put to death for desertion and acts of 'subverting the will of the people to fight' since September 1939. By June 1944, even before the Stauffenberg assassination plot, the figure had risen to a staggering 7,000. Despite the efforts of some to persuade the German Army to take a more humane look at battle exhaustion, little was achieved and the condition was never properly recognised, hardly an indication of a forward-thinking modern institution. With ever more reasons to fear extreme punishment and execution, German soldiers had little alternative but to dig in and grimly hang on as long as possible. Though factors such as tactical nous and ideological fervour played a part in sustaining German soldiers in the field, it is far from easy to disaggregate fear of retribution from any analysis of their morale, particularly as the summer of 1944 progressed. It was little wonder that many of the 200,000 prisoners taken by the Allies in Normandy displayed all the classic symptoms of extreme battle exhaustion.[97]

For the British Army in the closing days of July 1944 the Normandy campaign had become a drawn-out, tortuous and immensely frustrating experience. Its soldiers undoubtedly suffered a dip in morale as the fighting bogged down and little headway appeared to be being made, but levels of battle exhaustion and cases of desertion, insubordination, drunkenness and going AWOL, though showing some increases, did not generate panic, provoke a real crisis, or support later contentions that there was a morale problem in the British Army. For an army still finding its feet and with a large number of inexperienced troops in its order of battle this was no mean achievement. This is underscored when it is recognised that the static nature of the campaign exposed shortcomings in the firepower-based philosophy of Montgomery and his staff and laid a sharper and deeper burden upon the front-line fighting man, particularly the infantryman. Yet, though gloom and despondency were emerging across units in Normandy, by the beginning of August much had changed. Though it seemed highly unlikely to British troops in the aftermath of GOODWOOD, their work and sacrifices alongside those of their Allies were about to precipitate the denouement of the Normandy campaign and inflict a catastrophic defeat upon the enemy in France, throwing them all the way back to Germany itself.

6

BREAKOUT
Victory in Normandy

IN THE AFTERMATH of Operation GOODWOOD the British armoured divisions licked their wounds, began re-equipping, and absorbed replacements. Such new blood was technically well trained in how to operate tanks, but was tactically naïve and unversed in the realities of battle. Whilst some infantry formations continued to hold the line, the poor weather that set in on 20 July, as well as the need to recover, precluded much more. Some formations enjoyed the luxury of being rotated out of the line to recover their senses, enjoy hot baths, entertainment, fresh clothes and better food. Rations issued to troops in the front line were considerably improved from what had existed during the desert campaign when everything appeared to be bully beef and biscuits in some form or other, but even in the Northwest European campaign fresh food and bread were welcome alternatives to standard army fare.[1] Front line troops were occasionally disgruntled to see that such luxuries were standard for rear-echelon soldiers. Roland Jefferson, 8th Rifle Brigade, recalled:

> We were afforded the luxury of a change of clothing from the mobile laundry which appeared and a visit to the mobile showers. We even went to an ENSA concert and began to realise that these creature comforts were commonplace to the base wallahs and the HQ troops.[2]

But the break from action was short-lived for most troops. Montgomery was now under serious pressure following the disappointment of GOODWOOD, as his chief of staff, Freddie de Guingand, noted:

> My Chief undoubtedly suffered a lot from the criticism that appeared in the press and elsewhere about the slowness of progress in the bridgehead. 'Had we reached a stalemate?' 'Had Montgomery failed?'[3]

De Guingand, like Montgomery, was concerned that the troops would be picking up on this disgruntlement and would begin to question the leadership of the British forces in Normandy. Montgomery knew that the Americans were manoeuvring into place for another breakthrough attempt, Operation COBRA, but he also realised that with the GOODWOOD failure in the air it was politically impossible to allow the British and Canadians to be seen to be taking a breather. He intended to maintain pressure in the eastern sector where possible because he, like everyone else in the Allied leadership, did not expect COBRA to achieve what it eventually did, a strategic breakout; consequently, British and Canadian troops were on the move again soon after GOODWOOD.

A little-known yet significant action, Operation EXPRESS, took place on 22 July when a brigade of 43rd Wessex Division, supported by 7th RTR, was plunged into action in the Hill 112 sector once again, though this time in a more limited operation, to capture Maltot, a small village already battled over before in EPSOM and JUPITER. The Wessex Division had suffered in the JUPITER operation, but EXPRESS saw lessons learnt from previous actions being put into practice. The commanders and NCOs studied the task ahead of them with maps, photographs and sand models, discussed methods of infantry-armour cooperation, and conducted forward reconnaissance. The official divisional history later recorded: 'It has been said of this battle that it was a set piece in which all the precepts of the training manuals were fulfilled.'[4] There was still severe and hard close combat but the two Wiltshire Battalions in the van, supported by Churchill tanks, overcame the opposition and secured Maltot by the end of the day, beating off German counter-attacks and capturing some 400 prisoners. It was a fine example of excellent combined arms fused with determination and good leadership:

> When the dawn came, Maltot presented an appalling spectacle: the streets and fields were still strewn with the dead of the Dorsets and Hampshires who had fallen on July 10th [JUPITER] around slit trenches with hardly more than the turf removed; the houses were shattered; the roads cratered and full of debris; everywhere the sickly smell of death and destruction hung heavily over the ruins.[5]

EXPRESS was a great success on the part of British forces, amply supported by artillery who stuck to their training and achieved their objectives. The Wessex Division would be back in action a few days later, however, and the fighting would prove even more intense.

To the west of Caen, Dempsey's Second British Army took up positions alongside the Americans, whilst to the east, in and around the city, First Canadian Army was forming up under the leadership of Harry Crerar, becoming operational on 23 July. Crerar was not Montgomery's favourite commander, and Monty held a low opinion of his capabilities. He noted on 26 July following a squabble between John Crocker, I Corps commander, and Crerar: 'The real trouble is that Crerar wants to show at once that he is a great soldier . . . the truth of the matter is that he is a very poor soldier and has much to learn.'[6] Montgomery wrote to Field Marshal Alan Brooke, on the matter: 'He [Crerar] had a row with Crocker the first day, and asked me to remove Crocker. I have spent two days trying to restore peace.'[7]

Monty went on to state, rather uncharitably, that after taking over command at 1200 on 23 July, Crerar made his first mistake at 1205 and his second after lunch. He thought Crerar a personable chap, but not well suited to army command; in contrast he had great faith in Guy Simonds, the high-flying Canadian II Corps commander.[8] But Simonds soon blotted his copybook with the poorly prosecuted Operation SPRING, which began on 25 July, an action to the south of Caen intended to push troops on to the Verrières Ridge. Although a Canadian-led operation, two British armoured divisions, 7th and the Guards, were deployed to support the action and exploit any resulting opportunities. This was highly unlikely as the Germans held this pivotal position to the south of Caen in considerable strength and were wary of a possible push by the Anglo-Canadian forces towards Falaise, which could in turn open up the road to Paris. Ahead of II Canadian Corps lay troops of 1st, 9th and 12th SS and 2nd and 21st Panzers. It was also clear to Dempsey and Montgomery that SPRING was a holding operation, small in scale and intended to keep the Germans in place around Caen, whilst developing the Anglo-Canadian position by achieving the phase II objective originally set down for GOODWOOD. Richard O'Connor, commanding VIII Corps, impressed upon Allan Adair, commander of Guards Armoured, that caution was the order of the day with SPRING. Bobby Erskine, commanding 7th Armoured, had already demonstrated an unwillingness to take undue risks with Cromwells and Shermans against emplaced anti-tank guns, and was probably feeling the effects of weeks of action in Normandy in conditions he had neither planned for nor welcomed.[9]

Although SPRING enjoyed some medium-bomber and substantial artillery support, it was nowhere near as lavish as that provided to major operations, because of the limited objectives and expectation. Simonds' plan called for three infantry battalions to advance on to their objectives just before first light, guided through the darkness by searchlights, to be followed by a second phase of three further infantry battalions supported by the Shermans of 2nd Canadian Armoured Brigade and an artillery barrage, to be closely backed by the tanks of 7th Armoured Division ideally pushing on to Point 122. If successful, Guards Armoured Division would be unleashed to exploit the situation still further southeasterly towards Garcelles.[10]

The operation, like so many 21st Army Group plans thus far in Normandy, did not unfold quite as had been hoped. The infantry assaults proved to be too weak in most cases to carry their objectives and the armour support too dispersed. Although the Royal Hamilton Light Infantry seized Verrières itself, other battalions fared less well, in particular the Black Watch which suffered over 300 casualties, 118 being killed.[11] Erskine's 7th Armoured demonstrated considerable caution once again, following on from their hesitant commitment to GOODWOOD. Convinced that the ground and opposition arrayed against his units were both inappropriate for armour and too powerful, Erskine's Desert Rats advanced very cautiously. Guy Simonds did not push the 7th Armoured at all hard, preferring to use them piecemeal in a defensive role. Some losses were suffered and although a number of German tanks were claimed as destroyed, the armoured regiments took few risks.[12]

Simonds continued to batter away with his infantry battalions but with little effect other than to deplete them. His aggression and determination to make SPRING work, even when it was clear quite early on that it was stalling badly, did not show him in a good light. Brigadier Bill Megill, 5th Brigade, 2nd Canadian Infantry Division, later recalled:

> It was perfectly clear that the attack should have been called off at a very early stage in the morning. I suggested this not later than perhaps eight or nine o'clock. Instead the corps commander was pressing the divisional commander [Foulkes] and he was pressing us to get on with the attack which we knew was hopeless.[13]

Simonds, a man known for his violent temper, was reduced to tears by SPRING's failure, though he turned his ire on his junior commanders in later assessments, claiming they were responsible for the failure.[14]

SPRING had supposedly been a holding operation only, but its timing on 25 July fortuitously coincided with the much larger US operation, COBRA. The Germans were for a time confused by the dual operations and in view of the greater importance placed on the position around Caen, believed SPRING to be the greater threat. This quickly changed, however, when in the space of forty-eight hours or so COBRA delivered a huge success and broke open the front to the south of St Lô.

Operation COBRA was in many ways quite similar in concept to those grand-scale Anglo-Canadian operations that had preceded it, and it differed markedly from American-style operations. It was to begin with a heavy bombing raid followed by large-scale artillery bombardment, and would see a rapid infantry assault after which two armoured divisions would press through the gap and develop the breakthrough, hopefully precipitating a significant push to the south. After previous disappointments Bradley's staff at First US Army played down the likelihood of anything decisive occurring as a result of COBRA, and speculation over a breakout (as opposed to a breakthrough) was brushed aside.[15]

The operation began inauspiciously. It had been repeatedly delayed due to bad weather and positioning actions, and it was delayed again on 24 July on account of the weather, even though 1,600 heavy bombers were already en route to Normandy to begin the preliminary bombardment. Despite a recall, around 700 tons of bombs were dropped, some erroneously, killing 25 US soldiers and wounding over a hundred more. When COBRA properly launched the following day, short bombing again caused dismay with 111 more American soldiers being killed, including Lieutenant General Leslie McNair. Bradley was incensed as he had planned for the air forces to bomb laterally across the front line in order to minimise the risk of short bombing, but unknown to him the air forces had rejected this tactic.[16]

The bombing also inflicted severe punishment on the German troops defending the line. Wolfgang Maas, a radio operator of 902nd Regiment, recalled:

> Reasonably removed from the CP [command post], in a sunken road, our SPW [self-propelled weapon] was in cover, when a vast number of heavy bombers approached us. All of a sudden bombs detonated nearby. I was struck in the shoulder. Grasping instinctively up there, I held a shell splinter in my hand. As it was hot, I threw it away at once. Jacket and blouse were torn.[17]

General Fritz Bayerlein, commanding Panzer Lehr, saw his forces bear the brunt of the bombing, and his front-line units endured complete collapse and loss of all tanks:

> The whole place looked like a moon landscape; everything was burned and blasted.
>
> The survivors were like madmen and could not be used for anything. On 24 and 25 July I lost about 2,000 men either dead or missing from the bombing.

> On the evening of the first day, I collected the few reserves we had north of la Chapelle-en-Juger, and tried to re-establish the old line. I had received more infantry and about 800–1000 men in the line. The next day they too were destroyed. I don't believe hell could be as bad as what we experienced.[18]

Yet initial American advances were limited and by the end of the first day – 25 July – frustration was emerging amongst the senior US staff at First Army. Some units made better progress on 26 July, but it was not until a day later that it became clear that German elements were not just falling back but disintegrating. Seizing their moment, Bradley's forces drove through the gap now created and turned COBRA into a full-scale strategic breakout. On 1 August General George Patton's Third US Army activated and began an all-out drive to the Seine. This was a marked change from the original plan, which had called for a steady advance into Brittany in order to clear the Atlantic ports and open them up to the Allies for supply and reinforcement, preparatory to a steady advance to the Seine, but the situation was changing rapidly.

The collapse of the German lines between St Lô and the coast opened up greater opportunities for an immediate exploitation to the east, towards the Seine and ultimately Paris; Brittany could now be cleared by smaller forces as and when necessary. The German strategy of digging in and hanging on obdurately in Normandy had stymied the Allies for six weeks, but it had been at the cost of longer-term survival as units had had to be fed into the line piecemeal merely to maintain a generally static front. Now with few reserves left and all available units committed, collapsing or pinned in place, the German position in Normandy was on the point of meltdown.

Montgomery later tried to claim some credit for nudging Bradley into a more focused, narrower front attack for COBRA, something that the US forces had previously eschewed. Dempsey recalled the meeting of 10 July when Bradley received some gentle advice from Montgomery regarding tactics: 'Bradley had obviously made his own task the more difficult by trying to buck the whole line right along instead of concentrating and punching a hole in one important sector.'[19] Montgomery and David Belchem, 21st Army Group's chief of operations, also later claimed that following any breakout the notion of an exploitation by US Third Army towards the Seine and Paris, and not into Brittany, was always an imagined and planned-for possibility. As ever, Montgomery's perception of his importance and role in events was inflated: COBRA was Bradley's plan and an American success.[20]

Yet there is no doubt that Anglo-Canadian assaults had pinned the heavier German units in place around Caen and made the success of COBRA possible.

Field Marshal Von Kluge, and before him Rommel, had identified the Caen sector as fundamental to the viability of the German position in Normandy and therefore to be defended in greatest strength. The repeated attacks by British and Canadian troops from early June to late July had confirmed this view and forced the Germans to commit their reserves just to hold that position. Consequently, by 25 July British and Canadian forces faced 645 tanks in six panzer divisions along with 92 infantry battalions, whilst the Americans confronted two panzer divisions with fewer than 200 tanks and 85 infantry battalions.[21] The Americans, though facing lesser opposition, had had to deal with much worse terrain but as a result of COBRA were now out into more open country with crumbling opposition in front of them.

Montgomery's concern now focused on how best to support the unexpectedly spectacular success of COBRA with his British and Canadian forces. On 27 July, inspired by a plan put forward by Dempsey, he issued a new directive in which he identified the area around Caumont in the western sector of the Anglo-Canadian bridgehead, and largely inactive since early June, as the key area in which Second British Army could deliver a heavy blow to the now-reeling Germans, particularly as the panzer forces were all fixed in place east of Noyers in the Caen sector. He accepted that the First Canadian Army would require further support and incoming forces before any significant action could be played out on their front; in any case, Monty argued, an attack into where the Germans remained strong would be playing into their hands – better now to keep the front moving and break open the breach still further. A tentative earlier notion of keeping a corps in reserve to strike quickly down from Caen towards Falaise was therefore withdrawn.[22]

Strategically there was undoubtedly some merit on 27 July for the decision made by Montgomery and his team, though as events unfolded over the following week, and in particular because of the foolhardy attempt by the Germans to counter-attack towards Mortain in the American Sector, an immediate push down the Caen-Falaise highway might have yielded even greater results. This could not have been known at the time when Montgomery committed his forces to what was to become Operation BLUECOAT; on 27 July the position was not as conclusively in favour of the Allies as it was to appear even two days later, by which time Second Army's six divisions and two corps were fully committed. As a result of BLUECOAT, the more experienced British forces in Normandy which had been in action since early June were unavailable to support First Canadian Army's vital strike to Falaise on 8 August.[23]

The British Army had to react quickly to the changing strategic situation. Montgomery's initial directive called for BLUECOAT to launch on

2 August by the latest, but the German collapse against First American Army was apparent by the end of 27 July and BLUECOAT was expedited and began less than three days later. It was to be a two-corps operation, launched over a much wider three-division front than previous plans, with the overall intention of driving Second British Army on to and to the west of Mont Pinçon, the highest point in Normandy. This would provide flanking support for COBRA and break the hinge of the German position in the west. The assault would comprise a strike south by O'Connor's VIII Corps from Caumont towards Hill 309, high ground just to the east of St-Martin-des-Besaces, and then on southwards towards the Bény-Bocage Ridge and the vital town of Vire. O'Connor had only one infantry division, 15th Scottish, to perform this task, initially supported by 6th Guards Tank Brigade, with 11th Armoured Division in a supporting role. O'Connor was dismayed by having to use an armoured division early in his attack in what was essentially a task for infantry, but infantry was in short supply and little could be done. It helped that 15th Scottish and 6th Guards had trained in England and knew each other well, a situation which had not existed between the Scots and 31st Tank Brigade in EPSOM.[24]

The main thrust of BLUECOAT was to come from Gerry Bucknall's XXX Corps, initially towards Hill 361, high ground commanding the position to the west of Mont Pinçon, and then on to Mont Pinçon itself. Bucknall had 43rd Wessex and 50th Northumbrian Divisions in the lead mixed with 8th Armoured Brigade, and 7th Armoured Division in support. For XXX Corps this would eventually mean a return to battling through the area surrendered back in mid-June following the Villers-Bocage failure. Paradoxically, though the British sought Mont Pinçon first and foremost, Point 309, the initial objective of VIII Corps, was considered by General Erich Straube, commanding LXXXIV Corps which opposed the British in this sector, to be 'the key to the defence. It must not be allowed to fall into enemy hands.'[25] Controversially, Montgomery's 27 July directive propelled Second British Army's troops into an operation in the most difficult and unforgiving terrain they had yet experienced that was later regarded by the soldiers who fought there as the nastiest of the campaign. The country to the south of Caumont and towards Mont Pinçon was characterised by *bocage*, thick woods, hills and valleys, whilst the land further south was known as *la Suisse Normande*, a name that reflected the similarities with the steep hills and dense woods associated with Switzerland. It was not without good reason that commanders frantically preparing for action in BLUECOAT emphasised the necessity of close armour-infantry cooperation to their charges; it would be imperative that the different arms worked closely together in the dense terrain.

Richard O'Connor, commanding VIII Corps, said as much to 'Pip' Roberts, commander of 11th Armoured Division, who recalled later:

> I saw General Dick O'Connor and he told me that we were going to operate on the right flank of Second Army, right in the middle of *bocage* country. He said, and this was very relevant, that, 'You must be prepared for the very closest of tank/infantry co-operation on a troop/platoon basis.'[26]

Commanders and soldiers had to put into practice those lessons learned in previous fighting in Normandy, in particular how best to operate in terrain where advance by vehicle could only be managed along narrow roads with infantry embarked as tank riders, despite the inherent dangers. The first sign of enemy activity precipitated a rapid debussing of infantry to provide cover in flanking fields and eyes for the force. The tanks often employed what became known as 'snake patrol', with the leading tank in a troop being covered from a bend or a corner in the road by a halted second tank. Once the next covering point had been reached the second tank would close up to provide covering fire once again. 'It was the best way we could think of for advancing relatively safely,' noted Lieutenant Johnny Langdon, 3rd RTR.[27] Peter Carrington, Guards Armoured Division, and later Lord Carrington in Margaret Thatcher's administration in the 1980s, recognised the reorganisation and rethinking taking place:

> The result was that in every encounter a mix of tanks and infantry was available: tanks and infantry, furthermore, who came from the same regiment, who already knew each other and were quickly to know each other very well indeed.
>
> The upshot was a great improvement on what had gone before.[28]

Despite the daunting terrain, time was now of the essence. On 28 July Montgomery issued further instructions, imploring Dempsey to accept heavier casualties if necessary and to 'step on the gas to Vire':

> I ordered Dempsey to launch his attack from the Caumont area on Sunday 30 July; all caution to be thrown overboard, every risk to be taken, and all troops to be told to put everything into it.[29]

In the days leading up to BLUECOAT's launch the areas behind the front became a hive of activity as units frantically moved westwards to join up with 15th Scottish Division which was already in place around Caumont, having moved across to take over the sector from US troops on 23 July.[30] Bucknall's XXX Corps had been holding positions in the sector for much of the campaign, but VIII Corps had been placed in reserve following GOODWOOD, and were now reconstituted and established with alacrity in their new positions to the west of Bucknall's forces. It was a shock to the system at VIII Corps HQ, which had enjoyed a period of quiet and had acquired a 'strangely deserted air'. O'Connor remarked later on the great haste in mounting BLUECOAT and the speed and complexity with which British units had to shuffle about the bridgehead in less than forty hours. Soldiers marvelled at the efficiency of the pioneers and engineers in getting routes ready and sufficiently maintained for such a large number of units to move so quickly at short notice. The mobility of the British was something the Germans simply could not match. Though accomplished broadly according to the exacting requirements made of them, it was not easy. Tim Ellis of 4th King's Shropshire Light Infantry noted in his diary that the original order came to move out on the night of 28 July, but that it was not until 1100 the following day that they were able to do so: 'We might as well have spent the time in bed and got more sleep.'[31] Jack Thorpe, a co-driver in 2nd Fife and Forfar Yeomanry, remarked on seven hours' solid driving:

> The tanks were not allowed to use the metalled roads in the bridgehead as they were breaking up fast under the traffic supplying the Army and so we were driving on earth marked out tracks. This created a dense fog of dust clouds. It was hell trying to see and follow the tank in front of us.
>
> I could only keep awake by twisting my ear till it hurt or singing at the top of my voice.[32]

In spite of the rapid response by VIII Corps troops, when the attack began on 30 July the tail of the corps' forces were still on the east side of the Orne.[33]

Security was considered vital and a range of measures was put in place to conceal the depth of forces mustering at Caumont. The movement of 11th Armoured Division and 6th Guards Tank Brigade took place at night, radio activity was strictly curtailed, the White Knight symbol of VIII Corps HQ was removed from vehicles, only the guns of 15th Scottish were allowed to register, air observation post activity was restricted, and Second Army organised a deception plan employing decoy radio activity and dummy tanks. As ever it was difficult to assess the value of such measures; intelligence material gathered two days after BLUECOAT's start showed that a British patrol captured by the Germans on 29 July had given the game away to an extent, but the Germans, though alerted to the possibility of some increased activity on 29–30 July, never expected that such a major effort, let alone one with armour, would be mounted across such difficult terrain. Briefings offered to the newly arrived German troops of 326th Infantry Division, who were directly opposing the advance of VIII Corps, stated that they were confronting troops who had suffered heavy casualties with little armour, and that thoughts of deserting should be discarded as victimisation of their families at home would surely follow. The 326th Infantry had a nine-mile front to cover, though the positions had been well prepared with minefields, obstacles and strongpoints moulded on to the already defensive layout of the terrain.[34]

On the morning of 30 July XXX Corps got underway following the ubiquitous aerial bombardment and artillery barrages, but progress was uneven. The sector had been static for some weeks and many minefields had been sown and incorrectly marked – corps HQ could not provide adequate maps showing such locations and troops in the lead had to deal with these difficulties in addition to a well-prepared enemy.[35] Major General Ivor Thomas' 43rd Wessex Division had endured significant battalion and company commander losses in the fighting thus far in Normandy, but the leading battalions still made decent progress as they advanced in gloriously hot weather, despite hold-ups for the unmarked mines and other obstacles. The division had trained in the sunken lanes and thickets of Stone Street in Kent and had some idea of how to negotiate the *bocage*, but progress was steady at best. Corporal Doug Proctor noted:

> It was impossible to observe anything beyond the nearest hedgerow. It was a hopeless situation.
>
> The [illegible] we began to advance and immediately ran into a hail of small arms fire.
>
> One German soldier ran towards us from the left flank. His hands were raised as if surrendering but I could see he was still armed with a few stick grenades that were in his belt. His arm dropped and grasped a grenade; without the slightest hesitation or compunction, I shot him.[36]

Some battalions had particularly pressing matters: 5th Wiltshires, despite taking part in a relatively straightforward action, had their post lorry and second-in-command, Major Metcalf, captured by the enemy. The lorry was recovered some days later, embarrassingly by their sister battalion the 4th Wiltshires, but the Germans had smoked all the cigarettes from the parcels.[37] The 4th Somerset Light Infantry made some headway but 5th Dorsets were soon entangled in minefields and were able to push on only under the cover of darkness. The 7th Hampshires advanced southwards on Cahagnes and a German counter-attack was beaten off. Frustration followed and it took until the following day to secure Cahagnes. Some 180 prisoners were captured and another 100 killed.[38] Lieutenant Stuart Hills, Sherwood Rangers, passed through the place:

> Cahagnes was a terrible mess, like every other Normandy village we fought our way through: it had been bombed and then smashed up by the guns of the tanks. If any civilians were still there, they would have been hiding deep in their cellars.[39]

Even in this mayhem 4th Dorsets were still able to prosecute a set-piece attack on Montmirel to the south and for just a handful of casualties captured the village and took 87 prisoners of war. But overall the terrain, the opposition and the static defences hindered the assault and the main objectives were still some distance away. Unfortunately, 50th Northumbrian Division made still less headway against stiff opposition and equally noxious terrain. On 1 August 7th Armoured Division (the Desert Rats) entered the fray with orders to pass between 50th and 43rd Divisions and push on south to Aunay-sur-Odon, preparatory to a drive on Mont Pinçon. Orders emphasised the need for alacrity and risk, but the division was soon entangled in minefields, pockets of as yet unsuppressed opposition and traffic jams of troops, transports, equipment and supplies feeding the two already engaged divisions. The Desert Rats made only modest progress and the seizure of Aunay was repeatedly postponed. Gerald Verney had been warned about the poor road discipline of the Desert Rats and how the formation resented criticism of its methods, despite the setbacks so far in the campaign. Verney later recorded that 1st and 5th RTR were no longer having a go, the brigade commander (Hinde) was dead tired, and the infantry were crumbling under the pressure of heavy losses. Verney himself was unable to make much impression on the divisions when he became commander of 7th Armoured later in the campaign, and was moved on, which may in part explain his negative comments. But a combination of fatigue and grim operating conditions were clearly taking their toll on 7th Armoured.[40] Dennis Cockbaine, 5th RTR, recalled:

> A heavy mist made observation almost impossible and the inevitable happened when we had advanced about a mile and the mist lifted. We were on a forward slope with little cover and were faced by a large number

> of Pzkw IVs and Panthers who were well placed in hull-down positions. They picked us off throughout the day.
>
> For most of that eventful day we had a badly burned body of a fellow tankman on the engine cover at the back of my tank and I was very relieved to be able to bring him back to the regiment and to a decent burial.
>
> So ended an eventful and thoroughly unpleasant day.[41]

Fighting was confused and disjointed, with elements being cut off and losses suffered both in equipment and men. A lack of drive, indiscipline and obfuscation on the part of 7th Armoured prompted a tetchy exchange between XXX Corps HQ and Erskine's staff. There was fury at XXX Corps that 7th Armoured had signalled in the afternoon of 1 August that its armoured brigade had advanced much further than it really had, as this induced an order to move other troops along the route that had supposedly been vacated by 7th Armoured's tanks. When they all became entangled, Gerry Bucknall, commanding XXX Corps, visited Erskine's HQ to find out what was going on – in effect to reprimand him and tell him to get a move on. According to Brigadier Pete Pyman, XXX Corps' Chief of Staff: 'Corps commander instructed commander 7 Armoured Division to speed up action by taking any risks and by all means. He stated that corps artillery was available.'[42] The Desert Rats still made little discernible progress that day and XXX Corps' whole offensive appeared to be stalling. Dempsey's patience snapped; he pressed Bucknall for progress, prompting the latter to get on to Erskine once again later that evening: 'You may lose every tank you have got, but you must capture Aunay by midnight tonight.'[43] They failed and XXX Corps generally were making much less impact than O'Connor's VIII Corps, which made the situation look even worse. Montgomery had already impressed upon Dempsey the need for greater alacrity on 31 July, and Dempsey had warned Bucknall the previous day about 'getting on with it' following the sluggish start. Dempsey confided to Montgomery on the telephone that morning that he was tired of Bucknall, and in a meeting later that day the whole matter was clearly discussed. Montgomery stated in his diary:

> Bucknall of 30 Corps is very slow; he does his stuff in the end but it's always 24 hours late. I have several times told Dempsey that he must drive him along; if he cannot be quicker he will have to go.
>
> I am also becoming suspicious of Erskine 7th Armd Div; he is too cautious and will not fight his division all out; he may have to go too.[44]

Following the sluggish fighting and progress on 1 August and after a furious exchange of messages with Erskine and Bucknall on 2 August, Dempsey decided that Bucknall's time was up:

> That evening [2 August] when 30 Corps' progress was still unsatisfactory I told Bucknall he would have to go. The next day or the day after, I decided that Erskine and Hinde would have to follow.[45]

Montgomery and Dempsey had already met on 2 August, with Dempsey requesting the replacement of Erskine who had 'missed some good chances', as well as Bucknall:

> The Corps Commander has failed in the last seventy-two hours to produce the results which the situation demanded. I must therefore recommend with regret that Lieutenant General Bucknall be replaced in command of 30 Corps. In my opinion he is not fit to command a corps in mobile operations.[46]

Montgomery concurred and wanted Bucknall replaced with Lieutenant General Brian Horrocks. This was a rare admission of poor judgement on the part of Montgomery, who conceded that the selection of Bucknall to corps command, in the face of Brooke's misgivings, had been an error: 'Gen Bucknall was appointed to command a Corps at my request. I admit, frankly, that I made a mistake.'[47]

Bucknall did not go graciously, and the situation was not helped by the fact that the *Sunday Express* newspaper ran a positive piece on him the very day of his sacking.[48] He complained to Montgomery that the tasks set out for XXX Corps in BLUECOAT had been unrealistic, that VIII Corps had had an easier ride, and that he had stated all this to Dempsey before BLUECOAT had begun.[49] Bucknall then set out his grievances to the War Office on 4 August, blaming Erskine for the sluggish advance, and then a few days later he privately fixed the blame for his dismissal on Dempsey: 'I think that Dempsey was getting jumpy and nervy and I am sure he would secure a scapegoat if there were prospects of a check and further raised eyebrows from the press.'[50] Montgomery's decision to replace Bucknall was unsurprisingly formally ratified by the War Office on 18 August and Bucknall spent the rest of his career as military commander of Northern Ireland. Montgomery had also decided on 2 August to replace Erskine and signalled the War Office to that effect the following day:

> I consider that General Erskine is at present unfit to command an armoured division in battle. I have removed him from command of 7th Armoured Division.[51]

Whilst acknowledging that Erskine had done well prior to D-Day, he conceded that:

> . . . the Division has not done well since D-Day and I am satisfied that the fault lies with General Erskine . . . he has been too long on the same line [and] I also think he needs a rest.[52]

Erskine's career as a field commander may have stalled, but Montgomery still thought him a valuable officer and by the autumn he was back in Northwest Europe playing a political role as head of the SHAEF mission in Brussels. The sackings may have acted as markers to others but their value to the formations themselves remains unclear. There was certainly some disgruntlement, though Brigadier Harold 'Pete' Pyman, Bucknall's erstwhile chief of staff at XXX Corps, fully supported Montgomery and Dempsey's decision: 'The dismissal of Bucknall and Erskine was fully justified – they made no effort to push hard or carry out their orders.'[53]

In the aftermath of Bucknall's and Erskine's removal a hundred other senior officers were also shipped out by Montgomery and Dempsey in an effort to pep things up in XXX Corps and 7th Armoured Division. Brian Horrocks, Bucknall's replacement, was a favourite of Montgomery but had been recovering from wounds at the time of corps appointments for OVERLORD; now this popular character would get his chance. Erskine's replacement was to be Gerald Verney who, as Monty put it, 'has done very well and displayed tremendous drive and fighting spirit' as commander of 6th Guards Tank Brigade.[54] Horrocks' appointment proved popular and ultimately relatively successful, and XXX Corps turned its fortunes around; Verney struggled to have a similar impact but the Desert Rats took somewhat longer to get going once again.

In spite of the travails of XXX Corps, BLUECOAT did not flounder, for O'Connor's VIII Corps had enjoyed tremendous success in its operations to the west of Bucknall's forces. O'Connor had deployed 15th Scottish Infantry Division supported by 6th Guards Tank Brigade to strike south from the Caumont area towards Hill 309, with 11th Armoured Division offering flanking support. Despite poor weather hampering the first phase of bombing, the initial assault went particularly well. Major General Gordon MacMillan's Scots had engaged in some preliminary minor actions to reach the allotted start line for 30 July but the assaults proved effective, the co-operation between 15th Scottish and 6th Guards enhanced as a result of having previously trained together in the UK. The attack was to be supported further by a range of mine-clearing tanks and Churchill Crocodile flame-throwers.[55]

Because of the terrain restricting possible lines of advance for armour and the poor visibility imposed by the hedgerows, trees and woods, many battles quickly broke down into small-scale actions. Though there were the usual moments of combat friction the battalions of infantry and tanks pushed south, and though timetables rarely worked out fully, the commanders and troops seized particular moments to maintain the momentum. What was abundantly clear was the improved nature of infantry-armour cooperation now developing across many units in the British Army.

The first key decision made during BLUECOAT came when MacMillan and Verney met in Caumont to discuss progress. The infantry, embroiled in actions and hindered by the terrain, were unable to form up in time for the final drive on to the day's objective, Hill 309. Verney took the decision to press on with the tanks of the 4th Coldstream Guards and allow the infantry to catch up when possible. Assaulting through close terrain without infantry seemed a high-risk tactic, but German opposition was thinning out ahead of the Guards and was simply not expecting tanks to battle their way through such terrain. The Churchill tanks of the 6th Guards were ideally suited to such assaults, being designed with low centres of gravity for negotiating obstacles. It was still tough going, as recounted by Major Mark Millbank commanding 2nd Squadron:

> The high banks, surmounted by scrub, made a cross country ride remarkably uncomfortable! One climbed slowly up the face of a bank, balanced precariously on the top, warned the occupants to hold tight as one launched forth down the other side. In several tanks, men were knocked senseless by the battering.[56]

The Churchills pushed on through the appalling ground and by 7 p.m. had forced their way on to Hill 309 – or Quarry Hill as it was known – meeting little opposition; such resistance as there had been seemed to have fled during the bombing. The hill General Straube had announced could not be allowed to fall into enemy hands had indeed done so, due to initiative and dash. Throughout the evening and morning of 31 July, infantry filtered up on to the hill to secure the position. To the east the Churchills of 3rd Scots Guards along with infantry of 2nd Argyll and Sutherland Highlanders pressed on to Hill 226, enjoying similar experiences to the Coldstream Guards, but they had to hold back from joining their fellows on Hill 309 as the limited advance of 43rd Wessex to the east had opened up a potentially exposed flank. In the early evening an aggressive assault from three Jagdpanther tank hunters threatened the position on Hill 226; in a matter of minutes eleven Churchills had been knocked out, their thick armour protection proving no match for the modern 88mm guns carried by the German tank hunters. Captain Willie Whitelaw, later Margaret Thatcher's deputy prime minister, witnessed the attack:

> I saw the left hand tank of my left forward troops go up in flames closely followed by the other two.
>
> As I was driving up the field I saw all three tanks of my left flank troop go up in flames.
>
> All six tanks in my two left hand troops together with the Battalion Second-in-Command's tank had all been knocked out . . . in little over a minute.[57]

The Churchill tanks' armaments, a mixture of 75mm and 6-pdr guns, offered no realistic chance of defeating the frontal armour on the Jagdpanthers and hastened the British tactic of adding M10 17-pdr self-propelled anti-tank guns to bolster Churchill formations. On 30 July the Scots Guards were awaiting the arrival of towed 17-pdrs to secure the position fully, but these took much longer than self-propelled equipment to get forward and could take many hours to dig in and set up.[58] Despite the ferocity of the German attack the Jagdpanthers withdrew, giving up a potentially commanding position. German counter-attacks to recover Hill 309 the following day were also beaten off.[59]

Despite the success in seizing Hill 309, it was to be somewhat overshadowed by the even more spectacular progress made by 11th Armoured Division on 31 July. 'Pip' Roberts' armour and infantry columns had made good progress on 30 July, offering flanking support to the west of 15th Scottish Division. The mixed infantry and armour formations proved invaluable, and despite encountering initial problems of minefields and German infantry they managed to push through two-thirds of the way to the little town of Saint-Martin-des-Besaces which lay some 2 kilometres to the west of Hill 309. After a hard day's fighting, the troops of 4th King's Shropshire Light Infantry believed they were settling down for the night when orders came to make an immediate march through to be in place to assault Saint-Martin-des-Besaces at first light. The pressure to maintain the excellent tempo of operations achieved on the first day of BLUECOAT in the VIII Corps sector came directly from O'Connor, for as Roberts later put it, 'firm orders came from the Corps Commander that we could not relax'. Jack Churcher, now commanding 129 Infantry Brigade of 11th Armoured Division, concurred that the pressure came from O'Connor.[60] Roberts would have preferred to deploy his reserve of 3rd RTR and 8th Rifle Brigade, but they were fouled up in traffic jams in the rear. Hence, the order came to Churcher to get 4th KSLI moving again in the darkness. Max Robinson, commanding 4th KSLI, 'bellyached' as he later put it, and tried in vain to get the order changed: 'It will be realised that this was quite a tall order to receive, just as the Battalion, tired out by the day's exertions, was settling down and sorting itself out for the night.'[61] Churcher and Roberts pressed O'Connor to relent; he would not and assured his forces that latest intelligence indicated that the enemy had withdrawn, though it is far from clear how real this information actually was. Ned Thornburn, 4th KSLI, recalled:

> I don't know what information the Corps commander can have had. I doubt if it was more than a pious hope! But the real trouble was that the CO was not given any indication of the vital nature of this operation.
>
> Had we known that it was an attempt to cut off the Germans' lateral supply route and so unhinge his whole defensive position, we would have been much more ready to take the enormous gamble involved.[62]

In reality O'Connor could not have known on the evening of 30 July that the situation would develop as successfully as it did, but it does illustrate his drive and determination to push his troops, when necessary, to exploit an opportunity, perhaps something that Bucknall had lost. The 4th KSLI grudgingly shuffled off into the night and, despite the hazards and darkness, reached their allotted positions. Supported by tanks of 2nd Fife and Forfar Yeomanry, they pressed home a textbook assault which secured St Martin by 1100 on 31 July, against some initially determined opposition. The assault was further aided by the arrival of 3rd RTR and 8th Rifle Brigade from the north.[63] The whole German position in the VIII Corps sector now started to collapse. They were caught out by the sudden capture of Saint-Martin, principally because of the opening into the German lines that the capture of the town afforded to the British. As the battle for Saint-Martin progressed, reconnaissance elements of the 2nd Household Cavalry had been probing for weaknesses in the German positions with little success until an armoured car and a Dingo scout car, led by Captain Dickie Powle, slipped past the befuddled German defenders; they then drove southwards for some six miles and located a bridge crossing over the River Souleuvre, potentially opening up a route to Bény-Bocage, a key objective on high ground. Upon reaching the bridge Corporal Bland, commanding the Dingo scout car, recalled:

> It was decided that I should have a crack at crossing it, covered by the armoured car. It worked, and after quickly dismounting we slipped up behind a German sentry and quietly finished him off. We had to dispose of any such visitors in a similar way otherwise we were sunk as there was not a hope of holding any numbers off with just the two cars if the warning went off.[64]

Radio communication across such distances through rolling wooded terrain was difficult, but eventually the information was relayed to the main British forces which speedily pressed home the advantage. Roberts' 11th Armoured Division were soon rumbling southwards and as the day progressed they threw the whole German front into a ferment. The Germans were in part caught out because the line of advance taken by 11th Armoured was straight down the divisional and indeed army boundaries between the German 3rd Parachute and 326th Infantry Divisions and Seventh Army and Fifth Panzer Army. For once the Germans had erred and left the area largely uncovered; whilst they bickered over who should deal with it and how, 11th Armoured drove ever onwards. In the west the Germans were forced to fall back, allowing US V Corps to push forward on the immediate flank of the 11th Armoured Division. To the east O'Connor switched the intended line of advance of the Guards Armoured Division to one through St Martin, with 15th Scottish providing flanking support until such time as XXX Corps was able to get moving forward – VIII Corps were clearly now driving the strategy. Equally dynamic progress was set out in objectives for Roberts on 1 August by O'Connor, but Roberts was increasingly concerned that his division was out on a limb, his leading troops were now exposed on both flanks. Around midday he discussed the situation with the Australian journalist Chester Wilmot, who was reporting on the campaign and who later stated: 'He knew then that he had Beny Bocage but he said to me, "I'm not telling Corps this yet as they'll want us to go somewhere else." '[65] Wilmot thought this prevarication baffling, but did note that two days later O'Connor admitted that the position was not as fluid as he had originally thought. The troops who entered Beny Bocage were greeted by ecstatic crowds, as Noel Bell, 8th Rifle Brigade, recalled: 'Everybody was either shouting, waving, cheering, clapping, kissing one another, singing the "Marseillaise" or doing the whole lot at once.'[66]

It perhaps mattered that Beny Bocage had been little affected by the war so far, hence the contrast with receptions in other towns and villages which had been severely mauled by the fighting.

The advance of the Guards Armoured Division on 1 August, between 11th Armoured and 15th Scottish Divisions, struggled to make headway through the traffic jams caused by the other formations, and they then ran into more determined opposition in the form of the remaining elements of 21st Panzer Division. Progress was limited. Some officers in 11th Armoured regarded the progress of the Guards as somewhat disappointing compared to their own.[67]

Although British progress on 1 August was more limited than during the previous forty-eight hours, the Germans were well aware that their front was in ruins: 326th Infantry Division had effectively ceased to function and 21st Panzer Division was threatened with a similar disaster. Hans von Kluge, commanding German operations in the west, had few resources now left to play with and faced looming calamitous situations against both the Americans and the British. Which presented the greater threat? He was forced to decide between dispatching II Panzer Corps from the Caen sector to shore up Seventh Army as it battled to stem the American flow in the west or to deal with Second British Army's drive from Caumont. A collapse against the British courted total disaster in the west too, as all German forces there would be threatened from the rear if the Vire-Vassy area was overrun, so von Kluge had little option but to commit General Wilhelm Bittrich's II Panzer Corps to confront Second British Army to the south of Caumont.[68] The removal of this force from the area south of Caen would aid First Canadian Army's Operation TOTALIZE which launched a week later.

The German reinforcements could not begin to intervene forcefully until late on 2 August. Until then the Vire-Vassy road which lay to the south of Beny Bocage and which constituted a crucial east-west supply and communications route, as well as the major town of Vire itself, lay at the mercy of the Allies. Roberts decided that he must push on and that by waiting for his flanks to be secured he would pass up an opportunity to compromise the German position still further; he therefore pressed on southwards, taking a calculated risk. Matters were complicated by the terrain and the main network of communications routes which ran contrary to the intended line of advance desired by 11th Armoured. Roberts and his two brigadiers, Jack Churcher and Roscoe Harvey, had also decided in the aftermath of GOODWOOD that key geographical objectives in themselves, such as the Vire-Vassy road, were not necessarily the most appropriate places to halt and form up; it made much more sense to deploy advance units in accordance with physical terrain principles, such as on the Perriers Ridge which lay just to the north of the road and would provide dominating positions overlooking the local area. Seizing this position would allow forward units to attack traffic on the road but also to remain safely within range of supporting heavy artillery to be able to beat off likely German counter-attacks.[69] By midday leading units of 11th Armoured had pushed within sight of the Vire-Vassy road. They had been aided by diminishing opposition and by local French farmers who had marked out the positions of mines laid by the Germans. Lieutenant William 'Steel' Brownlie's troop from 2nd Fife and Forfars eventually reached the road and took up defensive positions, closing the route to the Germans, despite being mistakenly strafed by American fighter-bombers. More tanks later arrived, but the position was not tenable without serious reinforcement and this was not immediately forthcoming. By nightfall all but Brownlie's troop were pulled back to Perriers Ridge, much to the chagrin of Brownlie himself.[70]

Though 11th Armoured had seized the Perriers Ridge, Vire itself was not quickly captured. Dempsey had instead turned VIII Corps southeast, leaving Vire to the Americans as it lay in their sector, which Roberts, who believed the town to be at his mercy at that time, found particularly frustrating.[71] With the arrival of units of II Panzer Corps, opposition to the British intensified and 11th Armoured, though giving as good as they got, decided to dig in. O'Connor wanted more infantry brought forward to stiffen the defence of the salient and was concerned by the exposed eastern flank of VIII Corps, a consequence of XXX Corps' sluggish progress. Desperate battles ensued over the next few days as the Germans repeatedly tried to throw the British back from their newly won positions, but with no real success. Major J.J. How later wrote on the defence at Le Grand Bonfait by 4th KSLI and 3rd RTR:

> The attack burst with an unnerving shriek of falling missiles. The flash of exploding shells and mortar bombs darted erratically about the branches of the trees. Detonations shattered the air. Earth and stones fountained up, showers of leaves fluttered down. The tank crews were caught outside their tanks. With so much metal flying about they could only hug the earth . . . Then the din stopped as suddenly as it started.
>
> A distant sound impinged on the exaggerated silence, the faint clatter of tracks and the sound of running engines. There was a shot. A dozen or more tanks were advancing across the field towards them. There were fleeting glimpses, too, of infantrymen working their way forward using available cover.[72]

Repeated support from corps artillery underpinned the defence of the units of 11th Armoured and after three to four days of heavy fighting the pressure slackened as German units began to fall back in a general retreat to the Orne, with the intention of holding the line from the Bourguébus Ridge to Vire via Mont Pinçon.

This coincided with the growing momentum of XXX Corps' push south-east supported by XII Corps operations still further east. On 4 August 50th Northumbrian Division was at last able to capture Villers-Bocage which had been held by the Germans since 14 June, in the aftermath of the abortive Operation PERCH. There was little left to see of the town, which had been repeatedly hammered by Allied artillery and air strikes. The Desert Rats now maintained the push following the retreating Germans through the smoking ruins of Aunay-sur-Odon, where only the church and one other building were still standing, though they too were reduced to shells. Such was the damage that the Royal Engineers and Pioneers had to carry out a series of clearance actions before the vehicles of the division could carry on. The whole area was littered with decaying cattle and German corpses, with mines and booby traps lavishly deployed to hinder the advancing British.[73] Condé-sur-Noireau was the next objective but Mont Pinçon still had to be captured and that task was allocated to 43rd Wessex Division supported by 8th Armoured Brigade.

Initially expected to achieve this task by 1000 hours on 6 August, the battalions of the 43rd Division, now badly depleted after the heavy fighting over the past week, made only slow progress. It was a stiflingly hot day and the fighting was grim and intense, with the soldiers combatting the sun, thirst, hunger, the terrain and fatigue as well as the Germans. The 5th Wiltshires, despite being effectively reduced to two companies, battled forward to the westerly slopes of Mont Pinçon. Their commanding officer soon became a casualty and by late in the afternoon only 63 riflemen were left in action from the entire battalion of some 800 men.[74]

Consequently, it was to be the 4th Wiltshires that would take up the assault to the summit, but by 1800 they were still some 2 miles away from the starting point, and in a bold move Lieutenant Colonel Vincent Dunkerly commanding the tanks of 13/18th Hussars acting in support of 43rd Wessex Division, decided to push a force of Shermans up on to the slopes as quickly as possible, leaving the infantry to catch up later. Captain Noel Denny of A Squadron was therefore confronted with an assault denuded of infantry support, despite the lessons of the previous two months of fighting that intimate co-operation was fundamental to success:

> Therefore, realising that it would almost certainly be my job to command the half-squadron which would carry out the patrol, I viewed the future with the gravest of concern and gloom. However, hope, as ever, springing

> eternal in the human heart, I set off with Lieutenant Elliott's and Lieutenant Jennison's troops to patrol to the top.[75]

They eased up to the top of Mont Pinçon against little opposition and sat it out, awaiting the infantry that followed up later that evening, despite counter-attacks by German troops attempting to cut off the approach to the base of Mont Pinçon.[76] Alongside their achievement stood that of 4th Battalion Somerset Light Infantry, which infiltrated up on to the summit, bypassing German infantry in the murk of the later evening. Lieutenant Sydney Jary wrote:

> A cold and damp mist descended which with the fading light, gave us welcome cover but also wretched discomfort. We were still in our shirt-sleeves, which became damp from the sweat of our exertion climbing the steep lower slopes. Alert, with pistol in hand, I anticipated a sudden brush with an enemy post. Not a shot was fired. By some miracle we passed right through their positions without being detected. Our luck had changed.
>
> Up the hill we scrambled, through the trees, until we reached the rocky gorse-covered summit. Through the mist German voices could be heard calling to each other, unaware that by stealth we were now king of the castle.[77]

Private O'Connell recalled: 'If one braved the still falling mortars, bullets and occasional shells one could see a great view of France that was won, and the France still to be fought for.'[78] Far from relying on unimaginative and trusted methods of firepower-assisted assaults, both 13/18th Hussars and 4th Somersets had employed intuitive methods of infiltration and the success was consolidated the following day.

By the morning of 7 August, VIII, XXX and XII Corps had driven the Germans back towards the Orne, capturing Vire and Mont Pinçon. The fighting was bitter, perhaps the hardest and nastiest of the campaign.[79] But BLUECOAT was a great success, demonstrating that British forces could exploit German failings as ruthlessly as the Americans, and show dash and *élan* when required. The dramatic and forceful push of VIII Corps to the Beny-Bocage Ridge and then on to the Vire-Vassy road threatened the German position in Normandy to such an extent that von Kluge was forced to draw troops away from the Caen-Falaise sector. The attempted mustering of remaining forces for the Germans' disastrous Operation LÜTTICH, the so-called Mortain counter-offensive, was also seriously hampered by the threat posed by BLUECOAT's success. As the pressure from BLUECOAT intensified, the Germans committed the best part of four panzer divisions, two Tiger battalions, a Nebelwerfer brigade and three batteries of 88mm guns to the sector. BLUECOAT's contribution to victory in Normandy is not in doubt, but its place in defeating the Germans has been masked by the success of COBRA, the innovation of TOTALIZE and the denouement of the Falaise Pocket.

The campaign had moved increasingly quickly since the end of July, and with the success of BLUECOAT, and more obviously COBRA, the German position had started to collapse. Matters were not helped for von Kluge and his staff when they were committed by Berlin to prosecuting Operation LÜTTICH. As these German forces headed west to attack the Americans, their commanders knew they were heading for disaster but could do little to stop it. As a beacon of the dysfunctional nature of the German defence of France, the Mortain counter-offensive stands out above all others; it also illustrates the superiority of the Allies' chain of command, strategic accountability and political integration.

With the Germans therefore committed to the deployment of many of their remaining functioning units to western Normandy, propelling them further into the closing jaws of a trap, the pressure on the Allies to catch and destroy as many of them as possible became paramount. To the south General George Patton's Third US Army continued to hurry eastwards whilst General Courtney Hodges' First US Army absorbed the German offensive at Mortain. To the northwest Second British Army followed up BLUECOAT with a general push towards the River Orne and beyond. There remained the northern flank of the Allied forces, First Canadian Army, under the tutelage of Harry Crerar. Montgomery and the 21st Army Group staff now responded to the unfolding situation in Normandy by committing Crerar's forces to a drive southeast from Caen towards Falaise.

Crerar's army, although Canadian led, was a multinational amalgam of Polish, British and Canadian units, and it was this force that was to drive the Germans back southeastwards from the Bourguébus Ridge. The operational command fell to II Canadian Corps under the leadership of Lieutenant General Guy Simonds, a commander still smarting from the reverse suffered by the Canadians, and his reputation, in Operation SPRING. Conscious as Simonds was of certain self-evident shortcomings and weaknesses in Anglo-Canadian methods, his concept for the new operation, codenamed TOTALIZE and planned to begin on the night of 7–8 August, was radically different from previous 21st Army Group actions. Crerar had already started the process of rethinking how future operations might be conducted in a tactical appreciation issued to First Canadian Army on 22 July, but it was Simonds who drove the innovation.[80]

There were two fundamental principles behind TOTALIZE. First, Simonds recognised that the depth of German defences had repeatedly confounded Allied offensives and that any plan would have to take account of this; second, that in order to penetrate the first line of German defences quickly, tactical surprise was crucial, especially as the ground favoured the highly effective long-range anti-tank guns of the defenders. Consequently, Simonds' plan was to be a two-stage offensive, with a highly dangerous night-time advance through the primary German defences followed by a morning consolidation, before a heavy air strike blasted a further path through the remaining German lines, opening up a relatively clear route towards Falaise. Large-scale night offensives were generally eschewed as being too dangerous and far too difficult to coordinate. TOTALIZE attempted to circumvent this by deploying the initial break-in forces in deep, closely compacted columns of tanks, armoured vehicles and transports, which would push through the German defences in the darkness in conjunction with the first phase of bombing. The Germans, expecting a daybreak assault, would be at a low level of readiness at night, and by using various navigational aids such as searchlights, flares and radio beams, the advancing Anglo-Canadian troops would be through the German lines and in position ready for action at first light around the enemy positions. In order to overwhelm the Germans entrenched in villages and woods quickly, immediate Allied infantry support would be essential, and to facilitate this the infantry would be carried forward in converted fully tracked vehicles or armoured personnel carriers, as well as the other usual forms of cross-country capable transports, so that they would be definitely and immediately on-hand at first light to conduct assault and mopping-up operations.

That TOTALIZE was to receive the support of these valuable and scarce newly developed armoured personnel carriers, previously denied to O'Connor for GOODWOOD, indicated the relative expectations: TOTALIZE was considered to be a genuine breakthrough operation, unlike GOODWOOD. A second grouping of infantry would follow up, pin and then eliminate the German forward lines in order to allow the Allies' exploitation forces to advance rapidly into position on the morning of 8 August. Simonds believed that tactical surprise would be complete, and that genuine exploitation towards Falaise and possibly beyond was likely.[81] The second phase of the operation would then see two armoured divisions drive through the path blasted by the midday aerial bombardment, which would paralyse the remaining German defences. This was an aspect of the plan that Simonds thought essential especially as, in the days leading up to TOTALIZE, he had erroneously interpreted the late removal of 1st SS Panzer Division from the front line of German defences as an indication of the strengthening of this second line.[82]

The main British component of TOTALIZE was to consist of 51st Highland Division and 33rd Armoured Brigade, which together would form the eastern of the two deep columns intended to prosecute the night advance on 7–8 August. The western column would consist of Canadian troops and the two exploiting formations would be the 4th Canadian and 1st Polish Armoured Divisions, neither of which had yet seen battle. Richard O'Connor was greatly enthused by Simonds' approach and heartily supported it to Montgomery.[83]

Ahead of II Canadian Corps, initial German opposition would be provided by 89th Infantry Division, a formation of mixed troops of lower grade and questionable staying power formed just a year earlier in Norway. But backing them up would be Kurt Meyer's 12th SS Panzer Division, whilst 1st SS's position was thought by the Allies to be close enough to allow intervention. Allied intelligence inferred that the two SS divisions could now muster some 3,500 infantry and 160 tanks, of which fifty might well be Panthers. The fifty 88mm guns of III Flak Corps would also present a serious obstacle, but information on the Tiger tanks in the sector was scant.[84]

There is no doubt that the Allies held considerable advantages in resources and capabilities on the night of 7 August. Many decades later in the 1980s Soviet officers touring the battlefields of Normandy, as guests of the British Army, perused the TOTALIZE plan and announced that their preferred method of getting the job done quickly would have been to threaten the commanders of TOTALIZE with execution if they did not reach Falaise by the end of 8 August. Fortunately for Guy Simonds such draconian tactics were not standard in 21st Army Group in 1944.[85]

For the assembling troops on 7 August, although the weather was pleasant, their surroundings after so many battles and bombardments were not: 'It was a scene of dreadful desolation; a landscape of grey-white craters dominated by the tattered skeletons of the factories, crushed and tossed about by weeks of every sort of bombardment.'[86] For the troops of 51st Highlanders, TOTALIZE offered some opportunity to recover morale after the annoyance inflicted by Montgomery's sacking of Major General Charles Bullen-Smith as their GOC (General Officer Commanding), and the questions raised about the formation's fighting abilities. The new commander, Tom Rennie, proved to be a popular and effective choice, but as one Highlander claimed, it was TOTALIZE that put them back on their feet again.[87]

In the late hours of 7 August the armoured units began to form up. The columns were led by two navigation tanks, followed by mine-clearing Sherman Crabs using flails, whilst the tanks of the armoured regiments deployed four-wide behind them. The embussed infantry followed in their variety of armoured transports. The British forces formed up in two such columns, the east column consisting of 1st Northants Yeomanry and 1st Black Watch, the west 144th and 148th Royal Armoured Corps (RAC) with 7th Argyll and Sutherland Highlanders and 7th Black Watch, respectively. At 2300 hours the bombers began their attacks with a bombline 1,000 yards ahead of the columns – there were no friendly-fire incidents.[88] Forty-one minutes later the artillery bombardment kicked off and shortly afterwards the armoured columns began trundling forwards, initially keeping quite good order, despite the shortcomings of some of the navigational aids. The Bofors tracer streams lancing forward on to the objectives to guide the troops appeared to interfere with magnetic compasses, whilst 144th RAC could not locate the radio beams and 1st Northants Yeomanry found it to be a distraction. The air was thick with dust and smoke as well as being shrouded in darkness and the rate of 1–2 mph was slow walking pace. There was mixed German resistance and a sprinkling of tanks and armoured vehicles became casualties, though some fell foul of navigational indiscretions and terrain difficulties. When a 1st Northants Sherman was hit and disabled, Trooper Ken Tout later wrote:

> A louder crash once, twice, thrice. A fan of fire shoots high into the sky, silhouetting a distant Sherman tank. Tiny figures of crewmen come squirming from its turret like maggots out of a ripe Camembert cheese. A new puff of fire lifts the turret into the air. Then there is only a Roman Candle of flame spurting the usual fireworks.[89]

Yet the advance, in darkness, described by one participant as 'a bloody silly idea', achieved its objectives with only minor inconvenience. Lieutenant Colonel John Hopgood commanding 1st Black Watch was somewhat surprised by the success: 'Fuck me! We've arrived.' The British column seized 130 prisoners and suffered only 40 casualties.[90]

To the west the Canadians were less successful but by midday on 8 August five out of seven columns had secured their objectives while the remaining two were not far off. Behind them two of the five objectives for the follow-up foot infantry had been captured, with the others being won as the afternoon progressed. At the cost of 380 casualties TOTALIZE had achieved a penetration of the German front five miles wide by four miles deep. The British and Canadian troops consolidated their positions and awaited the expected

German counter-attacks. To the rear, units of 1st Polish and 4th Canadian Armoured Divisions began advancing to be ready to follow up the second wave of bombing due in the early afternoon.[91]

The German response was panic-stricken, for far from having a stoutly defended second line which remained to be breached by the Allies, as Simonds had expected, the initial TOTALIZE assault had ruptured the German defences in the sector. The Allies were unaware of this development, but even if they had been, they were not in an appropriate position to exploit it; the second phase of bombing was due a little after midday and such a commitment could not readily be cancelled at such short notice. Previous experience in Normandy, during GOODWOOD especially, had demonstrated the necessity of suppressing the deep defences of the Germans, particularly across open ground when the enemy's superior long-range gunnery could be brought to bear; the second phase of TOTALIZE would take place across such terrain towards high ground on which it was expected there would be arrayed a line of 88mm anti-tank guns ready to stop dead any armoured assault, as had occurred on 18 July in GOODWOOD. Quite simply, as there was no evidence to the contrary and every reason to suspect that the Germans had a hostile welcome ready for the Allies a little to the south, the second phase of bombing was still a vital necessity: only with the benefit of hindsight can a continuing push southwards throughout the morning of 8 August be viewed as a possible stratagem, and ultimately an unsustainable one as the troops were in no position to continue the push at that time.

Kurt Meyer, commanding 12th SS Panzer Division, was observing the Allies in the late morning of 8 August from positions at Urville and Cintheaux and, realising the parlous state of the German defences, ordered whatever forces were available to launch immediate counter-attacks, however sporadic and uncoordinated, in an effort to buy time for the Germans to reform their lines broadly along the position of the River Laison to the south. Meyer paints an implausibly colourful picture of these moments, including shaking the hand of Michael Wittman just before the esteemed tank ace headed north around noon to lead his Tigers into battle against the Anglo-Canadian forces. Meyer also wrote of rallying fleeing troops of 89th Infantry Division by sheer force of personality. In 1947 it was reported to British officers studying the TOTALIZE operation that:

> Meyer calmly lit a cigar, stood in the middle of the road and in a loud voice asked them [the retreating Germans of 89th Division] if they were going to leave him alone to cope with the Allied attack. One look at this

> impressive thirty-five-year-old Commander was enough and the men turned around.[92]

Such nonsense helped to build the image of Meyer as a dynamic and inspirational leader to be admired, despite his remaining an unrepentant Nazi to his final days. The troops of 89th Division saw it differently and greatly resented the power of the SS. Prisoners later captured on 9 August claimed: 'Yesterday morning the SS with pistols in their hands drove us into battle with the cry – "Push on, you dogs" – threatening to shoot our corporal because he did not advance fast enough with his group.'[93] Meyer and others later condemned the troops of the 89th Division for giving up on 8 August, but a number of units stubbornly held out well into the afternoon, most obviously in Tilly-la-Campagne, despite confronting overwhelming odds. Meyer also later castigated the Allies for apparently halting for no good reason that morning; he argued that the Allied front-line commanders were held back by the timetable acrobats in the planning staff and that it was simply not possible to lead an armoured assault from behind a desk in this manner. The latter point in other circumstances was entirely valid, but so is the point that it is not the place of the divisional commander physically to lead attacks; he is there to command the division's entire efforts, something Meyer repeatedly failed to grasp as many of his fellow senior commanders noted.[94]

Meyer also claimed that upon seeing an Allied aircraft dropping flares as markers for the oncoming heavy bombers, he acted quickly and decisively, and by advancing his counter-attacking forces immediately he saved them from the bombers. This is once again quite fanciful as the forces that acted in response to Meyer's initiative were already safely between the Allied forces and the bombline set just under a mile ahead of the leading Anglo-Canadian troops. What appeared to Meyer to be a consequence of his initiative and dynamism was in fact mere coincidence, though naturally Meyer never seems to have revised his view that his leadership saved the day for the Germans.[95]

Two counter-attacks ordered by Meyer assaulted the British forces that lunchtime, one led by Hans Waldmüller, the other by Wittman. The latter's attack amounted to a headlong charge by largely unsupported Tigers directly up the Caen-Falaise road straight into the teeth of the Anglo-Canadian forces. In one of the more famous incidents of the campaign five of the seven Tigers, including Wittman's, were picked off by 17-pdr-equipped Sherman Fireflys, though it remains unclear as to precisely who accounted for Wittman himself.[96] In the space of twelve minutes, Trooper Joe Ekins of 1st Northants Yeomanry fired the gun that destroyed three Tigers as his Firefly manoeuvred around orchards just south of Saint Aignan; his troop commander Captain

Boardman later described it as 'rather like practice no. 5 on the ranges at Linney Head'.[97] In a prime example of the advantages conferred by firing from defensive positions, even against heavily armoured opponents, the Northants Yeomanry, together with fellow units to the northwest, stopped the German attack dead in its tracks. Joe Ekins later stated: 'I had never heard of Wittman; didn't know who he was. It was six-to-seven years after the war before I knew what had happened.'[98] Ekins never directly claimed the 'kill' of Wittman, but many believed his gunnery had been responsible. He eschewed the attention that the fighting south of Caen brought his way for many years, and later stated to friends in the Northants Yeomanry that he wished he had 'never killed the bastard'.[99] Paradoxically, Ekins never fired a gun again, subsequently being moved into the radio-operator's role.

Further east, Waldmüller's attack was better coordinated, consisting of 20 tanks and some 200 soldiers. The fighting was fierce but the British prevailed, the Germans once again employing increasingly futile and desperate tactics:

> Shortly before 1400 hours the enemy infantry assault started. They advanced in mass formation, line abreast on a front of 1000 yards. The cornfields were black with them. The Squadron's Brownings opened up, everyone peppering away as hard as he could. The infantry went to ground . . . and crawled through the corn to the nearest place of safety. Many of them were observed in a wood which was heavily shelled and machine gunned by our tanks and shortly set on fire.[100]

Despite some success in accounting for 20 Shermans of the Northants Yeomanry, the attack petered out and was back on its start line before TOTALIZE Phase II had even started. Kurt Meyer always believed that his aggressive actions in ordering frantic counter-attacks against the Anglo-Canadians in the early afternoon of 8 August bought his countrymen enough time to stabilise the line and enabled them to repel the second phase of TOTALIZE. But this was a gross misreading of the situation; the counter-attacks did not delay the second phase at all, which began on time at 1355 hours. Yet TOTALIZE did indeed stall that afternoon, despite the very promising impact of Phase I. The anticipated exploitation by 1st Polish and 4th Canadian Armoured Divisions fell well short of expectations, with the latter advancing just 2.5 miles by dusk, the former a hugely disappointing mere mile or so.[101]

The Poles were confronted by a series of difficulties and complained of limited manoeuvring space, the effects of friendly-fire short bombing during the air attack, and having to assault a largely intact German defensive line. Simonds attempted to push his armoured commanders throughout the day, hectoring and badgering, arguably excessively micromanaging the situation. He even reputedly castigated the Poles for communicating in Polish rather than English, preventing him from assessing the ebb and flow of the battle. By nightfall Simonds was fuming and sought explanations.[102]

Undoubtedly, short bombing, which inflicted 315 casualties on Canadian and Polish troops assembling for Phase II, was a contributory factor, along with inexperience, as the great majority of these soldiers were entering battle for the first time. Some failure in communication and level of artillery support further hindered the advance and contributed to the cautious pace. The lines of advance were also quite constricted for the proper deployment of armour – both George Kitching (commanding 4th Canadian) and Stanislaw Maczek (commanding 1st Polish) had lobbied Simonds for more manoeuvring space in the planning of TOTALIZE but had been refused. Kitching's job was not aided by his finding one of his brigadiers asleep in his tank, possibly the worse for drink.[103] The Poles, though often experienced soldiers, had never fought together as the 1st Polish Armoured Division, and furthermore quickly advanced into a killing zone where they lost 40 tanks in short order; it was an initiation that inhibited their offensive spirits for a time. Lieutenant Tomasz Potorowski stated that:

> There was a certain lack of experience in the two armoured division entering the battle for the first time, but the major reason for the limited terrain gains obtained was the depth of the German defences unexpected at Army Group level.[104]

Some British troops in the area also found the Poles to be a disorderly and ill-disciplined bunch, nonetheless.[105]

Simonds' frustration led him to drive his units forward in darkness on the night of 8–9 August with mixed fortunes. Most infamously, a combined force of armour and infantry commanded by Lieutenant Colonel Don Worthington became horribly lost and isolated in the darkness behind enemy lines, and was destroyed the following day. Some further progress was managed throughout the day and on the night of 9 August, but the failure to secure Quesnay Wood, which was powerfully and obdurately defended by the Germans, continued to hinder TOTALIZE and by 10 August the operation had effectively blown itself out.

Whilst the British contribution was smaller in TOTALIZE, it nevertheless serves to consider the overall impact of Simonds' plan. It cannot be denied that II Canadian Corps failed to translate the success of Phase I into an operational breakout in Phase II and for this TOTALIZE must be seen as a partial success at best. The Anglo-Canadians had again demonstrated an ability to adapt and innovate, but equally this still proved to be a work in progress; experience of battle underpins chances of success in action and the troops available to exploit in Phase II did not yet have that experience.

In spite of the tactical innovation and application of clear thinking on the part of Simonds' team, events conspired against 21st Army Group on 9 August to limit the potential impact of the operation. It is true that the Germans reacted quickly to repair their ruptured lines in the afternoon of 8 August, but there was never a real opportunity for the Allies to push faster than they did to exploit the hole that Phase I had created without attributing to them a greater level of prescience than could be reasonably expected. Perversely, in retrospect, the GOODWOOD plan may well have served the Allies better on 8 August and the TOTALIZE plan better on 18 July, but counterfactual history is a largely futile endeavour, even if fleetingly interesting. TOTALIZE was still a considerable success and provided a greater advance than other previous 21st Army Group operations. Its impact on the Normandy campaign should not be underrated, despite the lingering myths about missed opportunities, dynamic German leadership and convoluted timetables that continue to undermine its place in the defeat of the German forces in France. Shortcomings it may have had, but TOTALIZE was another significant step towards victory.

By 11 August the campaign in Normandy had once again shifted gear. First Canadian Army had at the time of TOTALIZE intended to push towards Falaise and then turn eastwards to the Seine with the intention of crossing at Rouen and helping to trap German forces west of the river and north of the Loire. But even as TOTALIZE began, Montgomery and Bradley were changing their plans towards a determined effort to ensnare as many of the German units still committed to the west of Falaise in a large battle of encirclement. First Canadian Army was therefore committed to a follow-up operation to TOTALIZE, codenamed TRACTABLE, with the objective of capturing Falaise itself, whilst in the south and to the west the American First and Third Armies pushed ever eastwards with the intention of enveloping the Germans.[106] Second British Army was to continue its push from the northwest following up the success of BLUECOAT by shepherding the retreating Germans into the jaws of the trap; there followed days of remorseless smaller-scale actions that maintained progress but at heavy cost. To the north XII Corps pushed through the sector that had been fought over during EPSOM and JUPITER towards Thury-Harcourt; further south and west XXX Corps battled on from Mont Pinçon towards Condé-sur-Noireau; and further west and south still, VIII Corps drove on south and east from the Vire-Vassy road towards Tinchebray. On 6 August mixed German forces pressed their final ever attack on VIII Corps in Normandy but were again repulsed and O'Connor's staff noted that organisation in the enemy forces was collapsing quickly, such was the plethora of mixed troops that were being encountered and captured.[107]

Some actions were relatively cost free. Brigadier Jack Churcher of 11th Armoured Division recalled the capture of Vassy, where the Germans had cleared all the civilians from the town as it was considered critically important to their strategic position: 'Now this was an eerie experience. There wasn't a living person or animal to be seen, not even a cat.'[108] Most actions were not so straightforward. Considered the most junior infantry division in Second Army, 59th Staffordshire Division in XII Corps had nonetheless battled hard in generally non-glamorous roles, but in early August its 176th Brigade in particular displayed grit, determination and intelligence in securing and holding a crossing over the River Orne facing Brieux and Grimbosq. Timed for 1845 hours on 6 August, just as Mont Pinçon was being captured, 176th Brigade employed decoy smokescreens to throw the enemy (mostly consisting of 271st Infantry Division) off the scent of where the real assault crossing was taking place. Two battalions, 6th North Staffs and 7th South Staffs, forced their way across the river despite heavy enemy machine-gun fire, and during the night engineers quickly constructed a Bailey bridge in the face of mortar fire. The brigade's third battalion, 7th Norfolks, moved across during the night to reinforce the position, along with two squadrons of Churchills of 107th RAC, and though the Norfolks lost a company which became isolated and then eliminated by the enemy, the British tightened their grip on the east side of the river. Two counterattacks took place that morning in an effort to dislodge the British from their position on the east of the Orne, the second at battalion strength; both were beaten off. Further reinforcements were pushed into the bridgehead to aid the Staffs battalions, but on the evening of 7 August a series of determined assaults by 12th SS Panzer Division began, spearheaded by Panthers. The North Staffs were driven back to within 200 yards of the bridge, but held, whilst Lieutenant Colonel Ian Freeland, commanding 7th Norfolks, noted that 'at no point were our positions penetrated', though few of the supporting Churchills were left running.[109]

That night Major General Lewis 'Lou' Lyne, commanding 59th Division, pushed another battalion of infantry across the river and the third squadron of Churchills of 107th RAC, though only 11 tanks got across the river.

1 The future Queen Elizabeth II visiting troops before D-Day. Such inspections were considered valuable in bolstering morale, particularly in an army lacking much combat experience.

2 King George VI visiting Montgomery at his HQ near Portsmouth in the days leading up to D-Day.

3 Montgomery speaking to the troops of 15th Scottish Infantry Division prior to D-Day. Monty saw such visits as being crucial in boosting the confidence and morale of his forces. He did not always win popularity with his troops, but he usually instilled confidence.

4 Sherman Duplex Drive 'swimming' tank, a useful support weapon on D-Day and in other amphibious operations such as the Rhine crossing in March 1945. The British were highly adept at building such specialist armour and this proved to be a decided advantage.

5 Royal Marine Commandos of 4th Special Service Brigade, making their way onto 'Nan Red' on JUNO Beach, at St Aubin-sur-Mer at about 9 am on 6 June.

6 Royal Army Medical Corps nurses and women of the Queen Alexandra's Imperial Military Nursing Service carry a wounded soldier out of the operating tent at the 79th General Hospital at Bayeux, 20 June 1944. Medical support in the British Army was excellent and much superior to that of the Germans.

7 Riflemen B. O'Neill, George Wood and Jack Pearson of 8th Rifle Brigade (11th Armoured Division) move forward cautiously on a patrol in the Baron and Eterville area south west of Caen, July 1944. Such patrols were fraught with danger but provided much useful intelligence on the enemy.

8 Churchill visits senior commanders in Normandy, July 1944. Montgomery was irked by the Prime Minister's insistence on coming to Normandy at the height of the campaign, but in the aftermath of the relative failure of Operation GOODWOOD had little option but to accept it. *Left to right*: Lieutenant General Guy Simonds (commander II Canadian Corps), Churchill, Lieutenant General Miles Dempsey (commander Second British Army) and Montgomery.

9 Major General Francis 'Freddie' de Guingand, Montgomery's right hand man at 21st Army Group. As well as acting as chief of staff, a specialised post developed by Monty, Freddie acted as the linkman with the Americans. Sadly de Guingand's health was not good and when he was absent with illness, relations with Eisenhower, SHAEF and other US generals deteriorated.

10 Mike Hutchinson of the Somerset Light Infantry receiving an MC from Montgomery. Although some troops viewed the awarding of medals with some cynicism, senior commanders saw it as a useful tool to underpin morale.

11 Lieutenant General Miles Dempsey (commander of Second British Army) and Air Vice Marshal Harry Broadhurst (commander of 83 Group, RAF). Dempsey and Broadhurst co-operated highly effectively in 1944–5 and tactical air support for British forces was usually of a high standard, though it was never as effective as many imagined.

12 Troops stacking jerrycans, July 1944. An excellent logistical and supply network was fundamental to the way in which the British Army waged war in 1944–5. Troops wanted for little and commanders endeavoured to ensure that their frontline soldiers were supported by a plentiful supply of equipment, ammunition and fuel.

13 Senior 21st Army Group staff officers, in effect Montgomery's brains trust throughout the campaign. Many had already seen service with Monty in the Mediterranean and he brought them back to Northwest Europe to co-ordinate and run 21st Army Group because they had proved capable and trustworthy. *Left to right*: Joe Ewart (interpreter), Charles Richardson (plans), Freddie de Guingand (chief of staff), David Strangeways (R-Force, deception), Edgar 'Bill' Williams (intelligence) and John Drummond Inglis (engineers).

14 Civilians ride on Cromwell tanks as the British enter Brussels, 4 September 1944. The lightning advance by British forces from Normandy to the Low Countries outstripped even the rates managed by the Germans in the blitzkrieg of 1940. Some British tanks may have suffered from certain weaknesses, particularly in firepower, but they were reliable and quick.

15 Residence Palace, Brussels, where 21st Army Group's administrative HQ was established in 1944. It was quite a contrast with Montgomery's much smaller tactical HQ which was much closer to the front.

16 Eisenhower (*second from right*) and Bradley (*far right*) confer with Montgomery. Relations with the Americans were not Montgomery's forte, and matters were made worse when Eisenhower took over strategic responsibility for the land campaign on 1 September 1944. Twice Eisenhower issued veiled threats that he would move to have Monty replaced unless he buckled down, and Bradley point-blank refused to serve under Montgomery ever again.

17 Montgomery in the depths of winter 1944–5. By January 1945 Monty was becoming weary of his squabbles with Eisenhower and Bradley, but there was still time for further bickering even after the Rhine had been crossed.

18 Ken Tout, Northants Yeomanry. Since the Second World War, Ken has written many books on the campaign, including the acclaimed *Tank!*

19 The Comet, designed and built in the UK, and probably the best British tank to see service in the campaign. Alas it only arrived in theatre at the very end of 1944 and did not see serious action until 1945.

20 Monty's chief of staff, Freddie de Guingand, with senior RAF commanders in Brussels, 1945. The British Army fully recognised the vital role played by the RAF in beating the Germans, but Monty still managed to fall out seriously with both Tedder and Coningham. *Left to right*: de Guingand, Arthur Tedder (Eisenhower's deputy at SHAEF), Charles 'Peter' Portal (Chief of the Air Staff), Harry Broadhurst (commander of 83 Group) and Arthur 'Mary' Coningham (commander of 2nd Tactical Air Force).

21 Reg Spittles has written up many accounts of his time in the army and his experiences in the 1944–5 campaign. His work in touring schools and in educating post-war generations in the realities of life in the British Army in 1944–5 continues well into the twenty-first century.

22 21st Army Group's senior commanders. Montgomery (*second row, fifth from the left*) is flanked to the right by Harry Crerar (First Canadian Army) and to the left by Miles Dempsey (Second British Army).

23 Command briefing for the Rhine crossing, Operations VARSITY and PLUNDER, March 1945. British staff work and planning was much improved by the 1944–5 campaign, underpinned by excellent intelligence and administration.

24 Crossing the Rhine, 24–31 March 1945. Men of 15th Scottish Infantry Division leave their assault craft after crossing the Rhine and double up the east bank to their assembly point near Xanten. The Rhine was crossed relatively easily as German strength had been broken weeks earlier in the bitter fighting of Operation VERITABLE (February to March 1945).

25 The final act: Monty accepts the surrender of the Germans at Lüneburg Heath, May 1945. The Field Marshal exploited these moments with unalloyed glee, ordering the German delegation about, belittling them and reducing one of them to tears.

Throughout the morning of 8 August the Germans launched a series of furious counter-attacks which caused the British great concern. During the fighting 107th RAC lost 22 tanks, 17 burnt out, but despite the best efforts of 12th SS Panzers, the bridgehead held and by the following day the British were throwing out patrols to begin a further push. The key elements to the success of the battle were artillery support and excellent wireless communication, as well as the resolute spirit of the infantry.[110] As Lieutenant Colonel Freeland later noted: 'If any of these comms had failed the artillery fire could not have been called for and the bridgehead overrun.'[111]

The scale of the German losses was significant. Major General Lyne informed 176th Brigade on 10 August that:

> The division are once more advancing and have captured 200 prisoners already today. The forest [de Grimbosq] is literally strewn with the bodies of men of the 12th SS Division, killed during their repeated counter-attacks which you so ably repulsed.[112]

One German PoW reported that of 400 men from 25th Panzer Grenadier Regiment that began the attack on the bridgehead on 8 August, only 30 remained by the evening.[113] The stout defence by formations considered to be 'junior' in the British Army in Northwest Europe demonstrated that when units followed organised and effective battle doctrines, they could show resolve, initiative and boldness. That the Germans considered the bridgehead over the Orne a major irritation was confirmed by their willingness to throw some of their best troops at the situation, but to no avail. The battles at Grimbosq once again demonstrated that the British had a successful and effective method for dealing with the Germans.

By 11 August troops of 53rd Welsh Division were on the outskirts of Thury-Harcourt and the town was captured during the following two days, opening the road to Falaise. To the south and west XXX Corps continued to battle on to Condé-sur-Noireau. Once again 50th Northumbrian Division was in the van and encountering the desperate rearguard actions of the Germans. This was no easy period of fighting. Lieutenant Colonel Robin Hastings, 6th Green Howards, recalled:

> The Germans met in the last fortnight had been quite different from those of the coastal divisions. They came mainly from 12th SS Hitler Jugend and 130th Panzer Lehr Divisions and were, on the whole, young men who had been brought up as Nazis and were prepared to die rather than surrender; they were determined fighters.[114]

The British were improving their battle techniques still further, and an assault by 8th Battalion Durham Light Infantry (151st Infantry Brigade, 50th Division) from Le Plessis-Grimault on the road to Condé on 9 August was considered to be one of the best prosecuted by the unit in the war, validating the doctrines outlined in training and those gleaned from experience. It was noted afterwards that:

> One hundred and twenty prisoners had been captured and many Germans killed. In contrast Battalion casualties had not been heavy, and it bore out the truth of the CO's conviction – that infantry are reasonably safe provided they keep right up with the barrage.[115]

The attack had been successfully supported by the tanks of 13/18th Hussars with whom 8th Durhams had never before cooperated, indicating the increasing flexibility of British troops. On 11 August the brigade was advancing once more, this time with 9th Battalion Durham Light Infantry leading, aided by the carriers of 8th Battalion. Despite initial confusion caused by enemy action in the forming-up area, the assault again proved successful and two companies overtook the supporting tanks, such was the pace of their advance.[116]

On 13 August 43rd Wessex Division took up the push to Condé, forcing a crossing of the River Noireau two days later. The 7th Battalion Somerset Light Infantry dispatched reconnaissance patrols that day, and in conjunction with local French civilians secured key tactical advantages over the enemy. The reconnaissance team was hindered by the enthusiastic welcome of the local population rather more than by enemy action:

> The hubbub was amazing; everyone seemed to have heard about it [the arrival of the British], except the Germans. Captain Baden persuaded them to go quietly away, but Madame, who turned out to be 'not at all bad looking', skipped behind the door with more joy than modesty and changed into her Sunday frock. Then she was photographed in front of house between the two 'Tommies' not two hundred yards from the Germans.[117]

The gathered intelligence aided the crossing that night and by 16 August the 43rd Division were firmly across the river. A dashing assault up hill towards the village of Berjou by 1st Worcesters supported by the Shermans of the Sherwood Rangers completed the rout of the enemy:

> Supported by a tremendous weight of artillery and mortar fire, they swept up the slope in perfect formation to see the village on the flat tableland four hundred yards ahead. Before them the shells poured down; from behind came the full blast of the Sherwood Rangers. Excitement ran high. This was too much for the enemy. The few who stayed to fight were wiped out. For the most part they fled as the companies stormed the village.[118]

By 16 August the Germans were in full retreat from Normandy, and the troops of Second British Army noted a falling-off in the levels of resistance as they herded the remaining German forces eastwards. Canadian troops were in the suburbs of Falaise; to the south US troops were pushing northwards from Argentan; and the British were in Condé and Flers. As Monty stated in a letter to James Grigg, Secretary of State for War, on 14 August:

> These are great days . . . We have the bulk of the German forces partially surrounded; some will of course escape, but I do not see how they can stand and fight seriously again this side of the Seine.[119]

Over the ensuing period, order in the German forces largely broke down as they fled eastwards to evade being ensnared by the various Allied armies manoeuvring around them. Command was in turmoil, hardly helped by von Kluge's disappearance for a day at the height of the battle. At last Berlin accepted that a general retreat eastwards was now justified. Field Marshal Walther Model was appointed by Hitler to assume command of forces in the west, arriving in Normandy on 17 August to relieve von Kluge who had reappeared the day before. Believing that he would be implicated in plots against Hitler, von Kluge took his own life en route to Berlin, after imploring the Führer to bring an end to the war.[120]

The Allies desperately attempted to close the gap through which the Germans were fleeing, initially between Falaise and Argentan, then at Trun and Chambois a few miles further east, and their failure to do so quickly has resulted in harsh scrutiny of Montgomery, Bradley, and the Canadian and Polish forces striking down to Falaise and beyond. Criticism of Montgomery has bordered on the ludicrous and once again demonstrates the hostile feelings he aroused in some of those around him. The reality is that the gap could have been closed faster and earlier than it eventually was on 21–22 August, but it would have put US troops at risk, perhaps even more so than the Poles who fought furiously to close the gap at Mont Ormel. In any case both Montgomery and Bradley were more interested in securing victory in the campaign as a whole, and this meant the first priority was to clear the Germans from all territory west of the Seine.[121]

Though more Germans escaped across the Seine than might have been hoped for, many factors lay behind this, not just the failure to close the neck of the Falaise Pocket a day or two earlier. The retreating Germans were subjected to intense air and artillery bombardment, and casualties were heavy. Though claims of tank kills by pilots were later shown to be greatly exaggerated, they undoubtedly inflicted immense damage to soft-skin vehicles, transports, artillery pieces and personnel. Royal Air Force analysts made the case that though few tanks were physically destroyed in the air attacks, many had been abandoned intact and this was probably owing to the collapse in morale of the retreating Germans, caused by the air strikes which, studies had demonstrated, had a more profound effect on soldiers' ability to fight than other forms of bombardment and combat. Such a claim proved impossible to substantiate and army operational researchers disputed it, arguing that a combination of factors caused the loss and destruction leading up to and through the notorious 'corridor of death' at Moissy Ford, the choke-point in the German route eastwards.[122]

British soldiers following up in the wake of the German retreat through this area were variously shocked and appalled at the level of destruction. Michael Carver, commanding 4th Armoured Brigade, at this time attached to II Canadian Corps, wrote on his troops' advance into the area south of Trun on 21 August: 'They advanced into a mass of dying horses, abandoned vehicles and dead and dying Germans . . . Carnage is the only word to describe it. It was a revolting sight, and the stench was indescribable.'[123] Troops of 5th Dorsetshire Regiment witnessed miles and miles of burnt-out tanks, cars and vehicles, many looted from the French; 'Carts with horses [illegible] 7th Army.'[124] One British soldier recalled:

> The bloated corpses of unfortunate domestic animals also lay in our path, so we took to the fields and tried to make some progress across country. Each spinney and copse contained its quota of dead Germans lying beside their wrecked vehicles, and once we came across the body of what had been a beautiful woman lying sprawled across the back seat of a staff car.[125]

The Allies were forced to use bulldozers and mass graves to bury the dead, both human and other animals, in order to try and contain the spread of disease. The Germans who had stubbornly and desperately held out in

Normandy for so long were forced to pay a heavy price in the final days of the collapse: some 10,000 were killed and 50,000 captured in the rout.

In the Normandy campaign the Germans suffered the breakdown and loss of two complete armies – the 7th and 5th – and by the time they had fled in disarray across the Seine little was left of either. Out of seven armoured divisions, as few as 1,300 men and just 24 tanks may have made it across the river; Hans Speidel, chief of staff in German Army Group B, believed that no more than 100 functioning tanks were left, and Model reported that of eleven infantry divisions he could now only muster just four units with a smattering of equipment. Edgar Feuchtinger, commanding 21st Panzers, saw his entire front-line strength of 167 tanks and self-propelled guns written off, along with the loss of 12,000 men and 350 officers; only some 300 made it across the Seine.[126] In total the Germans may have lost in excess of 300,000 troops in Normandy, compared to Allied losses of a little over 200,000. But even in the closing days of the fighting in Normandy the British still sustained heavy losses; between 13 and 21 August there were over 5,200 military casualties.[127]

Yet there can be no doubt that the Allied victory in Normandy was a stunning success and within a few days of the closing of the Falaise Pocket, Paris was liberated by French and American troops. In a flat-out pursuit Allied troops swept across the Seine, quickly making up for the apparent sluggishness of the drive inland from the bridgehead in July. Hope grew that the war might be finished in just a few weeks. The British Army had been involved in a vicious and hard-fought campaign, one in which their largely inexperienced troops had adapted quickly to the excesses of war. Their officers and NCOs had recast a range of tactical doctrines, and senior commanders had modified their operational methods to cope with the German strategy of digging in and slugging it out in a firepower-based attritional battle that made little sense. That the British Army rose to this challenge with a high degree of success says a good deal about its flexibility, adaptability and its modern attitude to warfare. Normandy was a campaign won by firepower, planning, logistics, intelligence and operational grip as much as if not more than by straightforward close-combat techniques. The British Army may have still been shaking out its tactical doctrines 'in theatre' in the summer of 1944, but its overall grasp of modern machine-age warfare had prevailed against the predominantly martial-based attitudes of the Germans – and it continued to do so, a few mishaps not withstanding, through to the end of the war.

7

PURSUIT
The Race to the Frontier

As spectacular as the success had been in crushing the German forces in Normandy, the task of defeating the Third Reich was far from over in August 1944. Even as the Allied forces were pummelling the fleeing German forces in and around the Falaise Pocket, it was still imperative that the impetus be maintained and every advantage be taken from the chaos inflicted upon the enemy. To that end on 20 August Montgomery ordered 21st Army Group to race to the Seine as quickly as possible. First Canadian Army, which included John Crocker's I Corps, was then to cross the river in the vicinity of Rouen, whilst Second British Army headed for the region further south between Mantes and Louviers. From there the British would head north across the River Somme towards Amiens and the Pas-de-Calais, whilst the Canadians secured Le Havre and its hinterland.[1] Speed was crucial in this phase of the campaign, as Montgomery stated even more emphatically six days later:

> Speed of action and movement is now vital. I cannot emphasise this too strongly; what we have to do must be done quickly. Every officer and man must understand that by a stupendous effort now we shall not only hasten the end of the war; we shall also bring quick relief to our families and friends in England by over-running the flying bomb launching sites in the Pas-de-Calais.[2]

In order to move as quickly as possible the British transferred the transport assets of VIII Corps to XII and XXX Corps to maintain momentum; any slackening in the pace would allow the Germans breathing space to reform and dig in, or at least provide stiffer resistance. Consequently Lieutenant General Brian Horrocks' XXX Corps was to drive flat out to force a crossing of the Seine at Vernon, halfway between Rouen and Paris, whilst Lieutenant General Neil Ritchie's XII Corps was to cross to the northwest between Les Andelys and Louviers.[3] Both corps commanders had things to prove. Horrocks had largely missed out on the Normandy campaign, not taking over XXX Corps until early August when the campaign had already swung decisively in favour of the Allies. His impact on the HQ of XXX Corps had been decidedly positive, but he had not tested his grip of command in Northwest Europe in the same way that O'Connor, Crocker and Simonds had. Neil Ritchie was one of those rarities in military history, a commander afforded a second chance. He had been over-promoted by Claude Auchinleck in the North African campaign, being given command of Eighth Army for a short time in 1942 before being sacked. But Ritchie was favoured by Brooke, Chief of the Imperial General Staff, and upon return to the UK was given a divisional and then corps command for OVERLORD.[4] During the fighting in Normandy, XII Corps had played a predominantly supporting role, but with the pursuit came the opportunity to flourish.

During this race to the Seine and then beyond, both corps had the crucial support of the Royal Engineers, which provided two columns of bridging troops with river-crossing equipment – 6th Army Troops Engineers for XII Corps and 7th for XXX Corps. In an excellent case of forward thinking and long-term planning inherent in the British Army of 1944, the techniques required for passing large formations of troops and equipment across major waterways in the face of the enemy had been carefully studied by the Royal Engineers in pre-OVERLORD planning; not for the British was the often ad hoc approach of the Germans. Lieutenant Colonel L.R.E. Fayle, 15th GHQ Troop Engineers (attached to XXX Corps), recalled:

> So far as I was concerned, crossing the Seine really began in the summer of 1943 when my formation carried out experiments and training on the assault crossing and bridging of a wide tidal river at Goole [Yorkshire] and later in the year when I was involved in the paper exercise OYSTER in which the tactical and technical problems of the assault crossing were considered.[5]

Stormboats, close-support rafts and specially designed bridging equipment had all been developed in the UK, and on 11 August the engineers, by then in Normandy, had renewed detailed planning for the crossing of the Seine. Each column working with the two British corps had 366 vehicles designed for the purpose of supporting a one-divisional front-assault river crossing.[6]

In the XXX Corps sector the task of breaching the Seine fell to 43rd Wessex Division, following the corps advance to the river that had been bizarrely named Operation LOOPY. The crossing itself had to negotiate forcing a route across a river over 600 feet wide and 10 feet deep. Fortunately, opposition was estimated to be limited and otherwise focused on watching the movements of American reconnaissance troops who had been spotted in the area since Third US Army had crossed the Seine to the south a few days before.[7] The assault would pass through Vernon itself, as the road routes to and through the town would facilitate a faster advance, prior to forcing the crossing to Vernonnet which sat on the steeply sloped far east bank. The attack would be led by the reinforced 129th Brigade supported by the Shermans of 15/19th Hussars, reconnaissance and artillery units, and the engineers themselves. Planning and assembly had been conducted at breakneck speed and with the aid of just one air-reconnaissance photograph. It was testament to the flexible and increasingly efficient staff work being carried out that such an operation with all its equipment and units could be mounted in such a short time and with limited intelligence. The column of troops raced for Vernon; drivers were told, 'interval as close as you can get. Speed – flat out.' They arrived in the town shortly after 1300, hours on 25 August and were deployed for action by late afternoon.[8]

The assault was to begin at 1900 hours on 25 August, but as ever in the moments before an attack an air of unreality pervaded the atmosphere. At 1845 hours Sergeant R.C. Hunt, Royal Engineers, was watching the scene:

> I was standing under the trees lining the boulevard running down towards the Seine and watching the precipitous wooded far side of the river mounting upwards from the little town of Vernonnet. It was hard to imagine that an assault crossing was imminent – blue sky, bright sunshine and a lazy peaceful atmosphere prevailed. French civilians stood around and chatted.
>
> Apparently the entire police force of Vernon and odd civilians had joined the Maquis. They had procured an ancient MG34 [German machine gun] and were firing this madly in the general direction of the Germans.[9]

There was to be a short fifteen-minute bombardment, followed by ten more minutes of firing in which a smokescreen would be created, to provide cover for the assaulting troops. The risks inherent in these tactics were soon apparent and it was the troops of 5th Wiltshires who initially suffered. Having already been ordered to unload their exceptionally heavy Stormboats too far from the water, precipitating a tiring run to the water's edge on foot, they then proceeded to tackle the crossing itself:

> Under a smoke screen the two leading boats set off, but both grounded on a submerged sandbank . . . At that moment the wind dispersed the smoke, the boats were raked with machine-gun fire and Lt Selby and all but three of his men were killed or drowned.[10]

In spite of such mishaps the crossing progressed, and the 4th Somersets encountered much less opposition. Once across, troops had to push on up to the high ground above Vernonnet in darkness, carrying heavy equipment up to and through the village itself, against largely unknown opposition. The experience of previous combat in Normandy paid off in Vernonnet, as Lieutenant Sydney Jary later wrote:

> The Germans were expert at holding off opposition with a screen of Spandaus supplemented by the odd sniper and this is what I suspected they were doing here. Inexperienced troops can be held up for hours by these delaying tactics . . . I had discovered that, by pushing on as fast as possible and bypassing machine-gun posts, the enemy's screen invariably collapsed.[11]

It still took until midday for the village to be cleared completely, but by the end of 26 August British units were firmly established on the heights and woods overlooking the Seine from the east bank. Below them the Royal Engineers worked furiously through the day and night, despite all opposition, to complete the bridges and rafts, and during the following day these rafts transported two squadrons of tanks across the river to support the infantry. The first bridge completed was a lightweight folding-equipment Class Nine bridge capable of supporting nine tons. They also began reconstruction of roadways to make up for the damage the heavy vehicles had caused to the existing network. Two Goliath Class Forty bridges, each 840 feet long and capable of carrying forty tons at 80-feet intervals, were in operation by the end of 28 August, the first taking just twenty-eight hours to complete, to support the advance being prosecuted by the British forces already across the river. By nightfall tanks of 11th Armoured Division began pouring across the Seine to begin the next stage of the advance. As the vehicles surged across, the engineers considered it to be 'a wonderful and rewarding sight'. Speed, efficiency and forward planning had contributed to the success of the operation, alongside the drive of the infantry in the initial assault. The British

Army's ability to keep their forces moving forward at a pace across major obstacles, even when the enemy had blown or damaged existing bridges, was fundamental to the speed of the advance from Normandy to the borders of Germany in less than a month.[12]

Further northwest, XII Corps was also forcing a crossing over the Seine in the Louviers area, spearheaded by 15th Scottish Division and 4th Armoured Brigade. The approach to the Seine had been hampered both by the movement of US XIX Corps, which was falling back southwards to conform to army boundaries, and also by the ecstatic nature of the welcome from French civilians. On 27 August reconnaissance of the immediate approaches to the river around Louviers was quickly spotted by a local civilian:

> 'Oh boys, am I glad to see you!' The speaker, a vision in the brightest of summer wear, was standing for all to see at the river's edge. Having shoo-ed the radiant lady away, the Brigadier [Colville] carried out his reconnaissance.[13]

The news of the arrival of the British troops had quickly spread through Louviers and a major reception erupted with a carnival, dancing and gramophone music. Major General Colin 'Tiny' Barber (at six feet nine inches tall) had only recently taken over command of the division from Major General Gordon 'Babe' MacMillan, following the injuries suffered by the latter during BLUECOAT, but Barber quickly grasped the situation, as did Ritchie himself who had visited the division that afternoon. Despite the risks inherent in attacking in daylight, 15th Scottish Division pushed its first troops across the Seine at 1900 hours in order to prevent the Germans from having sufficient time to form any kind of significant defensive line on the eastern bank. Initially the assault stalled as the first three stormboats were shot up by German machine guns and the attack halted. The failure of the Germans to blow up a road bridge on the left flank changed a difficult situation and this was rapidly seized by the Highland Light Infantry; Brigadier Colville quickly switched the thrust of the attack to this point and soon British troops were establishing themselves on the far bank. The following day further crossings were forced and the division was soon firmly across the river. Once again, planning was done on the hoof, risks were taken, and the effective work of the Royal Engineers and the military police in keeping the roads open and running were fundamental to the success.[14]

By 29 August, 4th Armoured Brigade and 53rd Welsh Division were streaming across the river and driving the advance against slackening opposition. The leading elements of 4th Armoured Brigade quickly advanced

20 miles to Gournay where they encountered some unsavoury Maquis (French Resistance fighters), who appeared more interested in catching women they regarded as having been too friendly with the Germans, shaving their heads and parading them through the streets of the town. Despite wanting to intervene, the British troops were under too much pressure to maintain the pace of the advance to do so.[15]

Once the British were across the Seine the next step was to press on north-east towards the Somme and then into the Low Countries. Speed was again of the utmost importance, but there were limits imposed on the number of units that could maintain this pace given the available transport and supply assets of the army. Although the army was relatively well stocked with supply and transportation vehicles, increasing numbers were being devoted purely to supplying front-line units from depots still back in Normandy; as the rapid advance continued so the supply lines became ever more stretched. The further from the beaches and small harbour facilities on the Norman coastline, the fewer the units that could be maintained for the pursuit, and there was little likelihood of this situation being resolved in the near future.

Consequently, 43rd Wessex and 15th Scottish Infantry Divisions were effectively grounded and left in possession of the bridgeheads across the Seine as the rest of the troops in XII and XXX Corps sped on. To the left Ritchie's XII Corps led by 7th Armoured Division and 4th Armoured Brigade headed for the Somme at Picquigny and Longpré west of Amiens, whilst XXX Corps pressed 11th Armoured Division and 8th Armoured Brigade towards the river at Amiens itself.[16] In another display of excellent mobility Guards Armoured Division was lifted by transporters from Condé 120 miles west of the Seine and brought forward and into action for the push to the Somme by 30 August; they eventually moved alongside 11th Armoured Division, having advanced in total some 200 miles in just two days.[17]

Second Army's race to the Somme and beyond was not the only significant activity undertaken by British troops following the collapse of German resistance in Normandy. Attached to First Canadian Army, I Corps, commanded by Lieutenant General John Crocker, was presented with the thankless task of helping to push the Germans back along the coast of the English Channel through Le Havre and towards the Pas-de-Calais. Crocker was under the command of Lieutenant General Harry Crerar with whom he had had an initially tetchy relationship, matters not being helped by Crerar's suggestion during their spat in July that Crocker be replaced by either Ritchie or Bucknall. Montgomery had knocked their heads together, but relations remained edgy. Crerar employed a more 'hands-off' role with Crocker, which allowed things to tick over. Crocker later confided to Dick O'Connor that:

> We have had quite an interesting war since we left you – not quite the sort I'd have chosen for myself, but it has had the merit of being an almost independent role all the way. Too close or intimate supervision by my particular authorities would have been irksome indeed. As it was, flash-point was nearly reached once or twice.[18]

Crocker was not the only British commander to grumble about the Canadians. In early September Major General 'Bubbles' Barker, commanding 49th Division, complained about how the British role in First Canadian Army was passed over. After advancing on Le Havre he wrote in his diary:

> 4 Sept: I'm fed up learning that the Canadians are mopping up the Le Havre peninsula and have asked JC [Crocker] to have it stopped and merely have credit given where due. The 49 Div have done everything and got across the Seine under very difficult circumstances.

The following day Barker asked the public relations staff to do something about the matter, but three days later was still unhappy:

> 8 Sept: I only wish we could leave this Canadian Army. They have such an inferiority complex that they concentrate almost entirely on themselves. It's maddening not to be able to deal with [Le Havre] any quicker.[19]

Yet in the pursuit along the Channel coast, the British and Canadians appeared to cooperate effectively enough, though the rate of advance was much more sedate in comparison to the breakneck speeds being managed by the armour of XII and XXX Corps, in part being caused by having to traverse four rivers before reaching the River Risle, the left tributary of the Seine. The 6th Airborne Division, still under I Corps command and fighting as ground infantry as they had been since shortly after D-Day, had little in the way of motorised transport to support a rapid advance and had to march some 45 miles to the Risle. Major General Richard Gale, commanding the division and mindful that they would soon be withdrawn to be re-equipped and replenished to fight again in future airborne operations, was determined to minimise casualties and followed up the retreating Germans carefully, largely just mopping up small pockets of resistance. Gale was aware that morale in 6th Airborne was suffering on account of the longevity of their stay on the ground in Normandy and he had had to order his officers to 'ginger up' their units to eliminate slackness.[20] It was noted that NCOs did not always meet these requirements, as one officer said:

> In spite of considerable efforts in the maintenance of discipline whilst the battalion was fighting a prolonged defensive battle, it was noticeable that NCOs in a few cases failed in their duties when the move forward began. There were many instances of such breaches as smoking on the march and falling out to drink by the wayside. NCOs need continual instruction in their responsibilities in the field.[21]

By the time the division was withdrawn on 27 August it had had enough. In the meantime alongside 6th Airborne, 49th West Riding, 51st Highland and 7th Armoured Divisions had advanced to the River Risle by 25 August.[22] Greater urgency might have been imposed from above, but Montgomery saw I Corps' advance as subsidiary to the main thrust of 21st Army Group. Yet the fighting was not without incident and units suffered significant casualties; the opposition, not as badly mauled as the German units further south who were fleeing the Falaise Pocket, was better organised. Often what might appear as simple actions soon developed into full battalion assaults due to the obduracy of some German units. Private Ted Castle, 2nd Glosters, recalled:

> Having a right do at Epaignes. When we took it the town was in flames. The Germans fought in the town and it was a real rough house. I can remember Frank Clark and B Company there in town. We lost a lot of lads there which kept the battalion weak. A Company was sent in to relieve B and D Company who were taking a hammering.[23]

Private Tommy Short, 49th Reconnaissance Regiment, recounted how the levity of the occasion was rapidly cut short when his armoured car and the surrounding civilians were brought under 20mm-gun fire:

> The vehicle caught fire almost immediately – the ammunition inside exploding into an inferno. My chum Roy Ogleby and Roberts were burnt to death but I managed to get the low side door open and fell to the ground wounded. Roberts was a tall quiet lad who spent most of his free time at the end of a day's fighting writing long letters to his wife.[24]

The Glosters suffered over 50 casualties in that one action, though they accounted for 58 Germans killed and five captured. British units eventually reached the River Risle where they forced a number of crossings using a combination of guile and directness, pushing the remnants of German 7th Army against the Seine in the Forêt de Brotonne. Barker, commanding 49th West Riding Division, was satisfied that the opposition was now at the point of collapse and ordered 56th Brigade to finish off the job. A series of RAF Typhoon air strikes prepared the ground and all three battalions of the brigade pushed into the forest. They were amazed to see the wreckage and remains of large quantities of German equipment that the enemy had been unable to ferry back across the Seine; neither had they been afforded sufficient time to lay booby traps or sabotage much of the abandoned kit. The 2nd Essex battalion history captured the moment: 'The Forêt de Brotonne proved to be what everybody had hoped – the graveyard of the bulk of the equipment of the 7th Army.'[25]

Having arrived at the Seine, I Corps was now reorganised. The 7th Armoured were dispatched to XII Corps for the pursuit to Belgium and 6th Airborne were withdrawn back to the UK. This left 49th West Riding Division, 51st Highlanders (who had now moved forward following their capture of Lisieux, east of Caen), and two independent armoured brigades to press on across the Seine and head towards their primary objective, Le Havre. The city lay at the mouth of the Seine and offered crucial port facilities which would ease the supply crisis that was beginning to envelop the Allied armies as they pushed ever eastwards away from their sources of supply, which were still predominantly back in Normandy.

Le Havre was the second largest port in France, with 12 miles of quays, three petroleum wharves and three shipbuilding yards. It was defended by some 11,000 German troops, though some were of dubious quality; Allied estimates placed the garrison at nearer 8,700.[26] Approaches to the city were complicated by a tributary river feeding into the Seine to the east, the Seine itself to the south and the English Channel to the northwest. To the north, high ground and nineteenth-century forts, alongside the defensive measures created by the defenders, provided a further challenge. Colonel Eberhard Wildermuth, commanding the German defenders, had the usual orders of fighting to the last man but also to cripple the port facilities as much as possible to prevent their use by the Allies should the city fall.

The British had excellent intelligence on Le Havre and had spent some time preparing and planning for this eventuality. Crerar's First Canadian Army staff had studied the problem prior to D-Day and Crocker's team was also furnished with excellent air-reconnaissance photos and the fruits of interrogations of deserters and PoWs captured in the days since British forces had invested Le Havre. In addition, valuable information was provided by French civilians, as one account from Sergeant Dick Philips, 2nd South Wales Borderers intelligence section, noted: 'A Frenchmen came in. He was employed in the office of the Commander of Le Havre. He brought in "Most Secret" German documents showing every minefield and the defences.'[27]

Crocker's plan for the assault, codenamed ASTONIA, clearly demonstrated that operational planning had continued to develop in 21st Army Group. With some evidence of low morale in the German garrison, Crocker believed that an attack on morale could be decisive in capturing Le Havre and a bombing and propaganda leafleting plan was put in place. Though the bombing was simultaneously intended to weaken the physical defences too, Crocker and his staff believed that hard and bitter fighting might well be minimised by such measures. They proved to be correct. In any case, due to the need to reposition various units and bring up equipment and supplies at a time when transports were being allocated elsewhere, the assault would have to be delayed by some days, allowing time to undermine the German defenders' state of mind.[28] The British issued an ultimatum to the defenders to surrender to avoid unnecessary bloodshed, particularly as there were many civilians still in Le Havre – this was refused. So too was a German counter-request to secure a two-day truce to allow the civilians to be evacuated, as Crocker thought this would delay the capture of the city. Accordingly, some 1,500 civilians were to die during the siege and consequent assault.[29]

The final plan was outlined to I Corps on 5 September and would involve 49th and 51st Divisions supported by 33rd and 34th Armoured Brigades and specialist assault elements of 79th Armoured Division. Naturally there was an extensive fire-support plan involving two AGRAs alongside the divisional artillery assets, four bombing raids in the days leading up to the assault, and from the sea the monitor HMS *Erebus* and the battleship HMS *Warspite*. Elements of the communication link between the bombers and the ground forces had also been tightened up, influenced by Crocker's experience at CHARNWOOD. Troops throughout the assaulting forces were greatly impressed by the level of preparations and quality of the briefings, aided by a range of models, photographs and detailed maps.[30]

Despite the vile weather, the plan worked well with the final bombing causing considerable disruption to the defenders prior to the first wave of ground attacks beginning immediately afterwards at 1745 hours on 10 September; this again was a reaction to the problems generated by the long pause between bombing and assault in CHARNWOOD. Engineers and assault armour cleared lanes through the defenders' minefields and assorted obstacles, though not without losses, and mechanised infantry in Kangaroos and armour surged forward. Behind them the firepower of the British forces was again intended to subdue the enemy. The account of 1st Northants Yeomanry captured the atmosphere:

> Over the wireless came the Colonel's voice, 'Hello all stations. Stand by to fire. Five rounds gunfire . . . NOW! Simultaneously everyone of the 55 tank gunners pressed his firing button and each tank fired its five rounds as quickly as possible. The sound was terrifying.
>
> It is not surprising that captured German officers afterwards asked to see the Allied belt-fed artillery.[31]

The use of specialised armour was again impressive and helped to overcome a range of difficulties and problems. Flame-throwing Crocodiles caused the usual mayhem to the Germans, with reports of a whole platoon being wiped out by a single Crocodile.[32] Brigade Major Paul Crook, 147th Brigade, recalled the assault:

> Because of the need to breach the minefields the attack had to be carried out at night. And what a night! There were flail tanks flashing away detonating some mines and missing others. Armoured assault. Engineer vehicles were chuntering around and tanks following up. There were the noises and effects of our own supporting fire from a variety of weapons – finally, of course there was the din of battle, organised chaos and danger.[33]

The close involvement of the commanding officer of the Royal Engineers in 51st Division, Lieutenant Colonel H.R. Carr, aided the coordination of the crucial first phase of the break-in when pushing through the minefields and obstacles proved troublesome. Immediate on-hand command helped to resolve the issues.

Pummelled by the bombers, with communications failing and without the fanatical resolve of the SS, the German defences crumbled. As the outer defences melted away the British commanders seized the moment to exploit emerging opportunities. Tom Rennie, commanding 51st Highlanders, brought forward a later phase of the plan when his troops made excellent progress. By 11 September the British were in Le Havre and opposition came to an end in the afternoon of the following day, the formal surrender being offered by the German Commander Colonel Eberhard Wildermuth himself dressed in his pyjamas, though still sporting his medals. Over 11,000 prisoners were taken and the cost to the British was a mere 388 casualties, just 10 per cent of the number suffered in CHARNWOOD.

Crocker was well pleased with how Operation ASTONIA had gone; his emphasis on demoralising the enemy prior to the assault certainly paid dividends, and once the outer crust of defences had been breached the Germans were largely overwhelmed. ASTONIA was a well thought-out, properly structured, multi-service operation that demonstrated what the British were most effective at: set-piece battles underpinned by their firepower philosophy. Yet Crocker's plan had also demonstrated degrees of continuing innovation and improvement; great emphasis was placed on impetus and timing, key lessons he had drawn from CHARNWOOD. Crocker had also adapted the plan after absorbing the intelligence derived in the period leading up to the assault, particularly regarding the likelihood of the disintegration in the morale of the defenders. Crucially, commanders were of a mind to loosen up the normally cautious approach if the enemy appeared to be folding.

The damage to Le Havre's port facilities was heavy but not irreparable; within a month the port was operating effectively, for the most part bringing in supplies for the Americans. Further up the Channel coast the Canadians, having now crossed the River Somme, were advancing on the ports of Boulogne, Calais and Dunkirk, but to the east the advanced forces of Second British Army had been engaging in further headlong pursuit towards Belgium. For the troops in the van, the pace of the drive towards the Somme and then beyond was intoxicating. Major General Allan Adair, commanding Guards Armoured Division: 'The 600 tanks of 30 Corps were advancing on a frontage of fifty miles, scything passages through the enemy rear areas "like a combine harvester going through a field of corn".'[34] Opposition was now crumbling away. Trooper Austin Baker, 4/7th Royal Dragoons, recalled: 'The whole squadron was going flat out and there was no sign of Jerry. We took the risk of paying no attention to the flanks but simply going straight up the road.'[35] When the enemy was encountered opposition was slight: 'It was obvious that Jerry had been caught on the hop and had no idea that there were any British troops within miles.'[36]

With easy pickings ahead of them, the leading units of XXX Corps were pressed hard. By the late afternoon on 30 August, 11th Armoured Division had advanced to within 30 miles of Amiens, which lay astride the Somme itself. Brian Horrocks arrived at Major General 'Pip' Roberts' 11th Armoured Tactical HQ to urge them on, proposing a night advance to take the division to within striking distance of the city by first light, preparatory to its capture later the same morning. As it was later put, Eisenhower told Montgomery, 'Amiens tonight'; Monty told Dempsey, 'Amiens tonight'; Dempsey told Horrocks, 'Amiens tonight', who told Roberts, 'Amiens tonight': then the planning really started.[37]

Roberts quickly reorganised his units to make such a move possible. Brigadier Roscoe Harvey impressed the urgency upon Lieutenant Colonel

David Silvertop, commanding 3rd RTR, who was tasked with leading the right-hand column towards Amiens. He in turn communicated it to Major Bill Close, commanding A Squadron:

> 'Your squadron will lead Bill,' the CO had told me. 'Don't let anything stop you.'
>
> I told my No 1 Troop commander, 'Johnny [Langdon] your troop will lead. Don't stop for anything.'[38]

Langdon simply recalled his single thought being: 'Bloody hell!'[39] Major Ned Thornburn, 4th King's Shropshire Light Infantry, was also caught by surprise:

> Out of the blue our General's car drew up and Pip Roberts got out, presumably to stretch his legs and see his troops at first hand.
>
> After a routine enquiry about the wellbeing of my men he asked me: 'How would you like to be in Amiens?' 'That would be fine,' I replied, 'but surely the Germans will defend the Somme?' 'They may,' said the General, with almost boyish glee, 'but they'll get an awful shock when we arrive there in the morning.' And that was my first intimation of the night drive to Amiens![40]

Promised extra petrol supplies had not materialised by the time the first units headed off in now deteriorating weather conditions, rain hammering down on the Shermans. The overnight surge to Amiens went spectacularly well, with a number of startled German units being caught out and captured en route. Some German vehicles tagged on to the British column thinking they were fellow German troops fleeing eastwards; they were quickly put right. The overnight drive also swept up many senior German officers. Brian Horrocks, who met with Roberts later that day, recalled:

> Having given me his report he [Roberts] said, 'I have a surprise for you, General.' And from behind one of his lorries was led a scowling, unshaven and very ugly German officer dressed in a black uniform. I would have disliked him at first sight, even if he had not looked like a senior SS commander (which he wasn't).
>
> [Roberts] told me with great pride that his prize exhibit was General Eberbach, commander of 7th Army, whom the 11th Armoured had captured in his pyjamas during the night advance.[41]

Eberbach, formerly commander of Fifth Panzer Army and recently appointed to take charge of the remnants of Seventh Army, had been reconnoitring forward to assess the likelihood of defending the Somme, but was captured by the Fife and Forfar Yeomanry. He was the most important senior figure thus far captured by the Allies. Meanwhile, aided by the local Maquis, 11th Armoured pressed into Amiens itself. Major Bill Close recalled:

> The buildings grew taller and the hairs on the back of my neck grew pricklier but gradually, shooting now and then, we made our way to the river. And there it was. A large bridge. Deserted. I saw little sign of activity. The people of Amiens were sensibly lying low. So was the enemy.[42]

Though that particular bridge was blown after only one troop had crossed, another bridge was located and 3rd RTR was soon across, closely followed by the rest of the column, and then the division. The Guards Armoured Division crossed the Somme to the southeast, seizing an intact bridge at Corbie, but 7th Armoured spearheading XII Corps' advance to the northwest of Amiens found their bridges blown by the enemy. They cut back through the outskirts of Amiens and crossed there in order to continue their advance northeast towards Lille. Once across the Somme they encountered pockets of stiff resistance in the form of SS troops, particularly at St Pol, but effectively bypassed them leaving them to the follow-on forces of 53rd Welsh Division, which was making slower progress due to limited transportation facilities. The advance of XII Corps was again greatly aided by the work of the Royal Engineers who quickly built a Bailey bridge at Picquigny, northwest of Amiens.

Throughout these advances the British were scooping up thousands of prisoners as the daily war diaries of the units involved attest. Many such prisoners were handed over to the Maquis to hold until they could be ferried back west; with such pressures being placed upon the supply and transportation network of the British Army, there was little that could be dedicated to the movement of PoWs. Royal Army Service Corps (RASC) units and vehicles would sometimes move PoWs westwards after having dropped off supplies with front-line units. These runs involved long, hard driving, often through territory still littered with desperate German troops either fleeing or seeking ways to surrender safely, all the way from Normandy to the front line now heading towards Belgium. Sergeant John Hooper, 171st Company, RASC, recalled: 'Many of the PoWs looked in poor shape – hungry, tired, dirty and dispirited, especially those conscripted from the occupied countries, but in sharp contrast to those from SS formations who were smartly dressed, disciplined and arrogant.'[43]

The pursuit continued. On 1 September, 11th Armoured Division advanced some 50 miles and similar rates were maintained the following morning, only for the race to be halted temporarily as an airborne drop, Operation LINNET, was planned ahead of the advance. Roberts recorded his frustration at having to sit around for the best part of a day before the airborne drop was cancelled, its objectives having already been achieved by ground forces. Second British Army had reached Douai, Lille, Tournai and St Pol by 2 September, and orders were then issued for 7th Armoured to seize Ghent, 11th Armoured to capture Antwerp and the Guards Armoured Division to take Brussels, though at one stage 11th Armoured were initially allocated the Belgian capital.[44] As Brian Horrocks later recorded:

> My big moment came on 2 September when I arrived at the Headquarters of the Guards Armoured Division. The Guards make a fetish of understatement, and with long practice have developed a remarkable capacity for never showing any emotion under any circumstances. But on this occasion even they were slightly shaken when I gave their next day's objective as Brussels, for Brussels was seventy miles away.[45]

The announcement of the objective, initially linked with the aborted airborne drop LINNET, provoked great excitement throughout the two brigade groups tasked with leading the advance. Though the Guards had developed a reputation for limited drive, and would later earn criticism for their inability to link up with 1st Airborne at Arnhem, in assembling and then driving through to Brussels they showed great alacrity and determination. When the airborne drop was cancelled, the advance on Brussels was brought forward and began in earnest early on 3 September. Armoured cars of the division quickly reached the Franco-Belgian border and by the end of the day the Guards were firmly established in Brussels. It was a stunning surprise to the Belgian civilians in the capital city. One later remarked:

> I glanced out of the window quite incuriously, and then my attention became riveted. These tanks looked different. It couldn't possibly be the Americans or British? Yet could it? Suddenly I realised that we had been liberated, and like everyone else in Brussels that night I went mad.[46]

Most Belgians were unaware that the Allies were even in Belgium, let alone Brussels. It was an astonishing advance for the troops of the Guards Armoured Division, who just over four days earlier had still been in Condé in Normandy, some 330 miles to the west.

Although a little disappointed to have had the prize of Brussels allocated to them and then have it taken away, Roberts' 11th Armoured was in fact to play a more important and controversial strategic role in being tasked with the capture of Antwerp and its crucial deep-water port facilities. The division attempted to sweep past Lille but was hampered by retreating German units, and infantry of 50th Division had to be brought up and deployed to free up the armour for its advance. By nightfall the tanks of the 11th Armoured had reached the area around Alost, 30 miles short of Antwerp. In the early hours of 4 September Roberts' troops resumed their advance and, once again aided by local civilians, pushed on towards Antwerp, cheered on by locals flanking the route. The speed of the British Army's drive across Northern France and now into Belgium had caught intelligence support by surprise and commanders were forced to work with inadequate maps and limited knowledge of objectives. Accurate maps were now in short supply, as Lieutenant Colonel Ivor Reeves, 4th KSLI, recounted:

> We had been provided with plenty of excellent one-inch maps throughout the campaign, but such was the speed of the advance that I presume it had proved impossible to find time to distribute them since we entered Belgium, so we were now working off a 1/250,000 scale map on which Antwerp was about the size of a thumb-nail.[47]

Organising 'O' (Orders) groups with inadequate maps and often surrounded by ecstatic crowds with freely flowing alcohol, food and women was a challenge. But, as Brigadier Jack Churcher, commanding 159th Brigade in Antwerp, put it: 'If you ever have the problem of capturing and clearing a city of two-and-three-quarter million inhabitants, it is no good referring to military textbooks as the answers are not to be found there.'[48] 'Pip' Roberts also later admitted to working off small-scale maps which did not show the crucial key points in the city. It was to lead to a blunder as Roberts did not realise upon entering Antwerp that the main Albert Canal did not run through the centre, but to the north. On the evening of 4 September, therefore, his troops focused on securing the centre of the city and the docks rather than pushing out to capture key crossings over the Albert Canal itself. The Germans blew the main bridge the following day. German artillery was able to shell the city intermittently from the far side and the British would now have to force a crossing over the canal.

The troops of 11th Armoured eventually took control of the city itself, most importantly even the dock area and its important gates, again being helped by the efforts of local resistance fighters. The only instance of serious

German opposition in Antwerp itself took place in the main Central Park where a fierce battle resulted in 6,000 Germans being captured. But the obstacle of the Albert Canal remained, and in the euphoria born of the seizure of the city, a rapid and high-risk dart across the canal was conceived for later on 5 September. It was all planned 'on the hoof' and prosecuted by 4th King's Shropshire Light Infantry, who had already been involved in the fighting in the centre of the city. Hastily organised at an hour's notice, without suitable maps or proper reconnoitring, the crossing was a very risky venture, as Lieutenant Colonel Reeves, commanding 4th KSLI, acknowledged, and was entirely dependent on the enemy's lack of strength. During the night the battalion managed to establish a small bridgehead over the canal, but the position was parlous and the opposition much greater than had been expected, including tanks against which the Shropshires could deploy only poorly regarded PIATs (projector, infantry, anti-tank). Acting C Company commander Lieutenant Dick Mullock remembered:

> We were in a diabolical position, completely surrounded by buildings with no way in which we could retaliate except through various gaps, and then only with small arms fire. We had no anti-tank guns and soon ran out of PIAT ammunition, after which there was nothing we could do to check the enemy tanks.[49]

Reeves set up a small tactical HQ in the bridgehead – consisting of himself and his radio operator – but was repeatedly forced to relocate due to the enemy's ferocious attempts to drive the British back across the canal. He was at least able to call in artillery support from his battalion mortars and three medium and five field regiments, thanks to the surprising reliability of his battalion 18 radio set.[50] Attempts by the engineers to put across bridges to reinforce the Shropshires' position came to nothing owing to the intensity of the opposition and the minimal bridgehead that had been forged. Jack Churcher, commanding the brigade to which 4th KSLI was attached, recognised the immense difficulties being encountered as a result of this impromptu crossing, and fearing that one of his best battalions was being shot to pieces he requested it be withdrawn. It took until 7 September for this to be accepted, and the retreat across the canal was much better organised and accomplished without further loss.[51]

The failure to capture crossings over the canal on 4 September, or even very early the following morning, has since been the source of considerable criticism of Roberts, but also of Horrocks, Dempsey and Montgomery. By crossing the Albert Canal quickly and continuing to push northwards to

Woensdrecht, advanced units of 11th Armoured might have cut off large numbers of German Fifteenth Army units, perhaps some six divisions, which had been falling back across the River Scheldt to Beveland and Walcheren. These troops had initially been deployed around the Pas-de-Calais to resist a secondary cross-Channel attack, expected to be delivered by the phantom First US Army Group. When it became clear that such an attack was not going to take place, some units had been fed into the Normandy battle, but the remainder were now falling back as First Canadian Army advanced northeast towards them along the Channel coast. Their natural route of retreat would have been through Antwerp, but the speed of the British advance had now cut them off. They were therefore forced to retreat across the Scheldt estuary to the Beveland peninsula, from where they could contest control and use of the river and therefore the port of Antwerp. Admiral Bertram Ramsay, SHAEF's naval commander-in-chief, forcefully pointed out to Eisenhower and 21st Army Group on 4 September that if the Germans heavily mined the Scheldt and still controlled the north bank, the port would be useless. Clearly, capturing the port mattered little if the river feeding it was unusable. Until the Germans could be cleared from Beveland, this was not going to be possible.[52]

Yet their source of supply into Beveland passed perilously close to Antwerp – through the Woensdrecht region which lay just 20 miles to the north – and thus any strike across the Albert Canal by 11th Armoured threatened to bag much of the Fifteenth Army, or so it has been alleged by writers such as Cornelius Ryan, author of *A Bridge Too Far*. He and others have argued that the failure to push on from Antwerp immediately after 11th Armoured arrived there was a huge error that resulted in Fifteenth Army retaining control of the north bank of the Scheldt for many weeks afterwards, effectively making Roberts' early capture of Antwerp redundant. As Antwerp's port facilities were considered crucial to relieving the supply problems confronting the Allies, the chance of defeating Germany in 1944 was consequently lost as a result of this error as operations had to be scaled back and the enemy afforded more time to recover.[53]

Yet the reality is somewhat different. It is true that if better intelligence had been available to Roberts, his troops might have seized the Albert Canal crossing on 4 September. But in view of the ferocity of German resistance to 4th KSLI's crossing a little over a day later, it is highly unlikely that he had sufficient strength to exploit another 15–20 miles northwards and hold such a position. Even if that had been possible, Roberts still had to secure Antwerp itself, overcome its garrison, and seize its port facilities which were still threatened on 4–5 September. As 4th KSLI were the only infantry in the city for much of that initial phase of the battle, it is improbable that the British could have carried on and retained any firm control of all these objectives.

But it is true that seizing bridges over the canal on 4 September might have facilitated an easier push northwards in the ensuing days, and this might have threatened German occupancy of the Beveland peninsula. In this regard Roberts was right to admit his error, but German strength was increasing in the area and there were two divisions already across the Scheldt. It is highly speculative and therefore unlikely that much more could have been usefully achieved without serious and immediate reinforcement from Second Army and 21st Army Group, and this was not forthcoming. Though Roberts felt the capture of Antwerp had been sloppily handled by himself and his brigadiers, the advance of the division had, like that of the Guards, been startling. In six days since crossing the Seine the division had advanced over 250 miles, fighting on five of those days. All this had been accomplished without transporters and though a few of the tanks and self-propelled guns had fallen by the wayside, the great majority had driven all the way from the Normandy beaches, often well beyond the mileage prescribed for them. Though many critics of Allied armour have focused repeatedly on the weaknesses of British tanks (both American and UK designed), they have rarely acknowledged their reliability and dependability, crucial factors in this period of the campaign. Even heavy tanks such as the Churchills of 6th Guards Tank Brigade made rapid forward moves similar in distance to the Shermans of the Guards Armoured Division, without the use of transporters and with few mechanical failures or losses.[54] It is difficult to imagine German Panthers and Tigers making such a journey without breaking down through mechanical failings.[55]

As well as being dissatisfied by the tactical seizure of Antwerp, Roberts was also dismayed by the delays this and the aborted airborne Operation LINNET had caused. He later remarked that without these hold-ups his armour might have made a crossing over the Rhine itself at Wesel some 100 miles further east.[56] Yet such thinking was also optimistic; all such advances were likely to suffer some form of friction of war, for few military actions ever go entirely according to plan. But Roberts' comment regarding Wesel indicates the nature of the optimistic thinking that was developing in the British and other Allied forces in early September, thinking that would ultimately lead to the debacle that was Operation MARKET GARDEN.

On 1 September Eisenhower had assumed overall command of the ground forces in Western Europe from Montgomery, something that had initially been reported as a demotion for Monty, though it had always been part of the planned reorganisation of the Allied command structure that would follow the conclusion of the Normandy campaign. Montgomery was to command 21st Army Group in the north, Bradley 12th Army Group in the centre, later to be supplemented in the south by further US forces and a Free French Army. All this, and the air forces, were now to be coordinated by Eisenhower, through SHAEF. With the ever-increasing contribution of the Americans to the Allied forces fighting in Western Europe it was entirely politic and logical that Eisenhower should assume executive control, despite Monty's misgivings and lack of perspective over the measure.

Eisenhower has been heavily criticised over his initial handling of the campaign on the ground, from late August onwards, and particularly for his failure to get a grip on his headstrong commanders, most obviously Bradley, Patton and Montgomery. What Montgomery had predicted, that tight control of the campaign would wane once Eisenhower had assumed command, did come to pass; the problem was that it was Monty himself as much as anyone, who worked to undermine his chief. The central issue revolved around precisely how to deliver the *coup de grâce* to the Third Reich before the autumn set in and before the Germans could recover sufficiently to offer stronger resistance. Allied forces were now operating at the end of their tenuous supply lines, and some units had already been grounded to keep others mobile and sufficiently supplied. The further east they pushed the more the front-line fighting strength of the advance would have to be cut in order to maintain the momentum of fewer and fewer units. At some point resources would have to be focused even more in order to maintain the advance still further, and by the end of the first week in September that point had arrived. By mid-September, 21st Army Group's lines of communication had lengthened to 300 miles, near double the original estimates for which staff had planned. SHAEF administrative officers had claimed that current supply capability could support only 15 divisions across the Rhine in the north, a wholly inadequate number for finishing off Germany, and this at the expense of grounding a large number of divisions. It was decision time.[57]

Eisenhower has long been associated with what has been labelled the 'broad front' strategy, in which it is simplistically stated that he wanted a general push across the whole Western Front into Germany once the Normandy campaign had been won. This is unfair, as Eisenhower's concept was more nuanced than that. Prior to the rapid disintegration of German resistance in August, he had envisaged a thrust towards the Ruhr, the so-called Northern route into Germany, and simultaneously towards the Saar further south, the two being key industrial zones in western Germany. This was as much as anything else a device for drawing the remaining German combat forces into action and destroying them west of the Rhine. This would then open up the possibility of a more straightforward advance into Germany rather than a bitter and grim Rhine crossing against properly organised and stout defences.[58]

Montgomery's vision has long been associated with the 'narrow front' strategy, in which a compact 40-division force would rapidly leap at and cross the Rhine, preparatory to thrusting towards Berlin. It was Monty's view that this would offer the best chance of finishing off the Germans in 1944. Yet there was a key political weakness in this strategy, in that the narrow front thrust would gobble up available supplies and entail an advance to the north of the Ardennes by 21st Army Group and First US Army at the expense of any further movement by the other Allied forces to the south. This would in effect hand the victory march to a British commander, for the most logical leader for this venture would be Monty himself. He teasingly offered to serve under Bradley if necessary, but this was hardly serious and Dempsey regarded this ruse as 'a nonsense'.[59] Equally, the notion of Montgomery commanding a largely Anglo-Canadian force across the Rhine to win the war whilst most American troops sat watching in a passive and secondary role was, understandably, utterly unacceptable to the USA. General George Marshall, based in Washington and head of the US Army, had already been emphatically applying pressure on Eisenhower to stop Montgomery from seizing all the credit for the successes, whilst Bradley had no interest whatsoever in serving under Montgomery again. Matters were complicated still further by the headlong eastwards advance by Patton's Third US Army, which offered considerable opportunities in the south.

Eisenhower had to make sense of this situation and impose his preferred strategy. Alas, although he was to alight upon probably the most realistic and appropriate strategy by early September he was unable to make it stick, with recalcitrant and headstrong front-line commanders driving SHAEF rather than the other way round. Ike had shuffled his strategic cards once the Germans had been routed in Normandy, but the subsequent pursuit had progressed at lightning speed. SHAEF planning for post-Seine operations had therefore been binned following the lightning advance towards the Low Countries and the Franco-German border in late August, and Eisenhower and his team had to revise their thinking and fast. The original double thrust to the Ruhr and Saar was soon scaled back as supply problems prevented the possibility of allowing both to develop. Eisenhower met with his staff in a series of meetings from 20 to 23 August to develop a post-Normandy strategy, and he was persuaded by the unfolding situation as much as by Monty's badgering that the northern thrust should take precedence over the southern, but he did not close down the Saar route, merely directing Bradley to split Hodges' First Army, so that the greater part of it would work alongside 21st Army Group, and to scale back operations in the south. Yet Eisenhower also instructed Montgomery that Antwerp was fundamental to long-term sustained operations and that its capture was top priority. Forever the compromiser, Ike had sought a sensible and balanced plan, but had in fact infuriated Bradley, whilst simultaneously frustrating Montgomery who did not get the blank-cheque support he was hoping for. Both commanders grumbled. Bradley's unusually harsh assessment was:

> Monty's plan sprung from his megalomania. He would not cease in his efforts to gain personal command of all land forces and reap all the personal glory for our victory.[60]

Whilst Montgomery confided to Brooke:

> Ike has now decided on his course of action. I do not agree with what he proposed to do and have said so quite plainly.[61]

Brooke was already of the opinion that Eisenhower's strategy was likely to add three to six months to the war, so such correspondence did little to help.[62]

Yet despite instructing Montgomery to deal with Antwerp, Eisenhower had left enough wriggle room for Monty by failing to state in writing in unequivocal terms that dealing with Antwerp meant ensuring its use. When Monty issued his directive to 21st Army Group on 26 August, therefore, although the advance to the Ruhr was a secondary priority after Antwerp, the latter was to be secured 'as a base'.[63] Consequently, when Second Army's forces reached Antwerp there were no immediate and clear instructions to begin securing the northern bank of the Scheldt, something both Dempsey and Guy Simonds later thought to be a grave error.[64]

By then the situation had changed and despite Eisenhower's instructions, Montgomery now had other ideas. On 1 September the Canadians had captured Dieppe largely intact and the port was deemed capable of handling 7,000 tons of supplies per day, according to Major General Miles Graham, chief administrative officer for 21st Army Group, just sufficient to support Second Army's 14 divisions in a quick dash to the Rhine, without having to open up Antwerp.[65] Montgomery recognised the necessity of clearing the Scheldt but believed it could wait a few days, as the prospect of crossing the Rhine quickly was too good an opportunity to pass up. In any case, the task of opening up Antwerp could be taken up by the Canadians, leaving the British to press on across the Rhine, with First US Army working alongside and driving into the Ruhr. This decision was to have parlous consequences.[66]

Monty's hopes for such a major push towards the Rhine and the Ruhr with American forces again under his direction came apart on 3 September when Bradley informed him that following a meeting at Chartres the previous day, Eisenhower had only allocated a portion, albeit the greater portion, of First US Army to the northern route and that it would not be under 21st Army Group command. In addition, Patton's forces would continue to get an allocation of supplies to carry on his dash to the Saar region, as Bradley had already surreptitiously circumvented Eisenhower's plan himself by allowing Patton to continue.[67]

Montgomery was both furious and frustrated at the development of Allied strategy and decided to push his own agenda more aggressively. He told Brooke that he has going for the Rhine crossing as a matter of urgency and his operational outline issued on 3 September clearly indicated that opening up Antwerp by directing a substantial British force to clear the Scheldt estuary had been dropped.[68] So when Roberts' forces reached Antwerp on 4 September there was no direction from above to head north and then west and begin dealing with German forces in Beveland; instead Second Army began reorienting itself for a push northeastwards towards the Rhine.

There is no doubt that a concerted effort by British forces from Antwerp towards Beveland on or around 5 September would have made the task of opening up Antwerp that much easier and brought forward the date when the port would become operational, but the notion that this could have been achieved with little effort is optimistic indeed. It would still have taken a considerable allocation of forces to drive the Germans away from the Scheldt and there is every indication that they would have continued strongly contesting the use of the river.

Most importantly, such a move would have been at the expense of trying to get across the Rhine quickly and in force, and Montgomery was loathe to let this happen. The real failure came later in continuing with this notion and particularly of reaching Arnhem with a very risky airborne operation, when it started to become clearer by the day from 6 September onwards that the Germans had pulled themselves together.

In retrospect, it can be seen that opening up Antwerp might have been the best course of action for Second British Army, but by early September the campaign had swung so decisively in favour of the Allies that overconfidence, optimism and arrogance were clouding the judgement of 21st Army Group, particularly that of Montgomery himself. SHAEF and Eisenhower were also being swept along. Messages and notes bounced around and between 21st Army Group, SHAEF, London and Washington, illustrating the wave of optimism. In view of the collapse in German resistance, Monty claimed that Allied forces could be in Berlin in three weeks and that the war would soon be over if correct decisions were made. London and Washington also made premature claims about the strategic position and even the ultra-realist Brooke believed that with proper handling of Allied strategy Germany might be overwhelmed. With Romania and Finland also dropping out of the war, it seemed that a determined thrust at the heart of the Reich from the west following the defeat in France might well finish the Germans off. Eisenhower too had recognised the crumbling opposition in August, though his view became more realistic towards the end of the month, as indeed it seems did the view of Freddie de Guingand, Monty's chief of staff. But it was in this euphoric atmosphere that the notion of Operation MARKET GARDEN began to emerge.

8

ARNHEM
Conceptual Failure

THE ATTEMPT BY Second British Army and the First Allied Airborne Army to cross the Rhine at Arnhem in mid-September 1944 is, after D-Day, perhaps the most iconic event of the whole campaign to liberate Western Europe. Encapsulated so effectively in the phrase 'A Bridge Too Far' – a throwaway remark supposedly first uttered by Lieutenant General Frederick 'Boy' Browning who commanded the airborne elements of the operation, and which later spawned Cornelius Ryan's very popular book of 1974 and the film three years later – Operation MARKET GARDEN has everything: a bold plan with so many individual tales of courage, incompetence and resolve, with plucky British soldiers hanging on grimly whilst others battled their way through to relieve them, but which ultimately ended in magnificent disaster, as one recent account has been titled.[1]

In simple terms the plan called for three airborne divisions to lay a path across which a ground force would advance, linking up the three forces, the third of which would capture bridges over the Lower Rhine at Arnhem in the Netherlands. The plan depended on the seizure of bridges to facilitate the 60-mile advance by the ground forces in just three days. Ultimately, the prize would be Monty's route across the Rhine and into Germany, delivering a devastating blow to the Third Reich by threatening the Ruhr or indeed a deep penetration towards Berlin. And all this would be achieved without the use of Antwerp.

Yet in reality it was a poorly conceived, ill considered and deeply flawed plan which stood little chance of success before it had even begun. In the aftermath there were some unseemly attempts by many officers and senior commanders to apportion blame and evade responsibility for the failure of an operation that should never have been enacted in the manner it was. Ultimately, although there was a range of poor tactical and operational decisions, much debated and pored over since 1944, the fundamental weakness lay in the whole concept. First, the plan took little account of the actions of the enemy, or of their considerable ability to react quickly and decisively to situations. Whatever the severe structural failings of the German Army, its unerring strength in stitching together ad hoc defensive groupings to hinder and slow the rate of Allied advances was well known, and at the time of MARKET GARDEN the Germans were at last pulling themselves together. Gerd von Rundstedt had been reappointed as Commander-in-Chief of the West, allowing Walther Model, Hitler's so-called fireman, to focus on the specific activities of Army Group B facing the Allies in the north. Von Rundstedt was confident that Montgomery's temporary halt on 4 September whilst Second Army reorganised itself would afford a small window of opportunity to the Germans; if some forces could be cobbled together quickly, the rout could be halted. Kurt Student, who was appointed to command First Parachute Army in the Low Countries, obliged and was able to produce a variety of small groupings of forces, most not paratroopers at all, which plunged into the line ahead of 21st Army Group from 5 September onwards. With the arrival of other lower-grade units, the position ahead of Second Army along the Albert and Meuse-Escaut Canals suddenly strengthened. Efforts by the British to push on towards the Netherlands from 6 September onwards hit significant resistance and made only limited progress. The great pursuit was at an end it seemed. Yet the strengthening German positions ahead of the British forces, and indeed the ability of the Germans to react quickly to unfolding situations, impacted little upon the concept and development of MARKET GARDEN. The plan would work only if the Germans melted away once pressed as they had since the Seine had been crossed, yet the evidence strongly implied this was much less likely to happen after 6 September.

The second conceptual weakness of MARKET GARDEN centred on the very essence of the operation – it asked the British Army to do something for which it was not mentally equipped – drive 60 miles through enemy lines with little regard to flanks, and act well beyond the likely range of the great weight of supporting artillery normally provided. Rushing through enemy territory against broken opposition was one thing, but by 6 September it was becoming self-evident that the environment had changed. The British had proved well able to mount big set-piece operations with reasonable success, but only when properly bolstered by ground-based fire-support to ease the way forward and to break up enemy counter-attacks. When they drifted away from this technique at GOODWOOD and attempted to act beyond this protective cover, the wheels had come off. The only way MARKET

GARDEN could succeed would be if XXX Corps, spearheading the ground offensive, could throw off its operational frame of mind and embrace risk. It would be completely out of character for it to do so, yet this was a fundamental aspect of the plan.

The third fundamental conceptual weakness was the estimation of the efficacy of airborne operations. All large-scale airborne operations in the Second World War ended in brawls, though at times the confusion generated proved to be a strategically beneficial by-product, as had been seen with the American air drops on D-Day. Crucially, these airborne operations never came close to achieving all their specified operational objectives. Though much attention has been placed on the bold seizure of Pegasus Bridge on 6 June, most of the other airborne operations in support of D-Day were chaotic, just as most other previous airborne actions had been. Yet MARKET GARDEN would only work if *all* the key operational objectives were achieved: if one major bridge crossing was lost, say at Nijmegen, the whole plan would fail, and fail spectacularly. It was as if MARKET GARDEN was conceived without any awareness of what had happened in all previous airborne operations.[2]

The key question therefore is why, despite all these fundamental weaknesses and with an awareness of the shortcomings inherent in previous airborne operations, did the planners of MARKET GARDEN ever imagine it could succeed? The plan grew out of previous airborne schemes, all of which had been cancelled or heavily modified. When LINNET was jettisoned on 2 September, Montgomery and his staff revisited the idea of employing airborne troops in support of the advancing Second Army. The recently created First Allied Airborne Army, commanded by the American Lieutenant General Lewis Brereton, was keen to find an operational role to justify its existence and to prevent the reallocation of its air transport assets to supply work for the ground forces, something favoured by Bradley. Lieutenant General Frederick 'Boy' Browning, commander of I Airborne Corps attached to First Allied Airborne Army, was also keen to get into action. Browning had not hitherto commanded an operation and was desperate to do so before the war came to an end, which in early September 1944 seemed to be imminent. In later years Browning was held up as the villain of the piece and portrayed by Dirk Bogarde in *A Bridge Too Far* as a vain careerist who was fully aware of the great risks inherent in MARKET GARDEN but suppressed them in order to get into battle. There is little doubt that Browning was hugely ambitious but he was no different from the others around him in 21st Army Group in terms of brushing aside, though certainly not suppressing, the incoming intelligence about increasing German strength lying ahead of Second Army.

More important was Browning's inexperience in handling and planning airborne operations – because of this he was willing to commit to objectives and operations the efficacy of which other seasoned airborne commanders would have questioned. Even so, he was not alone in this. Brigadier General James Gavin, who was a critic of Browning and his staff for their gauche planning and poor appreciation of airborne operations, himself was to commit 82nd US Airborne to a series of wildly ambitious objectives around Nijmegen assigned to him by Browning in MARKET GARDEN, though perhaps not the most crucial one, the Nijmegen road bridge itself. In comparison, his compatriot Maxwell Taylor (commanding 101st US Airborne) point blank refused to be saddled with his range of grossly optimistic objectives, whilst Richard Gale, commander of British 6th Airborne, on seeing the MARKET GARDEN plan for the capture of Arnhem, supposedly claimed he would resign rather than implement it.[3]

On 4 September in the wake of LINNET's cancellation Browning, Montgomery, Dempsey and de Guingand began cooking up a new airborne operation to propel Second Army over the Rhine, soon to be codenamed COMET. This plan called for 1st British Airborne Division and the Polish Parachute Brigade to be dropped on the objectives later assigned to MARKET GARDEN, to provide a carpet to the Rhine over which Second Army would quickly advance. Arnhem was already identified as the ultimate objective, even though this route, rather than an option to advance to Wesel (45 miles to the southeast), would set Second British Army on a divergent course from Hodges' First US Army. It was later claimed that concerns over flak defences around Wesel eliminated it as a target, though there is little contemporary evidence of this, and the fact that Dempsey and Browning were still pressing for a push to Wesel rather than Arnhem for some days after the 4 September meeting, indicates that the decision was not so clear-cut. In retrospect COMET seems an even more foolhardy plan than its more famous successor, but it was planned to begin on 6–7 September, before it became abundantly clear that the Germans were reinforcing their positions ahead of Second Army, and in an atmosphere of the Germans routing faster than the British could advance. In addition, COMET envisaged the use of night-time *coups de main* landings to seize the key objectives immediately, with two subsequent daytime landings and air drops to secure the positions. The plan required all the airborne elements to be deployed well within a twenty-four-hour period, though even this limited operation required two main airlifts, as there were not enough transport aircraft available to achieve it in one fell swoop.[4]

It is clear that COMET was driven predominantly by Montgomery and that Browning was tasked with simply making it happen, though he was a willing collaborator. Monty was still pushing for a semi-independent advance by 21st Army Group to force Eisenhower's hand into supporting his narrow thrust, believing it inconceivable that Ike would order him to stop if the British had seized a crossing over the Rhine. A crossing at Arnhem would also lead the advance away from the American sector, leaving First US Army to mop up the Ruhr whilst Second British Army might drive on deep into Germany. Montgomery outlined such thinking to Eisenhower on 4 September, but claimed that he did not properly receive his chief's lukewarm endorsement until three to five days later, and then, due to communications issues, in a fractured manner.[5] But COMET was cancelled when, from 6 September onwards, German resistance grew along the Albert-Meuse-Escaut canal sectors ahead of Second British Army.[6]

Montgomery and his staff then began looking at an expansion plan to include the use of the entire First Allied Airborne Army, including 82nd and 101st US Airborne Divisions, but broadly with the same objectives as COMET. Dempsey was still doubtful about Arnhem, particularly in view of reports that the Germans had increased their strength there, including the deployment of the remaining elements of II SS Panzer Corps. He still preferred a push eastwards towards Wesel to link up with Hodges' First US Army. Crossing the Rhine at Wesel would also eliminate the need to cross the River Waal, unlike the route to Arnhem which necessitated negotiating this major obstacle. That Dempsey recorded his unease and doubts about Arnhem in his otherwise anodyne daily diary tells us a good deal about his concerns.[7] Browning too saw some merit in pushing towards Wesel, in spite of the apparent extra flak defences in the sector. As David Belchem, Monty's operations chief at 21st Army Group, later recalled, Monty 'knew that all of us from Dempsey downwards were against Arnhem'.[8]

In spite of this dissent, Montgomery remained fixed on Arnhem. The V2 rocket attacks on London that began on 8 September were a cause of some political concern and Monty argued that a drive northwards to Arnhem would ease this crisis as it would threaten the V2 launching pads in the Netherlands. Whilst this was true, Arnhem had already been targeted in COMET before the V2 attacks began, so this was at best an extra factor rather than the decisive one. Monty was clearly still looking to pursue his semi-independent strategy and he knew that if he went for Wesel he would have to share the success with the Americans and that such a move was targeted on the Ruhr rather than a leap towards Berlin.[9]

Montgomery secured the use of 82nd and 101st US Airborne Divisions for MARKET GARDEN at a fractious meeting with Eisenhower at Brussels airport on 10 September. Eisenhower was near bedridden following an injury, but Montgomery claimed that, due to pressures of command, his boss would have to come to see him rather than the other way round. Eisenhower was nevertheless unable to leave his aeroplane and the meeting took place inside. Adopting his usual strategy, Monty tried to see Eisenhower alone, but was unable to persuade Lieutenant General Humfrey Gale, a fellow Briton and SHAEF's senior administrative and logistics officer, to leave the plane. Gale was highly regarded at SHAEF but Monty had little time for him. Montgomery berated Eisenhower for the lack of a single-thrust strategy to which Ike, as ever the consummate diplomat, answered: 'Steady, Monty! You can't speak to me like that. I'm your boss.' Gale thought the meeting was a highly unsatisfactory one:

> at which General Eisenhower showed enormous forbearance and far too amenable an attitude. Montgomery was not sure of his facts, was vague in his proposals, and spent a lot of time drawing a train of red herrings across the path which did not help anybody.[10]

Gale considered Montgomery's narrow-thrust strategy so logistically unrealistic that it was probably a ruse merely to demonstrate later that he had been prevented from winning the war quickly by Eisenhower's caution. Montgomery's pessimistic supply outlook, intended to squeeze more resources out of Ike, was even contradicted by his own chief administrative officer in 21st Army Group, Major General Miles Graham, who argued that a drive to the Rhine was still possible based on current logistical considerations.

Montgomery backed off, and although he could make no real headway with Eisenhower on the main point of his argument – the narrow-thrust concept – he did get enthusiastic support for MARKET GARDEN from Ike, who not only approved the plan but insisted on it. The prospect of seizing a bridgehead over the Rhine seemed an excellent prospect to Eisenhower and he even accepted that MARKET GARDEN might delay the opening up of Antwerp, though he saw the ultimate importance of doing so quickly much more than Montgomery. Most importantly, Eisenhower saw MARKET GARDEN only as a chance to get across the Rhine before the year was out rather than as a break for Berlin, which he ruled out, much to the frustration of Montgomery. Ike followed up the meeting with a written outline issued to Monty on 13 September in which he again underlined the necessity of opening up Antwerp.[11]

The key outcome of the 10 September meeting was the green light for MARKET GARDEN, eventually pencilled in for launch on 17 September. Detailed planning continued from 10 September onwards, but the scale of the operation and the multiple issues to be resolved undermined the plan more and more as the day of MARKET GARDEN approached. Brigadier Charles Richardson, Monty's chief planning officer, claimed that 21st Army Group staff were simply handed the plan by Browning's team and told by Montgomery to implement it.[12] Perhaps the most debilitating shortcoming proved to be the air-power element of the plan. Although MARKET GARDEN involved a significant airborne element, there had been little immediate air staff involvement in putting the plan together. As problems with the airlift emerged, 21st Army Group staff, determined to make MARKET GARDEN a reality, rode roughshod over a series of related air-based problems, whilst air staff refused to budge on some fundamental aspects of the plan.

First, the airlift plan was based on COMET, itself pasted in from LINNET, but LINNET had been intended for use much closer to airfields in England where the airborne forces were based. MARKET GARDEN called for drops much further into continental Europe, which increased flying time and scuppered the American tactic of using one tug to pull two gliders. As a result further airlifts would have to be used on the two subsequent days to get everyone into position, weakening the element of surprise and requiring first-wave troops to hold second-phase airlift DZ/LZs (drop zones and landing zones) for that much longer. This would hinder the concentration of maximum force towards crucial objectives in the first few hours of the operation, the phase when most could be achieved cheaply. Delays in seizing key objectives only afforded more time for the enemy to react; airborne troops arriving in the second and third waves would have a diminishing impact as the element of surprise, a fundamental strength of airborne operations, would have been sacrificed. Montgomery did not become fully aware of this problem probably until 15 September, by which time it was far too late to change the plan. Insofar as Monty had failed to include the air staff properly in the planning process, this deficiency was self inflicted and he was paying the price for this approach. Consequently, the input of air staff and any scope for shaping the plan accordingly were limited.[13]

Furthermore, LINNET had been planned for late August/early September when daylight hours had been longer and it was this, along with the longer flying times and greater numbers of troops to be deployed, which necessitated the second and third airlifts, exacerbating the problems of the loss of surprise and delayed concentration of force still further. Another casualty of this rejigging of the airlift was the *coup de main* aspect of the plan. The COMET plan had required initial surgical assaults to seize the primary objectives which were to be held until the main forces arrived to strengthen the positions. Because the airlift would now take place in daylight and *coup de main* assaults in daylight were ruled out as unduly hazardous, they were abandoned. Even night-time *coups de mains* were viewed sceptically after the Normandy campaign, but were envisaged as crucial parts of COMET, despite RAF hostility. Now in MARKET GARDEN they were gone. A last-minute effort by Colonel George Chatterton, commander of the Glider Pilot Regiment, to reinstate the *coup de main* fell on deaf ears, with Browning insisting it was too late to change the already highly complex airlift plan and to overturn the RAF's objections. According to Chatterton, the commander of 1st Airborne Division, Roy Urquhart himself saw no need to press the idea either.[14]

This might not have been so bad if the DZ/LZs had been close enough to their objectives to facilitate rapid capture, but, alas, they were not. Infamously, 1st Airborne's DZ/LZs were close on 8 miles from the bridges in Arnhem and this was later held up as a key factor in the failure of the operation. Strengthening dispositions of flak defences to the north of Arnhem, particularly around Deelen, closed off some air routes, and doctrine regarding the dropping of paratroopers close to, or in, urban areas, as well as the perceived unsuitability of the terrain to the south of Arnhem, greatly limited the range of initial DZ/LZs available. These arguments were acknowledged by 1st Airborne in September 1944.[15] It is true that the Polish Parachute Brigade planned to arrive in the terrain south of Arnhem on 19 September, on the third day of MARKET GARDEN and much closer to the principal objectives, but not until *after* flak defences in Arnhem and Nijmegen had been suppressed; landing there before this had been achieved was ruled out as far too dangerous. Though the objections of the RAF to some of the options on DZ/LZs later proved to be largely unfounded, the available intelligence at the time seemed convincing. Urquhart certainly accepted the thinking behind the RAF's objections: 'The RAF, I think, quite rightly were not prepared to fly into this defended zone [between Arnhem and Nijmegen].'[16] Consequently, 1st Airborne's initial DZ/LZs would have to be at Wolfheze, 8 miles from the principal objectives.

Further complicating the planning process was Urquhart himself. He had no experience of airborne warfare and had been an odd choice to command 1st Airborne; Miles Dempsey did not think too highly of him, later commenting: 'Urquhart was the most vocal, but not the most able of the divisional commanders.'[17] Tasked with seizing and holding the bridges over the Lower Rhine at Arnhem, Urquhart attempted to solve the problem of landing so far from the primary objectives by planning to race his Reconnaissance Squadron in jeeps straight to the bridges ahead of the main body of paratroopers who would arrive later on foot. Gavin, commanding 82nd US Airborne, thought Urquhart's solution foolhardy, famously confiding to his intelligence officer, 'my God, he can't mean it' on hearing Urquhart's plan.[18] Yet Gavin made no such concessions in his planning and as his DZ/LZs were also some distance from the bridges at Nijmegen, he simply accepted they would have to be captured after the initial landings – despite the huge risk of this approach in that the enemy might destroy the bridges once they understood the principal thrust of Allied intentions, and compromise MARKET GARDEN completely.

As 1st Airborne's DZ/LZs were some distance away from the main objectives, and drops and landings were to take place on subsequent days, some of the initially landed force would have to be retained to hold and protect the DZ/LZs to ensure the safe arrival of follow-up forces, whilst other units were tasked with securing the northern perimeter. The main strike for the bridge would therefore be weakened. This was to prove another weakness in the plan, yet there was little dissent about the planned DZ/LZs at the time (other than from Chatterton), either from Roy Urquhart or his brigadiers or battalion commanders, though the allocation of the DZ/LZs was later cited as a key reason for the failure of MARKET GARDEN.[19]

Of course a crucial aspect of the plan, as with any airborne plan, was intelligence. Placing relatively lightly armed forces in perilous positions against significant enemy strength for any length of time courted disaster. Yet the MARKET GARDEN intelligence process fundamentally broke down, and Allied airborne troops were inserted into a much more hostile and dangerous environment than had been anticipated. The position of II SS Panzer Corps, those battered veterans of Normandy, surprisingly close to Arnhem on 17 September, has long been cited as a reason for the failure of the plan. That units such as 9th and 10th SS Panzer Divisions were encountered so quickly and so close to the objectives at Arnhem and Nijmegen was no surprise however; as early as 6 September the Allies had information that II SS Panzer Corps were in the vicinity of Arnhem, and Dempsey was concerned enough to use this as one of the reasons to argue that COMET/MARKET GARDEN should be switched towards Wesel. In fact, the presence of SS Panzer units in the area was one of the factors that prompted Montgomery to cancel COMET and initiate the much larger MARKET GARDEN to compensate.

Allied commanders from battalion upwards were also briefed about the likelihood of these SS units being in the vicinity. The real failure came in grossly underestimating the ability of such units to offer determined opposition. In part this was driven by the belief that II SS Panzer Corps had been effectively eliminated as a significant fighting force in Normandy. Both Second Army and XXX Corps intelligence officers wrote off the ability of II SS Panzer Corps to offer much resistance.[20]

It was clear that an atmosphere of victory disease had infiltrated intelligence assessments; it was not, as some have argued, that senior officers suppressed disturbing intelligence reports, but more that they failed to acknowledge their potential significance. Most famously, Major Brian Urquhart, I Airborne Corps' chief intelligence officer, later claimed that he had tried to make senior commanders such as Browning aware of the 'sudden' presence of II SS Panzer Corps around Arnhem in the days leading up to MARKET GARDEN, but had been ignored. Major Urquhart's recollection is somewhat at odds with the records, which indicate that his warnings came earlier than he later believed, probably at the time of the cancelling of COMET.[21] More importantly still, there was no great revelation in the few days prior to MARKET GARDEN's launch regarding II SS Panzer Corps; the British knew they were in the line ahead of them, but they chose to believe, erroneously as it transpired, that they did not pose a major threat. As Montgomery later claimed:

> We knew it [II SS Panzer Corps] was there [Arnhem]. But we were wrong in supposing that it could not fight effectively; its battle state was far beyond our expectation.[22]

This assumption was a product of overconfidence and arrogance, a failure of intelligence interpretation and processing, rather than gathering.[23]

Despite the worries of Dempsey, de Guingand, Belchem and Charles Richardson and others at 21st Army Group HQ, MARKET GARDEN launched on 17 September, following a series of preparatory air operations the previous night. The first airlifts began in the early afternoon with 101st US Airborne dropping at Eindhoven-Veghel, 82nd US Airborne at Nijmegen-Grave and 1st British Airborne at Arnhem. Partly because it was a daylight drop, and partly because of improvements in training, the concentration and delivery of the airborne forces were highly impressive. Though the airlift required some 1,500 air transports and 500 gliders, along with covering aircraft, the operation began well enough and the tactical success greatly exceeded that achieved in previous airborne insertions. In less than an hour some 19,000 troops had been landed, predominantly on to their targets. Confidence was high and Lieutenant Colonel John Frost, commanding 2nd Parachute Battalion of 1st Airborne, later recalled thinking:

> We were highly delighted to be given a really worthwhile task at last. This was the genuine airborne thrust that we had been awaiting and we felt that if things went according to plan, we should be truly instrumental in bringing the war to an end in 1944.[24]

The 101st US Airborne Division efficiently set about its tasks, rapidly seizing its primary objectives. The only serious setback proved to be the loss of the Son Bridge, destroyed as American troops closed to within 50 metres of it. It would now be imperative that XXX Corps bring their bridging equipment and engineers quickly into action to avoid debilitating delays in pressing on to Nijmegen. Maxwell Taylor, commanding 101st US Airborne, now set about pushing his troops into Eindhoven itself with the intention of linking up with XXX Corps.[25]

Brian Horrocks had given his senior XXX Corps officers their briefing for MARKET GARDEN at a conference held in the cinema at Bourg-Léopold at 1030 hours the day before. In keeping with his usual approach, in part adopted from Montgomery, he kept things informal, and delivered his initial outline sporting a high-neck woolly jumper, a battle-dress top and a camouflaged airborne smock. His appearance was quite in keeping with the decidedly non-standard attire worn by his staff and officers, a collection of individuals he described as motley. Overall, it was quite distinct from American briefings where a high degree of formality was expected.[26]

As some ten days had elapsed since the German rout had halted, allowing plenty of time for the enemy to improvise defences, Horrocks emphasised the need for speed as he had many concerns over the timetable he was expected to stick to. The task of keeping open the route to Eindhoven, Nijmegen, and ultimately Arnhem was daunting. The problems potentially confronting the Royal Engineers in particular were monumental. It was estimated that if all the bridges en route to Arnhem were destroyed, some 2,277 vehicles would be required to bring in sufficient equipment to keep the advance moving; even then, the capturing of barges on the various rivers would be crucial to the operation. Because of the axis of advance down a single road, such units and equipment could not be brought forward unless required and were therefore held back at the start line of XXX Corps' advance in Bourg-Léopold until needed. Coordinating this would be hugely demanding, especially as US forces used different communications equipment. All told, XXX Corps' advance would involve some 20,000 vehicles and therefore road discipline and military policing would be crucial to the success of the action.[27]

The following day XXX Corps, spearheaded by Adair's Guards Armoured Division, initially encountered much stiffer opposition than anticipated and their 13-mile advance towards Eindhoven to rendezvous with 101st US Airborne was slower than had been planned. The Guards had kicked off at 1400 hours, led by a 350-gun artillery barrage and supported by Cabrank

Typhoons of 83 Group, RAF. This was an impressive array of firepower, but EPSOM and GOODWOOD had enjoyed much greater concentrations of artillery support. The advance soon encountered delays and suffered mounting casualties which imposed friction on the timetable. The leading elements of the Irish Guards grouping quickly lost nine tanks in the initial break-in battle. One account suggests all hell had broken loose once the Germans began to react to the initial attack: 'One Guardsman plunged into a trench and found himself in the company of a fat and very frightened Hun, who at once made room for him, and offered him a large cigar.'[28] Though the Irish Guards battered their way through, they later encountered some improvised weapons pit traps filled with explosives that accounted for a variety of vehicles, initially quite mysteriously, until solved by the engineers.[29] By nightfall Brigadier Norman Gwatkin, commanding 5th Guards Armoured Brigade, had called a halt to the Irish Guards' advance at Valkenswaard, 6 miles short of Eindhoven. This has often been offered as evidence of the less than dynamic attitude of the Guards and XXX Corps in MARKET GARDEN, even though Valkenswaard was their intended first-day objective. Horrocks saw nothing wrong in Gwatkin's decision and as 101st US Airborne had not at that stage captured Eindhoven it mattered less than has been imagined. The engineers had in any case to bring forward equipment to bridge an unexpected gap across a crater and the river at Valkenswaard, a move that took some twelve hours. Dempsey was relatively pleased by the progress made and later objected to critical comments about Horrocks, the Guards Armoured Division and the tempo of MARKET GARDEN made by Lionel Ellis, the official historian of the campaign, in an early draft of *Victory in the West*. Dempsey remained quite clear that the ultimate failure of MARKET GARDEN did not lie with them. And the pace of the advance had surprised the Germans; the commander in Eindhoven telephoned the town clerk in Valkenswaard with orders for the German garrison to hold on at all costs, unaware that the village had already been captured.[30]

The German response was not so disjointed and hapless elsewhere. Within a few hours of the initial landings and even before the Guards were entering Valkenswaard, a coordinated response to MARKET GARDEN was developing, the speed and force of which was to surprise the Allies. Walther Model, Kurt Student and Willi Bittrich rapidly grasped the situation and initiated countermeasures, decisions which were in part informed by the capture of the MARKET GARDEN plan from a downed Allied aeroplane. Bittrich wanted to blow the bridges at Nijmegen immediately, before 82nd Airborne could seize them, in order to foil MARKET GARDEN. SS Colonel Heinz Harmel, commanding 10th SS Panzer Division, later stated:

> Model said don't blow the bridge because I need it for a counter-stroke. By that he meant a counter-attack at the higher operational level. Bittrich and I believed it should be blown straight away.[31]

Model may well also have been unwilling to perpetrate an act that might be misconstrued as defeatist and panic-stricken in Berlin. But Model's decision handed an opportunity to the Allies to reach Arnhem, whereas destroying the Nijmegen crossings would have finished MARKET GARDEN immediately; clearly the Allies did not have the monopoly on flawed judgements in September 1944.

German units around the Allied airborne carpet quickly began to firm up their opposition. General Kurt Student organised the resistance around Eindhoven, using available forces to tackle XXX and XII Corps as well as 101st Airborne; General Kurt Feldt's troops of Wehrkreiss VI were to contest control of the Groesbeek Heights, to the southeast of Nijmegen, with 82nd Airborne; whilst Bittrich's troops were to hold Nijmegen itself and assault the British at Arnhem.[32] The ground forces were quick to respond and resistance soon hardened as improvised units came together to offer stubborn if, at times, initially uncoordinated opposition. The German response was nonetheless underpinned by foresight and planning; local commanders had anticipated a possible Allied airborne assault and had established rapid-response plans and lines of communication, while II SS Panzer Corps had specifically prepared for anti-airborne actions.[33]

By 0600 hours on 18 September XXX Corps was again pushing northwards against limited, though irritatingly persistent, opposition and it was only at 1900 that the main force met with 101st Airborne at Eindhoven. Royal Engineers and their bridging equipment were rushing forwards to [illegible] over the River Son, having already been alerted about the problem of the downed bridge earlier that day. Once again, though wonderful to experience, the activities of the British and American troops were hindered by the welcome of the ecstatic Dutch crowds. The Royal Engineers were still able to establish a 110-feet Class Forty Bailey Bridge by 0615 hours on 19 September and XXX Corps were soon advancing once again, this time at much greater speed. The Grenadier Guards group, now in the van, raced through the corridor of airborne troops, passing from the 101st to the 82nd's area of control. The time lost in the sluggish advance to Eindhoven and across the Son was now being made up, and by early afternoon on 19 September 5th Guards Armoured Brigade was positioned in strength just 3 miles outside Nijmegen, itself just 11 miles from Arnhem. If the route through Nijmegen was clear, linking up with 1st Airborne at Arnhem on 20 September appeared possible once again.[34]

Alas, as Allan Adair later remarked:

> My orders had said that the Nijmegen bridge would be in airborne hands by the time we reached it, and we would simply sweep on through. Instead I found that 82nd US Airborne had dropped too far away from Nijmegen.[35]

The bridges indeed still remained in German hands two days after the initial landings. In retrospect it seems quite remarkable that James Gavin and his staff at 82nd Airborne had not fixed upon the immediate capture of the bridges at Nijmegen as the absolute priority for MARKET GARDEN to succeed – particularly when they had baulked at Urquhart's plan at Arnhem where the job of capturing the main bridges was made that much harder by the DZ/LZs being 8 miles away from their target, thus hindering a rapid capture. In his defence it can be said that Gavin had been allocated a whole series of ambitious objectives for MARKET GARDEN by Browning, but nothing concrete was done to focus on the fundamental requirement of capturing the crossings to allow XXX Corps to keep moving. Horrocks for his part believed 82nd US Airborne had done a remarkable job, which is, of course, true, except that the job was in part the wrong one.[36]

Gavin, and later Browning who joined him when I Airborne Corps HQ arrived on 18 September, were both fixated on the Groesbeek Heights which dominated the approaches to Nijmegen and the airborne corridor to the east. This important and crucial position was potentially threatened by German forces advancing out of the Reichswald Forest, if there proved to be anything substantial to advance with. Ironically, although there was conflicting intelligence on the strength of the German forces in the Reichswald Forest, it still should not have taken precedence over Nijmegen; if the Groesbeek Heights were lost MARKET GARDEN might fail, whereas if the Nijmegen bridges were lost MARKET GARDEN would definitely fail – the priority was clear. Yet the perceived risk of the Groesbeek Heights drew in focus and resources away from the Nijmegen bridges and resulted in only a token force attempting to seize the main road bridge in the first few hours of the operation, a force that was easily pinned down by the minimal numbers of defending Germans. Once this effort had come to nothing, Gavin focused on securing the Groesbeek Heights and other supporting objectives, believing he had sufficient time to capture the bridges before XXX Corps arrived. This, of course, risked the Germans destroying the bridges – a measure pressed for by Harmel and Bittrich – and contravened Lieutenant General Lewis Brereton's first principle of MARKET GARDEN: capturing the key bridges with 'thunderclap surprise'. A further limited attempt to seize the road bridge the following day again came to nothing.[37]

With the Nijmegen bridges still out of reach on 19 September, the success of MARKET GARDEN was hanging in the balance. Poor weather had interfered with follow-up airlifts causing delays and cancellations, communications had broken down in a number of places, and the position of 1st Airborne at Arnhem was already deteriorating rapidly. These failings were not complete surprises – getting three days of clear weather in a row in September in Northwest Europe was always unlikely – though the repercussions of this reality were not incorporated into the plan. Officers were already aware of weaknesses in radio equipment and networks, and the plan for 1st Airborne was fraught with communications risk before it got underway. But the enveloping disaster might yet have been averted, or so it appeared to senior commanders, if the bridges at Nijmegen could be captured quickly and XXX Corps pressed on immediately to Arnhem.

Unfortunately, the delay in acting against Nijmegen in sufficient strength had afforded yet more time for the Germans to strengthen their hand, and the task was to prove much more difficult and costly than Horrocks, Browning and Gavin had foreseen, especially once elements of Harmel's 9th SS Panzer Division began to stiffen the resolve of those already in Nijmegen. When Guards Armoured Division began arriving in the town, it became clear that the Germans intended to stand and fight. As Captain Peter Carrington (later Lord Carrington in Margaret Thatcher's first administration), Grenadier Guards, noted:

> Nothing slowed us down until we got to Nijmegen and [we] found ourselves in the middle of a battle. That brought the column to a halt and I remember meeting Chester Wilmot, the war correspondent, who helped drink my last bottle of liberated champagne.[38]

Adair and Gavin quickly put together a plan involving 82nd Airborne infantry and Guards tanks in a joint assault to begin at 1845 hours that evening. The Grenadier Guards provided 1st (Motor) Battalion and 2nd (Armoured) Battalion, whilst the Americans deployed 2nd Battalion, 505th Regiment. They were split into three armour/infantry formations, one to take the road bridge, one the railway bridge and one the Post Office, where local Dutch information indicated that the Germans had set up the equipment to trigger the demolition of the bridges.[39]

This assault, against determined opposition, had only moderate success, despite desperate fighting. Tanks were of limited value in built-up areas and Allied infantry avoided urban combat where possible; it was casualty intensive rather than firepower reliant, the antithesis of Allied, and particularly Anglo-Canadian, thinking. Horrocks met with Browning and Gavin to formulate another plan. The XXX Corps commander pressed for a river assault to seize the north end of the bridges in conjunction with a further simultaneous attempt to capture the south ends. A further attack force was assembled for the following morning, involving the Irish Guards as well as the Grenadiers. On this occasion the Grenadiers and US Airborne troops would continue to press the attack towards the bridges, whilst the Irish Guards along with 502nd US Regiment would clear the west of Nijmegen preparatory to the improvised river crossing in small boats with Major Julian Cook's 3rd Battalion, 504th Regiment. By attempting to capture the bridges from both ends simultaneously, the Allies hoped to confuse the Germans and catch them partially unawares. It was in reality a desperate measure precipitated by the failure of planning in MARKET GARDEN to insist that troops be initially deployed north and south of the bridges, which would have allowed both ends to have been seized in the first place, the responsibility for which fell to Browning and Gavin.[40]

The joint attack in the west set up the opportunity for the assault river crossing, which went in at around 1500 hours following further delays and was supported and covered by the guns of the Irish Guards. The boats used by Cook's troops, and the small supporting group of Royal Engineers, were flimsy and ill suited to such an endeavour, but in one of the most courageous and famous acts of the campaign they forced a crossing despite considerable losses, and turned towards the northern end of the bridges. The Germans were caught out by the audacity of the attack, and, under pressure from the south of the river too, began to fall back. Many of those resisting the paratroopers' initial river assault were fifteen-year-old boys or ageing old hands previously exempted from front-line service, and they soon began to retreat.

With the Americans pressing along the northern riverbank, British tanks forced their way across the main road bridge, spearheaded by a troop of Shermans led by Sergeant Peter Robinson of the Grenadiers. German troops, most likely engineers trying to fix the demolition charges on the bridge, fell victim to the tanks' machine guns as the armour charged forward. Peter Carrington was the first officer across, in the fifth tank, with Germans still in the superstructure of the bridge. Lieutenant Tony Jones of the Royal Engineers was ordered to neutralise the German demolition charges – a tense moment according to Adair – but the charges had already failed.

Heinz Harmel had taken matters into his own hands and given the order to detonate when he saw British tanks on the bridge, but the charges had not exploded. Despite the bravery and determination of the Allied assault, Harmel remained convinced that the key to the successful breakthrough across the bridge had been the weight of Allied artillery which pummelled and dispersed the array of German anti-tank gunners defending the north bank of the Waal: 'Artillery fire was decisive. Because of this the flak crews were dead, or had fled. That is why the tanks managed to get across!'[41] Despite having forced their way over the bridge to link up with the American paratroopers, the Guards were only across in quite limited numbers, darkness was falling, and the Germans were positioned in some strength ahead of them. Heavy criticism has since been levelled at the Guards for not immediately pressing on to Arnhem, yet even leaving aside armoured doctrine which demanded halting at night, the Allies were not established on the north bank of the Waal in anything like sufficient strength to press on, even if paratroopers had supported the few tanks already across the river.

This halt to strengthen the bridgehead, bring over reinforcements and prepare for a push to Arnhem the following day has led to some controversy. Carrington was, according to one account, taken to task by an American officer for not attacking immediately, and terms such as 'yellow-bellied cowards' were supposedly bandied about.[42] Curiously, Carrington later claimed to know nothing of such an exchange and wrote only of a friendly welcome from the US paratroopers. When the Guards did not make a lightning strike for Arnhem immediately after the capture of the bridges, and it later transpired that 1st Airborne were by then in serious trouble, some American troops recorded their frustration at what appeared to be further hesitation and delays on the part of the British forces. Gavin received reports that the British were sitting around drinking tea and he later told Horrocks that he and his troops felt 'let down' by the British for not sending a force straight on to Arnhem as soon as the bridges over the Waal had been crossed.[43]

Yet by then the likelihood of getting through to Arnhem in time to rescue the beleaguered paratroopers hanging on at the north end of the Arnhem bridge had already gone: the Guards tanks pushed across the main road bridge at Nijmegen at around 1900 hours on 20 September and there appeared to be no realistic way of getting through to Arnhem before the following day. Though it later transpired that German opposition between Nijmegen and Arnhem was thin indeed that night, there was no way the British could have known this, and to commit a scratch force of a handful of tanks and infantry along an unreconnoitred road in darkness when the bridgehead on the northern bank of the Waal in Nijmegen had yet to be secured made little sense. By the following day 1st Airborne had already lost their grip on the Arnhem bridge. Culpability for this failure might be placed against XXX Corps and 82nd Airborne, but the crisis confronting Urquhart's 1st Airborne was only becoming apparent to senior Allied commanders around 1500 hours on 20 September when more complete radio links were achieved.[44] The position of Urquhart's troops at Arnhem had begun to deteriorate almost immediately on arrival on 17 September. The plan was already fraught with risk, with units being assigned a variety of tasks on the assumption that the quick race to the Arnhem road bridge would be successful, that follow-up forces would arrive on time, and that the Germans would not react in strength until it was too late. All of these assumptions proved, to a large extent, to be false and as a result the overall plan quickly unravelled, each failure making the likelihood of the success of other parts of the plan less likely. To an airborne division fighting largely isolated from the rest of the army, the impact of such failings proved not just troublesome, but debilitating. Dempsey was certain in his own mind that the failure at Arnhem was down to inept planning on the part of Urquhart and his staff, claiming they were never in the battle as a coherent formation.[45]

The rapid capture of the main objectives, the road and rail bridges at Arnhem plus a pontoon bridge and ferry crossing points, failed to come together as planned. The machine-gun-equipped jeeps of 21st Reconnaissance Squadron either did not arrive with the first drop or quickly came to grief in a German ambush, and of the three battalions of 1st Parachute Brigade only one, 2nd Battalion commanded by Lieutenant Colonel John Frost, made it to the main road bridge as planned, though they were unable to capture the south end. Frost noted years later the foolishness of the plan to capture the bridge from the north only: 'The fundamental mistake of dropping airborne troops on the far side of a large water obstacle when you actually require them on both sides appears altogether too obvious now.'[46]

This mistake was relatively obvious in September 1944, but at Arnhem, as at Nijmegen, the Allies did not incorporate this principle into their planning. Frost's troops attempted to seize the southern end, but they found it was held in some strength and were forced to await supports from the rest of the brigade. The attempt left the spans and support of the bridge burning throughout the night in quite spectacular fashion. The Germans had destroyed the railway bridge before it could be captured and the pontoon bridge was already partially dismantled, rendering it useless. The other two battalions of the brigade became entangled with scratch German forces that emerged in the line ahead of the advancing paratroopers, though there is some evidence that greater energy and flexibility might have engineered a speedier passage towards the bridge at Arnhem.[47] Command, control and communications had already started to break down as the radios deemed suitable for use in an urban area proved not to be; not only was Urquhart unable to contact XXX Corps, First Allied Airborne Army HQ or 82nd Airborne, he could not maintain communications with his units heading into Arnhem itself. Urquhart was forced to press on personally behind the advancing battalions of 1st Parachute Brigade as they pushed into Arnhem, in order to gain a clearer picture of the situation. Unfortunately, he became embroiled in a battalion-level battle and was then cut off from his tactical HQ by infiltrating German units. The following day he was totally isolated after being forced to hole up in a house by German troops. His subordinates were not in strong positions to help either as Brigadier Gerald Lathbury (1st Parachute Brigade) was by then wounded, Brigadier Shan Hackett commanding 4th Parachute Brigade was held up in the UK by poor weather, and Brigadier 'Pip' Hicks commanding 1st Air Landing Brigade was still stuck defending the DZ/LZs some miles from Arnhem. When Hackett and his troops eventually arrived some hours later than planned on 18 September, they did so under fire from the roused German defenders. He and Hicks then clashed over command of the division in Urquhart's continued absence and how best to proceed. By the time Urquhart was able to escape back to his divisional HQ, now centred at the Hartenstein Hotel in Oosterbeek, and re-establish command on the morning of 19 September, the newly arrived troops from the previous day were already ensnared in vicious street fighting and making little headway in breaking through to the beleaguered 2nd Battalion still positioned at the north end of the road bridge in Arnhem. The Poles who were supposed to land to the south of Arnhem on 19 September were also then delayed by poor weather.[48]

Resupply was also proving a problem as the DZ/LZs had by then been given up, but radio links with the outside world had still not been properly established so the RAF was not aware of the changed situation and continued to unload its supplies on the pre-planned DZs straight into the hands of the Germans. The RAF was to suffer excessive criticism for its role in MARKET GARDEN, but in attempting to fly in supplies to 1st Airborne it certainly fulfilled its part of the planned bargain and suffered considerable loss in doing so; 84 transport aircraft were shot down on 601 sorties to Arnhem during the supply operation, even though over 90 per cent of the supplies fell into German hands due to the breakdown in communications. The Luftwaffe had also been effectively suppressed playing only a limited role in the battle, failing to interfere in any serious way with the airlift.[49]

The RAF was also later criticised for the lack of adequate tactical air support, yet this is also largely unfounded. The RAF's 2nd Tactical Air Force, which provided the air support for MARKET GARDEN, was, like the rest of the Allied forces, operating at extreme ranges by September 1944. The small number of short-range Typhoons and Spitfires immediately available were also flying from a limited number of bases close to the front line and were tasked with a wide range of roles and objectives, primarily on 17 September in support of XXX Corps. Dempsey had easily arranged all the air support he and Horrocks deemed fit for their part of MARKET GARDEN with Air Marshal Arthur Coningham (commanding 2nd Tactical Air Force) and Air Vice Marshal Harry Broadhurst (commanding 83 Group). These 21st Army Group/Second Army lines of communication, despite the breakdown in the personal relationship of Montgomery and Coningham – and indeed Tedder – had worked relatively effectively since D-Day in Normandy, but there was little in the way of similarly proven lines of communication between 2nd TAF and First Allied Airborne Army: air-support planning as a result suffered. Requests for air support had to be routed via XXX Corps' artillery net, then to Second Army, through 83 Group RAF, and then to the airfields. Unsurprisingly, the system was therefore not particularly responsive.[50]

Matters were not helped by the inadequate air-transportable radios utilised by the airborne forces, which failed to work effectively in MARKET GARDEN, though even if they had, they were simply not up to the task of linking ground and air assets properly. With limited numbers of aircraft available operating at long range, poor air-ground communications, and inclement weather on 18 and 19 September, it is little wonder that air power was unable to help the airborne forces as much as had been hoped. In reality these expectations were quite unrealistic, for the likelihood of tactical aircraft aiding troops on the ground in an urban environment effectively and safely was already low, and the breakdown in radio communications made matters still more challenging. In his after-action report Roy Urquhart argued that inadequate tactical air support had been a crucial factor in his troops not achieving their objectives in the first few hours of the landings. Yet Frost gave clear evidence of air support aiding his march into Arnhem on 17 September.[51]

By 20 September, German resistance and strength had increased to such a degree that 1st Airborne had been effectively dismembered; Frost's 2nd Battalion held on at the bridge at Arnhem until the morning of 21 September, whilst the rest of the division was penned back into a slowly shrinking position around Oosterbeek with their backs to the north bank of the Rhine. The situation of the troops in the pocket soon began to deteriorate. Lipmann Kessel was a surgeon parachuted into Arnhem with 1st Airborne and he commented on the soldiers he had to treat:

> They were almost silent; uncomplaining and close to indifference. For eight days none of them could have eaten a proper meal or slept more than three or four hours at a stretch. Their eyes were dull and scarlet-rimmed, their faces smeared and unshaven; some already had thick short beards, others merely a few straggling tufts. Through the normal reek of disinfectant came strong smells of sweat, dirty dressings and damp, mud-caked uniforms.[52]

The Polish Brigade eventually arrived south of the river on 20 September, but in much smaller strength than had been imagined due to the weather. It had been intended that they would make use of the Heveadorp ferry at Driel to pump troops and supplies into the bridgehead at Oosterbeek, but the ferry had been scuttled and though some units were pushed across the Rhine, the Poles could be of little substantive help. They, like the surviving elements of 1st Airborne, could only wait for the arrival of XXX Corps.

Having forged a path across the Waal on the evening of 20 September, XXX Corps and supporting American troops began to push the final few miles to Arnhem a little after noon the following day. But a number of crucial factors coalesced to hinder their efforts. The terrain ahead of the Allied forces between Nijmegen and Arnhem was extremely hostile for an armoured advance, with only a single raised road providing a route between flooded low-lying fields, impassable to vehicles. German strength did not need to be great to impede any assault by tanks in this scenario, but this was effectively all the Guards had, as the divisional infantry was still tied up in Nijmegen, as indeed were most of the US paratroopers. The Irish Guards, back in the van, soon hit SS troops, suffered the loss of five tanks, and concluded that this would have to be an advance spearheaded by infantry.

The decision was not in itself invalid but it required 43rd Infantry Division, following on behind Guards Armoured, to push through Nijmegen and position themselves ready to recommence the advance. This delay afforded yet more time for the Germans to strengthen their forces blocking the route to Arnhem, particularly as the road bridge there was now back in their hands, thus allowing yet further reinforcements to head quickly southwards towards Nijmegen. Slowing the progress yet more, the corridor leading to Nijmegen from the MARKET GARDEN start line was repeatedly threatened and at times closed by German forces pressing in from the flanks. The flanking troops of Second British Army, VIII and XII Corps, had been afforded little time and resources to prepare for MARKET GARDEN and now, when called upon to strengthen the Allied hand in the airborne corridor, could only partially fulfil their objectives. Clearly, the terrain between Nijmegen and Arnhem, and the realistic capability of the flanking forces for XXX Corps, were both factors that were known in the planning of MARKET GARDEN, but were disregarded.

In spite of significant shortages in artillery shells, units of 43rd Division and the Guards forced their way through to the Poles at Driel by 23 September, but there was little prospect of forcing a major crossing over the river without large amounts of equipment and a full complement of Royal Engineers – all of which were much too far to the rear of the corridor. Ivor Thomas, commanding 43rd Division, and Stanislaw Sosabowski, commanding the Poles, quickly clashed over what to do to aid 1st Airborne. Sosabowski's attitude was described 'as the reverse of co-operative', but Sosabowski considered Thomas to be rude and arrogant, a description of him that mirrored many others.[53] Horrocks eventually had to intervene and order the Poles to do what they could immediately. Some boats were made available to allow a limited reinforcement but, as Sosabowski argued, this was achieving very little other than chewing up Allied units piecemeal. Sosabowski was not thanked for his candour by the senior British leadership and was later to be regarded as having been difficult and unhelpful at this stage of the battle.

The Lower Rhine was subsequently crossed by 4th Dorsets further downstream from Oosterbeek, but this achieved little other than crippling a decent battalion. The contested river assault demonstrated the fierce resistance the Allies were encountering. Major M. Whittle, 4th Dorsets, later wrote:

> The enemy opened up with counter-fire and at least two of the ten boats in my company were holed badly before reaching the bank. We were launching the first boat when they opened up with MG fire from the opposite bank, the boat sank, and we had several casualties.[54]

Once across, they were forced to press on up a steep bank and by the time they reached the top they had suffered 50 per cent casualties. They remained pinned down for much of the following day.

In fact, MARKET GARDEN was long past salvaging by the time Thomas, Sosabowski and Horrocks started bickering. Realisation of this dawned when Browning too became fully aware of the parlous state of 1st Airborne Division in a communication from Roy Urquhart on 24 September:

> Must warn you that unless physical contact is made with us early 25 Sept consider it unlikely we can hold out long enough. All ranks now exhausted. Lack of rations, water, ammunition and weapons.

> Even slight enemy offensive action may cause complete disintegration. Have attempted our best and will do so as long as possible.[55]

Little could be done in time to prevent such a calamity and therefore the only realistic option, to withdraw what remained of 1st Airborne back across the Rhine, was finally accepted on 25 September. Dempsey had already authorised Horrocks to carry this out if it became obvious that pushing on across the Rhine was ruled out.[56] This decision sparked further querulous exchanges. Sosabowski's behaviour was once again called into question at the meeting of 25 September with Horrocks and Thomas:

> General Sosabowski's attitude at the conference cannot be described as cordial. Having heard the outline of the plan, he said: 'I am General Sosabowski, I command the Polish Para Brigade. I do as I like.' Lt General Horrocks and Maj Gen Thomas exchanged glances. Then Lt Gen Horrocks said: 'You are under my command. You will do as I bloody well tell you.'[57]

Grudgingly, Sosabowski complied, though his attitude, if accurately recorded, may well have been due to his misgivings over MARKET GARDEN, expressed before the operation and having been borne out by the prosecution of the battle. That his troops had suffered as a result clearly caused dismay on his part and he was willing to say so. Whether this was the time to express such views is perhaps another matter, but it was surely insufficient motive alone to warrant his sacking by Browning and Montgomery a few months later, a move which prompted some of the Polish troops to go on hunger strike in protest.[58] When the remnants of 1st Airborne were withdrawn under the cover of darkness and grim weather on 25–26 September, it proved to be perhaps the best-prosecuted action of the entire battle. The 1,700 or so remaining British and Polish troops escaped back across the river under cover of darkness in a well-organised action, with medics and wounded soldiers staying behind in Oosterbeek to conceal the withdrawal. By the morning of 26 September MARKET GARDEN was over and the opportunity to force a vital crossing over the Rhine, if it had indeed ever been anything more than an illusion, was gone.

The fall-out from MARKET GARDEN was considerable and undoubtedly it effectively finished Browning's operational career, and indeed that of Sosabowski – unfairly in the latter's case. Though many senior officers sought to evade responsibility and apportion blame, and though many operational and tactical errors had contributed to the failure of MARKET GARDEN, the real weaknesses had been in higher-level planning and thinking. Montgomery's usually excellent grip on command and overall strategy had failed him in MARKET GARDEN. He had driven through a plan, over which most of his senior staff held serious misgivings, in order to try and retain control over the unfolding strategy of the Northwest European campaign. Level-headed assessments of available intelligence, a more considered evaluation of the realistic prospects for deep airborne operations, and an inclusive and holistic attitude to grand strategy would have surely yielded the cancellation or severe modification of the plan. Such was the small chance of resounding success in MARKET GARDEN when it began on 17 September, that any analysis should not look for reasons for failure as they were all too apparent, but more for why it came as relatively close as it did to succeeding.

In MARKET GARDEN Montgomery and his staff had lost sight of what their forces excelled in and were capable of in 1944. The British were best suited to orderly operations, fought within means, properly supported and underpinned by good intelligence, and logistically sound. The linchpin of this was crushing superiority in firepower – ground and air based. The plan for the Arnhem operation cast this doctrine to one side, in the face of mounting evidence that the Germans were growing in strength and might not collapse as they had since the Seine had been crossed. Without the usual weight of artillery supporting them and with poor weather and issues in ground-air communications restricting air support, the ground forces struggled to inject sufficient energy into their push towards Arnhem, and it was a severe misjudgement on the part of Montgomery to expect them to do so. He had moulded and shaped the British Army in a particular way since 1942, imposing order, rigour and clear thinking to the extent that it produced highly effective results; in September 1944 it was as if he lost sight of the machine he had played a crucial part in creating.

There is no doubt that Montgomery and Eisenhower and many around them were being swept along by the desire to finish the war quickly and that this resulted in the commitment to MARKET GARDEN, but perhaps the greatest tragedy was that even if Arnhem had been reached in time and the bridges secured, this would anyway not have resulted in the collapse of German resistance and brought an end to the war. Far from being on the point of surrender, German strength was recovering, while the stretched supply lines of the Allies were continuing to hinder their operations and would in any case have soon curtailed Montgomery's dream of speeding on to Berlin. The weather was closing in and the British Army was in for a hard winter's campaigning.

9

WINTER
Frustration and Anxiety

WITH THE FAILURE of MARKET GARDEN the likelihood of the war continuing into the autumn and winter of 1944–5 became a stark reality for the British Army in September 1944. The rapid victory that some, though not all, had been imagining to be probable following the race to Antwerp and Brussels now became a distant prospect, and 21st Army Group had to reconcile itself to putting its house in order. The issue of the Scheldt estuary remained to be resolved, and the Arnhem gamble had rendered as most unlikely the prospects of opening up Antwerp speedily to ease the logistical headaches confounding Montgomery's administrative staff.

Eisenhower was unaware of how much damage had been done to the Antwerp question by MARKET GARDEN, but Montgomery was better acquainted with the realities and although he had been unwilling to accept the situation, he now had little option other than to do what the strategic situation demanded. He admitted in his memoirs that he had underestimated the level of the task confronting 21st Army Group in opening up Antwerp: 'I reckoned that the Canadian Army could do it *while* we were going for the Ruhr. I was wrong.' Dempsey also believed the lack of attention paid to opening up Antwerp to be a grave error on the part of his chief.[1] This misjudgement illustrates the overconfidence at 21st Army Group HQ in early to mid-September 1944, but the situation was now compounded by the commitment of much of Second Army to the continued fighting in the Nijmegen corridor for some time to come, preventing their redeployment to help with the Antwerp problem. Dempsey's forces were subjected to repeated attacks in the aftermath of MARKET GARDEN, in particular a determined effort from the northeast of the Reichswald Forest on 28 September and another south from Arnhem on 1 October. All were intended to recover the bridges at Nijmegen and were only driven back after bitter fighting. British firepower was here again a crushing advantage:

> In a three-battalion attack . . . only one company of one battalion crossed start line. Enemy called for truce to bury dead – refused. 82 United States Airborne Division offered to lend a bulldozer for the job.[2]

The Germans even managed to bring down the road bridge at Nijmegen following a daring frogmen raid, but the crossing was operational again within a day or so after rapid work by the bridging units of the Royal Engineers.[3]

With Second Army committed, Harry Crerar's First Canadian Army were left as the principal weapon for clearing the Scheldt estuary and opening up Antwerp. But they had also been undermined by the focus on MARKET GARDEN, as the administrative staff later acknowledged:

> Operation MARKET GARDEN had to commence for operational reasons at a time when the administrative resources were barely able to support it. The estimates of rail and other capacities had proved too optimistic with the result that although it was supported with . . . rations, petrol and ammunition, this was only achieved at the expense of ordnance and other stores for Second Army and of the build-up for First Canadian Army.[4]

Now that it had become clear that the war would not be over in the autumn of 1944, the pressure to open up Antwerp increased significantly. The administrative and logistical pickle in which the Allies found themselves towards the end of September was becoming more apparent by the day. Lieutenant General Humfrey Gale, the chief administrative officer at SHAEF, noted: 'The overall reason for our troubles is that we have outrun our bulk supply and the available stock of flimsy tins in the theatre – which is enormous – is insufficient to cover the great amount of territory over which we are now operating.'[5] The ordnance staff at 21st Army Group were also aware of the situation:

> It became plain that we should need to re-group and re-equip. Here then was another firm test of ordnance, for the main flow of stores and ammunition was still far from the Rear Maintenance Area, hundreds of miles away. Road transport simply did not exist in anything like sufficient quantity. The railways were only coming into operation, and were already over-taxed.[6]

Montgomery stated his concerns about the administrative problems confronting the Allies on 20 September, and saw Gale the following day. Monty singled out the problems facing General Bradley's 12th Army Group as being of most concern, though he remained convinced that they had brought the difficulties on themselves by allowing Patton's Third Army to continue its breakneck advance, thus gobbling up dwindling resources at the expense of a considered overall focused strategy – in short, Montgomery's northern narrow-thrust approach. Montgomery stated as much in a pointed message to Eisenhower the following day: 'From what Gale tells me it seems clear that 12 Army Group has been allowed to outstrip its maintenance and as a result we have lost flexibility throughout the battle area as a whole.'[7] The change in command on 1 September and Gale himself were to blame, according to Montgomery's analysis, but the consequence was that 'unless it [the administrative position] improves, the tempo of operations will have to be reduced'.[8]

Montgomery was being a little unfair on Gale, whose position at SHAEF was much less crucial to the supply situation than might be imagined, and who in contrast had considered Montgomery to be a fine commander with a firm grip, who issued clear orders and knew what he wanted. But Gale had been one of the key officers who presented Eisenhower with many reasons for blocking Montgomery's single-thrust drive for Berlin on supply grounds and was thus consigned to feel the ire of Monty.[9] Like his fellow British officers at SHAEF, Gale was in an invidious position, caught between the drive and determination of Montgomery and 21st Army Group on the one hand, and the political and diplomatic needs of the Anglo-American alliance on the other, with the War Office having to act as arbitrator on occasion. Gale's position was in part limited because 12th and 21st Army Group's teams effectively looked after their own logistical situations with a high degree of independence from SHAEF, though Gale coordinated such efforts. He always considered the Anglo-Canadians to be better organised logistically than the Americans, and this in part explained some of the issues now facing Bradley.

The port situation concerned Gale gravely, and he knew full well that in a matter of weeks the Mulberry Harbour back at Arromanches in Normandy would begin to decline in capacity, with further adverse consequences. He had been agitating about this eventuality since August: 'There are too many people with their fingers in this Mulberry pie and it is getting in a tangle as a consequence.'[10] In the days leading up to MARKET GARDEN Gale and his staff had been hammering home the pivotal nature of Antwerp to future operations and believed they had got Montgomery to accept the point. If he did he was still committed to reaching for the Rhine and risking a delay in opening up the port. Lack of fuel was also becoming acute by the time MARKET GARDEN began, further undermining any lingering hopes of 21st Army Group carrying on to Berlin, even if Arnhem and its bridges could be seized.[11] Major General Miles Graham, 21st Army Group's Chief Administrative Officer, noted on 16 September, '21st Army Group petrol situation was becoming critical. No bulk facilities existed except in Port-en-Bessin where bad weather might interfere with tanker discharge.'[12]

The railway and transport situation also caused consternation with Montgomery's senior staff who, annoyed at the perceived lack of progress, agitated for the replacement of Brigadier I.L.H. Mackillop as Deputy Quarter Master in charge of movement and transport at 21st Army Group. Both Montgomery and Graham wanted to bring in another North African veteran, Brigadier Arthur Rhé-Philipe, or Major General Charles Napier. Despite the reservations of Major General Alfred Godwin-Austen, Quarter Master General at the War Office, such measures were pushed through in order to pep up the supply situation, with Napier taking up the post. Gale also agitated for changes, advocating a new Director of Railways to deal with the problems being encountered on the rail network in France and Belgium, and even called for the employment of suitably qualified PoWs as engineers: 'make them mend the mess their people have made!'[13]

Ultimately, with the supply chain still catching up, the railway network and the rolling stock in tatters following months of aerial bombardment, particularly in France, and with the destruction meted out by the retreating Germans, there was little prospect of the logistical problems being resolved quickly. Consequently, 21st Army Group would have to open up Antwerp as soon as practicable and defend the Nijmegen salient with a sharply diminished capability.

But the British Army was neither inactive nor passive following MARKET GARDEN. In early October Second Army launched an operation to push back the eastern flank of the Nijmegen corridor, codenamed Operation CONSTELLATION carried out by VIII Corps. O'Connor's VIII Corps had previously made some progress offering flanking support to XXX Corps in MARKET GARDEN, even though it had had to rush forwards some 300 miles to be in position to do so. They had still advanced some 50 miles between 18 and 24 September, despite being short of the levels of artillery and air support usually afforded to British ground operations. By late September progress was slowing and the necessity of organising a set-piece battle seemed unavoidable. Once again 11th Armoured Division had proved itself to be a very effective formation, perhaps highlighting the case that they might have been a better choice to spearhead MARKET GARDEN. Even so, Major General 'Pip' Roberts' troops had suffered grievous losses when Lieutenant Colonel David Silvertop and Lieutenant Colonel Hubert Orr, commanding 3rd RTR and 3rd Monmouths, respectively, had been killed in an ambush on 25 September. The loss of such experienced and proven commanders was a serious blow to the division.[14]

O'Connor's forces had been intended to participate in a much larger action, Operation GATWICK, which was also to involve XXX Corps in a simultaneous effort to clear the Maas Pocket and the Reichswald Forest in one fell swoop. But Dempsey and O'Connor agreed that this was too ambitious for the troops and resources available, and they devised a smaller, though still grand, multi-divisional operation to replace it.[15] Operation CONSTELLATION was intended to clear up the remaining German forces west of the Maas river, in the so-called 'Peel' area, and was to involve two armoured divisions (11th and 7th US – attached to Second Army at this time), two infantry divisions (3rd and 15th Scottish) and two brigades (6th Guards Tank and 1st Belgian).[16] The terrain over which the operation would be fought was well suited to stout and stubborn defence, constituted as it was of reclaimed marshland and fields surrounded by deep drainage dykes which did not function as effectively as they might in the winter, leaving the ground a sticky quagmire. Local Dutch folklore maintained that no army had ever captured the region. The difficulty of the task was underscored by the problems encountered by the newly arrived 7th US Armored Division when it attempted to battle its way through to Venraij, some 30 miles east of Eindhoven, in the days before CONSTELLATION came together. The formation was inexperienced – one condescending British comment stated: 'Their morale was rather higher than their skill' – and although it was later to show itself to be effective and competent, it struggled at first. CONSTELLATION was in part born out of the difficulties endured by 7th US Armored.[17]

The advance of CONSTELLATION began on 12 October and was, as ever, firepower based with a heavy artillery barrage leading the way and the RAF again playing an important role. But air support was not as heavy as had been hoped for, owing to air assets being diverted east to Aachen in Germany, and key bridges behind the German lines remained intact, allowing the enemy to bring up reinforcements faster than anticipated. The German opposition was tough enough, 'first class infantry men, brave and tenacious in their defence', with the positions strengthened by parachute formations.[18] Though the fighting was grim and the weather inclement, the multi-divisional offensive began to achieve results. Despite the usual array of mines (including a newly encountered mine that was powerful enough to disable heavy Churchill tanks), obstacles, roadblocks and carefully positioned defensive positions, the Germans were driven back to Overloon by the initial assault. Once again engineers supported the armour and infantry, and together they battled their way through the Germans' prepared defences and Overloon was captured. Further exploitation to Venraij proved slower going; troops in 6th Guards Tank Brigade noted that the concentrations of minefields were the greatest they had yet encountered. The terrain was heavy with thick woods, the ground sandy and loose, whilst the artillery barrage seemed to have limited effects on the Germans. To the west, 11th Armoured were pressed into rapid action, with infantry units having to work with non-divisional artillery support at short notice, and as a result encountering friendly-fire incidents. They still achieved their goals, though they had a nasty surprise when encountering anti-personnel Schu-Mines for the first time. The 4th King's Shropshire Light Infantry noted sardonically: 'A PoW fortunately demonstrated the presence of Schu-Mines by inadvertently stepping on one.'[19]

The British battered their way into Venraij and suppressed the opposition by 18 October, after some days of fierce and unrelenting action. By then, German defences in the sector were crumbling and, when 7th US Armored began to advance more aggressively towards Venlo some 10 miles south of Venraij, the overall objective of clearing the Maas Pocket seemed imminent. This was indeed how O'Connor had planned the whole operation, and VIII Corps was about to deliver the knockout blow to the Germans with 15th Scottish ready to drive eastwards to the Maas at Roermond. Roberts considered O'Connor to be at his best during CONSTELLATION. Unfortunately, the strategic situation cut the ground from under O'Connor as he was ordered to withdraw 15th Scottish Division and 6th Guards Tank Brigade and despatch them westwards to aid operations intended to speed up the opening of Antwerp. Montgomery had finally and resolutely announced this as his top priority.[20]

Operation CONSTELLATION, although falling short of its primary aim, still demonstrated that British (and US) troops could make progress against a resolute foe in difficult and dense terrain, even when hindered by deteriorating weather and not supported by the usual lavish air assets. O'Connor expressed his dismay at not being able to finish off the task allotted to him: 'It has been very sad not being able to finish it off. It will have to be done sometime without doubt.'[21] This proved to be doubly true when a determined German counter-attack spearheaded by 9th Panzer Division fell on the 7th US Armored Division on 27 October, throwing the Allies backwards with the loss of Meijel, midway between Venlo and Eindhoven. The attack came as something of a surprise for the German build-up had been covered by a week of fog, but though some consternation was caused, O'Connor was able to bring in reinforcements and support the American formation, initially with artillery and then with the recalled 6th Guards Tank Brigade and 15th Scottish Division. The guns of 25th Field Artillery Regiment, RA, loosed off some 10,000 rounds in support of the US troops, who battled hard to fend off the German assault, suffering the loss of some 1,265 troops by 6 November. At one point O'Connor had to step in to assert clear control over the American division's plans. The pivotal period in the fighting came on 29 October when heavy Allied artillery once again proved devastating in breaking up the German attacks. The offensive petered out and the Germans slowly fell back.[22]

That the Allies could have been caught out in this way demonstrated once again that the Germans were far from finished and that over-confidence could lead to errors on the part of British high command; it underscored one of Montgomery's maxims that his army must not be 'off balance' in order to reduce the risk of the Germans delivering counterblows. With 21st Army Group's attention focused on the Scheldt estuary by late October, leaving VIII Corps at reduced strength to cover some 70 miles of front line following CONSTELLATION, the enemy had been afforded a decent platform with which to launch such an offensive blow. It was, however, testament to the strength in depth and mobility of 21st Army Group that they were quickly able to deal with the situation.

Yet there were substantial consequences at higher command level in the wake of the fighting. Montgomery had previously questioned the capabilities of US 7th Armored commander General Lindsay Silvester during CONSTELLATION and had lobbied Eisenhower to have him removed; now after the German attack had caught the American division unawares, Omar Bradley sacked Silvester before further Allied operations began in November. O'Connor was appalled, believing the Americans would think it was he who had pressed for Silvester's replacement when in fact, though thinking Silvester no Napoleon, he argued that the US commander and his team had done a decent job. O'Connor believed Dempsey and Montgomery had conspired to move Silvester on because they 'did not like his face'. It seems that Montgomery and Bradley were behind the measure rather than Dempsey, as he also recorded some support for Silvester, but to no avail. However, Brigadier Michael Carver, commanding 4th Armoured Brigade attached to 7th US Armored at the time, did not hold Silvester in similar esteem, and even Silvester's team did not expect him to last long in command.[23]

O'Connor felt undermined and compromised by this move and asked to be relieved of his command. His position at 21st Army Group had always been mildly uncomfortable as he was, in some ways, senior to Montgomery and not one of Monty's chaps. Yet although there were rumours of a whispering campaign against O'Connor, there is little evidence to support the allegation that Montgomery and Brooke conspired to move him on; indeed, Montgomery was usually publicly fulsome in his praise for O'Connor.[24] In any case, Dempsey persuaded O'Connor to carry on, and it was Brooke who decided that he should move O'Connor on to take up the position of GOC Eastern Command in India. The order was issued on 27 November and was technically a promotion, allaying O'Connor's fears that his offer to resign would finish his career. O'Connor was still dismayed that Montgomery did not appear to try and keep him in command of VIII Corps, something O'Connor would appear to have wished to retain. 'It was no doubt a young man's war, and perhaps I was getting too old for the job,' O'Connor later recalled.[25] Though Dempsey supported O'Connor, he later accepted the possibility that his VIII Corps commander had lost some of the drive that had made his name in the desert three years earlier.[26]

Earlier in November, 21st Army Group had once again turned its attention to clearing the Maas Pocket in what would be O'Connor's last operational command of the campaign. A combined XII and VIII Corps offensive comprising Operations MALLARD and NUTCRACKER committed British and Allied troops to fighting once again across flat, flooded terrain quite unsuited to heavy equipment and which placed a premium on the ability of the Royal Engineers to keep the battle moving. Air support was increasingly exposed to the vagaries of the November weather in Northwest Europe, and the ability to bring forward heavy and medium artillery was constrained by the limited transportation network. In order to ease the way forward, Second British Army allocated considerable assets from 79th Armoured Division to the battle along with armoured vehicles and equipment of the Royal Engineers (AVRE) and an ever-increasing use of Kangaroo armoured personnel carriers, now supplemented by Buffalo amphibious assault craft which were capable of carrying thirty soldiers. German resistance to XII Corps in MALLARD, which began on 14 November, was limited to delaying actions, and the British soldiers found that dealing with the vicissitudes of the terrain and weather generated the greatest problems. One account noted:

> It was an unhappy time of year in an unhappy countryside. Rain poured down on a chilly world of drenched fields and miserable villages which had been battered to pieces by both sides, and especially during the latest German attack.[27]

The Germans at last showed their hand on 17 November when they attempted to drive back the 51st Highlanders who had forced a crossing over the Uitwaterings (or Zig) Canal. The vicious counter-attack, supported by an unusually heavy concentration of fire support, was beaten off with a liberal application of artillery to support the 5th Cameronians in the defence. The Germans persevered with the attack, despite their casualties, but failed to make any useful impact on the British positions. The Highlanders then pushed on to their objectives in darkness through thick mud and driving rain, 'a thoroughly miserable experience' as one account put it in typically understated fashion; 'and none of those who survived ever forgot the terror that accompanied the dreaded crossing of the canals'.[28]

As MALLARD achieved its objectives, NUTCRACKER was launched on 19 November, spearheaded by 15th Scottish Division, followed three days later by 11th Armoured Division. Progress was steady and remorseless and the general intention was to avoid incurring heavy casualties. This often meant units halting and waiting in the line for some days whilst other units positioned themselves on the flanks or in different sectors. This left troops fixed in grim positions in heavy rain, cold and mud, with supplies limited by the wholly inadequate roads. Troops recalled the conditions as miserable, deflating and dispiriting. When 15th Scottish troops reached their first-phase objective, all that lay ahead of them were the Peel marshes: 'The prospect ahead looked grim enough. Seen through pouring rain and in the glare of fitful fires, the Peel was indeed the abomination of desolation.'[29] Steadily and surely the British maintained the pressure in what was essentially an infantry battle, with limited armour and fire support. The British forces pressed on, winkling out the defending Germans who continued to offer only limited resistance and frustrating delaying actions.

By the end of the month, the British had forced the enemy back to the Maas where the Germans continued to hold out in strength on the west banks around Venlo. In a set-piece action on 3 December even this final bastion fell, along with its garrison. This operation, codenamed GUILDFORD, was conducted principally by 15th Scottish Division, supported by as much panoply of equipment as could be mustered, including specialised armour, engineering units, Crocodile and Wasp flame-throwers and mine-clearing tanks. The operation was essentially textbook and despite the nature and level of obstacles, minefields, traps and trenches prepared by the Germans, the battle lasted only a single day. Of GUILDFORD, the 44th Brigade history later noted:

> Each time the recipe was the one learned at Blerick [the objective of GUILDFORD, on the west bank of the Maas adjacent to Venlo which was situated on the eastern bank] – meticulous preparation and planning,

> concentration of all available firepower, use of the 'Funnies' [79th Armoured Division's specialist armour] to overcome the obstacles and a quick, bold use of the infantry to exploit the advantage won by the success of the armour – if possible by moving straight into the heart of the enemy position. This recipe brought quick success at little cost.[30]

It was the failure of infantry exploitation that had confounded many attacks so far in the campaign, but experienced formations which had seen repeated action since D-Day, despite heavy losses in personnel, had developed effective methods that limited casualties, yet still yielded effective results.

It was still the case that had sufficient forces been available to Montgomery in mid-October during CONSTELLATION, the grim battles to clear the Maas Pocket in November might have been avoided; but the imperative of clearing the Scheldt estuary had taken precedence. Montgomery claimed in early October that 21st Army Group operations would have to be scaled back and attention focused largely on the Scheldt issue unless more forces were allocated to his command. Little was forthcoming, but it took another two weeks or so for 21st Army Group staff to acknowledge that more forces would have to be thrown at the Scheldt, and it was this that led to CONSTELLATION being scaled back.[31]

Hopes that the First Canadian Army could deal with the issue of the Scheldt estuary were wholly unrealistic as Crerar's forces were more limited in numbers than Dempsey's. The Canadian Army had to clear the Germans from the Breskens Pocket on the south bank of the Scheldt, and drive westwards from the neck of the Beveland peninsula towards the sea to capture Walcheren Island. Then the Allied navies would have to sweep the river to clear it of mines and obstacles before any shipping could make use of Antwerp's intact but idle port facilities. Confronting the Allies was the German Fifteenth Army, much of which had been ferried across the Scheldt to Walcheren and Beveland whilst 21st Army Group had been focused on MARKET GARDEN. By 23 September some 82,000 German troops, 530 guns and 4,600 vehicles had been shipped across the river, enhancing their defences on the north bank and on the island of Walcheren. There were still significant numbers of troops south of the river around Breskens to resist the Canadians, and much of the land had been flooded by the Germans, creating still further headaches. Many German divisions throughout the Scheldt area were seriously understrength and short of equipment and resources, but they could still muster considerable numbers of troops, many of whom were experienced in combat. Whilst the British forces to the east of the Nijmegen corridor had been confounded by the weather and terrain as much as the enemy in October and November, the same could not be said of the fighting to open the Scheldt.[32] Whilst II Canadian Corps focused on the Breskens Pocket, I Corps, commanded by John Crocker with 49th Infantry Division operating alongside 2nd Canadian Infantry and 1st Polish Armoured Divisions, attacked north out of Antwerp to close the land link between the enemy forces in Beveland and those beyond.

The advance by I Corps was resisted in considerable strength by German units, principally by Kurt Student's Parachute Army, and more Allied troops were fed into the line to hold the position as long as possible. Losses were heavy but the Germans were forced to give ground, if slowly. By the end of September the Allies had drained the enemy's reserves and captured the Turnhout Canal.

The next objective of Crocker's troops was Tilburg to the northeast, and the 49th Division worked closely with the Poles to begin the assault. The Germans were well aware of the seriousness of such a development for the long-term viability of denying the use of Antwerp to the Allies. German Fifteenth Army commander General Gustav von Zangen issued clear views on the vital nature of preventing the enemy clearing the Scheldt: 'each day you deny the port of Antwerp to the enemy will be vital'. He backed this up with reinforcements of some 3,000 keen and eager troops.[33]

Crocker was forced to scale back his next moves as Montgomery's attention was still focused elsewhere. Second Army shuffled its pack leaving too much for Crocker's troops to cover, causing further delays to the advance. Rumours of a shortage of ammunition in First Canadian Army did little to assuage fears that 21st Army Group was less than fully committed to opening up Antwerp as an immediate priority. Consequently, it took the Allies some ten days to 16 October to push through the 15 miles necessary to close the land link to the German forces remaining in Beveland, Walcheren and Breskens. Losses were considerable, particularly in the Canadian and Polish forces, the latter suffering a lack of infantry replacements despite combing out many Polish soldiers from enemy units captured during the rout from Normandy. The Canadians were simultaneously forcing their way into the Breskens Pocket. Two previous attempts had failed but on 6 October better progress was made, and despite stubborn resistance most of the pocket was eliminated by mid-October, though German resistance was not completely cleared until early November.

By mid-October the strategic imperative in 21st Army Group had also shifted, following another exchange between Eisenhower and Montgomery over the nature of high command in the Allied armies in Western Europe. Monty had complained to General Marshall on 8 October that all was not well with the central direction of the land campaign and had not been so since he had handed over command to Eisenhower. He laid out his thinking on the matter in a memo to SHAEF on 10 October, effectively criticising the whole command set-up in SHAEF:

> I do not believe it is possible to conduct operations successfully in the field unless there exists a good and sound organisation for command and control. I do not believe we have a good and sound organisation for command and control.[34]

Eisenhower rebuffed Montgomery's criticisms and offered to take the matter higher up the command chain if Monty was so dissatisfied – effectively telling Montgomery to toe the line or face being replaced. But Eisenhower was much more exercised by 21st Army Group's lingering non-committal attitude to the vital necessity of opening up Antwerp. Despite poor weather slowing down the rate by which supplies could be pumped into Europe, 21st Army Group's operational directives still hinted at wider objectives than just clearing the Scheldt; Monty outlined this attitude on 9 October and again five days later. On 15 October Montgomery received a direct and unequivocal order from Ike to focus everything on opening up Antwerp. Eisenhower pointed out that the difficult supply situation confronting 21st Army Group was as nothing compared to that facing Bradley's American forces. Montgomery, knowing that Eisenhower would be backed by Churchill and Marshall, and probably even Brooke, backed down completely. He replied to Eisenhower on 16 October:

> You will hear no more on the subject of command from me. I have given you my views and you have given your answer.
>
> I have given Antwerp top priority in all operations in 21 Army Group and all energies and efforts will now be devoted towards opening up that place.[35]

Montgomery instructed his commanders to give the matter complete priority over all others, 'without any qualifications whatsoever'. Yet he still grumbled to Lieutenant General Archie Nye, Vice Chief of the Imperial General Staff in London, that the whole matter was in part a result of the Q situation (supply) getting out of control since 1 September, when Montgomery had passed overall command to Eisenhower.[36]

To deal with Antwerp once and for all, Montgomery reined in O'Connor's Operation CONSTELLATION and committed a reinforced

XII Corps to link with I Corps in dealing with Tilburg and 's-Hertogenbosch. This would also protect the flank of II Canadian Corps, as this formation was soon to begin pressing along the South Beveland peninsula towards the island of Walcheren. All of this would be necessary to open up Antwerp. Plans were also stepped up to prepare for Operation INFATUATE, the joint services amphibious and land assault on Walcheren Island. I Corps' forces battled their way towards Breda on 20 October, beating off German counter-attacks and inflicting heavy losses. Neil Ritchie's XII Corps, in much greater strength, launched Operation PHEASANT two days later with the aim of capturing Tilburg and 's-Hertogenbosch and clearing the area as far as the Maas. These operations once again took place in awkward terrain with canals, rivers, low-lying ground and a paucity of useful roads along the axis of advance. Intelligence reports indicated that the Germans could muster some 56 battalions against XII Corps.[37] PHEASANT was another example of how the British Army functioned highly effectively in set-piece battles.

Yet again operations were enhanced by the embellishments of Kangaroos, Royal Engineer equipment, self-propelled artillery and other supporting units. One battalion alone had some 111 vehicles to aid the assault, creating a column some 1.5 miles long based on a standard 20 yards between each vehicle. Such support and careful detailed planning in the days leading up to the attack proved hugely beneficial. The operation began effectively and 53rd Division, leading the drive towards 's-Hertogenbosch, proceeded according to the operational timetable until 25 October, when progress slowed a little. Opposition was stubborn in places and two key bridges were damaged, hindering the assault, but by the evening of 26 October 's-Hertogenbosch had been effectively secured, partly as a result of a surprise penetration by 1st East Lancashire Regiment who under the cover of darkness managed to infiltrate 1.5 miles behind the Germans' forward defensive lines outside the town.[38] This manoeuvre severely compromised the German position and accelerated their collapse, a factor acknowledged later by the garrison commander. But resistance was still sustained over a period of four days before 's-Hertogenbosch was finally subdued. The whole operation to seize the town was another example of how the British Army had developed its practices; the integration of the various arms – infantry, armour, artillery and engineers, with only limited air support due to the inclement weather – showed that the army could handle itself well enough, even in difficult operating environments against a redoubtable enemy.[39] The 53rd Division's view was later recorded as:

> The attack on 's-Hertogenbosch is perhaps the best example in modern times of a successful assault on a large town held by a resolute and skilful

> enemy. Larger and more important towns were captured during the campaign, but they either capitulated at an early stage or were comparatively easily reduced.[40]

A few miles further south 51st Highland Division pressed forward flanking the moves of 53rd Division. They quickly seized the small town of Schijndel whilst suffering a heavy *Nebelwerfer* (rocket-propelled mortar) attack. The local Dutch population were as ever elated to be liberated, though some thought the Scots were Americans until indignant soldiers put them right. The effects of combat on communities became all too apparent to some troops. Private John Tough recalled on meeting a liberated Dutch family:

> When the joy subsided the farmer's family told us that their daughter had just been killed in the shelling. We were stunned. It made such an impression on me that these people could have given us such a welcome at a time when they were grieving for their child.[41]

When the division entered Vught, just outside 's-Hertogenbosch, on 26 October, many troops were horrified by the discovery of a concentration camp. Though abandoned (the inmates had been moved to Belsen), there was still a good deal of evidence of the atrocities perpetrated there. With the overall plan going well, 15th Scottish Division with 6th Guards Tank Brigade in support began their advance towards Tilburg, with the enemy falling back leaving only booby traps, mines and blown bridges to harass the British soldiers. The Royal Engineers again quickly provided replacement bridges, whilst AVRE equipment was also called into action. The advance pressed on. Tilburg was captured in the early hours of 28 October against very limited opposition, the enemy still conforming to the pattern of maintaining a semi-orderly retreat rather than offering anything other than sporadic opposition. The liberation was once again a memorable occasion for all concerned:

> The non-stop celebrations which the people of Tilburg kept up for thirty-six hours are beyond any description. Ninety-thousand men, women and children were in the streets – laughing, dancing, and singing.
> None could see these sights unmoved.[42]

By 28 October the enemy was falling back along the line in the face of a remorseless if steady advance by XII Corps, with 51st Highlanders and 7th Armoured Division delivering the final push. As the British approached

Raamsdonk to the north of Tilburg, enemy resistance intensified in order to try and keep the Pereboom Bridge route open as long as possible for retreating German forces to escape northwards across the Maas. A small counter-attacking force was despatched into and through Raamsdonk to halt the British advance. This was to little avail and a combined 1st Northants Yeomanry and 154th Brigade column of infantry in Kangaroos repelled the Germans and reached the Maas at Raamsdonk on 31 October.[43]

To the south and west, I Corps had continued to push the Germans back away from the flank of the Canadian forces pressing on to Beveland. As part of these operations, the 49th West Riding Division of Major General 'Bubbles' Barker was tasked with driving northwards towards the Maas along the coastal region. Liberation of towns and villages still brought enthusiastic civilians on to the streets with pleasing results. Gunner John Mercer noted the comments of a recently liberated civilian, who stated:

> When the Germans were here and we encountered them on the pavement we had to get out of the way always. But with your soldiers it is they who move out of the way and get into the road. This may seem trivial to you, but to me it is a mark of a civilised nation.[44]

The division was continuing to progress its tactical systems as the advance continued and the issue of infantry-armour cooperation was constantly being refined. More and more examples of textbook assaults with tanks and artillery combined with infantry were delivering low-casualty successes. Though the enemy was less intent on fierce and aggressive resistance in Belgium and the Netherlands, confused and naïve assaults by British troops could still result in Allied casualties; that these were fewer in number indicated the tactical progress.[45]

Urban fighting still caused heavy casualties, however, as the Allies' equipment and firepower superiority could not be deployed so readily. Vince Spring of 2nd Glosters recalled:

> The thing I detested most was house-to-house fighting. You had to move in, get the enemy out and move on to the next building. That was unpleasant. The majority of actions were uninspiring but dangerous, and if you had to clear an orchard or building or field you invariably had men killed or badly wounded.[46]

In the east Breda was captured and cleared by 1st Polish Armoured Division by 29 October; 4th Canadian Armoured Division seized Bergen op

Zoom on the coast; and 49th Division pressed on to Roosendaal midway between the two. This seemed as though it would be a daunting task as early encounters in the approach to the town proved costly, prompting Lieutenant Colonel Trevor Hart Dyke, commanding the 1/4th King's Own Yorkshire Light Infantry, to request a set-piece artillery and armour-supported assault. But a patrol under cover of mist infiltrated the town and discovered that the Germans had in fact pulled out.[47]

Field Marshal Gerd von Rundstedt sought permission in these desperate days for the Germans to withdraw Fifteenth Army across the Maas, whilst it still could get away. Berlin demurred, ordering that firm and stout resistance be maintained. But despite attempts to fix new defensive lines, circumstances repeatedly overtook German plans. By the beginning of November they had been driven back towards the Maas with only I Corps encountering serious opposition.

By 8 November the Maas had been reached and the objectives of I and XII Corps achieved. Yet the German retreat never collapsed into a rout and they employed excellent delaying tactics and occasional bouts of determined resistance. The British and Allied forces in the area could not be halted, however, and though they were unable to deliver a knockout blow and bag tens of thousands of prisoners, they were nonetheless able to achieve the principal result of clearing the enemy from the region between Antwerp and the Maas to secure Allied supply lines. The terrain and weather had been key factors in determining the pace of events; the work of the Royal Engineers was again pivotal, with a vast range and number of bridging duties to be performed. The Germans continually recorded their surprise at the speed with which the British were able to traverse obstacles such as canals, rivers and flooded land. Meanwhile the RAF was as ever playing a key role, but one limited by flying conditions.

In order to capitalise on the success, the rest of the Scheldt zone required clearing by the Allies before the job of sweeping the river of mines and other obstacles could begin. The Canadians began their advance along the Beveland peninsula with Operation VITALITY I on 24 October, followed by VITALITY II which was an amphibious outflanking manoeuvre designed to break German resistance on the Beveland Canal. These landings brought into action the British 52nd Lowland Division, which had been seeking an active role throughout the campaign. It had originally been developed as a mountain division with hard and testing training directed by tough, relatively uncompromising regular senior officers. Soldiers unable to endure the testing regime were shipped out. The commanding officer, Major General Edmund Hakewill-Smith, enforced strict discipline and believed his division to be the toughest, fittest and hardest in the British Army. The unfolding war appeared at one stage to be passing 52nd Division by, so Brooke transformed them into a partially air-transportable division, capable of being airlifted, though not dropped, into action. Hakewill-Smith's troops had been on stand-by to fly in to support the bridgehead over the Rhine at Arnhem, but, of course, that call had never come. At first the Scots of 52nd Division and the Canadians did not see eye to eye, with a cultural clash of untidy and 'undisciplined' Canadians against 'spit and polish' Scots. On taking over some Canadian positions in mid-October, Scottish officers commented: 'No one in Scotland would ask a pig to lie in the houses [recently vacated by the Canadians] on the south side of the canal.'[48] However, both sides soon came to recognise that high fighting capability could be engendered in both approaches.[49]

The landings in Beveland encountered difficult terrain but despite this and a shortage of Buffalo amphibious assault craft, 52nd Division forced the Germans into retreat. Resistance crumbled and the Allied advance drove the enemy back towards Walcheren, the last remaining bastion preventing the opening of the Scheldt. A thin 40-metre-wide causeway some 1,200 metres long linked Walcheren to Beveland, and was enough of a hindrance to immediate progress to warrant a more coordinated joint assault. Initial efforts to forge a crossing by 2nd Canadian Infantry Division were rebuffed, the Germans in situ showing they were not without resolve. Eventually on 2 November the Canadians, under considerable pressure and having suffered heavy casualties, managed to hold on to a small bridgehead on Walcheren itself.

Hakewill-Smith's 52nd Lowland Division took on the responsibility for establishing a fully fledged bridgehead. Rather than battering their way out of the causeway position, 52nd Division's engineers devised a plan to [illegible] the mudflats [illegible] the [illegible] which would outflank the Germans then pinning the Allies in place at the western end of the causeway. On the night of 2 November, 6th Cameronians jumped across the mudflats in a daring and surprise assault which thoroughly compromised the German defences.[50]

The situation on Walcheren itself had been prepared by the Allied air forces which had subjected the hapless place to a series of bombing raids throughout October, resulting in the flooding of much of the island. The German forces were isolated and movement only became possible via amphibious means, something largely denied to the enemy. But the remaining key strongholds still had to be reduced prior to the use of the Scheldt by transport shipping, as early attempts to traverse the route ended in failure.[51]

The Allies put together a series of daring and quickly planned assaults to capture Walcheren once and for all. The Anglo-Canadian troops now at the causeway from Beveland would initiate operations to force the Germans back towards Middelburg which lay near the centre of the island, while special forces would capture the coastal areas of Flushing and Westkapelle from the sea. A degree of criticism, with some justification, has been levelled at the British leadership in the Second World War, particularly Churchill, for investing too heavily in special or non-conventional forces, leading to a dilution of the leadership and fighting strength of regular units. But at Walcheren the actions of the 4th Special Services Brigade at Westkapelle and No. 4 Army Commando (leading 155th Brigade of 52nd Division into Flushing) demonstrated that there were also benefits to these choices. These operations were conducted with limited resources and relied on tactical initiative, resolve and flexibility.

The assault on Flushing, led by No. 4 Army Commando, required the commandos to cross the Scheldt from Breskens in assault landing craft, with limited air cover, seize a bridgehead in the harbour of Flushing through which units of 52nd Lowland Division would then pass as they forced their way through the largely flooded town and on to Middelburg at the heart of the island. The assault, which began on the morning of 1 November, worked well, supported by some 300 artillery pieces as well as air strikes preparing the ground. The commandos seized their objectives, overcame fixed defensive positions and then opened the route for the immediate follow-on forces, 4th King's Own Scottish Borderers, before the Germans had much opportunity to react. It was a daring operation that demonstrated considerable tactical capability and drive by both British units.

The following day more elements of the Lowland Division arrived and they were soon clearing up pockets of resistance in Flushing whilst other units pushed on towards Middelburg. Much of this was achieved despite having to negotiate the floods which often forced soldiers to wade about in water. German resistance folded in Flushing on 3 November, and intelligence based on local knowledge indicated that German morale was also collapsing in Middelburg; a gesture was all that would be needed to end the fighting. The following day resistance in Middelburg finally came to an end when a Buffalo-mounted assault closed on the town, precipitating an eager surrender from the German commander, General Wilhelm Daser.[52]

Despite the skills and determination displayed at Flushing, the capture of Westkapelle was even more daring, and based on the kind of drive and capability too often readily associated only with the German armed forces in the Second World War. The plan for the amphibious seizure of Westkapelle employed a fleet of 150 assault ships, 27 ships to provide close fire support, and a battleship bombardment force. Very poor weather precluded much in the way of air support and the Royal Navy later grumbled that it had to bear the brunt of the casualties in the assault because of the air force's unwillingness to take losses in suppressing the Germans' defensive batteries. The RN commander, Rear Admiral Anthony Pugsley, who had the authority to cancel the operation if he believed it too risky, went ahead, though he later complained that joint planning had been inadequate and that this generated poor understanding. Nine support ships were sunk and 11 more badly damaged in the landings on 1 November, with 297 casualties – 172 killed and 125 wounded. Despite this setback the 4th Special Service Brigade got ashore and began the process of whittling down the German positions.[53]

By 8 November, Operation INFATUATE, the name given to these operations, had delivered the capture of Walcheren, and the final land threat to the Scheldt estuary had been secured. Much of the fighting in these battles had been undertaken by the Canadian forces in 21st Army Group, but the British troops deployed had demonstrated tactical awareness, determination, guile and thrust. Yet Antwerp was still some weeks away from being usable, as the Royal Navy had to complete a hazardous mine-clearance task which occupied some 10 squadrons of minesweepers until 26 November before the channel was declared safe enough. Two days later a convoy of 19 Liberty ships became the first to dock at Antwerp and the logistical constraints that had threatened to undermine Allied strategic aspirations in the autumn of 1944 eased, though by that time the Allies had long since accepted that the window of opportunity to finish the war in 1944, if indeed it had ever existed, had closed.

Though Montgomery had gambled and taken a huge risk in committing his troops to attempting to cross the Rhine in September 1944, at the expense of focusing on the Scheldt problem, the long-term grand strategic consequences were minimal. There was no victory for the taking in the autumn of 1944. If 21st Army Group had turned its attention to Antwerp earlier, the task of opening the port would have been much easier, but it would not have been a pushover. It would also have eliminated any prospect of getting a bridgehead across the Rhine. Seizing a crossing over the Rhine was a possibility, but by attempting to reach Arnhem rather than turning to Wesel and linking up with First US Army, this chance faded too. Either way it would not have caused a German capitulation but merely made the task of finishing off the Third Reich somewhat easier.

For the front-line units tasked with carrying out 21st Army Group's strategy from September to the end of November, the consequences were more significant. Most obviously, those committed to MARKET GARDEN suffered more severely, 1st Airborne being the prime casualty. The most avoidable suffering was that imposed on VIII Corps' troops when CONSTELLATION was halted to switch units to supporting operations for the Scheldt campaign, just as it was about to deliver the *coup de grâce*. This then allowed a German counter-attack, the only significant example of its type against 21st Army Group, and later made the task of clearing the enemy to the banks of the Maas much more troublesome and protracted.

Though the overall campaign had gone remarkably well by the closing weeks of 1944, fatigue was beginning to tell on British troops, and the dreary and remorseless fighting in the Maas area and around the Scheldt estuary in dreadful and demoralising weather and operating conditions took its toll. Casualties mounted and the replacement shortages that had been flagged up in pre-OVERLORD planning now began to bite again. Such had been the optimism in August and September that Montgomery had provisionally agreed to the redeployment of 3rd Infantry and 6th Airborne Divisions, 6th Guards Tank Brigade and a corps HQ to Burma. By 2 October, following the failure of MARKET GARDEN and the increasing intensity of fighting on 21st Army Group's sector, he requested Brooke that the arrangement be cancelled:

> We have in front of us some very hard fighting. If we emerge successfully, I suppose we shall have about won the war. But if we are seen off the war is very likely to drag on.
>
> With our present resources . . . I do not see how we can fight two wars at the same time.[54]

Montgomery wrote to Brooke again in late October stating his concerns. He was worried about the impact the continuous fighting was having on his fighting forces, particularly infantry officers. Since D-Day his infantry divisions in 21st Army Group had suffered an average loss of some 7,500 casualties per division, approaching 40 per cent of the total strength of each division. Worrying as this was, in truth the situation was worse, because the figure equated to the initial front-line fighting strength of a division, and, of course, most casualties had been inflicted on the rifle companies in the vanguard:

> This sticky fighting is expensive in officers and I have some battalions with only 18. If the tempo of operations in this theatre is to be kept up it will be necessary to give it a high priority for infantry reinforcements and especially officers.[55]

Montgomery met with Dempsey on 26 October and the issue of manpower was once again a high priority. He had already accepted the effective disbandment of another infantry division (50th) in order to provide replacements, but Monty was still gravely concerned, as he outlined in notes to Major General Frank 'Simbo' Simpson, Director of Military Operations at the War Office, and Brooke that 'unless situation can be improved my future operations will be affected'. By the end of October, 21st Army Group was short of some 14,500 men and this figure was projected to rise to over 22,000 by the end of the year. Montgomery alighted on 50th Division as it had suffered heavy casualties, both physical and psychological, and he had concerns over its long-term viability. Churchill was dismayed at this further diminution of the apparent strength of 21st Army Group, both in military and political terms, and in early December he attempted to offer alternatives, such as using the Royal Marines to bolster 50th Division, but to no avail – the process was well underway and little could be done. He grumbled to Montgomery: 'I greatly regret the destruction of 50th Division as a fighting force, but as you have gone so far, I fear the process must be completed.'[56]

Churchill was incensed by Montgomery and considered that he had been forced into accepting the Field Marshal's decision as it was already being enacted when he became aware of the measure – which was not exactly true as Lieutenant General Archie Nye had informed the Prime Minister of the plan in early November. Still, Frank Simpson warned Montgomery that he had blotted his copybook with the Prime Minister.[57] Yet the loss of 50th Division was not in itself enough, and later in the autumn 21st Army Group began combing out as many soldiers as possible from other formations, arms and services to meet infantry replacement needs.[58]

Troops at the front line were all [illegible] fighting and the personnel shortages, particularly in officers. Lieutenant Colonel Martin Lindsay, 51st Highlanders, later wrote:

> I think we were all secretly dreading that there might be some sort of fiasco if there were casualties among officers, since each company now had only two instead of five.
>
> . . . it only needed one man to shout, 'this is murder, I'm getting out' and he would take half a dozen with him.[59]

Tired and war-weary NCOs were also proving less willing to step forward and take extra responsibilities in these situations. Even when fighting was considered to be merely 'holding the line', stress and pressure were all too apparent. Unlike the static phases of the First World War, there was little in the way of clearly demarcated lines which neatly divided the armies. Units were constantly having to engage in aggressive patrolling and countering infiltrations by the enemy. Even when rivers such as the Maas separated the armies, regular incursions took place. Charles Hanaway, 6th Royal Scots Fusiliers, recalled:

> Patrols by the enemy, made by swimming the bitterly cold river, just a couple of hundred yards in front of us, were a nightly event. The Germans at this stage were more active, and very aggressive. They would broadcast to us that 'Herman' and his patrol were coming over to collect a goose for their Christmas dinner.[60]

During this period of the campaign battalions relied heavily on intelligence gathering, communications, logistics, engineering and supporting firepower to combat the enemy. It was time-consuming and demanding work, but the more experienced battalions' supporting structures eased the pain considerably.

The Commonwealth forces had begun to tackle with increasing effectiveness the most troublesome threat on the battlefield in 1944–5: enemy mortars. Some 70 per cent of British Army casualties were inflicted by the enemy's highly effective use of mortars. In part this was due to the decreasing role of larger-calibre artillery in the German armed forces, but it was also due to the lethality of the weapon system and the difficulties in countering it.[61] One division said of the problem: 'It was most difficult to locate the enemy's mortars as they used a smokeless powder, and sound-bearings were often inaccurate. In addition to this, the mortars themselves were usually well dug in on the reverse slopes of dykes.'[62] In November 50th Division had issued its views: 'Enemy mortars cause serious casualties to our forward troops. It is these weapons that have made ground won in some attacks too costly to hold. When an enemy mortar becomes active, retaliation must be immediate to stop firing.'[63]

These appreciations were underscored by the staff of 21st Army Group's No. 2 Operational Research Section (ORS), which surveyed the problem and identified possible countermeasures. Operational Research staff had previously tried to impress upon senior officers in the Royal Artillery the potential of radar in aiding their efforts, but had met with a cool response. The value and importance of counter-mortar duties was also undervalued in pre-OVERLORD planning by Montgomery. The Royal Artillery branch at 21st Army Group had stated in May 1944:

> Ever since the 1942/3 operations in North Africa, German mortars had become an increasingly important menace to our infantry . . . this had pointed to the need for a counter-mortar officer [and small staff] in each division.
>
> However, in May the Commander-in-Chief [Montgomery] had ruled that these special arrangements were not required in 21 Army Group at that juncture.[64]

Provision was made to deploy such teams and staff if it proved necessary, and by July this was certainly the case. The Operational Research Section had already begun an investigation that month and concluded that location methods, although capable of some improvement and development, remained a serious weakness. It was particularly noted that available methods and equipment, including the GLIII radar and Four pen recorders, declined in effectiveness in the final stages of an assault, just when they would be needed most. FA3 10-centimetre radar equipment was identified as a possible solution for locating enemy mortars, though it would be October before the first three sets would be ready for deployment, with one allocated to each army (First Canadian and Second British) and one as a reserve.[65]

A Counter-Mortar Committee was formed at 21st Army Group HQ and on 8 August it began assessing the variety of measures that had been introduced and adopted in a rather ad hoc fashion by different units to combat the problem: 'Each showed some promise of success but it was clear that nothing short of a complete overhaul of the system would serve to enable effective countermeasures to be taken.'[66] By July I, XXX Corps had begun forming dedicated Counter-Mortar Groups with specific resources deployed at divisional level, consisting of a single heavy battery of 7.2-inch guns, a troop each of 5.5-inch and 3.7-inch guns. At brigade level 4.2-inch and 3-inch mortar platoons would be allocated to the task and all would be supported by divisional artillery if necessary. As the campaign continued, the level of importance within divisions attributed to counter-mortar activities grew as the senior officer responsible for such duties rose from lieutenant to major by October, whereupon allocations of firepower to the role and new training schemes to maximise the effectiveness of available equipment increased.[67]

The British Army tried to identify appropriate solutions and formulate new doctrine, but in late September the problem was still apparent.[68] By the autumn it was clear that radar was offering the best results, with GLIII sets providing location accuracy down to 50 yards, compared to listening posts that were three to four times less effective. The army, aided by the ORS, managed slowly to refine the use of radar in neutralising and suppressing enemy mortars and by the turn of 1945 had established still more effective radar-assisted countermeasures. Initially, these measures diminished the enemy's efforts by forcing repeated relocation, but later in the spring of 1945 they began to impose systematic losses on them. But the equipment was cumbersome and post-war analysis accepted that until lighter and more suitable radar sets were available, resources would be best based at corps level under a dedicated counter-bombardment officer, holding the rank of lieutenant colonel, who would direct all such operations; resources would be deployed down to brigade level only as situations demanded.[69] Ultimately, though mortars and *Nebelwerfers* continued to inflict casualties on Allied units, British and Canadian efforts served to bring the problem under control in a manner which the Germans could not match.[70] The view of the mortar issue from the other side of the hill was somewhat worse. Within the enemy's ranks mortar fire was equally reviled, but both in terms of the lethality of British mortars and in the intensity of counter-battery fire likely to be brought down by mortaring the enemy. One PoW claimed that his mortar crew suffered abuse from fellow infantrymen who recognised that deploying close to your own mortar crews was very dangerous, as the mortars would bring down the wrath of Allied counter-battery fire once they began firing.[71]

Rotation out of the front line and static warfare also allowed the British the opportunity to begin tackling the lingering bugbear of combined arms operations at the tactical level, in particular infantry-armour cooperation. Doctrine and practice for combining tanks and soldiers in the assault, linked with artillery and other supporting arms, had troubled many British formations since D-Day and has been viewed as the weakest link in British fighting methods in Northwest Europe.

Yet the army was neither complacent nor ossified in its thinking on this matter. Some units had arrived in Normandy with a better grasp of the issues than others, but experience gleaned from the fighting and a willingness to share useful common practice and refine methods had developed still further in the British and Canadian armies as the war continued into the autumn. Conferences, meetings and dissemination of ideas and learning continued apace, which then fed into the ongoing process of refining operating practices and doctrine still further. In mid-September Brigadier Jack Churcher's 159 Infantry Brigade, of 11th Armoured Division, produced a report on infantry and armour tactics to inform future operations and it emphasised the necessity of close teamwork. It also noted that units within the brigade and indeed the division were becoming more adept at interchanging structures, combining infantry and armour units and engaging with flexible tactics, such as tank riding: 'Initially it was found advisable to group regiments together, but once success in battle had been obtained and confidence between infantry and armour assured, the switching of regiments produced just as good results.'[72] Communication between tanks and infantry was identified as crucial, but not always easy due to technical and tactical difficulties. Staff at 34th Armoured Brigade noted in their review of fighting that intimate cooperation at tactical level (squadron/company) had left something to be desired, but that if higher-level planning did not impose unrealistically short briefing times prior to H Hours, situations could be managed.[73] Examples of best practice were also circulated through the Royal Armoured Corps branch of 21st Army Group, and by the Directorate of Military Training in the War Office, which brought together examples of good practice and then passed out such tactical thinking to units across 21st Army Group.[74] Battle schools were also employed to acquaint infantry commanders and units with armour tactics and methods, albeit with a slimmed-down syllabus.[75] Equally, it was impressed upon tank commanders in armoured divisions that close support of infantry was a fundamental role on the battlefield:

> While it is to be hoped that an armoured brigade will have ample opportunity to carry out its normal role of exploitation within the Armoured Division, nevertheless Armoured Regiments must be prepared to take on an infantry close support role when necessary.[76]

Not all such findings would be acted upon and the constant complaint of infantry division staff and the commanders of independent armoured and tank brigades remained – namely, that they were too often being moved around just as best working practices were being codified. Tom Rennie, commanding 51st Highland Division, noted the advantages of the close links and firm understanding that had been developed by his command with 33rd Armoured Brigade.[77]

The Royal Artillery was also considering its methods in the autumn of 1944 in an effort to refine and improve tactics. Accuracy and targeting still required refinement and it was in the sphere of counter-battery fire that close attention was required. As indirect fire – mortar, *Nebelwerfer* or traditional artillery – remained the biggest killer on the battlefield, suppressing the enemy's artillery during the assault phase of a battle, when Allied infantry would be at its most exposed, was crucial in reducing casualties. Current artillery practice argued that it took 170 rounds to place 100 rounds in an area of 100 square yards, but operational research indicated that it took over ten times that amount to hit that level of saturation. Suppressing enemy targets, even if the intelligence-gathering part of the problem had been worked through, was therefore much more difficult than had been thought. Measures to improve the accuracy in order to suppress enemy guns prior to and during assaults were therefore undertaken, with radar eventually proving to be the key, though it would take until the spring of 1945 for this initiative to prove fruitful. It remained the case that once operating ranges of over 6,000–7,000 yards were required, the available radar equipment became bulky and cumbersome. Such was the importance assigned to the role of counter-battery fire that yet further resources, both human and equipment, were channelled into meeting the problem.[78]

It was certainly true that combined-arms tactics had improved since D-Day and the battles in the autumn of 1944 complemented this experience; and, when allowed some time to assess these new findings, doctrine could be further refined and developed. New equipment such as Kangaroo armoured personnel carriers and Wasp flame-throwers (Churchill Crocodiles were already admired and feared by friend and foe alike) added to the perception that the British Army was further improving its fighting power. Yet more would be achieved in early 1945 to facilitate further tactical refinement in the battles to cross the Rhine, but as winter closed in by December 1944 there is no doubt that, even with heavy personnel losses in certain key areas, the British had forged an army more effective than that which had hit the beaches in June, one that had fixed upon the most appropriate tactics for dealing with the Germans, and one that was working hard to eliminate its weaknesses.

The manner in which front-line troops implemented the improvements in combined-arms tactics in the autumn of 1944 bolstered morale somewhat, despite the weather and terrain. And though the sodden and miserable autumn and winter of 1944–5 stretched human resources, static warfare did at least increase the likelihood of hot food, showers, concerts, letters and newspapers from home, and the chance of rotation out of the line to recharge batteries. Being close to centres such as Brussels and Antwerp brought many benefits. Sergeant Trevor Greenwood, 9th RTR, recorded in his diary on 15 November:

> We are now in fresh billets – in centre of town. An uninhabited café cum bar cum billiard saloon. Sgts' room downstairs – where I am writing – easy chairs, carpets, electric light, fire etc. Very comfortable Bar is open too, with large fire, and beer on sale to both troops and civvies. We have a wireless set. It all seems too good to be true.[79]

Soldiers were often billeted with civilians, providing mutual benefit, even in trying circumstances. Signalman Alex McLennan noted in his diary on 5 December:

> I was in Brussels one day last week. Both houses, the Stiernons' and the Goffaux' – are still partially uninhabitable. The roofs have been temporarily repaired. They were exceptionally pleased to receive the coffee. Food is still . . . very scarce, especially meat and butter.[80]

Troops could be positioned in rather bland and boring small towns, such as Valkenswaard south of Eindhoven, for weeks on end, though this brought the prospect of sleeping indoors and opportunities for visiting livelier centres such as Eindhoven itself. Leave was also a distinct possibility, especially for those who had been in action since June, and was warmly welcomed.[81]

A most significant fillip to soldiers' outlook and morale remained survivability in the field, even if wounded, and here the British Army supported its troops particularly well, a factor recognised by front-line troops:

> I think there's no doubt the RAMC [Royal Army Medical Corps] is doing a magnificent job in the forward areas, under very difficult conditions. Despite everything there must be many thousands of people who owe their lives to their initial treatment.
>
> Time and again they make remarks like 'Thank God we've got such a medical service.'[82]

Even when operating in poor weather conditions that might otherwise have precluded medical support or increased levels of sickness, the British Army served its troops well. In Operation BLACKCOCK in January 1945, despite the adverse weather and extreme cold, one division in action reported only twenty-five medical cases per day, with no evidence of any wounded man suffering from exposure in the battle. The extreme cold slowed down blood loss, and excellent medical support and attention, coupled with efficient evacuation in trying conditions, helped to limit death resulting from wounds to less than 2.5 per cent.[83]

The British Army managed to cut the impact of haemorrhage, sepsis and shock, the most important elements in battlefield casualties, to noticeably low levels in 1944–5 through the use of improved medical support. The use of blood supplies and improved surgical techniques, and, of course, the mass use of penicillin, dramatically improved the chances of survival once a soldier was wounded. Medical support was also fundamental in easing the personnel crisis as troops with flesh wounds usually had their wounds closed within three to five days and could be returned to the front line in around six weeks. Air support and evacuation again proved to be vital, particularly in the pursuit phase from Normandy to the Netherlands, though medical supplies and support were momentarily in crisis during the pursuit from the Seine to the Rhine, before measures were undertaken to correct the deficiencies.[84]

In contrast, medical support in the German Army, already inferior to the British, deteriorated markedly once order had broken down. Owing to the collapse in German medical support the numbers of PoWs with infected wounds increased dramatically in quantity in August and September. The German Army was generally both unable and unwilling to devote resources and effort to maintaining adequate, modern medical support to its soldiers with the consequence that survivability was much lower than in Western Allied armies. This weakened the chances of troops being returned to active service quickly, if at all, at a time when diminishing reserves of personnel, more than anything else, was undermining the German war effort. It also demonstrated the moribund and casual attitude to welfare inherent in the German armed forces and indeed in the Third Reich, not only to those around them, but to their own soldiers. The Germans resorted to enforcing discipline through fear. Whereas the death penalty had been withdrawn by the British Army in the 1930s for crimes other than murder and similar, the German Army enforced severe repression and coercion of its own troops, executing a staggering 13,000 to 15,000 of its own soldiers in the Second World War. In turn, German soldiers, brutalised and infected with a corrupt and distorted ideology, inflicted suffering on those around them all too often. An army that failed to recognise or appreciate battle exhaustion and treated individuals with such contempt was not an army to admire.[85]

As December 1944 drew on towards Christmas it appeared to the Allies that although the Germans were not yet ready to surrender, they were nonetheless beaten and it was just a matter of time. Montgomery himself stated on 15 December that the inadequacies of German manpower, equipment and resources precluded any offensive action on their part. In a similar vein American deployments lacked reserves and in-depth defences; such was the air of confidence at SHAEF. Ultra and other intelligence sources failed to provide any real warning of enemy intentions – though there were some hints – and just a few days before the Germans' Ardennes offensive Eisenhower and his staff met at Maastricht on 7 December to discuss future plans, oblivious to the build-up occurring ahead of them. Brigadier Bill Williams, 21st Army Group's chief intelligence officer, though noting that a German offensive was possible, regarded it as unlikely, perhaps attributing an air of rational thinking to German strategy when in reality it was being driven by delusional thinking in Berlin.[86]

On 16 December the Germans launched their surprise offensive that fell squarely upon the Americans, and which demonstrated once again that the Third Reich still retained desperate resilience and some not inconsiderable capability. Hitler's last gamble in the west saw some 200,000 troops, supported initially by around 500 tanks and 1,900 guns and mortars, crash through thinly held US lines in the Ardennes region, which threw Allied plans into a ferment. The front was driven back and within a few days the possibility of German troops pushing on to Antwerp emerged, though this would only have occurred if Allied resistance had collapsed almost entirely. Commanders such as Bradley and Montgomery, leading well-equipped and confident forces that had been forged in battle since D-Day, were never likely to allow this to happen – these Allied forces were not akin to those of 1940.

Eisenhower and Bradley attempted to impose order on the crumbling situation in the first few days of the offensive, but the weight of the German attack overwhelmed a number of American positions and eventually forced a more radical rethink. This drew in Montgomery as commander of the northern flank of the salient created by the German thrust, the salient which gave its name to the action, the Battle of the Bulge. Appointing Montgomery, by now viewed with resentment and suspicion in some American circles, as a commander of US First and Ninth Armies, however fleetingly, did not sit easily with Eisenhower, less so Bradley. Yet the strategic reasoning was sound; Bradley would grip the southern flank, Montgomery the north, though the overwhelming majority of Allied forces deployed in halting the German offensive would, of course, be American. As Bradley conceded, if Montgomery had been American the logic of appointing him to command the northern flank on a temporary basis would have been irrefutable, but he was British and, worse, he was Montgomery. Initially, Montgomery too had not fully recognised the parlous situation, and had been more concerned on 17 December that troops should not be drawn southwards away from the 21st Army Group sector, potentially delaying his next major operation, VERITABLE, pencilled in for 8 January 1945. Three days later, with greater realisation growing amidst the confusion, Montgomery was already asserting control, even before Eisenhower formally authorised him to do so.

Monty had despatched liaison officers to Courtney Hodges' First Army HQ on 19 December to uncover the reality of their position; they found an air of despondency and a dismayed Hodges who 'did not seem to know much about the situation and looked worn out'. In a frenetic and disjointed telephone conversation the following day, Eisenhower formally appointed Montgomery to take command of the northern flank, Monty noting that he was quite relieved when Ike was finally cut off as he was making little sense, talked wildly and seemed most excited. Montgomery met Crerar, Dempsey, Hodges and Bill Simpson, who commanded Ninth US Army, over the next few hours and began to establish a firm grip on the situation. He had already started to mobilise XXX Corps to resist any threat to the northern bank of the Maas, and he subsequently ordered 29th Armoured Brigade to cease re-equipping with new Comet tanks and begin moving back into the line to free up other forces, such as 51st Highland Division and 6th Guards Tank Brigade, to form a reserve for Simpson's forces.[87]

The position was stabilised over the next few days and for this Montgomery must take considerable credit; his efficient and disciplined system of controlling or gripping subordinates and wielding command was well suited to organising and instilling order into the situation. His desire to fight a defensive battle, largely absorbing the German assault, drew subsequent criticism from American commanders who argued that a more decisive victory might have been achieved if Montgomery had been more aggressive once the German offensive had petered out. Bradley was incensed by the transfer of First and Ninth US Armies to Montgomery's command, however temporary it might have been, and believed a great opportunity for slaughtering the Germans was missed because of Montgomery's caution:

> This was the darkest of times for me. Giving Monty operational control of my First and Ninth armies was the worst possible mistake Ike could have made. Owing to Monty's caution and conservatism, it practically assured that we would fail to cut off the German salient with a bold thrust form the north.[88]

But Monty preferred to await initiating offensives of his choosing, when he was ready. British troops directly involved in the fighting were quite limited in number, and when the campaign was over and the territory seized by the Germans had been recovered in mid-January, British losses amounted only to some 1,400, of whom 200 had been killed. Matched to US losses of around 80,000 and German losses perhaps numbering 90,000, the relative place in the fighting of the respective armies seems clear.[89]

Yet the history of the aftermath has been clouded and distorted, and further poisoned the relationship between Monty and the Americans. There is no doubt that Montgomery considered that he had brought higher command order to First and Ninth US Armies at a time when Bradley was otherwise engaged in working with Patton in the south. Monty noted to Frank Simpson at the War Office on Christmas Day:

> The American armies in the north, Ninth and First, were in a complete muddle; Bradley had not visited either Army since the attack began; there had been no grip, or tight control of the battle.

> I spared no effort trying to sort the thing out, and get a properly organised show in the American zone.[90]

But Monty blundered twice in his handling of the politics of the situation. First, he used the Bulge situation to bring up once again the question of Allied land command in the campaign. In effect he argued with Eisenhower and Bradley that the failure to deal with the German offensive quickly was in part due to the Allied command structure and Eisenhower's strategy. He lobbied Bradley about having a deputy to Eisenhower appointed to direct the whole land campaign, but found little support, once again because Bradley feared the idea of being commanded by Montgomery. George Marshall had also been at work, informing Ike that: 'The appointment of any British officer to be Deputy to Eisenhower for the land operations or to control the operations over the head of Bradley would be quite unacceptable in America.'[91]

Montgomery pressed on with the spat but was again threatened by Eisenhower with the ultimate sanction of taking the matter to the Combined Chiefs of Staff, who would undoubtedly have backed Eisenhower and sacked Montgomery. It took the personal intervention of Montgomery's likeable and affable chief of staff, Freddie de Guingand, to salvage the situation.[92] Monty backed down again, though he grumbled bitterly to Brooke, and even Churchill. In his diary he noted:

> The conduct of the war at the present time calls for the highest professional skill and the most careful control; we have not got it.
>
> Eisenhower cannot take on Rundstedt. He will be seen off every time; it is like an amateur trying to take on a very experienced and skilled professional.[93]

As with his previous attempts to change the command structure, Montgomery was both right and wrong; a single commander may well have driven Allied strategy more directly than, or at the very least somewhat differently to, Eisenhower. But that did not guarantee greater success; the fact that the Germans had been able to mount their December offensive in such strength underscored the view that the war could not have been won in the autumn of 1944. Montgomery also could not evade the fact that he too had been caught out by the German offensive and had not considered such a threat to be real prior to 16 December. Most importantly, of course, Montgomery's argument ignored the political and strategic reality that the Americans were by some distance the senior partners in the alliance – ever more so by December 1944 – and the idea of their armies being directed by a foreigner was simply untenable; Bradley in particular threatened to resign if forced to operate under Montgomery's tutelage once again.

Montgomery's second error was to give a press conference on 7 January 1945 in an effort to clarify the role of the British in the battle, as he put it; the role of Montgomery and British forces in the Ardennes battle had not been publicised until 5 January and there was growing speculation, particularly amongst the partisan UK press, about the role of the British. Monty's staff at 21st Army Group were gravely concerned at the prospect of the conference, knowing his propensity to say the wrong thing, even when he was not trying to make a barbed point. Matters were not helped by the absence due to illness of Freddie de Guingand, whose ameliorating influence might have tempered Monty's tone. Brooke and Churchill had cleared the conference, having, of course, only seen the intended text, and thus it went ahead. Though Montgomery endeavoured to praise the role of the American troops, he failed to give due credit to his fellow American generals, save Eisenhower, and supposedly gave the impression that he had saved a deteriorating situation. Brigadier David Belchem, Monty's head of operations, always considered that his chief was out of his depth with American reporters who had never taken to his stiff Englishness, and that it was they who stirred up the media storm that ensued. Yet even friendly journalists such as Chester Wilmot and Alan Moorehead were dismayed at Montgomery's performance. Moorehead, who had followed the path of Monty for much of the war, despaired of the Field Marshal's clumsy handling of press conferences: 'Often when he intended to be fair he simply neglected the other man's point of view. And when he was pleased and elated he could not disguise the fact.'[94] Monty's chief of intelligence, Brigadier Bill Williams, later stated of the 7 January conference: 'The text in a sense was innocuous; the presentation quite appalling.' This view chimes all too easily with Moorehead's assessment and that of Brigadier Charles Richardson, 21st Army Group's chief planning officer.[95]

Bradley, whose personal standing had already been undermined by the Ardennes situation and who was feeling vulnerable to external pressures and scrutiny, took severe umbrage at Montgomery's comments, seeing them as deliberate insinuations about his capabilities. The situation was gingered by rumours that Bradley had heard in the aftermath of the Ardennes battles that his own troops were stating that Montgomery always knew what he was doing whereas some American generals, including Bradley, did not. Bradley later claimed that, contrary to the Field Marshal's comments at the 7 January press conference, Monty had refused to deploy more than a single brigade in the Ardennes battles, and that he had failed to get clearance for his press conference from Eisenhower; neither of these points were true, but they do tell us something about Bradley's perspective.[96] Bradley was also fuming that Eisenhower, despite refusing Montgomery's proposal to retain complete control of the northern group of armies (including two American armies), had accepted that Bill Simpson's Ninth Army would remain under 21st Army Group control. These were difficult times for Montgomery's relationship with Bradley. Monty later conceded that it would have been better to have said nothing, as anything he did say was likely to be misinterpreted by a hostile US audience. Yet he did not consider that such hostility was largely a result of his previous conduct and comments.[97] As Eisenhower wrote after the war:

> I do not believe that Montgomery meant his words as they sounded, but the mischief was not lessened thereby.
>
> I doubt that Montgomery ever came to realise how deeply resentful some American commanders were. They believed he belittled them – and they were not slow to reciprocal scorn and contempt.[98]

Montgomery's insensitivity was not, of course, aimed particularly at Americans; he had infuriated a whole string of British officers too, making many enemies who were only too willing to undermine the Field Marshal when the opportunity arose.

These personal setbacks notwithstanding, by mid-January the position of the Allied forces had improved dramatically, for the Ardennes offensive had now drained many German reserves and would make the task of pushing on into Germany and crossing the Rhine that much easier. The final showdown with Hitler's Third Reich was at hand.

10

VICTORY
The Rhine to the Baltic

JANUARY 1945, THOUGH bitterly cold, brought the prospect of the Allied armies beginning the final push across the Rhine into Germany itself, and with it the near certainty of victory. German resources had all but been expended in the ultimately futile Ardennes offensive, and though the Allies had suffered embarrassment and some not inconsiderable dismay at being caught out by an enemy they had begun to dismiss as beaten, the battle had ultimately made their job of driving across the Rhine and finally breaking the Third Reich that much easier.

The principal aim of 21st Army Group in 1945 was to drive through the Reichswald Forest, reach the Rhine, and then to launch into the largely flat, easily traversable northern plain of Germany. Before such a concerted effort could be mounted to force a Rhine crossing, 21st Army Group had to consolidate its position, eliminate certain pockets of resistance, and clear the Maas-Rhine area. Some planned operations for December and early January had been postponed due to the Ardennes offensive and the inclement weather, but by mid-January Montgomery's forces were on the offensive once again.

Operation BLACKCOCK, conducted by Neil Ritchie's XII Corps, was planned to clear the triangular territory formed by the then front line, and the rivers Roer, Wurm and Maas. Ritchie's plan was for a night attack to begin on 15 January, heavily supported by artillery, and for a series of flanking attacks to prise the Germans out of their defensive positions. The initial assault would be spearheaded by 7th Armoured and 52nd Lowland Divisions, with 43rd Wessex to follow up, other support being provided by two independent brigades of armour and substantial artillery, as air support could not be guaranteed if the weather proved to be poor. Intelligence briefings concluded that initial opposition, provided by two Volksgrenadier divisions, was likely to be organised but would crumble due to inadequate reserves. The enemy had had plenty of time to prepare defences as these positions had been held since November, but German dispositions implied that they expected an attack from the right flank, as indeed original British intentions at that time had planned – however, the BLACKCOCK offensive would begin on the left.[1]

Once again rapid initial bridging, particularly on the left flank, would be vital to maintaining momentum in the early stages of the attack, as would the use of flail tanks to clear paths through enemy minefields. Flail tanks proved less effective in snow against anti-armour mines, but across frozen ground they would destroy anti-personnel mines quite effectively. Pressure on the road network would be considerable, so traffic discipline would be crucial, and if the ground remained frozen greater speed would be facilitated. Cross-country movement by tanks would be eminently possible providing there was no thaw, and this would free up the roads to other vehicles. Vehicles were painted white, though this often produced a muddy and grimy hue and crews found the process unpleasant, whilst white over-suits were also distributed to the troops.[2]

The start was postponed by Ritchie until the following morning (16 January) due to grim weather – extreme cold and lashing rain that produced a slippery film of water on top of a frozen crust, under which lay thick mud.[3] Initial advances met only limited opposition, but battles to secure and hold the bridges constructed under trying conditions proved hazardous thanks to enemy fire and treacherous operating conditions. When the ground began to thaw the approaches to newly constructed bridges were soon reduced to quagmires: 'On more than one occasion a bridge completed under fire was into by a tank, or other heavy vehicle, skidding on the approach and crashing into the bridge, and work had to start all over again.'[4] The thick mud often precluded the efficient movement of [illegible] The British were, however, sometimes able to keep the infantry advancing thanks to the use of Kangaroos and the full range of support vehicles and engineers, in conjunction with strict traffic management. The use of the new Weasel vehicles also aided the efforts in the operation, when deployed appropriately and not indiscriminately at lower level. For 7th Armoured Division, in the van of this operation, acknowledgement of excellent discipline was an indication of tactical improvement following the criticism levelled at them some months earlier. After-action analysis recorded:

> A most comprehensive traffic plan had to be initiated in order to ensure that the two main axes . . . were used to maximum advantage as soon as they were cleared by the leading troops.

> This system proved its worth throughout the operation and all traffic problems were quickly settled without confusion.[5]

The Desert Rats also utilised a flexible mixed-brigade system to facilitate infantry-armour cooperation and this proved fruitful as formations shuffled to meet particular emerging situations.

The experience of 52nd Lowland Division demonstrated that even when the mud confounded armoured support, and radio communications were damaged, determined troops ably supported by heavy concentrations of firepower could still carry their objectives. The absence of support vehicles such as Crocodile flame-throwers certainly increased casualties, nonetheless. The effectiveness of the enemy's Tiger tanks was also demonstrated to the troops of the 52nd Division. During a localised counter-attack in Waldfeucht, south of Roermond, on 21 January, just one Tiger stubbornly supported German troops in clinging on to their toehold in the village for some three hours, surviving hits by PIAT rounds and sticky bombs.[6]

The Germans for the most part fought a delaying battle and had by January 1945:

> Brought delaying actions by small bodies of infantry backed by SP [self-propelled] guns to a fine art.
>
> Working over country which he knew thoroughly, and behind his own mines, he used his SP guns boldly and to full advantage.[7]

The impact of the war on the German population now became transparent to British troops. Major General Edmund Hakewill-Smith's 52nd Division was the first to base itself in a German town and found that the human costs of war remained similar to any other settlement. After capturing Scheifendahl, some 5 miles north of Geilenkirchen, Lieutenant Sydney Jary, 4th Somerset Light Infantry, recalled:

> To my astonishment we found some German civilians still in their cottages. A young girl, her face streaked by tears, was trying to rescue her possessions from the cottage in which I set up my Platoon HQ. There was nothing any of us could do to comfort her. As night fell she finally left, bravely pushing her belongings heaped on an old pram with squeaking wheels. It was at times like this that I wished that we could fight our war in the desert.[8]

The effects of war were also still being acutely felt by non-German civilians, and the British were conscious of making matters worse, particularly when employing the vast arsenal of firepower available to them: 'In view of the enemy practice of evicting civilians from the cellars of non-German towns and villages, the possibility of killing numbers of civilians must be weighed against the military importance of the target.'[9]

BLACKCOCK went broadly according to plan with the objectives being achieved, though it took a little longer than expected, largely because of the weather. The Germans offered little in the way of sustained, determined opposition, save in a few pockets, and the 43rd Division's account later recorded: 'Indeed, an operation in which the enemy allows himself to be reduced piecemeal and almost at leisure can hardly be described as a battle.'[10] German PoWs, admittedly of lower quality than those that would be confronted after BLACKCOCK, were particularly intimidated by rocket battery attacks, weapons recently introduced by the Allies. Some captured Germans having endured such an attack:

> were just about able to talk but were so dazed that several walked into walls without seeing where they were going. Observers from our own lines commented on the way these salvos seemed to obliterate the areas on which they fell, and it was undoubtedly a most effective weapon.[11]

British casualties were limited, totalling around 1,500, whilst some 2,200–2,500 prisoners were taken. Armour losses were also relatively light, and 7th Armoured lost only 10 tanks to enemy action.[12] The support of the RAF in the initial assault phases against defended villages worked particularly well, and the ground forces employed short counter-flak artillery plans – code-named APPLEPIE – to suppress enemy anti-aircraft capability just prior to the fighter-bomber attacks going in, which kept RAF losses low, encouraging [illegible] from the air 'blind', directed by Signals Corps Type 584 radios. Ultimately, BLACKCOCK produced decent results and precipitated closer integration of new equipment and techniques, which proved fruitful when more serious opposition and larger-scale operations were mounted in the following weeks.

The nature of how future strategy was to be developed was once again causing friction between 21st Army Group and SHAEF. Montgomery had a two-operation plan in mind to finish the job west of the Rhine, before the Rhine crossing could be mounted. The first stage was to be VERITABLE, a thrust from the north through and around the Reichswald Forest, by a reinforced First Canadian Army mustering some 470,000 troops with many British troops under its command. Two days later the American Ninth Army, then under 21st Army Group command and with some 300,000 troops available, would strike northeast across the River Roer and converge on Wesel with the Anglo-Canadian forces. Montgomery had been planning Operations VERITABLE and GRENADE for some time: 'Operations VERITABLE and GRENADE will together be a terrific party and there will be little rest for most of us once we begin.'[13] He also believed that the fighting would be intense and ferocious, and warned the War Office of the necessity of finding more officer replacements to make good existing deficits and maintain strength when losses were incurred in VERITABLE. Plans were also underway to comb out as many spare officers from non-frontline units in 21st Army Group as possible. Montgomery was determined the two operations should be broadly connected, with GRENADE launching shortly after VERITABLE in order to maximise impact, but he was increasingly worried that continuing American fighting in the Ardennes would drain away resources from GRENADE, causing its delay and therefore pushing back the start of VERITABLE.[14] His concerns were focused on Eisenhower's directive on future strategy of 18 January. In this, Ike hinted strongly at continuing operations on Bradley's front in the Prüm-Eüskirchen sector, east of Luxemburg, and this dismayed both Montgomery and the British Chiefs of Staff. Monty wrote to Brooke on this point on 20 January:

> Instead of one clear and decisive plan there was great indecision and patchwork.
>
> Both Ike and Bradley are emphatic that we should not cross the Rhine anywhere until we are lined up along its entire length from Nijmegen to Switzerland. If we work to this plan we shall take a long time to get anywhere.[15]

Montgomery was further dismayed by the problems brewing further south in the Strasbourg area where, as he described it to Brooke: 'I understand the French divisions are not fighting properly. I also hear that Devers [6th Army Group C-in-C] is quite useless.'[16] Montgomery could see only dispersion of effort hindering operations, which would delay the main thrust, a strategy supposedly already agreed by Eisenhower. Despite his despair, however, Montgomery was not in a position to shape Western strategy, nor was he now particularly willing to try. He lamented to Brooke on 22 January:

> I am taking no part in it at all except to keep in close touch with Whiteley [General Jock Whiteley, the senior British Army liaison officer at SHAEF]. One has to preserve a sense of humour these days otherwise one would go mad.[17]

Whiteley's view was that Eisenhower had given the impression that he would maintain levels of activity in Bradley's sector for appearances' sake and that in the near future the main effort would indeed be focused in the north. This did not convince 21st Army Group or the British Chiefs of Staff, but by the beginning of February it appeared that SHAEF would give priority to VERITABLE and GRENADE.

With some two weeks to go before VERITABLE began, therefore, Montgomery organised a few days' leave citing fatigue and staleness: 'the last few weeks have been somewhat strenuous,' he confessed in a rather understated manner to Eisenhower. Dempsey also took leave before the next stage of operations got underway.[18] But when Montgomery returned from the UK he was still fretting over the commitment of Eisenhower. On 7 February Monty met with Tedder and raised the issue of SHAEF adhering to the plan for VERITABLE/GRENADE once more and was less than convinced by the reply. He confided to Brooke: 'Tedder visited me today and I rubbed this into him but I have little faith in any robust views being given out by him.'[19] But Monty's fears faded in the following days as VERITABLE began and he received assurances that Ninth US Army would remain with 21st Army Group for the rest of the war.[20]

Operation VERITABLE was conducted under the direction of First Canadian Army, although XXX Corps, which included five British divisions and totalled some 200,000 men for the action, was to take the lead role, after which II Canadian Corps would join the fray. VERITABLE was in essence a simple plan which aimed to hit the enemy still in place to the west of the Rhine hard and 'continue hitting him, night and day, until there was nothing left to hit'.[21] It was also a huge undertaking, the largest that Brian Horrocks, commanding XXX Corps, had thus far commanded, and one that he had to direct whilst suffering from illness that made him irritable and bad tempered. He was concerned that the Germans had heavily fortified urban centres such as Kleve and Goch, and that terrain features such as the Reichswald Forest, high ground known as the Nutterden feature, and flooded polder land to the north presented particular difficulties likely to hinder progress. The defences of the Siegfried Line, which consisted of three belts ranging from 500 to 1,000 metres deep, in conjunction with natural features and the weather, made VERITABLE potentially a severe challenge. Montgomery was fully aware that if the transport and communication network began to fail due to deteriorating weather, the advance would slow down to a methodical pace.[22]

The plan called for five divisions to attack in line with two more in reserve should they be required. In the opening phase of the operation, three British infantry divisions would launch themselves southeast from the Nijmegen area through and around the Reichswald Forest; the northern route would be taken by 15th Scottish, the southern by 51st Highlanders, and between them the 53rd Welsh. Further north two Canadian Divisions would also attack into and along the flooded region to the Waal River.[23] Support was as ever impressive with the Royal Engineers of 13 Army Group Royal Engineers (AGRE) initially building five special bridges, adding over 100 miles of new roads and reconditioning 400 miles of existing roads to take all the traffic required to mount VERITABLE.[24] Conditions were far from easy. Colonel F.C. Nottingham, commanding 13 AGRE, noted: 'Many of the roads were country roads and required considerable work. The period was one of continuous frost and major works were only done with great difficulty. Tarmac was out of the question.'[25]

The weather had started to improve by the time VERITABLE launched on the morning of 8 February, with a thaw having begun on 31 January. This brought major difficulties as many roads, tracks and routes, hitherto frozen and thus able to carry traffic, began to break up. Matters were further complicated by a period of rain in the few days leading up to the operation. Roads began to degenerate into thick mud, quite unsuitable even for tracked vehicles, and the predetermined 'thaw precaution plans' could not offer complete solutions. The required speed of concentration of force therefore placed great demands on engineering and construction capacity, and matters were exacerbated by yet more heavy rain in the period after 8 February which caused further deterioration in roads, particularly in the Reichswald Forest itself. The work of over 1,500 military police in enforcing good road discipline was therefore paramount in keeping the operation moving.

Whilst the Allies had identified fairly accurately the nature and type of the opposition confronting them, the enemy had a weak appreciation of the situation, despite a rare Luftwaffe reconnaissance sortie overflying the First Canadian Army sector two days before VERITABLE began. Senior German commanders such as Kurt Student and Gerd von Rundstedt, who were denied any reliable or effective intelligence to the contrary, remained convinced that the Allies' next move in the area would come from the Americans around Roermond, 20 miles southeast of Eindhoven.

In contrast, General Alfred Schlemm, commanding the troops in the Reichswald area, claimed after the war that he was convinced that the Allies would attack through the Reichswald, but his own patrols had failed to verify such an assessment. VERITABLE would come as a shock to the Germans, therefore, though for perhaps the last time on the Western Front they would act resolutely to salvage the situation.[26] A massive fire-support plan had naturally been put together for VERITABLE with over 1,200 guns – perhaps the largest British bombardment of the war – and a series of major air attacks had been organised.

Some of the targets such as the beautiful medieval town of Kleve, 20 miles east of Nijmegen, provoked some soul-searching on the part of Allied commanders, but with the difficulties of the operation increasing, all offers of support were taken up. The artillery plan included greater use of *Pepperpot* tactics, methods derived from operational analyses which showed that the number of guns firing into a given area for a sustained period of time was more effective than the actual weight of shell. After-action reports later indicated that *Pepperpot* had been highly effective, notwithstanding the increased ammunition required. The fire plan still worked to the assumption that at least six tons of ordnance would be delivered on to a specified target, and in many cases key enemy positions, such as enemy mortars, received over eleven tons. The counter-battery plan prevented all but one enemy artillery battery from firing in the period before the advance and 19 enemy mortars were located in the bombardment and, in total, 23 were attacked.[27]

The effects of the bombardment and air plan on the German defenders were noted in the First Canadian Army's after-action report as being particularly useful in severely undermining enemy morale. The artillery was also more effective because advancing Allied infantry leant into the barrage particularly well and surprised many German positions before they could recover from the bombardment – such tactical success had been harder to find in 1944:

> It is realised by the Inf[antry] that the risk of casualties from our own guns and aircraft must be accepted if the follow-up is to be close enough to succeed. The prolongation of the arty [artillery] programme to cover the digging in and reorganisation, in combination with intense counter-battery and counter-mortar activity, again proved of great value.[28]

Such tactics came at a heavy cost and one report filed in 1945 argued that perhaps as many as 19 per cent of Allied casualties from shrapnel may have come from friendly ordnance, and almost certainly not less than 7 per cent.[29]

Yet reports from No. 2 Operational Research Section calculated that the density of fire inflicted upon enemy troops had proved sufficient to achieve initial objectives and the fire plan in VERITABLE demonstrated the increasing sophistication of artillery tactics, and air-to-ground communications in coordinating and controlling air support.[30]

Despite the operating conditions and persistent rain, the initial assaults went relatively well and all initial objectives were seized by midnight on day one. Once again the benefits of the Kangaroo armoured personnel carrier were considerable, leading to one portentous assessment that: 'Since the substitution of the musket for the cross-bow, there has been no development in Inf equipment which is comparable to the KANGAROO.'[31] For VERITABLE, 21st Army Group had two regiments of armoured personnel carriers, both part of the 79th Armoured Division and each capable of carrying two infantry battalions. All but one squadron of Kangaroos were deployed and worked intimately with other mechanised assets and units to drive the initial advances forward. Such was the value placed on these vehicles that great demand was made on them, leading to their suffering the heaviest casualties of any armoured equipment in VERITABLE. Amphibious Buffalo transporters were also highly regarded, being pivotal to the operations of the Canadian troops in the flooded territory to the north.[32]

Assaulting infantry were heavily supported by specialist armour and vehicles – flail tanks, Crocodile and Wasp flame-throwers, and engineering equipment – but the mud and sodden conditions foiled the efforts of these units in a number of cases, and often it was left to the infantry to make as much use as possible of the artillery barrage to reach their targets.

The troops of 53rd Welsh Division were tasked with driving into and capturing the Reichswald Forest itself and they acquitted themselves well, though ultimately the operation was achieved at a heavy cost. They had trained in advance in combat techniques necessary for narrow-front assaults into forests and this preparation, partly based on lessons learned from previous actions in the Ardennes, as well as astute foresight, contributed greatly to the success of the initial assault. The division's preparations were reinforced by the establishment of dedicated intelligence and operations rooms organised to coordinate the logistical and transport effort. The effects of the massive bombardment were clear to all as they entered the Reichswald Forest, as a history of the 1st East Lancashires attached to 53rd Division noted:

> An almost overpowering smell of spent explosive hung like a cloud in the forest. Trees lay smashed and shattered; their broken branches strewn about, leaving stumps standing like grotesque scarecrows to discourage invaders.[33]

The terrain and operating conditions in many cases precluded the lavish use of supporting equipment and specialist armour in the forest fighting, forcing greater reliance on infantry firepower and determination; as one battalion commander who fought in the Reichswald said, 'it was Spandau versus Bren the whole way through'.[34] To their left and slightly north, 15th Scottish Division also achieved good progress, making highly effective use of the rolling artillery barrage which swept ahead of the advance, moving on 300 yards every twelve minutes in front of the infantry and supporting armour when it had not become bogged in the mud. They too forced their way on to the first-phase objectives.[35]

To the south 51st Highlanders endured a more difficult opening, with resistance offered by the Germans proving much more obdurate. This, fused with the devastated terrain, hampered progress no end. Major Martin Lindsay, acting commander of 1st Gordons, recalled:

> We climbed up the face of this steep ridge . . . but the wood was jungle, so many branches and trees having been felled by our shelling. We might well have been in darkest Africa. Every hundred yards took us about fifteen minutes and the confusion was indescribable.[36]

Lindsay reflected with dismay on the problems of exerting control over his charges in such terrain. Communications became a major issue and brigades and battalions had to employ a whole range of ad hoc measures to solve the difficulties, often taking valuable officers away from other roles and employing them in liaison duties. The necessity for battalion commanders to exercise such close control of sub-units was fundamental to success in forest fighting, but not easily achievable.[37]

German troops initially fell back and British units dug in for the night in the middle of the Reichswald Forest. Corporal Tom Renouf, Black Watch, noted:

> It was a terrible night. My trench mate and I took turns to stay awake. Scared as I was, sleep came easily, but staying alert when it was my turn for a sentry shift was a real problem . . . every little crackle, every snapping twig, set my nerves jangling again.[38]

Though further decent progress was made on 9 February, by the following day momentum was being lost. The practical difficulties in getting troops and equipment forward through a rapidly disintegrating road and transport network, alongside the withdrawal of wounded soldiers, were beginning to overwhelm the administrative capacity of the army to cope. Horrocks had also contributed to the congestion by pressing 43rd Division into action before 15th Scottish had opened up enough space and advanced sufficiently to warrant such a measure. Horrocks admitted his grave error after the war:

> I unleashed my first reserve, the 43rd Wessex Division, which was to pass through the 15th Scottish, to burst out into the plain beyond and advance towards Goch. This, however, turned out to be one of the worst mistakes I made in the war.[39]

Matters were further complicated by the enemy's actions, as Horrocks later claimed:

> The Germans added to our difficulties by blowing large gaps in the banks of the Rhine. The result was that the floods steadily increased and eventually two feet of water flooded across the Kranenburg road [a key arterial route for the operation].[40]

Kurt Student's paratroopers displayed fierce determination and resolve in the fighting, much to the dismay and incredulity of the British soldiers, resulting in the greater levels of resistance offered to the Highlanders, compared to the other two British infantry divisions in the early stages of the assault. One captured German commander noted that his soldiers knew 'nothing better than life at the front' and 'provided they got something to eat and smoke . . . would continue to fight'.[41] On 10 February German high command also acted to reinforce the position around the Reichswald and moved 116th Panzer and 15th Panzer Grenadier Divisions into the line, followed later by Panzer Lehr. Owing to Allied artillery the Germans were unable to mass these troops quickly enough, and the counter-attack only began on 13 February. Though these German units were defeated and driven back, as indeed later German initiatives would be, VERITABLE began to descend into a slog.

Von Rundstedt wanted to withdraw his forces back across the Rhine, but Berlin insisted on fighting for every position. The reality of enacting this policy at the front line was, of course, somewhat different and German units, pressed from above to have 85 per cent of personnel fighting in the front line, simply lied about available strength in order to convince those above that the order was being carried out. This supported Berlin's wholly unrealistic vision of what was happening at the front line. The reality of the German position was that available troops were being fed piecemeal into the battle to slow the Allies down, but at the expense of a considered and sustainable application of strength. Once again this forced the Allies into a slow, remorseless advance but consigned remaining German strength in the sector to a lingering death, the consequences of which would become apparent once the Rhine was crossed a few days after VERITABLE came to an end.[42]

The initial carefully organised Allied plan had compensated for the operating difficulties, but once the battle had been joined and became more confused the possibility receded of redeploying support forces, bringing through replacements, and coordinating firepower support effectively to re-energise the momentum of the assault. Poor weather hindered air operations, particularly medium and heavy bomber sorties, though only one day, 12 February, was blotted out completely. The weather brightened up on 14 February allowing the RAF to increase its support, only for it to be shut out again when the weather deteriorated once more a few days later.[43] Units also had to contend with town-clearance operations in VERITABLE, often when the town itself had been severely damaged by artillery or aerial bombardment, such as Kleve or Goch. For assaulting infantry, heavily damaged urban areas again proved to offer more headaches than solutions. After their town-clearance experiences in VERITABLE, Brigadier J.H. Wilsey's 158th Brigade, 53rd Welsh Division, reported:

> From our experience in a town not bombed to one that has been heavily bombed there is little doubt that the Infantryman would ask the airmen to go elsewhere, particularly as he does not kill or even frighten the defenders he is going to meet.[44]

The troops of 43rd Division fully concurred, complaining bitterly about the destruction in Kleve which, in their view, hindered the seizure of the town:

> What will always rankle in the minds of those who fought at Kleve is the oafish stupidity of the attack by Bomber Command, which with its deep cratering, completely blocked the roads within the town.[45]

Major Joe Symonds, 4th Dorsets noted:

> That evening we moved to Kleve and found that ancient town a mass of ruins. No house, building, or even tree was left intact. The roads were cratered everywhere, and dead German soldiers and civilians were numerous.[46]

The difficulties in fighting amongst urban environments were in any case already manifest. German forces, particularly determined and experienced paratroopers as were being encountered a few days into VERITABLE, would occupy key buildings, operating only from ground floors with excellent fields of vision. Booby traps were not prevalent, perhaps reflecting the limited amounts of time available to the enemy to prepare defences, but resistance was determined, skilful, and required equal countermeasures to avoid debilitating losses.

British and Canadian infantry forces adopted particular methods to deal with town and village clearance; such actions at night were eschewed in favour of first-light attacks to unhinge German positions in urban areas. Progress was still necessarily slow, arduous and very demanding.[47] Montgomery's initial enthusiasm had been tempered by the slower progress of VERITABLE from 10 February onwards, and with increasing casualties and the repeated delays to the second part of his plan for clearing the area to the west of the Rhine, Ninth US Army's Operation GRENADE, recognition dawned that this would be a more painful and drawn-out process than had been hoped for. The Germans' flooding of the area through which GRENADE was to be launched and the prevailing wet weather caused the River Roer to flood and precluded any possibility of starting the operation on time; it was repeatedly put back from 10 February onwards. This resulted in German reserves being drawn to the VERITABLE sector which, though it would ultimately facilitate the success of GRENADE when it eventually began, still made life much more difficult for British and Canadian forces fighting in and around the Reichswald Forest and on towards the Rhine.

A key turning point in VERITABLE came when 43rd Division advanced 10,000 yards, often with open flanks, to capture the Goch Escarpment, some 10 miles south of Kleve, a feature which overlooked the town of Goch from the north. By 17 February this thrust forced the enemy to withdraw from Staatsforst Kleve. The fighting was sustained and grim but brought about the capture of 2,400 prisoners and, in conjunction with troops of 15th Scottish and other units, the capture of Goch itself by 21 February.[48]

On 19 February Montgomery had noted in his diary that resistance to VERITABLE was stiffening and progress notably slowing, though 10,000 prisoners had been captured and 20,000 German troops accounted for. He was also concerned about the capability of Harry Crerar, commanding First Canadian Army which was directing VERITABLE, to keep the operation on track:

> The operations are now reaching a very critical stage and the next blow to be put in by the Canadian Army [codenamed BLOCKBUSTER] must be carefully staged and be exactly right. Crerar is not good at fighting an army battle . . . he fights two Corps battles and not one Army battle.[49]

Conscious of the need to initiate GRENADE quickly, Montgomery visited Bill Simpson's Ninth US Army HQ on 21 February to pep things up. He wrote:

> Bill Simpson could not decide whether to launch GRENADE. Fine day, country drying fast, river had fallen, engineers could do the bridging, weather forecast was good.
>
> So I decided for him.[50]

GRENADE finally began on 23 February and dramatically speeded up the clearance of German opposition west of the Rhine in the 21st Army Group sector. The Ninth US Army's offensive bore immediate fruit and town after town fell to the American troops, and though a river crossing over the Rhine between Wesel and Cologne proved unattainable, GRENADE was a great success. Bradley's forces were also making progress pushing across the Roer and on towards Cologne itself. Simpson's troops even sought permission to force an impromptu crossing over the Rhine but Montgomery refused, preferring to organise a full-scale set-piece operation to achieve this. Some at Ninth Army HQ grumbled about this decision, their optimism reflecting the speed with which they had rolled up the German positions in front of them in GRENADE, but Montgomery's usual caution was reinforced by the hard work that had been VERITABLE.[51]

For the British and Canadian forces, VERITABLE continued to grind away into early March, and it was II Canadian Corps which forced the pace from 25 February onwards, though British units continued to battle away too, both in XXX Corps and with the Canadians. With Canadian progress in BLOCKBUSTER German resistance against XXX Corps began to weaken. Intelligence indicated that though enemy artillery fire was as intense in VERITABLE as at any point in the campaign so far, it would slacken due to shortages of ammunition. Enemy mobility and air power were also increasingly affected by fuel shortages.[52]

The target of Wesel now lay just 15 miles away but the Germans continued to resist obdurately. By 3 March British troops had linked up with the Americans of Ninth Army and the Germans had been forced into a small pocket around Wesel. Even now British troops, particularly those committed in the later stages of VERITABLE, still regarded the fighting as intense with the Germans, even in the collapsing positions west of Wesel still providing stout and in some cases fanatical resistance. Troops of the highly regarded 11th Armoured Division, transferred across the Maas to support the final phase of VERITABLE, bemoaned the conditions and fighting, regarding it as: 'a slow, miserable and costly operation. We had been fighting our way through country where no armoured division could have been expected for one moment to fulfil a natural role.'[53] They nevertheless proved adept at adapting to the situation and demonstrated increasing flexibility. Despite being thrown together, 4th King's Shropshire Light Infantry (of 11th Armoured Division) and The Scots Greys (of 4th Armoured Brigade), formations that had not previously worked together, successfully prosecuted an attack in artificial moonlit conditions, a tactic increasingly employed by the Allies in 1945, with limited casualties. Units in the British Army were showing a high degree of shared tactical doctrine, allowing rapid interchanging of units.[54]

By 10 March organised German resistance on the west bank of the Rhine ceased and VERITABLE drew to a close having achieved its central aim. Horrocks' final comment on VERITABLE was most telling: 'My chief memories of the Operation are of mud, more mud and still more mud.'[55] German losses were considered by British intelligence as much more significant than had been considered likely when VERITABLE began. It was estimated that contesting the Rhineland so vigorously had cost the enemy 40,000 killed and wounded and 50,000 prisoners.[56] The victory had been achieved at considerable cost in British manpower too, and it was the infantry battalions that had suffered most as the effectiveness of the supporting arms fell away, exposing them to shouldering the burden of the offensive more and more. The 53rd Welsh Division suffered 2,445 battle losses in VERITABLE, over a quarter of the division's total casualties in the entire 1944–5 campaign. Even a division with a high reputation and limited exposure to the fighting in VERITABLE such as the 11th Armoured did not escape, with its infantry units displaying the highest battle-exhaustion rates of any formation in the battle. The psychiatrist attached to XXX Corps, Major John Wishart, noted the pressures playing on the British soldiers committed to VERITABLE. Up to a half of the battle-exhaustion cases were men who had previously been wounded, whilst many he saw were very young, some of whom had yet to shave. Few could be returned to combat in his view.[57] Battle-exhaustion casualties were often returned to front-line units, which bolstered fighting numbers, but as had already been noted by some commanders, this rarely helped actual fighting power. Lieutenant Colonel Trevor Hart Dyke said:

> They decided to 'patch up' these 'bomb-happy' cases which we had to evacuate, but I never found one, who, on his return, proved an asset to the battalion. True, they made the unit stronger on paper, but they made it weaker in actual fact, because their nervousness always recurred on going into battle, and this, of course, affected the others.[58]

The overall picture was still stable. Major General Miles Graham, 21st Army Group's administrative chief, reported shortly after VERITABLE that the incidence of sickness, including battle exhaustion, was down to 6.75 per 1,000 men. VD incidence was only 0.65 per 1,000 men, easily within manageable parameters, whilst rates of desertion were giving no cause for concern. Troops in the field had particular views on how desertions should be dealt with. Major Martin Lindsay presided over a court martial one morning in March 1945:

> They were the usual cases of desertion from the field of battle. We gave two ten years, two five years and one twelve months. We knew that when we awarded a ten-year sentence it would be reduced to three or four and that the man would serve perhaps six months. So if we thought a man should get, say, two or three years we passed a sentence of ten or fifteen.[59]

Most tellingly of all, cases of trenchfoot had barely reached 200 in the campaign, which in view of the conditions in VERITABLE was a remarkable comment on discipline and medical support in the British Army in 1945, and contrasted markedly with the American Army which suffered proportionally many more cases.[60]

During the closing stages of the fighting Montgomery received a visit from Churchill and Brooke. The Prime Minister took great boyish relish in urinating on the Siegfried Line, much to the amusement of the press. Yet, under the instruction of Churchill, they did not take pictures of the event. Monty was more concerned about fending off a rumour that Harold Alexander might now be appointed as deputy to Eisenhower at SHAEF, with responsibility for the land campaign. Churchill favoured the idea, being a firm supporter of Alexander whereas Brooke was not. Brooke nevertheless wanted Alexander out of Italy where he was acting as Army Group commander and, in Brooke's view, not very successfully. Montgomery told the Prime Minister that such an appointment would lead to trouble and the idea never bore fruit.[61]

Montgomery was nevertheless confident about how the remainder of the campaign would unfold. After VERITABLE, as he was working on the Rhine-crossing plans – PLUNDER and VARSITY – he publicly expressed his supreme confidence to the troops: 'The complete and decisive defeat of the Germans is certain; there is no possibility of doubt on this matter.'[62] As British forces prepared for what would be the last great set-piece operation of the campaign, they were afforded time to reflect upon and absorb key lessons of the fighting in VERITABLE to further refine their tactical methods. Infantry-tank cooperation was still under deep consideration with the lessons of previous actions being confirmed and slightly refined. In

34th Armoured Brigade the importance of units having previously worked together was once again borne out:

> The real benefit of the infantry/tank training lies in getting to know the infantry and the value of this cannot be overemphasised. Many attacks were laid on at short notice. On one occasion a successful battalion/squadron attack was laid on in 5 minutes and it is certain that this could not have been done without previous training and practice.[63]

Where possible, the 21st Army Group Royal Armoured Corps staff concluded, units unused to cooperating together should have twenty-four hours to devise mutual tactical understanding. To facilitate better infantry-armour cooperation, units also assigned squadron reconnaissance officers to act as liaison with infantry battalion HQs, whilst tank commanders recognised the value of dismounting to coordinate with infantry officers, even though this increased the risk of being wounded.[64]

The Rhine crossing was an operation that had been planned since the autumn of 1944, and by January 1945, following the collapse of the German Ardennes offensive, 21st Army Group was filling in the details. Although many British units and troops had been involved in VERITABLE, Dempsey's Second Army staff had not, because they had been tasked with putting together the overall plan for Operation PLUNDER, as the Rhine crossing was to be codenamed. This included the planning for Simpson's Ninth US Army, which would fight on the right flank of the British, and for the First Canadian Army which would play a more limited role on the left. PLUNDER was a major multi-corps set-piece operation with an array of engineering, amphibious and assault units deployed to smash the way across the Rhine and on to the North German Plain. Dempsey deployed Ritchie's XII Corps to the left, Horrocks' XXX Corps to the right, with VIII Corps to play a supporting role. Once across the Rhine all three corps would exploit northeast into the heartland of Germany. The crossing was also to be supported by a major airborne assault – codenamed VARSITY – involving 6th British Airborne and 17th US Airborne Divisions.

The whole assault was a vast undertaking in which everything that 21st Army Group had devised, developed and improved since Normandy would be utilised. Montgomery was determined that everything that could be put in place would be; risks were to be eliminated as far as possible, and thus casualties reduced to a minimum. Deficiencies in infantry and particularly junior officers continued to inform 21st Army Group thinking, even though a number of units and formations from the Italian front, including

I Canadian Corps, were now arriving in Northwest Europe to boost the final push.[65]

Yet the level of resources and time invested in organising and structuring PLUNDER/VARSITY proved excessive and reflected that 21st Army Group's operational technique, though serving the needs of the Anglo-Canadian armies well enough in 1944–5, could be inflexible. German units had taken such a battering in VERITABLE that early intelligence assessments of opposing strength for PLUNDER were downgraded. Initial studies had indicated that enemy forces would muster some 58,000 troops to oppose 21st Army Group's assault, but such were the heavy losses imposed on the Germans in clinging on in the Rhineland that on 23 March intelligence summaries reckoned that the figure was more likely to be around 30,000. American successes further south, including having already established a bridgehead over the Rhine at Remagen, had also drawn available German reserves, such as they were, away from the 21st Army Group sector. There was also evidence that the German position was so parlous that a continuous defence of the east bank of the Rhine was impossible and that such strength as was available was deployed to defend nodal points such as villages and towns.[66] US generals Courtney Hodges and George Patton railed at what appeared to be the pedestrian nature of British preparations in the north when available intelligence strongly implied that the Germans were spent. But Montgomery was unwilling to change his methods and stuck to his risk-averse plan, his thinking shaped by the losses his forces had endured in VERITABLE. Eisenhower was also unwilling to alter the strategy he had thrashed out with his army commanders that focused resources on the initial 21st Army Group crossing of the Rhine in the north.[67]

Second Army's build-up for PLUNDER involved 32,000 vehicles, including 4,000 tank transporters and the movement forward of 118,000 tons of stores. Royal Navy landing craft, Buffalo amphibious vehicles and duplex-drive swimming tanks were all deployed to ease the way across the river, whilst overhead, the Allied air forces mustered some 10,000 aircraft, outnumbering the Luftwaffe in the west by ten to one. A vast and complex fire-support plan was drawn up to blast the way forward for the assaulting forces, whilst units were fully briefed about conditions, potential obstacles and enemy dispositions; there were 8,000 engineers alone in XXX Corps to facilitate the crossing.[68] To support the intelligence battle German civilians had been evacuated 6 miles back from the west bank of the Rhine, but even at Montgomery's 21st Army Group TAC HQ, security was still a concern now that the British were operating in Germany. Monty's HQ detachments were based in woods, near Straelen, ideal for isolated German troops to cause trouble, but most were intent on simply keeping their heads down until the war passed them by.[69]

Security was also an issue as Churchill was determined to be present when the British Army crossed the Rhine. Brooke, who was to accompany the Prime Minister, was far from pleased:

> I am not happy about this trip, he [Churchill] will be difficult to manage, and has *no* business to be going on this trip. All he will do is to endanger his life unnecessarily and to get in everybody's way and be a damned nuisance to everybody. However, nothing on earth will stop him.[70]

Both Churchill and Brooke were therefore in place to witness the opening of the battle. When PLUNDER eventually began on the night of 23–24 March, British units met little opposition and swept across the Rhine under cover of the firepower of 3,500 pieces of artillery, quickly establishing firm bridgeheads. In the north XXX Corps, spearheaded by 51st Highlanders (with 9th Canadian Brigade also under command), made excellent initial progress. Urban areas presented greater problems as German troops, especially the remaining paratroopers, continued to offer stiff resistance. First Gordons, 51st Highland Division, crossed the Rhine with barely a casualty only to be forced to engage in fierce street fighting in Rees, which they did not secure for three days. The Highlanders also suffered the loss of Major General Tom Rennie, their commanding officer, in the period of the crossing. He had helped to rebuild the reputation of the division following its difficulties in Normandy and, though a strict disciplinarian, proved popular with the troops. Like a number of other senior figures in the British Army, he did not conform to standard dress codes and usually wore a tam o'shanter and naval duffle coat, with hands jammed in the front pockets. Montgomery believed that such displays helped to provide high-profile characters for the troops.[71]

To the south XII Corps swiftly crossed the Rhine supported by similar levels of firepower and equipment. The lead division, 15th Scottish, had even played out a test river crossing in Exercise BUFFALO in early March where many of the practicalities and issues likely to be encountered were dealt with. In PLUNDER the division encountered few difficulties and units and troops were quickly transported across the river in the face of little opposition. Lieutenant Colonel Hopkinson, 8th Armoured Brigade, recalled: 'Soon the river was full of tanks looking rather like floating hip-baths, drifting down stream. One tank was hot as it left the shore and sank like a stone (the crew abandoned ship rather quickly).'[72] The 44th Brigade historian later wrote:

> The scene at the river was like Henley of the Thames at Oxford in 'Eights Week'.
>
> The storm-boats, rafts and Buffaloes plied backwards and forwards with their loads, every moment landing more stuff on the east bank; and the DD tanks, like strange canvas boxes, dived into the water and swam slowly across, emerged on the far bank, shook themselves, deflated, and then miraculously appeared as Sherman tanks again.[73]

Wesel was assaulted by 1st Commando Brigade, which suffered fewer than 100 casualties in crossing the Rhine, though it took until late on 25 March for the town to be declared captured, matters being helped by the assistance of elements of 17th US Airborne Division. The Allies took 850 prisoners and the German garrison commander, General Deutsch, was killed in the fighting. Further south still, Ninth US Army crossed without mishap, captured Dinslaken, and built the first bridge across the Rhine in 21st Army Group.[74]

Operation VARSITY, the airborne element of the Rhine crossing, had been carefully planned in great detail, and many of the lessons of MARKET GARDEN were incorporated. The two airborne divisions, 6th British and 17th US, comprising General Matthew Ridgway's XVIII Airborne Corps, had been intimately involved in the detailed planning of the air assault and had particularly focused on communications, speed of insertion and resupply. In early March a limited exercise was conducted by IX Troop Carrier Command to examine potential issues, and the extended time given over to the planning process squeezed much of the risk out of the plan. Yet the inherent dangers in airborne operations always remained.[75]

The air insertion in VARSITY was carried out in fine weather conditions but was hindered by the smoke and dust thrown up by the bombardment. [illegible] anti-aircraft artillery capability, but was not entirely successful. Sixth Airborne's parachute drop was nevertheless precise and, though some glider pilots overshot their targets, the landings went particularly well with 92 per cent reporting successful releases. Lieutenant Colonel P.E.M. Bradley, 6th Airborne's signals chief, noted:

> There was a bump and we were down, bumping along the ground. The Chief Clerk and the Signals NCO had loosed their straps and were already trying to open the door. They were thrown all over the place. When we eventually came to rest, it seemed an age before the door would open – in reality only a few seconds. We all tumbled out and lay flat to get our bearings.[76]

Concentration of forces on the ground was successful – 9th Parachute battalion gathered together 85 per cent of its strength in time to advance on its first objectives, whilst 8th Para's commanding officer, Lieutenant Colonel Hewetson, believed the entire 3rd Parachute Brigade was on the ground in less than ten minutes. The situation around the drop zones (DZs) was aided by the timing of the PLUNDER assault and the airdrop. The enemy had recognised that an air assault was likely and had correctly identified the areas likely to be used by the paratroopers, but by 0900 hours on 24 March with no airdrop in sight, German troops defending the potential DZs had been ordered forward to defend the river, making the landing of the paratroopers when it came that much easier.

Losses in the first two hours of the air landings were still considerable, each brigade suffering around 20 per cent casualties, predominantly due to unsuppressed German artillery and mortars. Yet the airborne forces soon secured their positions, and over the next day they beat off a small number of German counter-attacks, whilst linking up with the ground forces that had crossed the Rhine and were now massing preparatory to a breakout into Northern Germany from their bridgehead.[77]

The airborne landings had suffered the type and number of casualties likely to be incurred in a major operation of that nature in the Second World War, even if successful. In view of the spotty and limited response of the Germans, the likelihood of which was appreciated by Allied intelligence before VARSITY began, the necessity of such a dangerous airborne operation is open to question. PLUNDER and VARSITY had inflicted 30,000 casualties on the enemy, whilst Second British Army suffered just over 3,000 losses in the period 24–31 March. It was an overwhelming success, but one that could have been achieved more quickly and with less complexity. Montgomery's approach of sticking to his concept and the methods that had hitherto worked so well was exposed as being too inflexible in the Rhine crossing. As would be demonstrated in the next few weeks of operations, German resistance was collapsing and a fluid and flexible attitude to mopping up the remains of the Third Reich's fighting forces was now entirely appropriate.[78]

On 28 March, Second British Army broke out of its bridgehead on a two-corps front, with a third corps providing flanking cover, and began a push towards the River Elbe in order to win control of the North German Plain. To the north the Canadians advanced into the Netherlands, whilst to the south Simpson's Ninth US Army wheeled to the right to link up with Hodges' First US Army, thus encircling Model's forces in the Ruhr. With the Soviets closing on Berlin and German forces also falling back in the south, the end of the conflict was in sight.

There was still time left in the war for a further spat between Montgomery and Eisenhower, or more accurately on this occasion between the British and the Americans. On 29 March Eisenhower cabled Montgomery informing him that SHAEF strategy was to be amended, and that the major push in the north was to be reduced in favour of an advance in the centre towards the Leipzig-Dresden area, spearheaded by Bradley's 12th Army Group. What made matters worse for Montgomery was the transfer of Ninth US Army back to Bradley's command to reinforce this central thrust. To British eyes this downgraded the role of 21st Army Group, as Montgomery outlined with great suspicion in his personal diary on 29 March:

> With victory in sight, the violent pro-American element at SHAEF is pressing for a set-up which will clip the wings of the British group of armies and relegate it to an unimportant role on the flank; the Americans then finish off the business alone.[79]

Despite complaining to Brooke about the 'tragedy' of the situation, there was little that could be done. Montgomery despatched Freddie de Guingand to talk to Ike's Chief of Staff, Bedell-Smith, but to no avail. The pressure was telling on de Guingand again; he was taking sleeping tablets once more, and Montgomery thought he might be cracking up.[80]

Brooke saw national identity as being behind the measure, as there was little material difference other than that Ninth Army was now nominally under Bradley's command rather then Monty's. Brooke confided to his diary on 1 April:

> Most of the changes are due to national aspirations and to ensure that the USA effort will not be lost under British command. It is all a pity and the straightforward strategy is being affected by the nationalistic outlook of allies.[81]

Eisenhower was also responding to the emerging situation in Germany and working on the assumption that Berlin was going to fall to the Soviets anyway, much to the chagrin of Churchill, Montgomery and Brooke. Ike was now focused on heading off the possibility of a fanatical endgame being played out in the Alps by the remaining hard-core Nazi forces. Montgomery was unimpressed and still saw the measure as politically motivated: 'It seems that the doctrine that public opinion wins wars is coming to the fore again,' he wrote to Brooke on 1 April.[82]

Arthur Tedder, Ike's deputy at SHAEF, tried to justify the change to the British Chiefs of Staff on 3 April, by blaming a directive issued by Monty that had clouded the Western Allies' strategy and could cause problems with Stalin. His explanation cut little ice with Brooke: 'I said that I was astonished that Ike found it necessary to call in Stalin in order to control Monty!'[83] Though Montgomery considered that the new central strategy would prolong the war, there is little evidence to support this as, once the Allies had broken out from their Rhine bridgehead, German opposition began to disintegrate. British troops in XII and VIII Corps were driving on towards the Elbe, and though pockets of resistance were encountered, there was nothing akin to a single cohesive front being offered by the enemy. It was still territory for integrated armour-infantry cooperation, as Major General 'Pip' Roberts, commanding 11th Armoured Division, conceded after initially once more trying to operate with a separate armour and infantry brigade, in light of the demands for haste. The disjointed style of fighting forced a reversion to the mixed-brigade structure, particularly as the greatest threat to Roberts' armour, even the new excellent Comet tanks, no longer came from orthodox gunnery, but from hand-held *panzerfaust* weapons, useful only at point-blank range in close terrain. Intimate infantry support for the tanks was therefore essential.[84]

There were still shows of foolhardy bravado from German troops, all the more futile on account of Germany's impending collapse. Lieutenant Sydney Jary, 4th Somerset Light Infantry, recalled:

> I was briefing my runner, Private Thomas, behind a house when I heard the cry: 'Sir, they are charging at us'. Sure enough, from about one hundred and fifty yards ahead, a well spread out line of about twenty Germans were putting in a bayonet charge. Brave lads, they didn't stand a chance. I gave no orders except 'Cease fire'. Not one got within seventy yards of us.[85]

As Lieutenant Geoffrey Picot recounted:

> Our advance was somewhat easier than it had been in the Escaut-Arnhem area and much easier than it had been in Normandy. But danger attended us at every stage.[86]

The landscape through which British troops passed was bleak. William Lawrenson, 7th Armoured Division, noted:

> The German towns through which we've passed have been terribly knocked about; almost on the same scale as Villers-Bocage. Most of the German civilians we've seen have been women, many of them wheeling handcarts which carry their only remaining belongings. You can't feel too sorry for them, having seen the like in France – and to some extent in England (during the air raids). No doubt, however, they are beginning to feel sorry for *themselves*.[87]

Lieutenant Bill Bellamy recalled similar thoughts on seeing the destruction in Osnabrück:

> I was stunned by the totality of it and, despite my anger, horrified at the suffering which it had brought in its wake. Whatever the German people had done, I couldn't gloat over their anguish, or get satisfaction from a feeling of revenge.[88]

Bellamy's views, like those of so many others around him, changed radically in mid-April when advancing British troops began to uncover the realities of Hitler's Germany.

Against severe opposition Roberts' 11th Armoured Division had forced a crossing over the River Aller to the west of Winsen on 11 April, and were planning to move on to their next objective when they began to become aware of the concentration camp at Belsen. As the British troops advanced, a German party came to negotiate a truce to hand over the camp, in which 60,000 inmates were suffering from disease, malnutrition and appalling mistreatment, whilst 10,000 corpses of murdered victims lay about the camp and in open pits. Although it would mean a delay in taking proper control of the situation, the first British combat units in the vicinity of the camp mostly kept their distance, largely under orders, due to the need to contain the communicable diseases at work in Belsen, and even though it would, in the short term, leave the inmates at the mercy of the remaining SS and Hungarian guards.[89] But some British soldiers ventured in to see for themselves. Major Bill Close, 3rd RTR, recalled:

> I was not prepared for the horrific sights, even in the first few hundred yards of the camp. The huts were full of almost naked inmates, some dead, some only just alive and pitifully thin. There were bodies everywhere – lying in the small ditches around the huts; the stench was indescribable.[90]

Other camps such as Sandbostel were also uncovered by British forces in April and May 1945 with similar tales of appalling brutality and mistreatment, but none were on the scale of Belsen. At the time of the agreed handover 9,000 of the prisoners were already sick, though the scale of the problem was to become clearer when two British Field Hygiene Sections, a Light Field Ambulance and a Casualty Clearing Station under the command of Brigadier Glyn Hughes, Deputy Director of Medical Services in Second Army, arrived on 15 April to assess the situation. Hughes quickly devised a plan of containment, management and treatment, but the Royal Army Medical Corps (RAMC) struggled at first – they lacked sufficient personnel and know-how. The former was a matter of having simultaneously to support the British Army in the field, whilst the latter was due to shock, as nothing comparable to what the liberating forces confronted at Belsen had been catered for in planning.

Second Army's medical units had done an excellent job in the campaign, but they were initially unprepared for the scale of the job at Belsen. British troops rushed standard army food and supplies to the camp in order to feed the starving, laudably believing it to be the first matter to attend to. Tragically, army food was highly unsuitable for such malnourished inmates and caused diarrhoea and other complications which contributed to the deaths of some 2,000 souls.[91] Despite the best efforts of the RAMC, death rates at the camp remained high, with 600 inmates dying each day in the immediate aftermath of the liberation. Yet when coupled with greater understanding, better facilities, and when more resources were allocated, the problems were brought under control, though it would be a horrific process.[92]

There remains some controversy over the three days' delay in deploying medical support to the camp. It has been alleged that it was a reflection of the Allies' lack of concern for the fate of the Jews, but this oversimplifies the situation. Front-line units in Second Army had no understanding of the scale and nature of the horrors awaiting them, and although some information was emerging about the liberation of Auschwitz, little had filtered through to the West and next to nothing to the British Army in Northwest Europe. The fact that the war was still raging in the area around Belsen, that there was a pressing need to contain the problem of disease, and the sheer scale of the tragedy, explains the response of the British Army. That they were able to accommodate 9,000 patients within three weeks of liberation tells us something of the capabilities and determination of the collective response to the crisis, however ill-judged aspects of it were at the start.[93]

The British Army was also taking on greater responsibilities for government, a problem made more acute by the increasing numbers of German civilians falling under British control. As Second Army's combat units swept across Northern Germany, the scale of the task grew. Displaced persons (DPs) had been a constant issue for 21st Army Group, but by early April the problem was growing as units sped across the Rhine:

> This problem has been our greatest concern. It was not one of finding accommodation, collecting stores, getting organised and awaiting the DPs. The problem was one of a green detachment finding itself surrounded with DPs, with more coming in every minute, in a shattered town, with all the language difficulties attendant on lack of Allied LOs [liaison officers]. A single officer has on more than one occasion had to tackle the job.[94]

From the beginning of PLUNDER to 7 April, Second Army had accommodated over 25,000 displaced persons, about 10–15 per cent being ex-PoWs and 20 per cent those simply heading west away from the advancing Red Army. Orders from the British Army for DPs to stay put went largely unheeded, but Second Army had established five DP camps to control the situation. Crocker's I Corps had been stood down from combat operations and was devoted to lines of communications, supplies and civil affairs – three of the DP centres were organised by I Corps. It was a major multinational problem and on 7 April there were some 3,500 Russian DPs in British centres. Special provisions were made for them to be transferred into USSR units and to receive preferential treatment. Italian DPs proved curiously troublesome and ill-disciplined.[95]

Paradoxically, German civilians were causing little concern: 'The stage we are entering on is important. It is only a temporary stage and it offers the only opportunity of gaining a grip [illegible] while the population is still somewhat stunned and therefore docile.'[96] Civil Affairs reports noted that the morale and attitude of the German population varied, but that occasional claims of having been liberated, as had been found in the Rhineland, were much less frequent. In towns attitudes were recorded as sullen, if obedient. The depth of Nazism within an area was often a determining factor in guiding the attitudes of the locals, but more often than not fear of reprisals from ex-slave workers proved more a source of concern.[97]

Looting proved to be more of an issue during the advance, as XII Corps noted:

> Looting continues to be widespread. Though the behaviour of our own troops leaves much to be desired, all the blame cannot be attributed to

> them. As soon as the battle moves on, the civilians emerge from their cellars and wholescale looting commences.
>
> It is to be hoped that the looting by troops, and what is worse, the vandalism and wanton destruction will be suppressed.[98]

British detachments used loudspeakers with some success to warn civilians about the consequences of looting, and there was evidence that German soldiers had also been strongly implicated. Looting by troops and civilians alike was causing great difficulties for the Monuments, Fine Arts and Archives (MFA & A) branch of the army allocated to securing and safeguarding important and valuable works of art, ancient documents and collections. Though the conduct of British units was generally disciplined, it was not always so. At Schloss Anholt, MFA & A troops arrived to find the important collection of porcelain, paintings and other works of art ransacked and looted by a British unit that had passed through the area at the beginning of April. The damage was extensive, despite the efforts of the owner and archivist to intervene:

> The castle steward was forced at the point of a revolver to open up all the locked rooms in the cellars, which were sacked and the contents removed. She said that she had appealed to the officers who, although sympathetic, told her that they were unable to control their men.[99]

The loss of archives and documents in Germany was acute and many records of the location of artefacts were found to be inadequate, whilst SHAEF intelligence reports were also found to be incomplete.[100]

The chaos inflicted on German society by the British advance was clear for all to see. In many towns law and order was undermined by the disappearance of senior German police officials, especially if ardent Nazis, as British troops arrived, whilst public health concerns grew as hospitals were sometimes found to be in poor condition, overcrowded and hotbeds of disease with many staff and public health officials absent. The containment of communicable diseases was nevertheless well managed by the British Army in 1945, despite the movement of displaced persons. Cordons were established along frontiers to prevent the spread of diseases such as typhus and this prevented the outbreak of epidemics in Western Europe.[101]

The conflicting pressures on the British forces of fighting and governing in enemy territory as they advanced deeper into Northern Germany began to limit what Montgomery deemed safely achievable. Eisenhower issued another directive on 16 April ordering 21st Army Group to turn north towards Kiel, Denmark and the Baltic coast; there was growing concern at SHAEF that Soviet troops might beat the Allies into Denmark and so create a politically difficult situation. Montgomery despaired of the shifting politically motivated strategies emanating from SHAEF, believing that decisive military results were being delayed. In addition he wrote on 16 April: 'I cannot possibly go up into Denmark and also put under military government the large area of Germany we now occupy.'[102] Eisenhower therefore once again adapted his strategy and allocated three American divisions to support 21st Army Group's push north-eastwards.

British units pressed on with their drive towards the Elbe, encountering less and less in the way of sustained opposition. Advancing units often swept past straggling German troops, who laid low and away from main communications routes until the battle seemed to have passed by before re-emerging to harry British transport and supply units. In liberated territory this had been less of a problem as resistance groups mopped up straggling Germans, but in Germany itself this obviously did not occur. Horrocks considered this enough of a problem to slow the pace of his advancing formations to allow enough time to eliminate bypassed German troops. Whilst VIII and XII Corps forces encountered less resistance, for XXX Corps there were more troublesome, costly and futile acts of obduracy to deal with. On 15 April, 43rd Division crushed a final organised attack against its troops in the vicinity of the River Lethe. With only 200 soldiers and two panzers a German force pressed home an attack but suffered heavy losses before the force disintegrated:

> Later in the day, when the advance was resumed, old men and women emerged from the woods and neighbouring villages to carry away their dead, who lay in long rows in front of the Worcestershire's position. Many were young boys, others were old men who had been hurriedly pressed into uniform. It was a sombre scene, pathetic in its utter futility even to the battle-hardened troops of the Division.[103]

British commanders were finding it difficult to motivate their troops with the end of the war so close. Exhaustion and fatigue were taking their toll on soldiers, particularly in the case of the old hands who became increasingly wary of taking risks.[104] Montgomery, still conscious of unnecessary losses, refused to push too hard. On 19 April, 21st Army Group forces bypassed Bremen and reached the River Elbe, but Monty wanted to bring up sufficient equipment and supplies to make the crossing easier.[105] Whilst this was organised, four infantry divisions – 3rd, 43rd, 51st and 52nd – closed in on Bremen. From 20 April onwards, British troops advanced towards and into the city, encountering some stubborn resistance. It took until 26 April for opposition in the city to come to an end, but such was the chaos due to bombing, fighting, milling displaced persons, and looting that 52nd Division had to allocate an entire brigade to bring some order to the city:

> For two or three days towards the end of April 1945 Bremen was probably among the most debauched places on the face of God's earth: all sanctions broken down among those Germans who rioted in their shocking inability to accept the consequences of their own political stupidity.[106]

Horrocks' XXX Corps now pressed on past Bremen heading for Cuxhaven and the North Sea coast, whilst Ritchie's XII Corps advanced towards the Elbe and Hamburg. Dempsey planned for a fully organised assault crossing of the Elbe on 1 May, but the operation was brought forward as intelligence started to gather of masses of refugees converging on Lübeck, who were being swept westwards by the advancing Red Army.

Eisenhower was also feeling more political pressure about reaching the Baltic and impressed more urgency on Montgomery, who did not take such nudging particularly well: 'SHAEF began to fuss about the need for more speed in getting to Lübeck. This made me angry.'[107] Lieutenant General 'Bubbles' Barker's VIII Corps began Operation ENTERPRISE early on 29 April and started to cross the Elbe in force, led by 15th Scottish Division and 1st Commando Brigade. Opposition was slight and two bridges were soon under construction by the Royal Engineers. As the weather improved, RAF support increased and some irritating enemy fighter-bomber activity was driven away. By 1 May, 11th Armoured Division was across the river too and soon breaking out northwards towards the Baltic. To the east 6th Airborne Division and XVIII US Airborne Corps were also soon across the Elbe and striking northeast towards Wismar. The following day Dempsey ordered 11th Armoured to hurry on to Lübeck with all speed, partly to stop the Soviets from passing on towards Denmark but also because he believed it would push the Germans into a capitulation – Hitler was now dead and enemy troops were not just surrendering in pockets, they were beginning to give up en masse. In mid-afternoon on 2 May elements of 2nd Fife and Forfar Yeomanry and 1st Cheshires entered Lübeck and began to receive mass surrenders of German troops – 11th Armoured counted 18,000 PoWs by the end of the day, whilst 5th Division received the surrender of the entire 245th German Division.[108]

British and American troops had smashed a corridor northwards to Wismar in the east and Lübeck in the west, carving Northern Germany in two and sealing off the Danish peninsula from the Soviets by about six hours. Montgomery recorded the state of confusion and chaos that was being encountered by his rapidly advancing forces. On 2 May he wrote:

> North of the Elbe we have an eastern flank from Wismar southwards to the Elbe . . . German troops and civilians are surging against this flank trying to escape from the advancing Russians . . . great congestion and confusion; the roads are crowded with troops and civilians who have come in from the east; we must have taken 200,000 prisoners today.[109]

The following day 11th Armoured Division reached the Baltic at Travemunde, but the threat of the Red Amy getting into Denmark persisted. Churchill continued to fret (or bellyache as Monty called it) about Denmark and tried to badger Montgomery into sending troops north to shore up the pro-Western elements, even after the surrender ceremony at Lüneburg Heath.[110]

The collapse of the German forces was complete and with it came the surrender and Victory in Europe Day on 8 May. The principal objective of the British Army in Northwest Europe had been achieved, and though the challenges of switching from an instrument of war to an army of military government and occupation would be great, for such a well-organised, balanced and disciplined army as the British in 1945 this would be carried out in a most professional manner.[111]

Montgomery wrote of winning the peace and the challenges ahead when issuing his victory address to the troops under his command, but for most soldiers the primary objective now that victory had been won was simply to go home:[112]

> Men who for months had walked with danger, who had risen each day not knowing whether they would be there to see the day's end, just thought to themselves, 'So it's all over! Now I know that sooner or later I shall see my home again.'[113]

Some had to take on roles in the administration of the conquered Germany for many months after the war ended and grumbled about their lot. Captain Andrew Burn, 5th Royal Horse Artillery, recalled:

> Those of us who were not career soldiers were becoming bored with the pointlessness of peacetime soldiering and were straining every nerve to get out of the Army and begin our life's work – whatever that was.[114]

Many soldiers would stay in the army, though not all as they had imagined. Major Bill Close, 3rd RTR, was a professional who had won a field commission in 1942 and had commanded a squadron from Normandy through to the Baltic, fighting in EPSOM, GOODWOOD, BLUECOAT, leading into Antwerp, MARKET GARDEN, the Rhineland battles, then into Germany and all the way to the Baltic. Yet, he was passed over for a permanent commission in the Royal Tank Regiment shortly after the war, being offered an opportunity to revert to an NCO. He declined.[115]

The price paid by the British Army for victory in Northwest Europe in 1944–5 was one that by twenty-first-century standards seems appalling: over 30,000 soldiers were killed, with nearly 100,000 more wounded. Yet by the standards of the Second World War that price was not high; German losses were much greater and, of course, the loss of life in the Red Army was of a different order altogether. The comparatively low loss of life within the British Army reflected the manner in which it had conducted the campaign, and is testament to the adaptability, determination and professionalism of the troops who fought.[116]

11

RETROSPECTIVE

In the period leading up to the invasion of Normandy in June 1944, Churchill had, directly or indirectly, set out two principal goals for Montgomery's forces in the forthcoming Northwest European campaign. First, they needed to make a significant enough contribution to the defeat of the Third Reich to warrant a seat at the post-war conferences. If the British Army evaded its responsibilities in battling against the German armed forces, hiding behind the might of the USA, the position of the British in shaping the post-war settlement would be seriously weakened. How could the Americans and the Soviets take seriously a power that claimed to be first rate yet could not commit to determined fighting to underpin such a contention? Secondly, and in sharp contrast to the first requirement, Churchill realised the parlous state of British military strength by 1944 and that any costly and bitterly attritional campaign in Northwest Europe was unsustainable, particularly with a possible campaign in Burma and Malaya to come. Montgomery's forces would have to fight a war in Europe that could not be allowed to hollow out the manpower of the British Army – there could be no repeat of the Great War's bloodletting.

These two policies appeared to be diametrically opposed and provided a serious conundrum for those tasked with leading the campaign. This was a delicate balancing act for any army, and one fully recognised by its senior leadership, the Chief of the Imperial General Staff Alan Brooke and the Adjutant General Ronald 'Bill' Adam in London, as well as Montgomery and his 21st Army Group team preparing to lead the British Army into battle against their most feared foe. The leadership of 21st Army Group were fully apprised of the issues confronting them, as well as of the more obvious directly relevant difficulties of defeating an experienced and recalcitrant enemy in combat. That the British Army had a broad concept of how to achieve this is not in doubt – Montgomery, Dempsey and his corps commanders were aware of the methods to be employed and how they would attempt to defeat the Germans in battle, ideally without the need for heavy losses in Allied personnel. Firepower and superiority in resources were the cornerstones of British methods, underpinned by strengths in logistics, engineering, planning, medicine and intelligence, all attributes that it was hoped would achieve the overall objectives with tolerably low casualties. The approach suited British needs and attitudes, and reflected a holistic and modern attitude to the conduct of 'war', as opposed to the fighting of 'battles'.

Although the operational methods adopted by the British Army for the 1944–5 campaign might be seen as being born of weakness, they were in reality principally adopted because they reflected the strengths of the army and the political and strategic environment at that time. Far from being driven by weakness they were reflections of what the British Army did well and of the politico-strategic pressures at play in 1944. The approach was also born of earlier experience and a determination to limit the loss of life where possible. Senior officers and commanders, such as Montgomery and Dempsey, as well as Churchill himself, carried with them the burden of the Great War, the so-called 'Shadow of the Somme', and did not want to repeat the severe loss of life endured in the great battles of 1916 to 1918 if it could be avoided.

There was also a practical element underpinning this approach, because senior British officers believed that their predominantly conscript troops lacked the killer instinct and brutalised attitude to war of their German adversaries. Consequently, fighting methods based on firepower, equipment and superior resources would take some of the pressure off the troops at the sharp end and limit the necessity for them to match the Germans in close combat until greater experience allowed them to do so more evenly. Ultimately, the senior leadership of the army wanted to deploy metal rather than flesh to win their battles and this reflected the strengths of the British Army in 1944.

How successfully had the British Army achieved these aims by 1945? Whilst it is irrefutable that the principal aim was achieved in that the British were on the winning side, and on schedule by mid-1945, this in itself is not enough to validate the success or otherwise of the British Army – it was after all only one small part of an overall alliance of nations and arms working together to defeat the Third Reich. It is nevertheless obvious that the British Army began fighting on D-Day in June 1944 and was still successfully playing an important role in May of the following year. It was active throughout the campaign from the darkest days of Normandy when stalemate appeared to be descending – though this was never actually the case – through the rain, mud and snow of the winter, and into the grinding slog of Operation VERITABLE. Montgomery also lobbied hard to have 21st Army Group play the main role in delivering the knockout blow to the enemy in the period from September 1944 onwards – he could hardly be accused of shielding British forces from the front line, despite the grumblings of Bradley in January over Montgomery's refusal to commit his forces to counter-attacking the Germans in the Ardennes battles. Even in Normandy when some American voices hinted that US forces were doing most of the fighting whilst the Anglo-Canadians were too static around Caen, the reality was quite different. The 21st Army Group repeatedly hammered away for well over a month at the deepest and most determined concentration of German forces the Allies faced throughout the entire Northwest European campaign, pinning the enemy in place, inflicting heavy casualties and opening up the prospect of an American breakout, an opportunity that was skilfully seized upon by Bradley and Patton from Operation COBRA onwards. There is no doubt that the British Army made a major contribution to the defeat of the German armed forces in 1944–5. That the army was also in reasonable shape in 1945 at the time of the German capitulation is also self-evident; British troops moved seamlessly into occupation and retained a formidable presence in Germany for many years to come.

But the British Army also carried with it obvious weaknesses in the 1944–5 campaign, the most telling being an inability to translate break-in and break-through operations into breakouts and exploitations. On a number of occasions greater success might have been achieved if the army, from top to bottom, had thrust forwards more energetically and seized emerging opportunities on the battlefield. Yet the army was conceptually unsuited to this type of dynamism because it had adopted operational and tactical methods that emphasised risk aversion, where possible only committing to battle when the weight of Allied resources and firepower could reduce the likelihood of heavy casualties. By fighting its battles in this way, Montgomery believed, the British Army could drastically reduce the possibility of the Germans catching them off-guard, keep friendly losses down, and still win the war; there was no great benefit to be derived from undue risk taking. Any benefits that might accrue from such risks would be outweighed by the possibility of the inexperienced, citizen-based army suffering debilitating and morale-sapping setbacks. Montgomery reckoned that all could be won by the Allies as long as they did not relent in the employment of operational methods that had proved successful since 1942 and against which the Germans had no answer.

What then of the fighting power of the British Army in 1944–5? To what extent does the criticism that the British Army demonstrated a weaker grasp of modern warfare bear close scrutiny? This criticism is predicated first on the notion that fighting a campaign is founded solely on close-combat capability, and secondly that in this area the British proved weak. The evidence from the campaign of 1944–5 refutes both notions. The British Army's approach to fighting was more akin to a modern concept of conducting campaigns, one in which success was generated over the long term by focusing on the full range of an army's activities – intelligence, engineering, medicine, administration and planning, all areas in which the British were more adept than the Germans. By thinking about the campaign in this way, rather than fighting one battle at a time, the British Army was able to reach the end of the war intact whilst still having achieved its goals. The British Army also treated its most valuable asset, its troops, with a degree of respect, refusing to enforce compliance through fear alone, providing excellent medical care and logistical support, and creating an atmosphere in which lives would rarely be wasted unduly in futile or risky operations. Montgomery may not have been universally popular with the troops, but most at least accepted that he knew what he was doing and would do everything possible to win with low casualties.

The capabilities of the British Army in managing a campaign through efficient supply and organisation may seem of lesser importance, but contrast the British experience in 1944–5 with that of German campaigns in the earlier stages of the war. The German Army and the Luftwaffe committed to the invasion of the USSR in 1941 knowing full well they could neither feed nor supply their forces in the medium to long term and would have to resort to seizing resources from the civilian population to survive; it was accepted that this would lead to the starvation of over 1 million Russians.[1] Leaving aside the ethical and moral implications of this decision, if that is possible, it was also a gross strategic blunder. The plan caused widespread resentment and fury, resulting in huge administrative and logistical issues that compounded the already deeply flawed assumption that the war would be won within a few months. The British and their Allies embarked on a more considered and balanced strategy for dealing with civilians, liberated and conquered alike, and consequently there were few headaches for the British Army of this nature in 1944–5.

This wider view of campaigns and the vital place of the supporting arms underpinned British success. The Royal Engineers played a pivotal role in the operational methods of 21st Army Group, particularly in the pursuit from Normandy to the Low Countries and then in the atrocious weather of the winter of 1944–5. British Army methods placed great weight on deploying vehicles, equipment and supplies to feed the appetite of the firepower-based fighting machine forged by Montgomery. Building bridges, often under fire, clearing minefields, maintaining roads in the depths of winter and keeping open supply lines were just some of the crucial roles fulfilled by the engineers, allowing the army to function as it did.

The British Army greedily, and at times wastefully, ate its way through supplies, reflecting the Western approach to the conduct of war. But whereas the Germans were just able to maintain fighting strength via their overworked and overstretched supply network, the British, in spite of the voracious demands made on their supply chain, ensured that their troops had greater resources in order to maintain their adopted operational methods. The Western Allies placed much greater importance on keeping their armies balanced, maintained and nourished. From this, it was believed, morale and capability would be underpinned and there would be no long-term disintegration of the army, a vital requirement of British strategic needs.

What of the claims that the British Army demonstrated poor battlefield craft in the campaign? Basil Liddell Hart wrote in 1952 that whilst Montgomery and Dempsey had done a decent job in leading the army, the soldiers themselves had not performed well and lacked determination and resolve in combat. For this, he blamed a range of factors, but not least a 'national decline in boldness and initiative – from decreasing vitality or increasing domestication'.[2] There is no doubt that the greater investment in the supporting arms, and the wider demands of the war effort, drained skilled manpower from the combat arms of the army, particularly the infantry. It was also obvious that the majority of the fighting troops would begin the campaign untested in battle. Fighting methods had to suit the human resources available and allow a developmental period in which units and soldiers came to terms with battle and learned their trade. The use of artillery, air power and the support of mobile armoured fire support to cover advances was intended to meet the needs of the broader operational concept, but it also allowed soldiers to find their way in the campaign.

The British Army's operational methods resolved more problems than they created, but they were far from flawless. Firepower underpinned British methods throughout the campaign and was feared by the enemy more than any other element of the Allied arsenal. It imposed attrition and paralysis on the enemy, though rarely both simultaneously, and proved to be fundamental in defeating the German armed forces, especially when crushing counter-attacks. Yet, along with air support, it was no panacea and suffered from marked limitations; the evidence of the battles across the campaign demonstrates that against dug-in enemy forces the effectiveness of artillery and air support was less than planners had hoped for. Techniques improved and new tactics were adopted, and in the counter-battery role progress was obvious and valuable, but firepower alone was never enough. Air support faded in poor weather and though artillery was effective in the early stages on an assault, it tailed off afterwards. Even in Operation VERITABLE such problems were still apparent. Though artillery remained the most destructive weapon on the battlefield in 1944–5, its lavish application came at a price. Reliance on firepower caused sluggishness in offensives with troops going to ground too quickly, whilst tactical methods focused heavily on working with firepower and less on infiltration and other low-level tactics. Narrow and heavy concentrations of firepower also devastated terrain and retarded the speed of advancing troops, hindering follow-up forces, and working against armoured formations trying to exploit the situation. Successful though Monty's methods were, they came at a cost.

Tactical doctrines in the summer of 1944 were also in a state of flux. Although nearly five years of war had passed, the British Army's exposure to sustained combat against the Germans in Europe had been surprisingly limited and experiences in the desert were not always appropriate. The British Army's laissez-faire attitude to the imposition of doctrine had also resulted in an uneven adoption of suitable fighting techniques by June 1944. In Normandy the army proved at times to be predictable in its operational methods and confused in its tactics. Some aspects of operations worked devastatingly well, most obviously in defeating enemy counter-attacks from the time of Villers-Bocage and Operation EPSOM onwards, but in other areas such as infantry-armour cooperation and coordination of artillery with infantry assaults, much still had to be learnt and standardised across the army.

Yet the British Army was not static in its approach to operational and tactical matters, and innovation and flexible thinking can be detected from the first few days of the campaign onwards. Combat in Normandy forced units to reconsider their tactics where they were proving flawed, and develop and learn new approaches. The army's flexible attitude to doctrine, though in some ways a weakness, also proved to be a strength as it fostered a problem-solving attitude which quickly began to bear fruit. Supported by its growing experience, British formations, especially those which had previously cooperated together, developed workable and effective practices that solved many of the initial tactical problems. Formations and commanders constantly reviewed methods and practices, and by the autumn of 1944 new doctrine was being disseminated throughout the army to reinforce the learning process of the Normandy campaign. This process was both top-down and bottom-up;

Montgomery issued a series of pamphlets in late 1944 outlining his thinking on aspects of higher command, but brigades and upwards were also holding conferences to refine techniques and share thinking and learning.

Operational methods also improved. Though EPSOM suffered from tactical frailties, it conformed to the classic Montgomery set-piece battle and established a pattern and style that was to be too often repeated in Normandy of artillery bombardment at first light followed by rolling barrages leading infantry and armour on to objectives. By late July the Germans knew how to limit the effectiveness of these techniques, though they could not stop them completely. But from BLUECOAT and TOTALIZE onwards 21st Army Group operations began to display greater flexibility and incorporated new tactics and equipment to resolve some of the difficulties thrown up by the first few weeks of fighting. By the autumn battles in the Maas and Scheldt sectors, British and Canadian forces had a range of effective operational and tactical methods that, if properly supported, could overcome German resistance in most circumstances. These methods, which saw greater use of night attacks, armoured personnel carriers, flame-throwers and the support of engineering and close-support equipment, all covered by lethally responsive and heavy artillery and air support, could get the infantry on to their objectives more effectively than in the summer of 1944. These developments have largely been obscured by the focus of historians on Normandy and Operation MARKET GARDEN and a corresponding lack of attention on fighting in the autumn and winter of 1944–5.

Notwithstanding all these improvements and refinements, close-combat troops, and particularly infantry, were still central to success and failure in battle. Montgomery's operational methods and the British investment in artillery, mechanised support and new equipment and technologies, all aided the work of the soldiers in the rifle companies, but theirs was still the most dangerous and demanding job in the army. The task of the infantryman became that much harder when terrain and weather limited the effectiveness of the supporting arms. In close, rugged terrain where the enemy could dig in and evade the worst excesses of Allied firepower, such as in Normandy, and when the weather limited the effective deployment of air support and use of much of their mechanised supporting equipment, such as in the Rhineland, the burden fell emphatically on the infantry to carry the day. The intensity of the fighting for infantrymen was demonstrated by the fact that, despite constituting around 15 per cent of the army, they suffered over 70 per cent of the total casualties. Even in the spring of 1945 casualties were still heavy enough for soldiers heartily to accept that the bombing of Dresden was strategically warranted as their war was grinding on remorselessly. Ultimately, far from being a campaign in which the army simply blasted its way to victory, the fighting in 1944–5 imposed stresses on the front-line soldier as great as any in British history.

Yet even with these pressures there is no convincing evidence that morale was very seriously affected or undermined during the campaign. Intense phases of fighting such as in the middle part of the Normandy battle and in the Rhineland saw increases in battle-exhaustion and desertion rates, but never to seriously damaging levels. There was obvious concern in July 1944 when morale appeared to be dipping as the success of D-Day faded and static, attritional fighting set in, but the crisis abated and though senior commanders continued to support morale as much as they could throughout the campaign, it was never again such an issue.

Firm and impressive leadership was crucial in supporting morale in the British Army, as well as driving the forces to victory. Whilst Montgomery's idiosyncratic style of command brought some weaknesses, it yielded greater benefits. His grip and dominance over the command structure in 21st Army Group brought a singular and unwavering drive to the way in which the British and Canadian forces operated, and his adherence to the basic principles he imposed on the Commonwealth forces on taking senior command in 1942 served British soldiers well in 1944–5. Yet there was a price to pay, and missed opportunities such as at Falaise, the Scheldt and bouncing the Rhine in March 1945 are examples of where Monty's risk-averse culture impacted negatively on the campaign. In contrast, the one occasion when Montgomery lost sight of what kind of army he had at his disposal, and when he rode roughshod over all the checks and balances that existed to rein him in at 21st Army Group HQ, resulted in the MARKET GARDEN debacle.

Montgomery generally maintained a balanced understanding of the forces at his disposal and matched them effectively to the strategic objectives set for the British Army in Northwest Europe in 1944. The army grew into the campaign, overcoming a series of deficiencies, and managed its persistent weaknesses to the extent that they rarely impacted on the conduct and outcome of the war. Though the troops had to contend with initially imprecise battle doctrines, limitations on capability imposed by some equipment shortcomings, and operational methods that did not always yield the expected benefits, the performance of the British Army in 1944–5 was impressive. It matched resources with objectives, developed proficient fighting power sufficient to overcome the enemy, and delivered a victory to the British state that has for too long been downplayed by the passage of time.

Notes

1 Introduction – The Test of Time

1. Derek Knee, interview in *The Daily Telegraph*, 6 May 2005.
2. R. W. Thompson, *Montgomery: The Field Marshal: The Campaign in North-West Europe 1944–5* (London: Allen & Unwin, 1969), p. 310.
3. Memoir of Bob Ray, SOE officer in May 1945 attached to Montgomery's staff. *World War Two Veterans of Enemy Surrender* at www.biglotteryfund.org.uk.
4. Alan Moorehead, *Montgomery: A Biography* (London: Hamish Hamilton, 1967 edn.), p. 229.
5. Viscount Montgomery of Alamein, *The Memoirs of Field Marshal Montgomery* (London: Collins, 1958 – Companion Book Club edition, 1960), pp. 311–13; IWM LMD 70/28, Montgomery Papers. The colourful account is largely based on Montgomery's ten-year anniversary lecture on D-Day, 6 June 1954.
6. Recollection by Sergeant Bert Williams in Owen Boycott, 'Confusion and Tears among Germans on Lüneburg Heath', The *Guardian*, 5 May 2005.
7. Johnny Henderson with Jamie Douglas-Home, *Watching Monty* (Stroud: Sutton, 2005), pp. 144–5; UK NA WO 205/1226, Report on the death of General of Infantry Kinzel (June 1945).
8. Montgomery, *Memoirs*, pp. 315–16.
9. Russell Miller with Renate Miller, *VE Day: The People's Story* (London: Tempus, 1995), p. 56.
10. Recollection of [illegible] in [illegible], The [illegible], 5 May 2005
11. Albert Ricketts, *Memoirs* (unpublished).
12. Diary of Peter Hall, Duncan Rogers and Sarah Williams (eds), *On the Bloody Road to Berlin: Frontline Accounts from North-West Europe and the Eastern Front, 1944–45* (Solihull: Helion, 2005), p. 224.
13. UK NA WO 277/12, *Manpower Problems*, p. 80.
14. Lionel F. Ellis, *Victory in the West, Vol. II* (London: HMSO, 1968), p. 407; UK NA WO 285/13, Casualties and Ammunition, Second Army 1944–5; WO 106/4348, Operational Research in Northwest Europe, June/July 1944; John Ellis, *The Sharp End of War* (London: Compendium, 1990), p. 158; Sydney Jary, *18 Platoon* (privately published, 1987), p. 1.
15. See Max Hastings's views on the German Army throughout *Overlord: D-Day and the Battle for Normandy 1944* (London: Michael Joseph, 1984), and *Armageddon: The Battle for Germany 1945* (London: Macmillan, 2004). Also Trevor Dupuy, *A Genius for War: The German Army and General Staff, 1807–1945*. (Englewood Cliffs, NJ: Prentice Hall, 1977), and Martin van Creveld, *Fighting Power: German and US Army Performance, 1939–45* (London: Arms and Armour Press, 1983). Richard Holmes

described the German Army in these terms during a public lecture tour of the UK, January 2007 in Shrewsbury.
16. Hastings, *Armageddon*, p. 30.
17. Hastings, *Armageddon*, pp. 32, 90 and 392.
18. Hastings, *Overlord*, p. 211, and *Armageddon*, p. 24.
19. Antony Beevor, *D-Day* (London: Viking, 2009), p. 15. Academic sources criticising the British Army include: John Ellis, *Brute Force: Allied Strategy and Tactics in the Second World War* (London: Andre Deutsch, 1990); David Fraser, *And We Shall Shock Them: The British Army and the Second World War* (London: Hodder & Stoughton, 1983); Williamson Murray, 'British Military Effectiveness in the Second World War', in Allan Millett and Williamson Murray (eds), *Military Effectiveness – Vol. III: The Second World War* (London: Unwin Hyman, 1988); Raymond A. Callahan, 'Two Armies in Normandy: Weighing British and Canadian Military Performance', in Theodore A. Wilson (ed.), *D-Day 1944* (Lawrence, KS: University Press of Kansas, 1994); Russell A. Hart, *Clash of Arms: How the Allies Won in Normandy 1944* (Boulder, CO: Rienner, 2001).
20. Robert Citino, *Blitzkrieg to Desert Storm: The Evolution of Operational Warfare* (Lawrence, KS: University Press of Kansas, 2004), p. 108.
21. Alexander McKee, *Caen: Anvil of Victory* (London: Souvenir Press, 1964), chapters 3 and 4.
22. Hastings, *Overlord*, pp. 271–82; Beevor, *D-Day*, chapter 13; McKee, *Caen: Anvil of Victory*, p. 263.
23. Peter Beale, *The Great Mistake: The Battle for Antwerp and the Beveland Peninsula, September 1944* (Stroud: Sutton, 2004), and John A. Adams, *The Battle for Western Europe: Fall 1944 – An Operational Assessment* (Bloomington, IN: Indiana University Press, 2010), are two such examples.
24. Cornelius Ryan, *A Bridge Too Far* (London: Simon and Schuster, 1974), is the obvious example, though there are many others that seek to apportion blame for the failure of MARKET GARDEN.
25. Hastings, *Armageddon*, pp. 424 and 431.
26. Lionel F. Ellis, *Victory in the West, Vol. I* (London: HMSO, 1962 and 1968), p. 491.
27. See Montgomery of Alamein, *Normandy to the Baltic: A Personal Account of the Conquest of Germany* (London: Hutchinson, 1947), and *Memoirs* (London: Collins: 1958); Francis de Guingand, *Operation Victory* (London: Hodder & Stoughton, 1947), and Ellis, *Victory in the West*.
28. Basil Liddell Hart, *The Other Side of the Hill* (London: Cassells, 1951). On Liddell Hart as a historian see Alex Danchev, *Alchemist of War: The Life of Basil Liddell Hart* (London: Weidenfeld & Nicolson, 1998).
29. LHCMA Liddell Hart 11/1944/43–52, 'Lessons of Normandy' (1952); UK NA WO 285/29, Basil Liddell Hart to Miles Dempsey, February 1952.
30. Chester Wilmot, *The Struggle for Europe* (London: Collins, 1965 edition – first published 1952).
31. Wilmot, *Struggle for Europe*, p. 339 and pp. 427–8, 463–4.
32. S. L. A. Marshall, *Men Against Fire* (New York: Morrow, 1947). Criticism has been levelled at this work by Roger Spiller, 'SLA Marshall and the Ratio of Fire', in *Journal of the Royal United Services Institute*, 133/4 (winter 1988), and Terry Copp, *Fields of Fire, The Canadians in Normandy* (Toronto, ON: University of Toronto Press, 2003), pp. 10–12.
33. H. F. Joslen, *Orders of Battle 1939–45* (London: HMSO, 1960).
34. Marshall's work was a key part of Trevor Dupuy's analyses, which in turn informed that of Martin van Creveld's.
35. See Giffard Le Quesne Martel, *East versus West* (London: Museum Press, 1952), as an example.
36. Mungo Melvin, 'The German Perspective', in John Buckley (ed.), *The Normandy Campaign 1944: Sixty Years On* (London: Routledge, 2006); Trevor N. Dupuy, *A Genius for War: The German Army and the General Staff 1807–1945* (Englewood

Cliffs, NJ: Prentice Hall, 1976); Martin van Creveld, *Fighting Power: German and US Army Performance 1939–45* (London: Arms and Armour Press, 1983).

37. Omer Bartov's study, *The Eastern Front, 1941–45, German Troops and the Barbarisation of Warfare* (London: Palgrave, 2001), offers an indication of the nature of the German Army in the Second World War.
38. An excellent analysis of Montgomery's approach is Stephen Hart's *Montgomery and Colossal Cracks: 21st Army Group in Northwest Europe 1944–5* (Westport, CT: Praeger, 2000).
39. LHCMA Liddell Hart 11/1944–45 Canadian Land Forces Staff Course, *Normandy Battlefield Study* (1988).
40. My thanks to Professor Gary Sheffield for this insight into the army's teaching methods of the 1980s.
41. Ryan, *A Bridge Too Far*, and Richard Attenborough's United Artists film of the same name (1977).
42. Hastings, *Overlord*, p. 280.
43. Carlo D'Este, *Decision in Normandy* (London: Collins, 1983).
44. Wilmot, *Struggle for Europe*, pp. 337–9; Robin Neillands, *The Battle of Normandy 1944* (London: Cassell, 2002), pp. 179–81; Nigel Hamilton, *Monty: Master of the Battlefield 1942–44* (London: Coronet, 1985 – first published 1983), chapter 6, Lord Tedder, *With Prejudice* (London: Cassell, 1966), p. 555; Vincent Orange, *Tedder: Quietly in Command*, (London: Frank Cass, 2004), pp. 266–71.
45. Norman Gelb, *Ike and Monty: Generals at War* (London: Constable, 1994), pp. 440–3.
46. S. Hart, *Colossal Cracks*, pp. 3–4.
47. See Ronald Smelser and Edward J. Davies II, *The Myth of the Eastern Front: The Nazi-Soviet War in American Popular Culture* (Cambridge: Cambridge University Press, 2008), in particular chapters 7 and 8.
48. An example of which is Tim Ripley, *The Wehrmacht: The German Army of World War Two, 1939–45 (Great Armies)* (London: Routledge, 2003). Other written sources which present this orthodoxy are: Ellis, *Brute Force*; Fraser, *And We Shall Shock Them*; Murray, 'British Military Effectiveness'; Callahan, 'Two Armies in Normandy'; Russell A. Hart, *Clash of Arms*; Citino, *Blitzkrieg to Desert Storm*.
49. BBC TV documentary, *Weekend Nazis* (2007).
50. Jonathan Bailey, *Field Artillery and Firepower* (Oxford: Military Press, 1989); Martin Van Creveld, *Supplying War: Logistics from Wallenstein to Patton*, 2nd edn. (Cambridge: Cambridge University Press, 2004), chapters 5 and 6; Russell A. Hart, 'Feeding Mars: The Role of Logistics in the German Defeat in Normandy 1944', *War in History*, vol. 3, no. 4, 1996.
51. J. P. Harris, 'The Myth of Blitzkrieg', *War in History*, 1995, vol. 2, no. 3, pp. 335–52.
52. David French, *Raising Churchill's Army: The British Army and the War Against Germany 1919–1945* (Oxford: Oxford University Press, 2000); S. Hart, *Montgomery and Colossal Cracks*; John Buckley, *British Armour in the Normandy Campaign 1944* (London: Frank Cass, 2004); Terry Copp, *Fields of Fire*, and *Cinderella Army: The Canadians in Northwest Europe 1944–5* (Toronto, ON: University of Toronto Press, 2006).
53. Colin Hall, *Dropped In It: The Autobiography of a Cotswold Boy and Arnhem Veteran* (privately published, 2010), p. 85.

2 Preparation – The Road to D-Day

1. Lionel F. Ellis, *Victory in the West, vol. I* (London: HMSO, 1962), pp. 132–3.
2. Gary Sheffield, 'The Shadow of the Somme: The Influence of the First World War on British Soldiers' Perceptions and Behaviour in the Second World War', in Angus Calder and Jeremy Crang (eds), *Time to Kill: The Soldier's Experience of War in the West 1939–45* (London: Pimlico, 1997), pp. 29–39.
3. Austin Baker, 4/7 Royal Dragoon Guards, *Unpublished Memoir*, p.11, and interview with author, April 2003.

4. Geoffrey Picot, *Accidental Warrior: In the Frontline from Normandy till Victory* (London: Guild, 1993), p. 44.
5. Captain Trevor Jenks, interview with author, August 2011.
6. Jack Swaab, *Field of Fire: Diary of a Gunner Officer* (Sutton: Stroud, 2005), p. 133.
7. Bill Bellamy, *Troop Leader: A Tank Commander's Story* (Sutton: Stroud, 2005), p. 17.
8. Quote in Patrick Delaforce, *Churchill's Desert Rats: From Normandy to Berlin with the 7th Armoured Division* (Sutton: Stroud, 1994), p. 12.
9. David French, ' "Tommy is No Soldier": The Morale of Second British Army in Normandy, June to August 1944', in *Journal of Strategic Studies*, vol. 19, no. 4 (December 1996); John Buckley, *British Armour in the Normandy Campaign 1944* (London: Frank Cass, 2004), pp. 203–6.
10. Ellis, *Victory in the West, I*, pp. 534–5.
11. See for example Williamson Murray, 'British Military Effectiveness in the Second World War', in Allan Millett and Williamson Murray (eds), *Military Effectiveness, Vol. III: The Second World War* (London: Unwin Hyman, 1988); Russell A. Hart, *Clash of Arms: How the Allies Won in Normandy 1944* (Boulder, CO: Rienner, 2001); and Robert M. Citino, *Blitzkrieg to Desert Storm: The Evolution of Operational Warfare* (Lawrence, KS: University Press of Kansas, 2004).
12. J.R.M. Butler, *Grand Strategy, Vol. II* (London: HMSO, 1971).
13. UK NA WO 199/1334, memo from Major General Gilbert Watson [DMP] to C-in-C Home Forces, December 1943; John Peaty, 'British Army Manpower Crisis 1944', PhD King's College London (2000), see introduction, p. 6; UK NA WO 163/162, War Office comments on morale, report May–July 1944; UK NA CAB 78/21; Carlo D'Este, *Decision in Normandy* (London: Collins, 1983), pp. 252–5.
14. I.W.M. Bucknall 80/33/1, diary 1 June 1944; UK NA WO 204/1895, School of Infantry Training Conference, April 1944.
15. UK NA WO285/2, Montgomery to DCIGS Weeks, 19 March 1944; CAB 106/313, Montgomery to Weeks, 19 March 1944; LHCMA Liddell Hart 9/28/24, interview with Chester Wilmot, 18 May 1946.
16. Compare D'Este, *Decision in Normandy*, chapter 15, 'The Manpower Problem', with Stephen Hart, *Montgomery and Colossal Cracks: 21st Army Group in Northwest Europe 1944–5* (Westport, CT: Praeger, 2000), Introduction and chapter 2, 'Casualty Conservation'.
17. LHCMA Alanbrooke, 6/2/6, Wavell to Brooke, 31 May 1942, and Brooke to Wavell, 5 July 1942; LHCMA Alanbrooke, 14/61/9, Montgomery to Brooke, 27 November 1942; LHCMA Allfrey, 4/6, Lessons learnt by 4th Armoured Brigade in Italy, September 1943.
18. LHCMA Alanbrooke, 6/2/6, Wavell to Brooke, 31 May 1942.
19. Sheffield, 'The Shadow of the Somme'.
20. IWM Montgomery Papers BLM 161, *Morale in Battle: An Analysis*, April 1946.
21. LHCMA Alanbrooke 10/20, War Office Exercise *Evolution*, notes from Montgomery, p. 7, August 1946.
22. Captain Andrew Burn, 5RHA, 7th Armoured Division. Interview with author, May 2002.
23. IWM BLM 41/5, 'Some Notes on Morale in an Army', August 1943.
24. Montgomery of Alamein, *Memoirs* (London: Collins, 1958–1960 Book Club edn.), p. 321.
25. Montgomery quoted by Michael Howard in 'Monty and the Price of Victory', The *Sunday Times*, 16 October 1983.
26. Interview with Williams cited in Max Hastings, *Overlord: D-Day and the Battle for Normandy 1944* (London: Michael Joseph, 1984), p. 180.
27. LHCMA Allfrey 3/1, diary 17 January 1943; UK NA WO 205/1165, Captain H. B. Wright RAMC and Captain R. D. Harkness RAMC, *A Survey of Casualties amongst Armoured Units in Northwest Europe*, No. 2 Operational Research Section, 21st Army Group, 1945.
28. Kurt Meyer, *Grenadiers: The Story of Waffen SS General Kurt 'Panzer' Meyer* (Mechanicsburg, PA: Stackpole, 2005), pp. 275–6.

29. UK NA WO 259/77, Churchill to Grigg, 6 November 1943; UK NA PREM 3/342/5, Churchill to Grigg and Brooke, 6 November 1943.
30. IWM LMD 66/54, Churchill to Montgomery, 12 December 1944.
31. Kenneth Strong, *Intelligence at the Top* (London: Cassell, 1968), p. 149.
32. Montgomery of Alamein, *Memoirs*, p. 332.
33. Basil Liddell Hart (ed.), *The Rommel Papers* (London: Collins, 1953), pp. 486–7.
34. S. Hart, *Colossal Cracks*, chapters 4 and 5.
35. Mungo Melvin, 'The German Perspective', in John Buckley (ed.), *The Normandy Campaign 1944: Sixty Years On* (London: Routledge, 2006).
36. National Archives, Canada (NAC), *Operational Policy – 2nd Canadian Corps*, 17 February 1944, RG 24, vol. 10797. Replies from Dempsey and Montgomery appended.
37. IWM LMD 66/1, M535, Montgomery to Brooke, 17 November 1944.
38. LHCMA O'Connor 11/14, obituary of General R. McCreery.
39. UK NA CAB 106/1037, Notes of a Staff Conference, 13 January 1944.
40. LHCMA Verney IV 2 & 3, *Some Notes in the Conduct of War and the Infantry Division in Battle* (November 1944), and *The Armoured Division in Battle* (December 1944); Robin Dunn, *Sword and Wig: Memoirs of a Lord Justice* (London: Universal Law, 1993), p. 91; Churchill College Archives, Cambridge (CCA) RLEW 7/7, Miles Dempsey to Ronald Lewin, 15 November 1968; UK NA WO 277/25, Gravely, *Signals*, pp. 382–3; Lord Carver, *Out of Step: The Memoirs of Field Marshal Lord Carver* (London: Hutchinson, 1989), pp. 94–6; UK NA WO 205/39, Notes on a Visit to the Mediterranean, July 1943; G.P.B. Roberts, *From the Desert to the Baltic* (London: William Kimber, 1987), p. 94.
41. LHCMA Alanbrooke 6/2/22, Montgomery to Brooke, December 1943; James Grigg, *Prejudice and Judgment* (London: Jonathan Cape, 1948), pp. 421–5.
42. Montgomery, *Memoirs*, pp. 236–7.
43. John A. English, *The Canadian Army and the Normandy Campaign: A Study in the Failure of High Command* (London: Praeger, 1991), p. 208; IWM LMD 60/13, Montgomery to Brooke, 14 July 1944; Paul D. Dickson, 'The Hand that Wields the Dagger: First Canadian Army Command and National Authority', *War and Society*, vol. 13, no. 2 (1995); LHCMA Alanbrooke 6/2/22, Montgomery to Brooke, 28 February 1943, 6/2/23, Montgomery to Brooke, 28 December 1943.
44. Interview with Edgar 'Bill' Williams cited in D'Este, *Decision in Normandy*, p. 353.
45. Dempsey's obituary in *The Times*, June 1969.
46. LHCMA Alanbrooke 6/2/26, Montgomery to Brooke, 7 July 1944; see also Peter Caddick Adams, 'General Sir Miles Christopher Dempsey: Not a Popular Leader', *Journal of the Royal United Services Institute* (October 2005).
47. Alex Danchev and Dan Todman (eds), *War Diaries 1939–1945: Field Marshal Lord Alanbrooke* (London: Weidenfeld & Nicolson, 2001), p. 538; Stephen Badsey, 'Faction in the British Army: Its Impact on 21st Army Group Operations in Autumn 1944', *War Studies Journal*, vol. 1, no. 1, 1995, pp. 13–28; LHCMA O'Connor 5/4/4, Dempsey to O'Connor, 19 February 1944; Allan Adair, *A Guards' General: The Memoirs of Major-General Sir Allan Adair*, ed. O. Lindsay (London: Hamish Hamilton, 1986), p. 136; UK NA CAB 101/73, FSV Donnison interview with Brian Horrocks for the official history of civil affairs, 21 January 1958.
48. Murray, *Military Effectiveness, Vol. III: The Second World War*, p. 125.
49. Timothy Harrison Place, *Military Training in the British Army, 1940–44: From Dunkirk to D-Day* (London: Frank Cass, 2000), pp. 147–50.
50. Bob Hope, quoted in Grigg, *Prejudice and Judgment*, pp. 366–7.
51. LCMSDS (Laurier Centre for Military Strategic and Disarmament Studies Archive, Wilfrid Laurier University, Waterloo, Canada), M. Swann, 'A Comparison of the British and German 3-inch Mortars', 1943.
52. Harrison Place, *Military Training in the British Army 1940–44*, chapters 4 and 5.
53. UK NA WO 204/1895, 'Infantry Training Conference: Record of Discussions', 15 May 1944; see also Terry Copp, *Fields of Fire: The Canadians in Normandy* (Toronto: Toronto University Press, 2003), pp. 28–9.

54. This tactic had been imposed by the inadequacy of weaponry in training and had not been properly refined when more modern tanks were introduced in 1943.
55. Buckley, *British Armour*, chapter 4.
56. Buckley, *British Armour*, p. 74.
57. Richard Stokes, *Some Amazing Tank Facts* (privately published, 1945), p. 3.
58. Robert Boscawen, *Armoured Guardsmen: A War Diary, June 1944–April 1945* (Barnsley: Leo Cooper, 2010), p. 9.
59. UK NA WO 171/1, 21st Army Group HQ, War Diary, 1943; PREM 3/427/7, Supply Policy; WO 205/151, Availability of vehicles and equipment, 5 May 1944; IWM 21st Army Group pamphlet, 'The co-operation of tanks with infantry divisions in offensive operations' (November 1943); IWM BLM 52/18, Montgomery's notes on Pyman's 21st Army Group pamphlet, February 1944; RAC Tank Museum Archive, Bovington, Dorset (BOV), RAC Half-Yearly Reports, January to June 1943, Montgomery to War Office, 16 April 1943; BOV AFV Tank Liaison committee meetings, 9 March, 13 April, 11 May and 25 May 1943; PREM 3/427/1, appendix C, in Tank Policy memorandum by James Grigg and Andrew Duncan for Defence Committee (Supply) meeting, 30 April 1943; Buckley, *British Armour*, chapter 7 and pp. 153–7; David Fletcher, *The Universal Tank: British Armour in the Second World War, (Part Two)* (London: HMSO, 1993), p. 82; Major Bill Close, 3RTR, interview with author, 2002.
60. The greatest concentrations of artillery firepower would be brought down by the AGRA formations, in use since 1942. Each AGRA consisted of some 4,400 troops and contained one heavy and three medium regiments, and in some cases one or more field regiments. For OVERLORD, 21st Army Group could call upon six AGRAs, and the rule of thumb for operations was an allocation of one AGRA per corps plus one spare. Ellis, *Victory in the West, I*, pp. 523 and 537.
61. Jonathan Bailey, *Field Artillery and Firepower* (London: Routledge, 2004 edn – originally published in 1989), pp. 204–6; UK NA WO 277/25, T.B. Gravely, *Signal Communications 1939–45* (1950), pp. 138, 270 and 307; WO 201/2596, Middle East Training Memorandum no. 8, Lessons from Operations, October–November 1942; NA WO 279/200, A. L. Pemberton, *The Development of Artillery Tactics and Equipment* (London: HMSO, 1950), pp. 158–9 and 197; LHCMA Allfrey 2/5, Address by Allfrey, July 1944; NA WO 201/431, Royal Artillery Notes on the offensive by 8th Army, 23 October to 4 November 1942; NA WO 279/200, Pemberton, *The Development of Artillery Tactics*, pp. 217–32.
62. UK NA WO 279/200, Pemberton, *The Development of Artillery Tactics*, pp. 12, 37; WO 163/183, General Staff Policy on Field, Medium and Heavy Artillery, 31 July 1942; WO 106/2223, NTW no. 4, Cyrenaica, November 1941–January 1942, May 1942; WO 163/183, General Staff Policy on Field, Medium and Heavy Artillery, 31 July 1942; WO 279/200, Pemberton, *The Development of Artillery Tactics*, p. 37; Ian V. Hogg, *British and American Artillery of World War Two* (London: Greenhill, 2002), p. 47; IWM Montgomery Papers BLM 117/10, address by C-in-C 21st Army Group to senior officers of the Royal Artillery, Larkhill, 30 April 1944.
63. Bill Partridge, 4th Somerset Light Infantry, interview with Matthew Lucas, 2011.
64. Dennis Avey, 2nd Rifle Brigade, interview with Matthew Lucas, 2012.
65. Colin Hall, *Dropped In It: The Autobiography of a Cotswold Boy and Arnhem Veteran* (privately published, 2010), p. 53.
66. Charles Hanaway, *The PBI: Memoirs of an Infantryman* (privately published, 2002), p. 26.
67. Lieutenant Dickie Cox, 4th Somerset Light Infantry, interview with Matthew Lucas, 2012.
68. Lance Corporal Stan Proctor, 43rd Wessex Division, interview with Matthew Lucas, 2012.
69. Private Harry Askew, RAMC, interview with Matthew Lucas, 2012.
70. Jeremy Crang, *The British Army and the People's War 1939–1945* (Manchester: Manchester University Press, 2000), explains many of these issues.
71. Leonard Watkins, *A Sapper's War* (London: Minerva, 1996), p. 37.

72. Trooper Joe Ekins, Northants Yeomanry, interview with Matthew Lucas, 2012.
73. Bill Partridge, 4th Somerset Light Infantry, interview with Matthew Lucas, 2011.
74. Trevor Hart Dyke, *Normandy to Arnhem: A Story of the Infantry* (privately published, 1966), p. 1.
75. Major Johnny Langdon, 3rd Royal Tank Regiment, interview with author 2002.
76. Captain Robin Lemon, 3rd Royal Tank Regiment, interview with author 2002.
77. James Sims, *Arnhem Spearhead: A Private Soldier's Story* (London: Sphere, 1980), p. 41.
78. Major General Roy Dixon, 5RTR, interview with author, 2002.
79. David French, *Raising Churchill's Army: The British Army and the War Against Germany 1919–1945* (Oxford: Oxford University Press, 2000), pp. 133–4; S.P. Mackenzie, *Politics and Military Morale* (Oxford: Oxford University Press, 1992), pp. 91–3.
80. Ekins, interview with Matthew Lucas, 2012.
81. Montgomery, *Memoirs*, p. 485.

3 Bridgehead – The First Step to Liberation

1. L.F. Ellis, *Victory in the West, vol. I* (London: HMSO, 1962), pp. 217, 223 and 504–7.
2. RAC Tank Museum Archive, Bovington, Dorset (BOV), Patrick Hennessy, *Young Man in a Tank* (undated manuscript), p. 35.
3. Letter quoted in Russell Miller, *Nothing Less than Victory: The Oral History of D-Day* (London: Michael Joseph, 1993), pp. 53–4.
4. Edward Wilson, *Press on Regardless: The Story of the Fifth Royal Tank Regiment in World War Two* (Staplehurst, Kent: Spellmount, 2003), chapter XIII, 'Shaker's Wood', is a good example.
5. Robin Neillands, *The Desert Rats: 7th Armoured Division 1940–45* (London: Weidenfeld & Nicolson, 1991), p. 212.
6. J.L. Moulton, *Haste to the Battle* (London: Cassell, 1963), pp. 56–7.
7. David Holbrook, *Flesh Wounds* (London: Methuen, 1966), pp. 98–9.
8. Leonard Wills, *None Had Lances* (24th Lancers Old Comrades Association, 1986), p. 133.
9. Lord Lovat, *March Past* (London: Weidenfeld & Nicolson, 1978), p. 305.
10. Ian Hammerton, *Achtung Minen! The Making of a Flail Tank Trooper* (London: Book Guild, 1991), pp. 71–5.
11. Montgomery of Alamein, *Memoirs* (London: Companion, 1960 edn – first published, 1958), p. 230.
12. UK NA WO 205/118, Operation OVERLORD: Appreciation on possible developments of operations to secure a lodgement area, May 1944.
13. UK NA CAB 44/261, Second Army Operational Order No. 1, 21 April 1944; LHCMA Liddell Hart 9/28/84, Chester Wilmot interview with Miles Dempsey, n.d. but *c.*1946.
14. UK NA PREM 3/339/1, Montgomery to Dempsey and Bradley, 14 April 1944.
15. CCA (Churchill College Archives, Cambridge, UK), PJGG 9/8/5, Montgomery's notes on his address to senior commanders, 21 May 1944.
16. A point even Carlo D'Este recognised. D'Este, *Decision in Normandy* (London: Collins, 1983), p. 80.
17. CCA RLEW 7/7. Interview and notes with Miles Dempsey by Ronald Lewin, 4 November 1968.
18. Francis de Guingand, *Operation Victory* (London: Hodder & Stoughton, 1947), p. 106.
19. UK NA WO 171/613, 8th Armoured Brigade War Diary, 25 May 1944; Norman Scarfe, *Assault Division: A History of 3rd Division from the Invasion of Normandy to the Surrender of Germany* (London: Collins, 1947), p. 66.
20. John Ferris, 'Intelligence and OVERLORD', in John Buckley (ed.), *The Normandy Campaign 1944: Sixty Years On* (London: Routledge, 2006), p. 196; UK NA WO 285/3, Dempsey Papers, Second Army Intelligence Summaries, May 1944.

21. UK NA WO 205/972B, BAOR, *Operations of Second Army in Europe 1944–45 – Part I*, 1945, p. 78. Extracts from I Corps operation order No. 1, May 1944.
22. Airborne Forces Museum Archives, Aldershot, 1/15, CoS (44) 230(O), 'Policy as to the Organisation and Employment of Airborne Forces', 6 March 1944; Richard Gale, *With the 6th Airborne Division in Normandy* (London: Samson Low, 1948); see John Greenacre, *Churchill's Spearhead: The Development of Britain's Airborne Forces in World War Two* (Barnsley: Pen & Sword, 2010), for the best treatment of this subject.
23. Lloyd Clark, *Orne Bridgehead* (Stroud: Sutton, 2004), p. 40.
24. Annette Tapert, *Despatches from the Heart* (London: Hamish Hamilton, 1984), p. 96.
25. P. Warner, *The D-Day Landings* (London: William Kimber, 1990), p. 37.
26. Terence Otway, *Airborne Forces* (London: HMSO, 1951), chapters XIV and XV; Peter Harclerode, *Wings of War: Airborne Warfare 1918–1945* (London: Weidenfeld & Nicolson, 2005), chapter 9.
27. Ellis, *Victory in the West, I*, pp. 153–5; Terence Otway, video interview displayed at Merville Battery Museum, Normandy.
28. UK NA WO 171/425, 6th Airborne Division War Diary, 6 June 1944.
29. UK NA WO 205/118, Operation OVERLORD: Appreciation on possible developments of operations to secure a lodgements area, May 1944; Ellis, *Victory in the West, I*, p. 222.
30. Douglas Reeman, *D-Day: A Personal Reminiscence* (London: Arrow, 1984), p. 10.
31. Ellis, *Victory in the West, I*, p. 161.
32. F.H. Hinsley et al., *British Intelligence in the Second World War: Its Influence on Strategy and Operations, Vol. III (Part 2)* (London: HMSO, 1988), p. 130.
33. UK NA WO 291/243, AORG post-war report on D-Day bombardment; United States Strategic Air Forces in Europe, *Survey of Effectiveness of Bombing of the Invasion Coast*, July 1944; Terry Copp (ed.), *Montgomery's Scientists: Operational Research in Northwest Europe* (Waterloo, ON: University of Toronto Press, 2000), chapter 9.
34. See Ian Gooderson, *Air Power at the Battlefront: Allied Close Air Support in Europe, 1943–45* (London: Frank Cass, 1998).
35. Max Schoenfeld, 'The Navies and NEPTUNE', in Theodore A. Wilson (ed.), *D-Day 1944* (Lawrence, KS: University of Kansas Press, 1994), p. 111; NA Canada, RG24, vol. 10673, 'Naval Fire Support in Operation OVERLORD'; Copp, *Montgomery's Scientists*, chapter 9.
36. UK NA WO 205/972B, *Operations of Second Army in Europe, I*, (1945), chapter I.
37. Warner, *D-Day Landings*, p. 115.
38. UK NA WO 106/4469, *79th Armoured Division Final Report*, p. 64; Anon., *The Story of the 79th Armoured Division* (British Army of the Rhine, 1945), chapter 2.
39. Interview with Bert Scaife, cited in Robert Kershaw, *D-Day: Piercing the Atlantic Wall* (London: Ian Allan, 2004), pp. 264–5.
40. Stephen Badsey, 'Terrain as a Factor in the Battle of Normandy, 1944', in Peter Doyle and Matthew Bennett (eds), *Fields of Battle: Terrain in Military History* (London: Kluwer, 2002), p. 356.
41. Paul Lund and Harry Ludlam, *The War of the Landing Craft* (London: Foulsham, 1976), p. 162.
42. NA WO 171/163, 8th Armoured Brigade War Diary, June 1944.
43. Robin McNish, *Iron Division* (HQ, 3rd Division, 2000 – third edn), p. 100.
44. John Buckley, *British Armour in the Normandy Campaign 1944* (London: Frank Cass, 2004), p. 19 and chapter 4.
45. Letter to Carlo D'Este, 27 August 1982, cited in *Decision in Normandy*, p. 129.
46. UK NA WO 171/1325, 2KSLI War Diary, 6 June 1944; Alexander McKee, *Caen: Anvil of Victory* (London: Souvenir Press, 1964), p. 61.
47. UK NA WO 171/1325, 2KSLI War Diary, 6 June 1944.
48. LHCMA Liddell Hart, 'Special interrogation report of General Edgar Feuchtinger', undated.

49. Interview with Major General Nigel Tapp, cited in D'Este, *Decision in Normandy*, pp. 139–40.
50. David Isby (ed.), *Fighting in Normandy: The German Army at D-Day* (London: Greenhill, 2000), pp. 76–80.
51. Isby, *Fighting in Normandy*, p. 80; NARA ML 488, RG 407, Box 24154, Seventh Army War Diary, 11–12 June 1944.
52. D. Kahn, *Hitler's Spies: The Extraordinary Story of German Military Intelligence* (London: Arrow, 1980), pp. 387–99.
53. IWM LMD 59/1, Montgomery's Diary, 6 June 1944. Also Nigel Hamilton, *Monty: Master of the Battlefield 1942–1944* (London: Coronet, 1985), pp. 612–15.
54. Niklas Zetterling, *Normandy 1944: German Military Organisation, Combat Power and Organisational Effectiveness* (Winnipeg, Manitoba: J.J. Fedorowicz, 2000), pp. 386–90; Helmut Ritgen, *The Western Front: Memoirs of a Panzer Lehr Officer* (Winnipeg, Manitoba: J.J. Fedorowicz, 1995), pp. 36–44.
55. Arthur Reddish, *Normandy from the Hull of a Sherman* (London: Battlefield Associates, 1995), p. 29.
56. Interview with Corporal Frederick Spencer, quoted in B.S. Barnes, *The Sign of the Double T: The 50th Northumbrian Division – July 1943 to December 1944* (York: Sentinel Press, 1999), p. 110.
57. David Irving, *The War Between the Generals* (London: Penguin, 1981), p. 177.
58. Montgomery to Major General Frank 'Simbo' Simpson, 8 June 1944, quoted in D'Este, *Decision in Normandy*, p. 164.
59. UK NA WO 285/1, Dempsey Papers; IWM Montgomery Papers, LMD 59/1, Montgomery's Diary, June 1944, and LMD 59/3, Montgomery to de Guingand, 9 June 1944.
60. UK NA WO 205/5D, Montgomery to de Guingand, 12 June 1944, 21st Army Group correspondence.
61. Gale, *With the 6th Airborne Division*, p. 101.
62. IWM LMD 59/1, Montgomery's Diary, 10 and 18 June 1944; J.B. Salmond, *The History of the 51st Highland Division* (London: Blackwood, 1952), pp. 142–3.
63. Letter from Major General G.T. Armitage to Carlo D'Este, 29 April 1982, cited in D'Este, *Decision in Normandy*, p. 174.
64. IWM Bucknall Papers, folder 14, Bucknall's correspondence with Chester Wilmot, 1947.
65. UK NA WO 285/9, Dempsey Papers, diary 12 June 1944; IWM Bucknall Papers, folder 14, Bucknall's correspondence with Chester Wilmot, 1947.
66. UK NA WO 205/5D, Montgomery to de Guingand, 12 June 1944, 21st Army Group correspondence.
67. Letter from Major General G.T. Armitage to Carlo D'Este, [illegible] June [illegible], cited in D'Este, *Decision in Normandy*, p. 177.
68. The best account of the action in Villers-Bocage is Daniel Taylor, *Villers-Bocage Through the Lens* (London: Battle of Britain Press, 1999); Trooper Stan Jones, 4th CLY, taped interview, University of Wolverhampton, 1997.
69. IWM Montgomery Papers, LMD 59/1, Montgomery's Diary, 13 and 15 June 1944.
70. UK NA WO 285/1, Dempsey Diary, 14 June 1944.
71. LHCMA Liddell Hart 15/4/85, Notes on 22nd Armoured Brigade operations, 6–15 June 1944, compiled by Brigadier Robert Hinde, 15 June 1944.
72. Taylor, *Villers Bocage Through the Lens*.
73. See Michael Reynolds, *Steel Inferno: I SS Panzer Corps in Normandy* (London: Spellmount, 1997); pp. 96–113 is an informative study of the command decisions in the action.
74. Letter from Lieutenant Colonel S.F.T.B. Lever to Carlo D'Este, quoted in D'Este, *Decision in Normandy*, p. 183, note 3; UK NA WO 171/439, 7th Armoured Division War Diary, 13 June 1944.
75. LHCMA Liddell Hart 9/28/84, Chester Wilmot interview with Miles Dempsey, n.d. but *c.*1946.

76. Even Carlo D'Este is culpable in *Decision in Normandy*, chapter 11, but most recently Antony Beevor regurgitated the same myths. See *D-Day: the Battle for Normandy*, pp. 192–3.
77. Major General Roy Dixon, then with 5th 5RTR, interview with author, November 2002.
78. IWM Bucknall Papers, folder 14, Bucknall's correspondence with Chester Wilmot, 1947.
79. IWM Bucknall Papers, folder 9, Bucknall to Oliver Leese, 23 June 1944.
80. UK NA WO 171/1257, 3rd Irish Guards War Diary, 13 July 1944; Earl of Rosse and E.R.H. Hill, *The Story of the Guards Armoured Division 1941–45* (London: Geoffrey Bles, 1956), p. 190.

4 Caen – The Cauldron

1. Interview with Squadron Leader A.E.L. Hill, quoted in Alexander McKee, *Caen: Anvil of Victory* (London: Souvenir Press, 1964), p. 135.
2. Jack Swaab, *Field of Fire: Diary of a Gunner Officer* (Stroud: Sutton, 2005), p. 144.
3. Lionel F. Ellis, *Victory in the West, Vol. I* (London: HMSO, 1962), p. 274.
4. UK NA WO 285/3, Dempsey Papers, Second Army Intelligence Reports No. 18, 22 June 1944.
5. Nigel Hamilton, *Monty: Master of the Battlefield 1942–1944* (London: Coronet, 1985 – first published 1983), p. 668.
6. IWM Montgomery Papers LMD 59/1, Montgomery's Diary, 18 June 1944.
7. IWM Montgomery Papers LMD 59/10, 21st Army Group conference, 22 June 1944.
8. Helmut Ritgen, *The Western Front 1944: Memoirs of a Panzer Lehr Officer* (Winnipeg, Manitoba: J.J. Fedorowicz, 1995), p. 52; Hubert Meyer, *The History of the 12th SS Panzer Division Hitlerjugend* (Winnipeg, Manitoba: J.J. Fedorowicz, 1994), pp. 93–4.
9. LHCMA Liddell Hart 15/4/85, O'Connor's notes on EPSOM, 5 September 1944; John Baynes, *The Forgotten Victor: General Sir Richard O'Connor* (London: Brassey's, 1989), pp. 190–5.
10. Erroneously spelt Charndonnerette by the British in 1944.
11. UK NA WO 171/527, 51st Highland Division War Diary and Intelligence Summary, 24 June 1944; WO 171/1270, 5th Own Queen's Cameron Highlanders War Diary, appendices A and B; Hans von Luck, *Panzer Commander: The Memoirs of Colonel Hans von Luck* (New York: Dell, 1989), pp. 186–7; J.B. Salmond, *The History of the 51st Highland Division* (London: Blackwood, 1953), pp. 142–3; Ellis, *Victory in the West, I*, p. 275.
12. Trevor Hart Dyke, *Normandy to Arnhem: A Story of the Infantry* (privately published, 1966), p. 14; Patrick Delaforce, *The Polar Bears: Monty's Left Flank* (Stroud: Sutton, 1995), p. 69.
13. UK NA WO 171/223, 1/4th King's Own Yorkshire Light Infantry War Diary, June 1944; Leonard Wills, *None Had Lances: The Story of the 24th Lancers* (Old Coulsdon: 24th Lancers Old Comrades Association, 1985), p. 136.
14. Rex Flower, quoted in Delaforce, *Polar Bears*, p. 77.
15. Meyer, *History of the 12th SS Panzer Division*, p. 94.
16. Robert Woollcombe, *Lion Rampant* (London: Chatto & Windus, 1955), p. 39.
17. Memoirs of Sergeant Hugh Green, quoted in Ian Daglish, *Operation Epsom: Over the Battlefield* (Barnsley: Pen & Sword, 2007), p. 41.
18. Quoted in J.J. How, *Hill 112: Cornerstone of the Normandy Campaign* (London: William Kimber, 1984), p. 34.
19. H.G. Martin, *History of the 15th Scottish Infantry Division, 1939–1945* (London: Blackwood & Sons, 1948), pp. 34–5.
20. G.S. Jackson and VIII Corps Staff, *Operations of Eighth Corps: An Account of Operations from Normandy to the River Rhine* (London: St Clements Press, 1948), p. 33.
21. Memoirs of E.A. Powdrill, acting troop leader of D Troop, H Battery, 13th Royal Horse Artillery, quoted in Daglish, *Operation Epsom*, pp. 51–3.

22. UK NA WO 291/986, Lieutenant Colonel A.G. Packer and Major H.G. Gee, *The Operational Effectiveness of the Flamethrower Tank (Crocodile)*, Military Operational Research Report No. 44, June 1947; US NAII RG331/210A/1, Lieutenant Colonel John Routh, HQ 12th Army Group, to Colonel Wright, notes on use of Churchill Crocodiles at Brest on 20 September 1944, report dated 3 October 1944.
23. Major Ned Thornburn, *The 4th KSLI in Normandy* (Shrewsbury: Castle Museum, 1990), pp. 35–6.
24 LHCMA Churcher I, Jack Churcher, *A Soldier's Story* (1984), p. 36.
25. UK NA WO 171/456, 11th Armoured Division War Diary, intelligence summary, 26 June 1944.
26. LHCMA Liddell Hart 9/28/84, Roberts to Liddell Hart, 30 January 1952.
27. Royal Armoured Corps Museum Archive, Bovington (BOV), William Steel Brownlie, *And Came Safe Home*, unpublished personal memoir.
28. Meyer, *History of the 12th SS Panzer Division*, p. 112; Jackson, *8 Corps*, p. 37.
29. LHCMA Churcher I, *Soldier's Story*, p. 36.
30. Thornburn, *4th KSLI in Normandy*, p. 25.
31. G.P.B. Roberts, *From the Desert to the Baltic* (London: William Kimber, 1987), pp. 164–5; LHCMA Churcher I, *Soldier's Story*, pp. 36–7; Thornburn, *4th KSLI in Normandy*, pp. 25 and 41.
32. UK NA WO 205/972B, BAOR, *Second Army Operations in Europe, Vol. I* (August 1945).
33. Post-war interrogation of Hausser, quoted in Jackson, *8 Corps*, pp. 51–2.
34. How, *Hill 112*, p. 114.
35. Laurier Centre for Military Strategic and Disarmament Studies (LCMSDS), Wilfrid Laurier University, Ontario, Canada, War Diary, Panzer Group West, 30 June 1944; Steiger Report No. 50 and 58, quoted in Terry Copp, *Fields of Fire: The Canadians in Normandy* (Toronto, ON: University of Toronto Press, 2003), p. 86.
36. UK NA WO 171/286, VIII Corps War Diary, intelligence summary, 1 July 1944.
37. Roberts, *Desert to the Baltic*, p. 166.
38. Major Bill Close, interview with author, September 2002.
39. Thornburn, *4th KSLI in Normandy*, p. 50.
40. Kevin Baverstock, *Breaking the Panzers: The Bloody Battle for Rauray, Normandy, 1 July 1944* (Stroud: Sutton, 2002), pp. 157–9.
41. Churchill College Archives (CCA), Cambridge, PJGG Papers of Sir James Grigg.
42. Max Hastings, *Overlord: D-Day and the Battle for Normandy 1944* (London: Michael Joseph, 1984), pp. 177–80; Copp, *Fields of Fire*, p. 86.
43. Martin, *History of the 15th Scottish Infantry Division*, p. 56.
44. LHCMA O'Connor 5/3/37, O'Connor to Lieutenant General Allan Harding, 19 August 1944; LHCMA Liddell Hart 9/28/84, Roberts to Liddell Hart, 30 January 1952, Roberts, *Desert to the Baltic*, p. 160.
45. Ellis, *Victory in the West, I*, p. 309; Meyer, *History of the 12th SS Panzer Division*, p. 140.
46. Copp, *Fields of Fire*, pp. 100–1.
47. UK NA AIR 37/1057, Allied Expeditionary Air Force minutes, 7 July 1944.
48. Major General Nigel Tapp, letter to Carlo D'Este, 1 July 1982, quoted in D'Este, *Decision in Normandy* (London: Collins, 1983), p. 316.
49. Meyer, *History of the 12th SS Panzer Division*, p. 141; Kurt Meyer, *Grenadiers: The Story of Waffen SS General Kurt 'Panzer' Meyer* (Mechanicsburg; PA: Stackpole, 2005), p. 145.
50. David Orr and David Truesdale, *The Rifles are There: 1st and 2nd Battalions The Royal Ulster Rifles in the Second World War* (Barnsley: Pen & Sword, 2005), p. 54.
51. UK NA AIR 37/1255, Solly Zuckerman and E.J. Kingston-McCloughrey, 'Observations on Bomber Command Attack on Caen, 7 July 1944'; WO 232/51, T.C. Trail to Air Vice Marshal H.E.P. Wigglesworth, 7 July 1944.
52. Meyer, *History of the 12th SS Panzer Division*, p. 140.
53. Ellis, *Victory in the West, I*, p. 316; C.P. Stacey, *The Official History of the Canadian Army in the Second World War, Vol. III* (Ottawa, ON: Queen's Printer, 1960),

pp. 161–4; Michael Reynolds, *Steel Inferno: I SS Panzer Corps in Normandy* (London: Spellmount, 1997), p. 155; Tony Foulds to Terry Copp, letter, April 1999. Foulds was a troop commander in the engagement.

54. Second Battalion Lincolnshire Regiment, account quoted in Michael Reynolds, *Eagles and Bulldogs in Normandy 1944* (Staplehurst: Spellmount, 2003), p. 168.
55. McKee, *Caen: Anvil of Victory*, p. 217.
56. Meyer, *Grenadiers*, pp. 146–8.
57. Orr and Truesdale, *The Rifles are There*, p. 53.
58. Meyer, *Grenadiers*, p. 150.
59. Quote from Fifth Panzer Army War Diary, 11 July 1944, quoted in Ellis, *Victory in the West, I*, p. 318.
60. UK NA WO 171/868, 7RTR War Diary, 10 July 1944; WO 171/1372, 4th Somerset Light Infantry War Diary, 10 July 1944.
61. Lord Carver, *Out of Step: The Memoirs of Field Marshal Lord Carver* (London: Hutchinson, 1986), pp. 193–4.
62. UK NA WO 171/633, 31st Tank Brigade War Diary, July 1944.
63. O'Connor's notes on Operation JUPITER, 5 September 1944, author's collection.
64. UK NA WO 205/644, 'Review of the situation D+30', Brigadier Charles Richardson, BGS Plans, 21st Army Group, 7 July 1944; LHCMA Liddell Hart 15/4/85, Dempsey's notes on GOODWOOD, revised, 28 March 1952; Alanbrooke 6/2/27, General Operational Policy, Montgomery to Brooke, 10 July 1944.
65. IWM LMD 60/8, 'The General Situation', 21st Army Group Tac HQ, 10 July 1944.
66. Charles Richardson, *Flashback: A Soldier's Story* (London: William Kimber, 1985), p. 181; CCA RLEW 7/7, correspondence between Richard Gale and Ronald Lewin, 24 August 1968.
67. CCA RLEW 7/7, Lewin's notes on interviews with Dempsey, 1968.
68. LHCMA 1/230, correspondence between Liddell Hart and Dempsey 1952; LHCMA Roberts, 'The Origins and Objects of Operation GOODWOOD', notes by Major General Pip Roberts, 3 July 1977; CCA RLEW 7/7, Lewin's notes on interviews with Dempsey, 1968.
69. Hamilton, *Monty: Master of the Battlefield*, chapter 12; CAB 106/1037, Notes from 21st Army Group conference, 13 January 1944.
70. UK NA WO 285/9, Dempsey's diary, 12 July 1944.
71. LHCMA Alanbrooke 6/2/27, operational objectives for GOODWOOD issued by Montgomery to Dempsey and then O'Connor, 15 July 1944.
72. CCA RLEW 2/7, Notes on talk with Montgomery 28 January 1969; LHCMA Liddell Hart 1/230, correspondence with Dempsey, 1952; IWM LMD 60/19, Notes on Second Army Operations 16–18 July, issued to Dempsey and O'Connor 15 July 1944.
73. LHCMA Pyman 18/1/18, Notes on the objectives of Operation GOODWOOD, 5 February 1954; LHCMA Liddell Hart 15/4/85, Dempsey's notes on GOODWOOD, revised, 28 March 1952.
74. LHCMA Roberts, 'The Origins and Objectives of Operation GOODWOOD', notes by Roberts, 3 July 1977.
75. IWM LMD 60/14, Eisenhower to Montgomery 12 July 1944.
76. Interview of Brigadier Charles Richardson, BGS Plans 21st Army Group, by Carlo D'Este, 13 November 1979, cited in *Decision in Normandy*, pp. 363–4.
77. LHCMA Roberts Papers, correspondence between Roberts and Belchem, November 1978.
78. CCA RLEW 7/6, O'Connor to Lewin, 15 August 1978; RLEW 7/9, Kenneth Macksey to Lewin, 31 August 1968.
79. LHCMA Roberts, correspondence between Roberts and Belchem, 23 November 1978.
80. LHCMA Liddell Hart 9/28/84, Roberts to Liddell Hart 30 January 1952; Roberts, *From the Desert to the Baltic*, pp. 169–71.
81. Interview with Dempsey, quoted in D'Este, *Decision in Normandy*, p. 387.
82. UK NA WO 171/78, 153 Brigade War Diary, July 1944; Salmond, *The History of the 51st Highland Division*, pp. 145–6.

83. Colonel J. W. Tweedie, unpublished report, Stirling Castle archive, courtesy of Ian Daglish.
84. G. S. C. Bishop, *The Story of the 23rd Hussars* (privately published, Germany, 1946), p. 69.
85. Letter from Tony Sergeaunt to Terry Copp, 22 June 1990, and paper, 'The Evolution of Tank Tactics during the Second World War'. I am indebted to Professor Terry Copp for this information; US NA II 331/210A/1, 'Intelligence Reports on Tanks Rendered Inoperative to Enemy Actions', June to August 1944, First US Army; BRL MR-798, quoted in Roman Jarymowcyz, *Tank Tactics: From Normandy to Lorraine* (Boulder, CO: Rienner, 2001); John Buckley, *British Armour in the Normandy Campaign 1944* (London: Frank Cass, 2004), p. 125.
86. Ellis, *Victory in the West, I*, p. 339.
87. Freimark von Rosen, interview at Staff College, Camberley, 1979.
88. UK NA WO 205/1165, Captain H. B. Wright, RAMC, and Captain R. D. Harkness, RAMC, *A Survey of Casualties Amongst Armoured Units in Northwest Europe*, No. 2 ORS 21st Army Group, 1945.
89. Major Bill Close, interview with author, September 2002; Bill Close, *A View from the Turret* (Bredon: Dell & Bredon, 1998), p. 117.
90. Interviews with Majors Johnny Langdon and Bill Close, September/October 2002; see Ian Daglish, *Operation GOODWOOD: Over the Battlefield* (Barnsley: Pen & Sword, 2005), pp. 71–2.
91. Close, *View from the Turret*, p. 118; interview with author, September 2002.
92. Captain Robin Lemon, interview with author, September 2002.
93. LHCMA Roberts 2, extract of uncompleted manuscript for book on Operation Goodwood by Major J. J. How, author of *Hill 112* and *Normandy: The British Breakout*, p. 7.
94. Roberts, *Desert to the Baltic*, p. 173.
95. UK NA WO 171/627, 29th Armoured Brigade War Diary, 18 July 1944.
96. von Luck, *Panzer Commander*, p. 193; von Luck, Staff College interview, Camberley, 1979.
97. See Christopher Dunphie, *Pendulum of Battle: Operation GOODWOOD July 1944* (Barnsley: Pen & Sword, 2004).
98. See Daglish, *Operation GOODWOOD*, appendix 9, for an in-depth discussion.
99. John Thorpe, *A Soldier's Tale*, the Personal Diary of Trooper John Thorpe quoted in Daglish, *Operation GOODWOOD*, p. 118.
100. David Stileman interview, Staff College, Camberley, 1979.
101. Jim Caswell, *A Cat has Nine Lives* (unpublished personal memoir), pp. 25–6; interview with author, September 2004.
102. Major Johnny Langdon, interview with author, October 2002.
103. Major John Gilmour, quoted in Dunphie, *Pendulum of Battle*, p. 99.
104. Daglish, *Operation GOODWOOD*, pp. 164–7.
105. Roberts, *Desert to the Baltic*, p. 177.
106. Close, *A View from the Turret*, p. 129.
107. McKee, *Caen: Anvil of Victory*, p. 263; R. A. Hart, *Clash of Arms: How the Allies Won in Normandy*, chapter 8; Major Bill Close, interview with author, September 2002; UK NA WO 171/139, 21st Army Group War Diary, 18–22 July 1944; UK NA WO 171/182, 21st Army Group War Diary, Deputy Judge Advocate General records.
108. IWM AL 1901/2, Tagesmeldung, 18 July 1944, Panzer Group West.
109. LCMSDS, Panzer Group West War Diary, 21 July 1944.
110. Jean-Luc Leleu, *10th SS Panzer Division 'Frundsberg'* (Bayeux: Heimdal, 2001), p. 108.
111. Harry Butcher, *Three Years with Eisenhower* (London: Heinemann, 1946), p. 531.
112. Interview with Brigadier Edgar Williams by Forrest Pogue for *Supreme Command*, quoted in D'Este, *Decision in Normandy*, p. 392.
113. IWM LMD 60/1, Montgomery's Diary, 27 July 1944.
114. D'Este, *Decision in Normandy*, pp. 328–30.
115. IWM LMD 60/1, Montgomery's Diary, 21 July 1944; LMD 60/27, M512 General Situation, 21 July 1944, 21st Army Group TAC HQ.

5 Stalemate? – Frustration in Normandy

1. Geoffrey Picot, *Accidental Warrior: In the Frontline from Normandy till Victory* (London: Guild, 1993), p. 115.
2. Joe Ekins, Northants Yeomanry, interview with Matthew Lucas, 2012.
3. John Ellis, *The Sharp End of War* (London: Compendium, 1990 – first published 1983), p. 158.
4. Royal Artillery Archive, Woolwich (RAA), Royal Artillery Notes on Recent Operations No. 2, 1944; UK NA WO 366/39, Report by officer commanding 102nd Light Anti-Aircraft Regiment, 11 July 1944, cited in A.L. Pemberton, *The Development of Artillery Tactics and Equipment* (London: War Office, 1950), p. 224.
5. Notes on 8th Army Operations, Sicily, 23 August 1943, cited in Pemberton, *Development of Artillery Tactics*, p. 186.
6. Jonathan Bailey, *Field Artillery and Firepower* (London: Routledge, 1989), pp. 194–208.
7. RRA, Royal Artillery Notes No. 23, 1944; UK NA WO 205/404, Royal Artillery Notes on recent operations, 25 June 1944.
8. IWM collection, Army Training Manual No. 50, August 1944.
9. George G. Blackburn, *The Guns of Normandy: A Soldier's Eye View, France 1944* (London: Constable, 1998), p. 231.
10. UK NA WO 291/848, 'Material and Moral Effect of Bombardment', No. 2 ORS Report, 1945; UK NA WO 291/1318, No. 1 ORS Report, No. 1/24/A, 'Effect of Artillery in Attacks in Mountainous Country', *c.*November 1944; UK NA WO 291/1331, No. 2 ORS Report No. 26, 'Fire Support in Operational VERITABLE'; Terry Copp, ' "If this war isn't over, and pretty damn soon, they'll be no-body left in this old platoon: First Canadian Army, February to March 1945', in Paul Addison and Angus Calder (eds), *Time to Kill:The Soldier's Experience of War in the West 1939–45* (London: Pimlico, 1997), p. 154.
11. UK NA WO 291/1330, 'Probability of Hitting Targets with Artillery Fire', No. 2 ORS Report, 1944; *Notes from Theatres of War*, No. 14, 'Western Desert and Cyrenaica (August to December 1942)'; Terry Copp (ed.), *Montgomery's Scientists: Operational Research in Northwest Europe* (Waterloo, ON: LCMSDS, 2000), part II.
12. UK NA WO 232/10A, interrogation of General Jahn, Directorate of Tactical Investigation, undated but probably 1945; Basil Liddell Hart (ed.), *The Rommel Papers* (London: Collins, 1953), pp. 330 and 486; Shelford Bidwell, *Gunners at War: A Tactical Study of the Royal Artillery in the Twentieth Century* (London: Arrow, 1972), p. 209.
13. John Terraine, *The Right of the Line: The Royal Air Force in the European War 1939–1945* (London: Hodder & Stoughton, 1985), pp. 648–9; Lionel F. Ellis, *Victory in the West, Vol. I* (London: HMSO, 1962), pp. 487–8; Ian Gooderson, *Air Power at the Battlefront: Allied Close Air Support in Europe, 1943–45* (London: Frank Cass, 1998), see conclusions in particular.
14. UK NA WO 291/1331, *Rocket Typhoons in Close Support of Military Operations*, No. 2 ORS 21st Army Group Joint Report No. 3 (1945); Alfred Price, 'The Three-Inch Rocket: How Successful Was it Against the German Tanks in Normandy?', *RAF Quarterly*, Summer 1975, p. 129; Terry Copp, 'Operational Research and 21st Army Group', *Canadian Military History*, vol. 3, no. 1 (1994), pp. 79–80.
15. UK NA WO 291/1331, *Air Attacks on Enemy Tanks and Motor Transport in the Mortain Area, August 1944*, No. 2 ORS Report No. 4; UK NA AIR 37/61, *Investigations of the Operations of 2 TAF Aircraft in the Mortain Area, 7th August 1944*.
16. UK NA WO 291/1331, *Rocket Typhoons in Close Support of Military Operations*, No. 2 ORS 21st Army Group Joint Report no. 3, conclusions (1945).
17. UK NA WO 291/1331, *Bombing in Operation GOODWOOD*, No. 2 ORS Report no. 6.
18. IWM AL510/1/2 von Rundstedt to OB West – Rommel's report to Keitel was attached; Rommel to Keitel, 12 June 1944, quoted in Chester Wilmot, *The Struggle for Europe* (London: Collins, 1952), p. 313.

19. Martin Pöppel, *Heaven and Hell: The War Diary of a German Paratrooper* (Staplehurst: Spellmount, 1996), p. 209.
20. Ewald Klapdor, *Die Entscheidung: Invasion* (privately published 1984), p. 219, quoted in Richard Hargreaves, *The Germans in Normandy* (Barnsley: Pen & Sword, 2006), pp. 88–90.
21. US NA II 331/210A/1, 'Intelligence Report of Tanks Rendered Inoperative due to Enemy Action', June to August 1944, First US Army; BRL MR-798, quoted in Roman Jarymowycz, *Tank Tactics: From Normandy to Lorraine* (Boulder, CO: Rienner, 2001), p. 270; UK NA WO 291/1331, *Analysis of 75mm Sherman Tank Casualties Suffered Between 6th June and 10th July 1944*, No. 2 ORS Report, 21st Army Group HQ, 1944; Peter Beale, *Tank Tracks: 9th Battalion Royal Tank Regiment at War 1940–45* (Stroud: Sutton, 1995), p. 145.
22. W. Steel Brownlie, *The Proud Trooper* (London: Collins, 1964), pp. 364–5.
23. Stephen Dyson, *Tank Twins: East End Brothers in Arms 1943–45* (London: Leo Cooper, 1994), pp. 46–7.
24. UK NA WO 205/1165, H.B. Wright and R.D. Harkness, *A Survey of Casualties Amongst Armoured Units in Northwest Europe*, No. 2 ORS Report, 21st Army Group HQ, 1945.
25. UK NA WO 205/1165, Wright and Harkness, *A Survey of Casualties*; UK NA WO 291/1331, *Analysis of 75mm Sherman Tank Casualties Suffered Between 6th June and 10th July 1944*, No. 2 ORS Report, 21st Army Group HQ, 1944.
26. UK NA WO 291/2384, 21st Army Group, No. 2 ORS Report, *Examination of Tank Casualties – Causes of Fires in Shermans*; US NA II RG 331/240E/14, Major Millard Thompson, 1st Armoured Group, report on 'sand-bagging' M4 tanks for added protection, March 1945; RAC Archive Bovington (BOV), 21st Army Group technical reports, no. 16, October 1944.
27. UK NA WO 205/1165, Wright and Harkness, *A Survey of Casualties* UK NA WO 291/1331, *Analysis of 75mm Sherman Tank Casualties Suffered Between 6th June and 10th July 1944*, No. 2 ORS Report, 21st Army Group HQ, 1944; BOV, Box 623–438, Operation OVERLORD, reports on equipment, ADAFV(T) 2nd Army to DDAFV(D); US NA II RG 331/210A/1, 'Intelligence Report of Tanks Rendered Inoperative due to Enemy Action', June to August 1944, First US Army.
28. Patrick Delaforce, *The Black Bull: From Normandy to the Baltic with the 11th Armoured Division* (Stroud: Sutton, 1993), p. 13.
29. Technically, it was the cordite propellant that exploded.
30. BOV, Box 623–438, Operation OVERLORD, reports on equipment, Lieutenant General Ronald Weeks DCIGS, Report 324/5 and report by Major Matthews (RAC) and RAC Half-Yearly Reports No. 9, 1 January to 30 June 1944; Patrick Delaforce, *Monty's Marauders: Black Rat 4th Armoured Brigade and Red Fox 8th Armoured Brigade* (Stroud: Sutton, 1993), p. 73.
31. UK NA WO 291/1331, *Analysis of 75mm Sherman Tank Casualties Suffered Between 6th June and 10th July 1944*, No. 2 ORS Report, 21st Army Group HQ, 1944.
32. UK NA WO 291/2384, 21st Army Group, No. 2 ORS Report, *Examination of Tank Casualties – Causes of Fires in Shermans*.
33. US NA II RG 331/210A/1, operational information on M4 medium tanks, HQ 26th Infantry Division to XII Corps, 1 December 1944; BOV, Effects of Enemy Projectiles on Sherman and Churchill Tanks, Major General Percy Hobart, 79th Armoured Division, 26 August 1944.
34. Delaforce, *The Black Bull*, p. 13.
35. Delaforce, *The Black Bull*, pp. 13–14.
36. A. Wilson, *Flamethrower* (London: privately published, 1974), p. 54.
37. UK NA WO 291/1331, No. 2 ORS Report No. 17, *Analysis of German Tank Casualties in France 6 June–31 August 1944*.
38. UK NA WO 205/422, Lieutenant Colonel J.R. Bowring, Immediate Report IN 20, 'Impressions on Fighting in Normandy', 17 June 1944.

39. UK NA WO 205/422, 21st Army Group combat reports, Brigadier H.E. Pyman (BGS) XXX Corps to Major General Erskine, 7th Armoured Division, 16 June 1944.
40. UK NA WO 205/422, Erskine to XXX Corps HQ, 17 June 1944.
41. Richard Rapier Stokes MP, *Some Amazing Tank Facts* (London: privately published 1945); John Buckley, *British Armour in the Normandy Campaign 1944* (London: Frank Cass, 2004), p. 209; see also David Fletcher, *The Great Tank Scandal: British Armour in the Second World War (Part One)*, and *The Universal Tank: British Armour in the Second World War (Part Two)*, (London: HMSO, 1989 and 1993, respectively).
42. UK NA WO 205/5b, de Guingand to Montgomery (TAC HQ 21st Army Group), 24 June 1944; LHCMA Alanbrooke 6/2/25, Montgomery to Brooke, 27 June 1944, and Montgomery to Dempsey, 25 June 1944.
43. UK NA WO 205/422, Major General G.W. Richards to 2nd Army and 21st Army Group HQ, 22 June 1944.
44. CCA (Churchill College Archives, Cambridge), PJGG 9/8/11, Papers of Sir James Grigg, Montgomery to Grigg, 25 June 1944.
45. IWM Bucknall Papers, folder 9, Bucknall to Oliver Leese, 23 June 1944.
46. UK NA WO 291/2384, AORG Report No. 1/21, *Examination of Tank Casualties* by No. 1 ORS Report, autumn 1943; Major Bill Close, interview with author, September 2002; correspondence with Captain Robin Lemon, 3 RTR, December 2002.
47. LHCMA Liddell Hart 15/4/85, 22nd Armoured Brigade, notes on operations, 6–15 June 1944.
48. UK NA WO 171/1257, 3rd Irish Guards War Diary, 13 July 1944; Earl of Rosse and E.R.H. Hill, *The Story of Guards Armoured Division 1941–45* (London: Geoffrey Bles, 1956), p. 190; G.P.B. Roberts, *From the Desert to the Baltic* (London: William Kimber, 1987), p. 164.
49. T.M. Lindsay, *Sherwood Rangers 1939–45*, (London: Burrup, Mathieson & Co., 1952), p. 107.
50. Trooper Austin Baker, 4/7th Royal Dragoon Guards, personal account supplied to author 2003.
51. Trooper Austin Baker, 4/7th Royal Dragoon Guards, interview with author, April 2003; Ellis, *Victory in the West, I*, p. 252; Delaforce, *Monty's Marauders*, pp. 149–50.
52. UK NA WO 171/862, 1st East Riding Yeomanry War Diary, June–July 1944; LHCMA Allfrey 4/5, XIII Corps conference, 'Need for a Common Doctrine for Infantry-Tank Co-operation', 8 April 1944.
53. Lindsay, *Sherwood Rangers*, p. 108.
54. Major Johnny Langdon, interview with author, October 2002; Geoffrey Bishop, *The Battle: A Tank Officer Remembers*, quoted in Ian Daglish, *Operation BLUECOAT: Battleground Normandy* (Barnsley: Pen & Sword, 2003), p. 71.
55. Major General Roy Dixon, interview with author, 2002.
56. Major Bill Close, interview with author, September 2002.
57. UK NA WO 171/153, 21st Army Group liaison letter No. 2, 6 September 1944.
58. UK NA WO 205/152, Estimates of availability of Allied units and manpower, February 1944 to May 1945; WO 162/116, Europe: Western and Northwestern, British Battle Casualties notes.
59. LHCMA Dempsey 2nd Army Intelligence Reports, No. 2, 15 August 1944.
60. For an in-depth discussion on the issue of infantry tactics, see Timothy Harrison Place, *Military Training in the British Army 1940–44: From Dunkirk to D-Day* (London: Frank Cass, 2000), chapters 4 and 5 in particular.
61. Picot, *Accidental Warrior*, pp. 20–22.
62. NTW No. 20, *Italy 1943/44* (May 1945), chapter 5.
63. UK NA WO 231/16, 'El Alamein to Messina: Lessons Learned by 152nd Infantry Brigade during the Years of Fighting from El Alamein to Messina'.
64. Harrison Place, *Military Training*, p. 33.
65. UK NA WO 204/1895, School of Infantry, 'Infantry Training Conference', 15 May 1944.
66. S. Whitehouse and G.B. Bennett, *Fear is the Foe: A Footslogger from Normandy to the Rhine* (London: Robert Hale, 1995), p. 153.

67. Sydney Jary, *18 Platoon* (privately published, 1987), pp. 19 and 53; UK NA WO 291/474, No. 2 ORS Report no. 126, 'The Rate of Fire of the LMG', *c.*April 1944.
68. Picot, *Accidental Warrior*, p. 116.
69. Stuart Hills, *By Tank into Normandy: A Memoir of the Campaign in Northwest Europe from D Day to VE Day* (London: Cassell 2002), p. 116.
70. Joe Ekins, Northants Yeomanry, interview with Matthew Lucas, 2012.
71. Tom Renouf, *Black Watch: Liberating Europe and Catching Himmler – My Extraordinary World War Two with the Highland Division* (London: Little, Brown, 2011), p. 134.
72. Bill Close, *A View from the Turret* (Bredon: Dell & Bredon, 1998), p. 68, and in conversation with the author, September 2002.
73. Les Taylor, unpublished manuscript, quoted in Ken Tout, *A Fine Night for Tanks: The Road to Falaise* (Stroud: Sutton, 1998).
74. John Majendie, interview quoted in Sean Longden, *To the Victor the Spoils: D Day to VE Day, the Reality behind the Heroism* (Moreton, Gloucs: Arris, 2004), p. 179.
75. CCA Grigg 9/8/12, Montgomery to Grigg, 2 July 1944, with report by Lieutenant Colonel A. Turner, 'Report on state of 6DWR (49 Div) as on 30 June' appended; WO 166/15096, 6th DWR War Diary, June–July 1944; R. Lamb, *Montgomery in Europe 1943–5: Success or Failure?* (London: Buchan & Enright, 1983), p. 106.
76. See Terry Copp and Bill McAndrew, *Battle Exhaustion: Soldiers and Psychiatrists in the Canadian Army, 1939–45* (Montreal and Kingston: McGraw-Hill, 1990), pp. 42–3.
77. UK NA WO 177/321, Major D.J. Watterson, report by psychiatrist attached to 2nd Army, July 1944, 5 August 1944.
78. Hills, *By Tank into Normandy*, p. 130.
79. Joe Ekins, Northants Yeomanry, interview with Matthew Lucas, 2012.
80. UK NA WO 205/972B, BAOR, *An Account of the Operations of Second British Army in Europe 1944–45*, Vol. 1, p. 482; National Archives of Canada (NAC) RG 24, vol. 12, 631, address by Major General Edward Phillips to 21 AG Psychiatrists, 13 January 1945.
81. UK NA WO 177/405 and WO 177/377, Medical War Diaries for 3rd British and 51st Highland Divisions, June and July 1944.
82. UK NA WO 177/335, I Corps Medical War Diary, minutes of conference, Cobham, 27 April 1944, and operational instruction no. 4, 9 July 1944; WO 177/343, VIII Corps Medical War Diary, appendix I, 17 July 1944; WO 177/356, 21 AG DMS Medical War Diary, 4 July 1944.
83. Dyson, *Tank Twins*, p. 65.
84. Major General Roy Dixon, interview with author, November 2002; David French, '"Tommy is No Soldier": The Morale of Second British Army in Normandy June–August 1944', in Brian Holden Reid, *Military Power: Land Warfare Theory and Practice* (London: Frank Cass, 1997).
85. Dyson, *Tank Twins*, p. 67.
86. IWM Browne 86/41/1, field report by Major A.T.A. Browne on self-inflicted wounds and negligent wounding, 24 August 1944.
87. UK NA WO 222/275, British Second Army, reports of Judge Advocate General, July 1944–June 1945.
88. UK NA WO 171/321, Watson, 2nd Army monthly report, psychiatry, August 1944; see also David French, 'Discipline and the Death Penalty in the British Army in the War against Germany during the Second World War', *Journal of Contemporary History*, 1998, vol. 33, no. 4.
89. LHCMA Churcher I, 'A Soldier's Story', personal memoir of Jack Churcher, p. 36; George Kitching, *Mud and Green Fields: The Memoirs of Major General George Kitching* (St Catherine's, ON: Vanwell, 1993), p. 195.
90. IWM Bucknall Papers, folder 9, Bucknall to Oliver Leese, 23 June 1944.
91. UK NA WO 171/182, War Diary, Deputy Judge Advocate General, 21st Army Group, April–December 1944.

92. UK NA WO 163/53/AC/G (44)39, War Office Committee on Morale in the Army, June–August 1944, 15 November 1944.
93. Brian Horrocks, *Corps Commander* (London: Sidgwick & Jackson, 1977), pp. 28–9.
94. LHCMA Liddell Hart 9/28/84, correspondence between Liddell Hart and Roberts, February and March 1952.
95. IWM LMD 60/18, Montgomery to Brooke, 15 July 1944.
96. Niklas Zetterling, *Normandy 1944: German Military Organization, Combat Power and Organizational Effectiveness* (Winnipeg, Manitoba: J.J. Fedorowicz, 2000), p. 78; P.E. Schramm, *KTB des OKW Bd IV: 1.1.1944–22.5.1945* (Frankfurt am Main: Bernard & Graefe, 1961), p. 330.
97. Manfred Messerschmidt, *Nazi Political Aims and German Military Law in World War Two* (Ottawa, ON: Jackson Wegren, 1981); Dr B. McNeel interview, quoted in Copp and McAndrew, *Battle Exhaustion*, p. 127.

6 Breakout – Victory in Normandy

1. Major Bill Close, interview with author, September 2002.
2. Roland Jefferson, *Soldiering at the Sharp End*, private memoir, quoted in Ian Daglish, *Operation Bluecoat: Over the Battlefield* (Barnsley: Pen & Sword, 2009), p. 15.
3. Francis de Guingand, *Operation Victory* (London: Hodder & Stoughton, 1947), p. 397.
4. UK NA WO 171, 43rd Wessex Division War Diary; H Essame, *The 43rd Wessex Division at War: 1944–5* (London: Clowes, 1952), p. 48.
5. Essame, *43rd Wessex*, p. 49.
6. IWM LMD 60/1 Montgomery's Diary, 26 July 1944; LMD 60/31, Montgomery to Crerar, 26 July 1944.
7. LHCMA Alanbrooke, Montgomery/Brooke correspondence, July 1944.
8. LHCMA Alanbrooke 6/2/22, Montgomery to Brooke, 28 February 1943; 6/2/23 Montgomery to Brooke, 28 December 1943; 6/2/26, Montgomery to Brooke, 6 July 1944.
9. LHCMA O'Connor 5/3/22, O'Connor to Adair, 24 July 1944.
10. Terry Copp, *Fields of Fire: The Canadians in Normandy* (Toronto, ON: University of Toronto Press, 2003), pp. 163–5.
11. Charles P. Stacey, *The Victory Campaign: The Operations in Northwest Europe 1944–45*. (Ottawa: Queen's Printer, 1962), p. 192.
12. UK NA WO 171/439, 7th Armoured Division War Diary, July 1944; Dominick Graham, *The Price of Command: A Biography of Guy Simonds* (Toronto, ON: Stoddart, 1993), p. 143.
13. Brigadier W.J. Megill, interview with Professor Terry Copp, quoted in *Fields of Fire*, p. 182.
14. Roman Jarymowycz, 'General Guy Simonds: The Commander as Tragic Hero', in Bernd Horn and Stephen Harris, *Warrior Chiefs: Perspectives on Senior Canadian Military Leaders* (Toronto, ON: Dundurn Press, 2001), p. 119.
15. Carlo D'Este, *Decision in Normandy* (London: Collins, 1983), chapters 19 and 23, are an excellent analysis of COBRA.
16. D'Este, *Decision in Normandy*, pp. 401–3.
17. Wolfgang Maas, quoted in Helmut Ritgen, *The Western Front 1944: Memoirs of a Panzer Lehr Officer* (Winnipeg, Manitoba: J.J. Fedorowicz, 1995), p. 101.
18. Frederick Steinhardt, *Panzer Lehr Division 1944–45* (Solihull: Helion, 2008), p. 89. Translation and notes of the interview with Fritz Bayerlein, conducted 7–9 August 1945.
19. LHCMA Liddell Hart, notes on correspondence between Liddell Hart and Dempsey, 1952.
20. Montgomery of Alamein, *Memoirs* (London: Book Club Edition, 1960 – first published 1958), p. 241; David Belchem, *All in the Day's March* (London: Collins, 1978), p. 207, and *Victory in Normandy* (London: Chatto & Windus, 1981), p. 51.
21. Montgomery, *Memoirs*, p. 239.

22. UK NA WO 285/9, Dempsey's Diary, 25 and 26 July 1944; LMD 60/27, Montgomery to Dempsey, Bradley, Crerar and Patton, General Situation M512, 21 July 1944; LMD 60/37, Montgomery to Dempsey, Bradley, Crerar and Patton, General Situation M515, 27 July 1944.
23. This argument has been put forward by Terry Copp in *Fields of Fire*, p. 188.
24. LHCMA Liddell Hart 15/4/85, O'Connor's notes on BLUECOAT.
25. UK NA WO 205/972B, BAOR, *Operations of 2nd Army in Europe, 1944–5 – part 1* (1945), pp. 166–7; Freiburg, Miltärgeschichtliches Forschungsamt, B–824, notes by General Straube, quoted in J.J. How, *Normandy: The British Breakout* (London: William Kimber, 1981), p. 22.
26. G.P.B. Roberts, *From the Desert to the Baltic* (London: William Kimber, 1987), p. 184.
27. Major Johnny Langdon, interview with author, November 2002.
28. Lord Carrington, *Reflect on Things Past: The Memoirs of Lord Carrington* (London: Collins, 1988), p. 51.
29. IWM LMD 60/1, Montgomery's Diary, 28 July 1944.
30. H.G. Martin, *History of the 15th Scottish Infantry Division, 1939–1945* (London: Blackwood and Sons, 1948), pp. 121–3.
31. Ned Thornburn, *The 4th KSLI in Normandy: June to August 1944* (Shrewsbury: Castle Museum, 1990), p. 85.
32. John M. Thorpe, *A Soldier's Tale: To Normandy and Beyond*, unpublished memoir.
33. LHCMA Liddell Hart 15/4/85, Richard O'Connor's notes on Operation BLUECOAT, n.d. but probably August/September 1944.
34. G.S. Jackson and VIII Corps staff, *Operations of Eighth Corps: An Account of Operations from Normandy to the River Rhine* (London: St Clements Press, 1948), pp. 120–2; LHCMA Liddell Hart 15/4/85, Richard O'Connor's notes on Operation BLUECOAT, n.d. but probably August/September 1944.
35. IWM Bucknall Papers, XXX Corps Intelligence Summary, 30 July 1944.
36. Corporal Doug Proctor, quoted in Patrick Delaforce, *The Fighting Wessex Wyverns: From Normandy to Bremerhaven with 43rd Division* (Stroud: Sutton, 1994), p. 92.
37. N.C.E. Kenrick, *The Wiltshire Regiment in the Second World War: 4th/5th Battalions*, 2nd edn (Salisbury: RGBW, 2006), pp. 8–9.
38. Essame, *43rd Wessex*, pp. 55–6.
39. Stuart Hills, *By Tank into Normandy: A Memoir of the Campaign in Northwest Europe from D Day to VE Day* (London: Cassells, 2002), p. 121.
40. Robin Neillands, *The Desert Rats: 7th Armoured Division 1940–45* (London: Orion, 1995), pp. 230–1.
41. Dennis Cockbaine, quoted in Edward Wilson, *Press on Regardless: The Story of the Fifth Royal Tank Regiment in World War Two* (London: Spellmount, 2003), pp. 370–1.
42. IWM Bucknall Papers, folder 12, Pyman to Bucknall, 2 August 1944.
43. IWM Bucknall Papers, folder 12, Pyman to Erskine, 1 August 1944.
44. IWM LMD 60/1, Montgomery's Diary, 31 July 1944.
45. LHCMA Liddell Hart 15/15/159, notes on Chester Wilmot's interview with Miles Dempsey.
46. IWM BLM 119/14, notes from Dempsey on Bucknall, 2 August 1944.
47. IWM BLM 119/14, report on Lieutenant General Gerald Bucknall, 2 August 1944.
48. IWM Bucknall Papers, folder 13, *Sunday Express*, 2 August 1944.
49. IWM Bucknall Papers, folder 12, Bucknall to Montgomery, 3 August 1944.
50. IWM Bucknall Papers, folder 8, Bucknall's diary, 5 August 1944; folder 12, Bucknall to Colonel Browne, 15 August 1944.
51. IWM Erskine Papers 75/134/1, Montgomery to War Office, 3 August 1944.
52. IWM Erskine Papers 75/134/1, Montgomery to War Office, 3 August 1944.
53. LHCMA Liddell Hart 9/28/84, Pyman interview with Liddell Hart, 13 February 1952; Harold Pyman, *Call to Arms* (London: Leo Cooper, 1971), p. 74.
54. UK NA CAB 106/1066, Montgomery to Brooke, 2 August 1944.

55. LHCMA Verney I/i/3, O'Connor to Verney, 3 August 1944, and Liddell Hart 9/28/84, Pyman interview with Liddell Hart, 13 February 1952; UK NA WO 205/972B, BAOR, *Operations of Second Army, I*, pp. 168–71.
56. Major Mark Millbank, quoted in Daglish, *Bluecoat*, p. 48.
57. Captain William Whitelaw, quoted in BAOR's Operation BLUECOAT battlefield tour guide – directing staff edition, 1947.
58. UK NA WO 291/1336, 'Self-propelled artillery in 21st Army Group – analysis of the opinions of users', November 1944.
59. LHCMA Verney I/i/3, 'Account of part played by 6th Guards Tank Brigade in Operation BLUECOAT, 30 July 1944'.
60. LHCMA Churcher I, Jack Churcher, *A Soldier's Story* Churcher memoir, p. 41; Roberts, *Desert to the Baltic*, p. 187.
61. Max Robinson, quoted in Thornburn, *4th KSLI in Normandy*, p. 93.
62. Thornburn, *4th KSLI in Normandy*, p. 93.
63 UK NA WO 171/1326, 4th King's Shropshire Light Infantry War Diary, August 1944; Thornburn, *4th KSLI in Normandy*, pp. 93–6.
64. Account of Bland, quoted at http://daimler-fighting-vehicles.co.uk/DFV-File%20Part%20D001a-Houshold%20Cavalry%201939–1945.pdf.
65. UK NA CAB 106/1113, Wilmot's notes on the breakthrough.
66. Noel Bell, *From the Beaches to the Baltic: The Story of G Company, 8th Rifle Brigade* (Aldershot: Gale & Polden, 1947), p. 33.
67. How, *Normandy: The British Breakout*, p. 79; Thornburn, *4th KSLI in Normandy*, p. 106.
68. How, *Normandy: The British Breakout*, pp. 80–2; Michael Reynolds, *Sons of the Reich: II SS Panzer Corps* (London: Spellmount, 2002), pp. 58–60.
69. UK NA WO 171/627, 29th Armoured Brigade HQ War Diary, GOODWOOD conference notes, 25 July 1944; Roberts, *Desert to the Baltic*, pp. 192–3.
70. RAC Museum, Bovington, (BOV), William Steel Brownlie, *And Came Safe Home*, private memoir.
71. Roberts, *Desert to the Baltic*, p. 192.
72. From an account supplied to Joe How in 1976, quoted in Thornburn, *4th KSLI in Normandy*, pp. 111–12.
73. UK NA WO 177/367, 7th Armoured Division Medical War Diary, August 1944.
74. UK NA WO 171/1395, 5th Battalion Wiltshire Regiment War Diary, 6–7 August 1944; Major A.D. Parsons, comments quoted in Delaforce, *Fighting Wessex Wyverns*, p. 107.
75. Captain N.N.M. Denny, quoted in C.H. Miller, *History of 13/18 Hussars, 1922–1947* (London: Bradshaw, 1949), pp. 121–2.
76. N.C.E. Kenrick, text contained in *The Wiltshire Regiment in the Second World War, 5th Battalion* (Salisbury: Rifles Wardrobe and Museum Trust, 2006), pp. 9–11; UK NA WO 171/1395, 5th Battalion Wiltshire Regiment War Diary, 6–7 August 1944.
77. Sydney Jary, *18 Platoon* (privately published, 1987), p. 10.
78. O'Connell, quoted in Delaforce, *Fighting Wessex Wyverns*, p. 108.
79. Johnny Langdon, Bill Close and Roy Dixon, interviews with author, 2002.
80. IWM LMD 60/29, Lieutenant General Harry Crerar, Tactical Directive, 22 July 1944.
81. National Archives Canada (NAC), Crerar Papers, CP2, vol. 2, Operation TOTALIZE, Simonds' notes 1, August 1944, and memo, 6 August 1944. The best treatment of the planning is S.A. Hart, ' "The Black Day Unrealised": Operation TOTALIZE and the Problems of Translating Tactical Success into a Decisive Breakout', in John Buckley (ed.), *The Normandy Campaign 1944: Sixty Years On* (London: Routledge, 2006), chapter 8.
82. NAC, Crerar Papers, CP2, vol. 2, notes of telephone conversation, 4 August 1944.
83. LHCMA O'Connor 5/4/1, O'Connor to Montgomery, 24 August 1944.
84. BAOR, *Operation TOTALIZE – Battlefield Tour, Directing Staff Edition*, 1947, pp. 6–7.
85. My thanks to Professor Gary Sheffield for this insight.
86. Raymond Bird, *XXII Dragoons 1760–1945* (London: Gale & Polden, 1950), p. 206.

87. Charlie Robertson, Black Watch, 51st Highland Division, quoted in Ken Tout, *A Fine Night for Tanks: The Road to Falaise* (Stroud: Sutton, 1998), pp. 54–5.
88. Stacey, *The Victory Campaign*, pp. 213 and 218.
89. Ken Tout, *Tank! 40 Hours of Battle, August 1944* (London: Robert Hale, 1985), p. 61.
90. Brian A. Reid, *No Holding Back: Operation Totalize – August 1944* (Toronto, ON: Robin Brass Studio, 2005), p. 184; BAOR, *Operation TOTALIZE*, p. 22.
91. UK NA War Diaries WO 171/640, 33rd Armoured Brigade, WO 171/859, 1st Northants Yeomanry; WO 171/878, 144th RAC; WO 171/880, 148th RAC; Hart, 'Black Day Unrealised', p. 107; BAOR, *Operation TOTALIZE*, pp. 21–2.
92. BAOR, *TOTALIZE*, p. 101.
93. BAOR, *TOTALIZE*, Appendix M, p. 101.
94. Meyer interview, quoted in John English, *The Canadian Army and the Normandy Campaign: A Study in the Failure of High Command* (London: Praeger, 1991), p. 292, fn 9; see also Hart, 'Black Day', pp. 107–8; Kurt Meyer, *Grenadiers* (Winnipeg, Manitoba: J.J. Fedorowicz, 1994), p. 259.
95. See Reynolds, *Steel Inferno*, for a near-reverential treatment of these events, pp. 233–8.
96. Brian A. Reid provides the most forensic account in *No Holding Back*.
97. Anon., *The 1st and 2nd Northamptonshire Yeomanry – 1939–1946* (Brunswick, Germany: Meyer, 1946), p. 35.
98. Joe Ekins interview with Matthew Lucas, 2012.
99. Reg Spittles interview with Matthew Lucas, 2012.
100. Anon., *The 1st and 2nd Northants Yeomanry*, p. 39.
101. Reid, *No Holding Back*, pp. 281–90.
102. Evan McGilvray, *Man of Steel and Honour: General Stanislaw Maczek* (Birmingham: Helion, 2012), pp. 146–52.
103. George Kitching, *Mud and Green Fields: The Memoirs of Major General George Kitching* (St Catherine's, ON: Vanwell, 1993), p. 193.
104. IWM 06/38/1, Tomasz Potorowski, *Army Days 1943–1945: Recollections and Reflections of a Polish Soldier in the Time of Katyn, the Warsaw Uprising and Yalta* (second printing, 1997), pp. 51–2.
105. Martin Lindsay, *So Few Got Through* (London: Arrow, 1960), pp. 42–6.
106. IWM LMD 61/5, Operational Directive M518, 21st Army Group HQ, 11 August 1944.
107. UK NA WO 205/972B, BAOR, *Operations of Second Army – Part I*, pp. 172–81; G.S. Jackson and VIII Corps Staff, *Operations of Eighth Corps: An Account of Operations from Normandy to the River Rhine*, (London: St Clements Press, 1948), pp. 138–9.
108. LHCMA Churcher I, Jack Churcher, *Soldier's Story*, p. 43.
109. Staffordshire Regiment Museum Archives (SRMA), 59th Division, Major [illegible], 'Liberation of Thury-Harcourt' – account of Lieutenant Colonel Ian Freeland, CO 7th Norfolks; Peter Knight, *The 59th Division: Its War Story* (London: Muller, 1954), pp. 63–6.
110. SRMA, 59th Division, account of Lieutenant Colonel Ian Freeland, CO 7th Norfolks; BAOR, *Operations of Second Army – Part I*, pp. 172–3; Anon., *The Story of 34th Armoured Brigade* (1945), phase II.
111. SRMA, 59th Division, account of Lieutenant Colonel Ian Freeland, CO 7th Norfolks.
112. SRMA, 59th Division, Major General L.O. Lyne to Brigadier R.W. Fryer, 10 August 1944.
113. SRMA, 59th Division, account of Lieutenant Colonel Ian Freeland, CO 7th Norfolks.
114. D. Hastings, memoir 1991, quoted in B.S. Barnes, *The Sign of the Double T: The 50th Northumbrian Division – July 1943 to December 1944* (York: Sentinel Press, 1999), p. 132.

115. P.J. Lewis and I.R. English, *8th Battalion The Durham Light Infantry 1939–1945*, (privately published 1949), p. 268.
116. David Rissik, *The DLI at War: The History of the Durham Light Infantry, 1939–1945* (London: Naval and Military Press, 2004), pp. 252–3.
117. J.L.J. Meredith, *The Story of 7th Battalion Somerset Light Infantry – Prince Albert's* (privately published, 1946), pp. 55–6.
118. Essame, *43rd Wessex*, p. 87.
119. Churchill College Archives (CCA), Grigg Papers, PJGG, Montgomery to Grigg, 14 August 1944.
120. Lionel F. Ellis, *Victory in the West*, I (London: HMSO, 1962), pp. 432–4.
121. D'Este, *Decision in Normandy*, pp. 449–58; Richard Rohmer, *Patton's Gap* (London: Beaufort, 1981), p. 225.
122. UK NA WO 291/1331, Reports of No. 2 ORS 21st Army Group, especially report No. 15, and AIR 37/61, Reports of ORS RAF 2nd Tactical Air Force.
123. Michael Carver, *Second to None: The Royal Scots Greys, 1919–1945* (London: McCorquodale, 1954) p. 133.
124. G.R. Hartwell and M.A. Edwards, *The Story of 5th Battalion, the Dorsetshire Regiment in Northwest Europe* (privately published, 1945), p. 16.
125. Comments quoted in Eversley Belfield and H. Essame, *The Battle for Normandy* (London: Pan, 1967 – 1st edn in 1965), p. 238.
126. Martin Blumenson, 'General Bradley's Decision at Argentan (13 August 1944)', in *Command Decisions*, online edn, Center of Military History, Department of the Army, Washington, DC, 2000 (originally published in 1959); Hans Speidel, *We Defended Normandy* (London: Jenkins, 1951), p. 149; Model's comments quoted in Eddy Florentin, *The Battle of the Falaise Gap* (New York: Hawthorn, 1967), p. 335; LHCMA Liddell Hart interrogation of Lieutenant General Edgar Feuchtinger, 21st Panzer Division.
127. UK NA WO 205/972B, BAOR, *Operations of Second Army*, p. 181.

7 Pursuit –The Race to the Frontier

1. IWM LMD 61/3, Montgomery's Diary, 20 August 1944.
2. IWM LMD 62/3, 21st Army Group General Operational Situation and Directive M520, 26 August 1944.
3. UK NA WO 205/972B, BAOR, *Operations of Second Army in Europe 1944–45, Part I* (1945), p. 182.
4. Alex Danchev and Daniel Todman (eds), *War Diaries 1939–1945: Field Marshal Lord Alanbrooke* (London: Weidenfeld & Nicolson, 2001), p. 280.
5. Lieutenant Colonel L.R.E. Fayle, account in BAOR, *Royal Engineers Battlefield Tour – Normandy to the Seine* (privately published, Germany, 1946), p. 128.
6. UK NA WO 205/972B, BAOR, *Operations of Second Army in Europe*, pp. 184–5; BAOR, *Royal Engineers*, pp. 61–2.
7. UK NA WO 171/339, XXX Corps Operational War Diary, August 1944; WO 171/480, 43rd Division Operational War Diary, August 1944.
8. UK NA WO 171/480, 43rd Division War Diary, 25 August 1944; H. Essame, *The 43rd Wessex Division at War: 1939–1945* (London: Clowes, 1952), pp. 93–4.
9. Sergeant R.C. Hunt, account in BAOR, *Royal Engineers*, p. 127.
10. N.C.E. Kenrick, *The Wiltshire Regiment in the Second World War – 5th Battalion* (Salisbury: Rifles Wardrobe and Museum Trust, 2006), p. 12.
11. Sydney Jary, *18 Platoon* (privately published, 1987), p. 27.
12. BAOR, *Operation NEPTUNE: 43rd Wessex Division's Crossing of the Seine, 25–28 August 1944 – Battlefield Tour* (privately published, Germany, 1947); Essame, *43rd Division*, chapter VI; BAOR, *Royal Engineers*; memoir of Roy Young, 72nd Field Company, Royal Engineers, contributed to BBC People's War on-line programme, June 2005, http://www.bbc.co.uk/history/ww2peopleswar/stories/72/a4281572.shtml.

13. H.G. Martin, *History of the 15th Scottish Infantry Division, 1939–1945* (London: Blackwood & Sons, 1948), p. 114.
14. UK NA WO 171/466, 15th Scottish Infantry Division Operations War Diary, 27–30 August 1944; WO 171/476, 15th Scottish Provost Company War Diary, August 1944; WO 171/469, 15th Scottish Royal Engineers War Diary, August 1944.
15. Patrick Delaforce, *Monty's Marauders: Black Rat 4th Armoured Brigade and Red Fox 8th Armoured Brigade* (Stroud: Sutton, 1993), p. 85.
16. UK NA WO 205/972B, BAOR, *Operations of Second Army*, *I*, pp. 189–91.
17. UK NA WO 171/376, Guards Armoured Division War Diary, August 1944.
18. LHCMA O'Connor 5/4/49, Barker to O'Connor, 2 October 1944.
19. IWM Barker Papers, personal diary, September 1944.
20. IWM, Barker Papers, folder I; see also Andrew Robinson, *The British Sixth Airborne Division in Normandy 6 June–27 August 1944* (University of Birmingham MPhil, 2008), pp. 66–7.
21. UK NA WO 171/1239, 9th Parachute Battalion War Diary, Major Parry, 'Lessons Learned'.
22. Trevor Hart Dyke, *Normandy to Arnhem: A Story of the Infantry* (privately published, 1966), pp. 42–3, and Terry Copp, *Cinderella Army: The Canadians in Northwest Europe 1944–5* (Toronto, ON: University of Toronto Press, 2006), pp. 21–3.
23. Ted Castle, 2nd Glosters, interview 2008, quoted in Andrew Holborn, *The 56th Infantry Brigade and D-Day: An Independent Infantry Brigade and the Campaign in North West Europe 1944–45* (London: Continuum, 2010), p. 149.
24. Tommy Short, quoted in Patrick Delaforce, *The Polar Bears – Monty's Left Flank: From Normandy to the Relief of Holland with the 49th Division* (Stroud: Sutton, 1995–2003 edn), pp. 150–1.
25. A.A. Vince, *The Pompadours: 2nd Battalion Essex Regiment – D Day to VE Day in Northwest Europe* (originally late 1940s – reprinted in 1987), p. 30; UK NA WO 171/5188, 2nd Battalion Essex Regiment War Diary, August 1944.
26. UK NA CAB 106/958, Operation ASTONIA, 10–12 September 1944.
27. Dick Philips, interview with Andrew Holborn 2006, in Holborn, *56th Infantry Brigade*, p. 157.
28. The best recent analysis of this battle is Douglas E. Delaney, *Corps Commanders: Five British and Canadian Generals at War 1939–45* (Toronto, ON: UCB Press, 2011), pp. 160–7.
29. *After the Battle No. 139: The Capture of Le Havre* (Essex: Battle of Britain Press, 2008).
30. UK NA WO 171/259, I Corps War Diary, 5 September 1944; Castle interview in Holborn, 56th Infantry Brigade, 2006.
31. Anon., *The 1st and 2nd Northamptonshire Yeomanry* (Brunswick, Germany: Meyer, [illegible]), p. [illegible]
32. BAOR, *Royal Engineers Battlefield Tour*, pp. 57–61.
33. Paul Crook, *Came the Dawn: Fifty Years an Army Officer* (London: Spellmount, 1989), pp. 35–6.
34. Oliver Lindsay (ed.), *A Guards' General: The Memoirs of Major-General Sir Allan Adair* (London: Hamish Hamilton, 1986), p. 153.
35. Austin Baker, personal memoir written in 1997, p. 44, and interview with author, 2002.
36. Baker, memoir, 1997, p. 44.
37. G.P.B. Roberts, *From the Desert to the Baltic* (London: William Kimber, 1987), p. 202.
38. Bill Close, *A View from the Turret* (Bredon: Dell & Bredon, 1998), p. 137.
39. Major Johnny Langdon, 3rd RTR, interview with author, October 2002.
40. Ned Thornburn, *First Into Antwerp: The Part Played by 4th Battalion King's Shropshire Light Infantry in the Liberation of the City in September 1944* (Shrewsbury: Castle Museum Trust, 1987), p. 8.
41. Brian Horrocks, *A Full Life* (London: Collins, 1960), p. 198.
42. Close, *A View from the Turret*, p. 141; Major Bill Close, interview with author, September 2002.

43. Interview with John Hooper, quoted in Delaforce, *The Black Bull: From Normandy to the Baltic with the 11th Armoured Division* (Stroud: Sutton, 1993), p. 122.
44. Roberts, *From the Desert to the Baltic*, p. 206; UK NA WO 171/208, Second Army message logs, September 1944.
45. Horrocks, *A Full Life*, p. 198.
46. Civilian account, quoted in Horrocks, *A Full Life*, pp. 200–1.
47. Lieutenant Colonel Reeves, quoted in Thornburn, *First into Antwerp*, p. 19.
48. LHCMA Churcher I, Jack Churcher, *A Soldier's Story*, unpublished memoir, p. 50.
49. Lieutenant Dick Mullock, quoted in Thornburn, *First into Antwerp*, p. 40.
50. UK NA WO 171/1326, 4th King's Shropshire Light Infantry War Diary, September 1944.
51. Thornburn, *First into Antwerp*, pp. 42–51; UK NA WO 171/691, 159 Infantry Brigade War Diary, September 1944; Anon. (Captain Edgar Pallamountain), *Taurus Pursuant: A History of 11th Armoured Division* (privately published, Germany, 1945), p. 59.
52. UK NA WO 171/177, 21st Army Group, GS (Ops), September 1944; W.S. Chalmers, *Full Cycle: The Biography of Admiral Sir Bertram Home Ramsay* (London: Hodder and Stoughton, 1959), p. 244.
53. Cornelius Ryan, *A Bridge Too Far* (London: Simon & Schuster, 1974–1975, Coronet edn), pp. 61–4; Peter Beale, *The Great Mistake: The Battle for Antwerp and the Beveland Peninsula, September 1944* (Stroud: Sutton, 2004), chapters 1, 10 and 13.
54. Patrick Forbes, *6th Guards Tank Brigade: The Story of Guardsmen in Churchill Tanks* (London: Sampson Low, Marston & Co., 1946), p. 42.
55. Pallamountain, *Taurus Pursuant*, p. 57.
56. Roberts, *From the Desert to the Baltic*, pp. 210–11.
57. BAOR, *Administration History of 21st Army Group in Europe 1944–5* (privately published, Germany, 1945), p. 47; Roland G. Ruppenthal, *Logistical Support of the Armies, Vol. 2* (Washington, DC: Government Printing Office, 1954), pp. 10–11.
58. UK NA WO 219/259, Post-OVERLORD planning, May 1944; John A. Adams, *The Battle for Western Europe: Fall 1944 – An Operational Assessment* (Bloomington, IN: Indiana University Press, 2010). Chapter 3, is an excellent outline of the issues.
59. Churchill College Archives (CCA), RLEW7/7, notes of interview of Miles Dempsey conducted by Ronald Lewin, 4 November 1968.
60. Omar N. Bradley and Clay Blair, *A General's Life: An Autobiography by General of the Army Omar N. Bradley* (New York: Simon & Schuster, 1983), p. 316.
61. LHCMA Alanbrooke 6/2/30, Montgomery to Brooke, 24 August 1944.
62. Danchev and Todman (eds), *War Diaries 1939–1945*, p. 583.
63. IWM LMD 62/3, 21st Army Group Operational Directive, 26 August 1944.
64. CCA RLEW 7/7, notes of interview with Miles Dempsey by Ronald Lewin, 4 November 1968.
65. Nigel Hamilton, *Monty: Final Years of the Field-Marshal, 1944–1976* (London: Hamish Hamilton, 1986), p. 126.
66. Montgomery of Alamein, *Normandy to the Baltic: A Personal Account of the Conquest of Germany* (London: Hutchinson, 1947), pp. 128–30.
67. Bradley and Blair, *A General's Life*, pp. 313–17.
68. LHCMA Alanbrooke 6/2/31, Montgomery to Brooke, 3 September 1944; IWM LMD 62/12, Montgomery's Diary, General Situation, 3 September 1944.

8 Arnhem – Conceptual Failure

1. Cornelius Ryan, *A Bridge Too Far* (London: Simon & Schuster, 1974); United Artists' film, *A Bridge Too Far*, directed by Richard Attenborough, 1977; David Bennett, *A Magnificent Disaster: The Failure of Market Garden, The Arnhem Operation, September 1944* (Newbury: Casemate, 2008). The phrase was originally attributed to Major G.G. Norton.

2. Sebastian Ritchie, *Arnhem: Myth and Reality* (London: Robert Hale, 2010), is the best analysis of this aspect of the plan.
3. William F. Buckingham, *Arnhem 1944* (London: Tempus, 2002), p. 69; Gavin's diary, 6 September 1944, quoted in Willem Ridder, *Countdown to Freedom* (Bloomington, IN: Author House, 2007), p. 451; James M. Gavin, *On to Berlin* (New York: Viking, 1978 – Bantam edn, 1985), p. 147.
4. UK NA WO 285/9, Dempsey's Diary, 4 and 5 September 1944; WO 205/692, Operation COMET, HQ Airborne Troops Instruction, 6 September 1944.
5. Montgomery of Alamein, *Memoirs* (London: Collins, 1958), pp. 252–4.
6. LHCMA Alanbrooke 6/2/31, Montgomery to Brooke, 9 September 1944.
7. UK NA WO 285/9, Dempsey's Diary, 9–13 September 1944.
8. Churchill College Archives (CCA), RLEW 2/13, David Belchem to Ronald Lewin, 21 August 1980.
9. Montgomery, *Memoirs*, p. 254; Brigadier Edgar Williams, Chief Intelligence Officer, 21st Army Group, quoted in Richard Lamb, *Montgomery in Europe 1943–5: Success or Failure?* (London: Buchan & Enright, 1983), p. 224.
10. LHCMA Gale II/22, Gale's Diary, 10 September 1944.
11. LHCMA Liddell Hart 15/15/47, Chester Wilmot's papers on Eisenhower and Montgomery for *Struggle for Europe* (London: Collins, 1965); Stephen Ambrose, *Supreme Commander: The War Years of General Dwight D. Eisenhower* (London: Doubleday, 1970), p. 518.
12. Charles Richardson, *Flashback: A Soldier's Story* (London: William Kimber, 1985), pp. 186–7.
13. Peter Harclerode, *Arnhem: A Tragedy of Errors* (London: Caxton, 2000), p. 50; Ritchie, *Arnhem*, pp. 205–6.
14. Harclerode, *Arnhem*, pp. 51–2; Ryan, *A Bridge Too Far*, p. 93.
15. Roy Urquhart, *Arnhem*, (London: Pan, 1958), pp. 7, 9 and 23; John Frost, *A Drop Too Many* (London: Sphere edn, 1984 – first published 1980), p. 200.
16. UK NA CAB 106/1133, Urquhart to Harris, 22 November 1952.
17. UK NA WO 285/29, Dempsey to Ellis, 7 July 1966.
18. Gavin, *On to Berlin*, p. 150.
19. Frost, *A Drop Too Many*, pp. 198–9; Ritchie, *Arnhem*, pp. 178–9.
20. UK NA WO 285/3, Second British Army Intelligence summary, 6 September 1944, and WO 171/341, XXX Corps Planning Staff, intelligence summaries no. 494 and no. 496, 6 and 8 September 1944, respectively.
21. Ritchie, *Arnhem*, pp. 132–3, offers a convincing analysis of this aspect.
22. Montgomery, *Memoirs*, p. 275.
23. Ritchie, *Arnhem*, chapter 2.3.
24. Frost, *A Drop Too Many*, p. 198.
25. Bennett, *Magnificent Disaster*, pp. 61–5; Lionel F. Ellis, *Victory in the West, II* (London: HMSO, 1968), p. 32; Robin Neillands, *The Battle for the Rhine: Arnhem and the Ardennes – the Campaign in Europe* (London: Weidenfeld & Nicolson, 2005), pp. 98–9.
26. Brian Horrocks, *Corps Commander* (London: Sidgwick & Jackson, 1977), pp. 96–7. The scene is stirringly depicted in the film *A Bridge Too Far*.
27. 21st Army Group report on Operation MARKET GARDEN (1945), author's collection; UK NA WO 205/972B, BAOR, *Operations of 2nd Army*, pp. 227–9; BAOR, *Royal Engineers – Battlefield Tour*, pp. 95–100; Horrocks, *Corps Commander*, pp. 98–9.
28. Anon., *Club Route: XXX Corps in Europe* (Germany, privately published, 1946), p. 70.
29. Brigadier C.P. Jones, commander Royal Engineers in Guards Armoured Division, account in BAOR, *Royal Engineers*, p. 107.
30. UK NA WO 285/29, Miles Dempsey to Lionel Ellis, 28 June 1962, and Ellis to Dempsey, 5 July 1966; Horrocks, *Corps Commander*, p. 103; Anon., *Club Route*, p. 71; O. Lindsay (ed.), *A Guards' General: The Memoirs of Major General Sir Allan Adair* (London: Hamish Hamilton, 1986), p. 164.

31. Interview with Heinz Harmel, quoted in Robert Kershaw, *It Never Snows in September: The German view of MARKET GARDEN and the Battle of Arnhem, September 1944* (London: Ian Allan, 2004 edn, first published 1990), p. 233.
32. Stephen Badsey, *Arnhem*, in Julie Guard (ed.), *Airborne* (Oxford: Osprey, 2007), pp. 265–7; Ritchie, *Arnhem*, pp. 189–90; Ryan, *A Bridge Too Far*, pp. 190, 272, 274.
33. *Airborne Operations: A German Appraisal*, Office of the Chief of Military History, Department of the Army (1950), pp. 54–5; Kershaw, *It Never Snows in September*, pp. 38–43.
34. UK NA WO 205/972B, BAOR, *Operations of Second Army*, p. 231; UK NA WO 171/605, 5th Guards Armoured Brigade War Diary, 19 September 1944.
35. Lindsay (ed.), *Guards' General*, p. 164.
36. Horrocks, *Corps Commander*, pp. 106–9.
37. Neillands, *Battle for the Rhine*, pp. 102–3; James A. Huston, *Out of the Blue: US Army Airborne Operations in World War II* (West Lafayette, IN: Purdue, 1998), pp. 13–20.
38. Comments of Lord Carrington, quoted in Neillands, *Battle for the Rhine*, p. 114.
39. Lindsay (ed.), *Guards' General*, pp. 165–6; UK NA WO 171/1253, 1st Battalion, Grenadier Guards War Diary, September 1944, and WO 171/1254, 2nd Battalion Armoured Regiment, Grenadier Guards War Diary, September 1944.
40. Horrocks, *Corps Commander*, pp. 110–12.
41. Interview with Heinz Harmel, 27 October 1987, quoted in Kershaw, *It Never Snows in September*, p. 241.
42. Attributed to the colourful Lieutenant Colonel Reuben Tucker, commanding 504th Regiment, 82nd Airborne.
43. Gavin, *On to Berlin*, p. 181; Horrocks, *Corps Commander*, p. 117.
44. Charles B. MacDonald, *The Siegfried Line Campaign* (Washington, DC: Government Press, 1947), pp. 183–5; UK NA WO 205/972B, BAOR, *Operations of Second Army*, pp. 231–2; Neillands, *Battle for the Rhine*, pp. 121–5; Kershaw, *It Never Snows*, p. 272.
45. UK NA WO 285/29, Miles Dempsey to Lionel Ellis, 18 June 1962.
46. Frost, *A Drop Too Many*, p. 211.
47. UK NA WO 171/592, 1st Parachute Brigade War Diary, September 1944; WO 205/693, Operation MARKET GARDEN, reports; see also William Buckingham, *Arnhem 1944*, pp. 113–22.
48. UK NA WO 205/972B, BAOR, *Operations of Second Army*, pp. 231–3; Bennett, *Magnificent Disaster*, pp. 95–7.
49. UK NA AIR 37/1214, Allied Expeditionary Air Force, 'Report on Operation MARKET GARDEN', 1944.
50. UK NA AIR 37/1214, Allied Expeditionary Air Force, 'Report on Operation MARKET GARDEN', 1944; Bennett, *Magnificent Disaster*, pp. 232–3.
51. Ritchie, *Arnhem*, p. 212; Badsey, *Arnhem*, p. 84; Frost, *A Drop Too Many*, pp. 203–26.
52. Lipmann Kessel, *Surgeon at Arms: Parachuting into Arnhem with the First Airborne* (London: Heinemann, 1958), p. 3.
53. H. Essame, *The 43rd Wessex Division at War, 1944–5* (London: Clowes, 1952), p. 131; Stanislaw Sosabowski, *Freely I Served* (London: William Kimber, 1982), pp. 182–3.
54. Account by Major Whittle, quoted in G.J.B. Watkins, *From Normandy to the Weser: The War History of the 4th Battalion the Dorset Regiment, June 1944 to May 1945*, regimental museum reprint.
55. IWM LMD 63/25, Urquhart to Browning, 24 September 1944, Montgomery Papers.
56. UK NA WO 285/10, Dempsey's Diary, 24 September 1944; WO 285/29, Dempsey to Ellis, 18 June 1962.
57. Essame, *History of 43rd Wessex Division*, pp. 132–3.
58. Sosabowski, *Freely I Served*, p. 203.

9 Winter – Frustration and Anxiety

1. Montgomery of Alamein, *Memoirs* (London: Book Club Edition, 1960 – first published 1958), p. 275; Churchill College Archives (CCA), Cambridge, RLEW 7/7, notes of Ronald Lewin's interview with Dempsey, 15 November 1968.
2. UK NA WO 171/210, Second Army Operations War Diary, October 1944.
3. Montgomery of Alamein, *Normandy to the Baltic: A Personal Account of the Conquest of Germany* (London: Hutchinson, 1947), pp. 147–8.
4. BAOR, *Administration History of 21st Army Group in Europe June 1944–May 1945* (Germany, privately published 1945), p. 36.
5. LHCMA Gale II/22, Gale's Diary, 12 September 1944.
6. J. Lee-Richardson, *21 Army Group Ordnance: The History of the Campaign* (Germany, privately published 1946), p. 49.
7. IWM LMD 63/14, Montgomery to Eisenhower, 21 September 1944.
8. IWM LMD 63/1, Montgomery's Diary, 20 and 21 September 1944.
9. LHCMA Gale II/22, Gale's Diary, 5 September 1944.
10. LHCMA Gale II/21, Gale's Diary, 16 August 1944.
11. IWM Montgomery Papers, LMD 63/9, Montgomery to Eisenhower, 20 September 1944; LHCMA Gale II/22, minutes of meeting of Chief Administrative Officers, 22 September 1944.
12. LHCMA Gale II/22, minutes of Military Shipments Priority Committee, 16 September 1944.
13. IWM Montgomery Papers, LMD 63/16, Montgomery to Brooke, *c.*18/19 September 1944; Major General Miles Graham to Major General Godwin-Austen, War Office, 22 September 1944.
14. UK NA WO171/287, VIII Corps Operational War Diary, September 1944; G.S. Jackson and VIII Corps Staff, *Operations of Eighth-Corps: An Account of Operations from Normandy to the River Rhine* (London: St Clements Press, 1948), pp. 155–6; G.P.B. Roberts, *From the Desert to the Baltic* (London: William Kimber, 1987), p. 217.
15. UK NA WO 285/10, Dempsey's Diary, September 1944.
16. IWM Montgomery Papers, LMD 63/50, 21st Army Group General Operation Directive M530, 9 October 1944.
17. Anon., *The Story of the 23rd Hussars 1940–46* (Germany: privately published 1946), p. 162.
18. Jackson, *VIII Corps*, p. 160.
19. Patrick Forbes, *6th Guards Tank Brigade: The Story of Guardsmen in Churchill Tanks* (London: Sampson Low, Marston & Co, 1946) pp. 51–3; BAOR, *Operations of Second Army in Europe 1944–5, part I* (Germany: privately published, 1945), pp. 250–3; Ned Thornburn, *After Antwerp: The Long Haul to Victory – The Part Played by 4th Battalion King's Shropshire Light Infantry in the Overthrow of the Third Reich, September 1944 to May 1945* (Shrewsbury: Castle Museum, 1991), pp. 37–9.
20. UK NA WO 171/213, Second Army message logs, 15 September 1944; Roberts, *From the Desert*, p. 220.
21. John Baynes, *The Forgotten Victor: General Sir Richard O'Connor* (London: Brassey's, 1989), p. 237.
22. Jackson, *VIII Corps*, pp. 162–3; letter from Field Marshal Lord Carver to John Baynes, 6 August 1988, quoted in Baynes, *Forgotten Victor*, p. 243.
23. Baynes, *Forgotten Victor*, p. 243.
24. See Stephen Badsey, 'Faction in the British Army: Its Impact on 21st Army Group Operations in Autumn 1944', *War Studies Journal*, vol. 1, no. 1 (1995).
25. IWM BLM 119/32, Montgomery Papers, Dempsey to Montgomery, 31 October 1944; LHCMA O'Connor I/7–8, O'Connor to Dempsey, 20 October 1944, and notes of J.K. Nairne of conversation with O'Connor for official history; letters from O'Connor to his wife, quoted by Baynes in *Forgotten Victor*, pp. 240–2.
26. CCA, RLEW 7/7, Ronald Lewin's notes on conversations with Dempsey, 15 November 1968.

27. J.B. Salmond *The 51st Highland Division – 1939–45* (London: Blackwood, 1952), p. 195.
28. Tom Renouf, *Black Watch: Liberating Europe and Catching Himmler – My Extraordinary World War Two with the Highland Division* (London: Little, Brown, 2011), p. 189.
29. H.G. Martin, *History of 15th Scottish Division 1939–45* (London: Blackwood & Sons, 1948), p. 207.
30. Martin, *History of 15th Scottish*, p. 216.
31. IWM Montgomery Papers, LMD 63/46, Notes on the Situation, 7 October 1944; LMD 63/50, 21st Army Group Operational Situation and Directive M530, 9 October 1944.
32. Lionel F. Ellis, *Victory in the West, Vol. II* (London: HMSO, 1968), p. 69; Terry Copp, *Cinderella Army: The Canadians in Northwest Europe 1944–5* (Toronto, ON: University of Toronto Press, 2006), pp. 124–31.
33. Von Zangen, quoted in Robin Neillands, *The Battle for the Rhine: Arnhem and the Ardennes – The Campaign in Europe* (London: Weidenfeld & Nicolson, 2005), p. 164.
34. IWM Montgomery Papers, LMD 63/51 to 63/59. See run of correspondence between Montgomery and Eisenhower, 9 to 16 October 1944.
35. IWM Montgomery Papers, LMD 63/51 to 63/59. See run of correspondence between Montgomery and Eisenhower, 9 to 16 October 1944.
36. IWM Montgomery Papers, LMD 63/1, Montgomery's Diary, Montgomery to Nye, 15 October 1944.
37. UK NA WO 205/972B, BAOR, *Operations of Second Army*, pp. 254–5.
38. Anon., *The East Lancashire Regiment 1939–45* (privately published, 1953), pp. 104–7.
39. UK NA WO 171/554, 53rd Division Operational War Diary, October 1944.
40. G.N. Barclay, *The History of the 53rd Welsh Division in the Second World War* (London: Clowes, 1955), pp. 85–7.
41. John Tough, quoted in Renouf, *Black Watch*, p. 156.
42. Martin, *History of 15th Scottish*, p. 184.
43. Anon., *The 1st and 2nd Northamptonshire Yeomanry 1939–1946* (Brunswick, Germany: Meyer, 1946), p. 71.
44. John Mercer, *Mike Target* (London: Guild, 1990), p. 82.
45. A.A. Vince, *The Pompadours: The 2nd Battalion Essex Regiment – D Day to VE Day in Northwest Europe* (first published late 1940s – reprinted 1987), p. 31; UK NA WO 171/1295, 2nd Battalion Essex Regiment War Diary, October 1944.
46. Vince Spring, interview with Andrew Holborn, quoted in Holborn, *The 56th Infantry Brigade and D-Day: An Independent Infantry Brigade and the Campaign in North West Europe 1944–45* (London: Continuum, 2010), p. 176.
47. Trevor Hart Dyke, *Normandy to Arnhem: A Story of the Infantry* (privately published, 1966–1987 edn), pp. 65–71.
48. National Army Museum, London, UK, Hakewill-Smith Papers, correspondence between Lieutenant Colonel J. Hanky and Hakewill-Smith, 18–19 October 1944.
49. Copp, *Cinderella Army*, pp. 162–3.
50. UK NA WO 171/543, 52nd Lowland Division War Diary, CRA, October 1944; George Blake, *Mountain and Flood: The History of 52nd Lowland Division 1939–1946* (Glasgow: Jacksons, 1950), p. 97.
51. Ellis, *Victory in the West, II*, pp. 115–17.
52. J.L. Moulton, *The Battle for Antwerp* (London: Book Club, 1978), pp. 143–52.
53. Laurier Centre for Military Strategic and Disarmament Studies Archives (LCMSDS), Wilfrid Laurier University, Ontario, Canada, AORG Report No. 229, *The Westkapelle Assault on Walcheren*, October 1945; Moulton, *Battle for Antwerp*, pp. 153–70; Ellis, *Victory in the West, II*, pp. 119–23.
54. IWM Montgomery Papers, LMD 63/33, Montgomery to Brooke, 2 October 1944.
55. IWM Montgomery Papers, LMD 63/32, 21st Army Group notes, 2 October 1944; LMD 63/60, Montgomery to Brooke, 19 October 1944.
56. UK NA WO 216/101, Churchill to Montgomery, 12 December 1944.

57. IWM Montgomery Papers, LMD 67/4, Frank Simpson to Montgomery, 19 December 1944.
58. IWM Montgomery Papers, LMD 66/7, Montgomery to Brooke, 26 October 1944, and LMD 66/9, Montgomery to Simpson, 27 October 1944; UK NA WO 171/155, 21st Army Group Royal Artillery Branch, Operation SPARK report, December 1944.
59. Martin Lindsay, *So Few Got Through* (London: Arrow, 1960), pp. 122–3.
60. Charles Hanaway, *The PBI: Memoirs of an Infantryman* (privately published, 2002), pp. 84–5.
61. UK NA WO 171/155, No. 2 ORS Report, 'The Location of Enemy Mortars', 30 July 1944.
62. Blake, *Mountain and Flood*, p. 120.
63. UK NA WO 171/518, 50th Division counter-mortar staff, Standing Operating Instruction No. 3, 24 November 1944.
64. UK NA WO 171/155, 21st Army Group Royal Artillery Branch War Diary, appendix A, May 1944.
65. UK NA WO 171/155, No. 2 ORS Report, 'The Location of Enemy Mortars', 30 July 1944 and 21st Army Group Counter-Mortar Committee, minutes of first meeting, 8 August 1944.
66. UK NA WO 171/155, 21st Army Group Royal Artillery Branch War Diary, August 1944.
67. UK NA WO 171/518, 50th Division counter-mortar staff, Standing Operating Instruction No. 2, July 1944.
68. UK NA WO 171/155, 'Summary of Views Expressed at an RA Conference', 21st Army Group HQ, 27 September 1944.
69. UK NA WO 171/3893, 'Notes on BRA Second Army Artillery Conference', 17 May 1945, p. 18.
70. Best materials on this are held at the LCMSDS, Wilfrid Laurier University, Ontario, Canada. See particularly the Swann Archive; Terry Copp (ed.), *Montgomery's Scientists: Operational Research in Northwest Europe* (Waterloo, ON: LCMSDS, 2000).
71. UK NA WO 171/513, 50th Division Intelligence Summary no. 39, 29 July 1944.
72. UK NA WO 171/691, 159 Infantry Brigade War Diary, Infantry Training as a Result of Operations, 30 July to 10 September 1944, 19 September 1944.
73. UK NA WO 171/153, Notes of Conference held by 34th Armoured Brigade, September 1944.
74. UK NA WO 171/153, RAC 21st Army Group reports and letters, September to December 1944; WO 32/11034, 21st Army Group – operations narratives, report no. 56.
75. UK NA WO 171/4257, 51st Highland Division Battle School notes, January 1945.
76. UK NA WO 171/153, annex to 21st Army Group RAC Liaison letter no. 2, 6 September 1944.
77. UK NA WO 171/4252, 51st Highland Division War Diary, January 1945.
78. UK WO 291/1330, *Probability of Hitting Targets with Artillery Fire*, Operational Research Section reports, 1944; UWO 291/1321, ORS Report No. 24, *Accuracy of Predicted Shooting*, 1944; UK NA WO 171/3893, 'Notes on BRA Second Army Artillery Conference', appendix A, 17 May 1945.
79. Trevor Greenwood, *D-Day to Victory: The Diaries of a British Tank Commander* (London: Simon & Schuster, 2012), p. 271.
80. Alex McLennan, *Signals Home – 1944–46* (Salisbury: Quay, 1995), pp. 51–2.
81. William Lawrenson, *Of Straw and Stripes* (Edinburgh: Pentland, 1998), pp. 181–3; Hanaway, *PBI*, p. 87.
82. Robert Barer, *One Young Man and Total War – From Normandy to Concentration Camp: A Doctor's Letters Home* (Edinburgh: Pentland, 1998), p. 118.
83. LHCMA de Guingand 2/2/1, Report on Operation BLACKCOCK, 21st Army Group, 1945, p. 22.
84. Mark Harrison, *Medicine and Victory: British Military Medicine in the Second World War* (Oxford: Oxford University Press, 2004); chapter 6, is the best source

on this aspect of the campaign. See also F.A.E. Crew, *The Army Medical Services – Campaigns, Vol. IV: Northwest Europe* (London: HMSO, 1962).
85. UK NA WO 177/316, Brigadier E. Bulmer, 21st Army Group consulting physician Quarterly Report, autumn 1944; Manfred Messerschmidt, 'German Military Law in the Second World War', in W. Deist (ed.), *The German Military in the Age of Total War* (Leamington Spa: Berg, 1985), pp. 323–5.
86. Ellis, *Victory in the West, II*, pp. 170–3.
87. IWM Montgomery Papers, LMD 67/1, Montgomery's Diary, December 1944; LMD 67/8, 'Liaison Visit to General Hodges night 19/20 December 1944'; LMD 67/13, Montgomery to Brooke, 20 December 1944; LMD 67/18, Montgomery to Brooke, 21 December 1944.
88. Omar N. Bradley and Clay Blair, *A General's Life: An Autobiography by General of the Army Omar N. Bradley* (New York: Simon & Schuster, 1983), p. 368.
89. Ellis, *Victory in the West, II*, pp. 194–5.
90. IWM Montgomery Papers, LMD 67/28, Montgomery to Frank Simpson, 25 December 1944.
91. IWM Montgomery Papers, LMD 67/1, Montgomery's Diary, 31 December 1944.
92. Francis de Guingand, *Operation Victory* (London: Hodder & Stoughton, 1947), pp. 432–6.
93. IWM Montgomery Papers, LMD 67/1, Montgomery's Diary, 31 December 1944.
94. Alan Moorehead, *Montgomery: A Biography* (London: Hamish Hamilton, 1946), pp. 220–1.
95. David Belchem, *All in the Day's March* (London: Collins, 1978), pp. 255–7; Chester Wilmot, *The Struggle for Europe* (London: Collins, 1952), pp. 610–12; Bill Williams, interview, quoted in Nigel Hamilton, *Monty: Final Years of the Field-Marshal, 1944–1976* (London: Hamish Hamilton, 1986), p. 304; Charles Richardson, *Flashback: A Soldier's Story* (London: William Kimber, 1985), p. 189.
96. IWM Montgomery Papers, LMD 67/62, General Frank 'Simbo' Simpson to Montgomery, 20 January 1945; Omar Bradley, *A Soldier's Story* (New York: Holt, Rinehart and Winston, 1951), p. 416.
97. Montgomery of Alamein, *Memoirs*, p. 291.
98. Dwight Eisenhower, *Crusade in Europe* (London: Heinemann, 1948), p. 389.

10 Victory – The Rhine to the Baltic

1. LHCMA de Guingand 2/2/1, Report on Operation BLACKCOCK, 21st Army Group, 1945; H. Essame, *The 43rd Wessex Division at War, 1944–5* (London: Clowes, 1952), p. 195.
2. LHCMA de Guingand 2/2/1, Report on Operation BLACKCOCK, 21st Army Group, 1945.
3. UK NA WO 205/972C, *Operations of Second Army in Europe 1944–5* (Germany, privately published 1945), pp. 315–16.
4. LHCMA de Guingand 2/2/1, Report on Operation BLACKCOCK, 21st Army Group, 1945, pp. 5–6.
5. LHCMA de Guingand 2/2/1, Report on Operation BLACKCOCK, 21st Army Group, 1945, p. 9.
6. George Blake, *Mountain and Flood: The History of the 52nd Lowland Division 1939–46* (Glasgow: Jacksons, 1950), pp. 128–30 and p. 135; Gerald Verney, *The Desert Rats: The 7th Armoured Division in World War Two* (London: Greenhill, 1996 edn – first published 1954), pp. 265–9; LHCMA de Guingand 2/2/1, Report on Operation BLACKCOCK, 21st Army Group, 1945, pp. 19–20.
7. LHCMA de Guingand 2/2/1, Report on Operation BLACKCOCK, 21st Army Group, 1945, p. 27.
8. Sydney Jary, *18 Platoon* (privately published, 1987), p. 94.
9. LHCMA de Guingand 2/2/1, Report on Operation BLACKCOCK, 21st Army Group, 1945, p. 28.

10. Essame, *The 43rd Wessex Division*, p. 199.
11. LHCMA de Guingand 2/2/1, Report on Operation BLACKCOCK, 21st Army Group, 1945, p. 18.
12. Lionel Ellis, *Victory in the West, Vol. II: The Defeat of Germany* (London: HMSO, 1968), p. 247; LHCMA de Guingand 2/2/1, Report on Operation BLACKCOCK, 21st Army Group, 1945, p. 15.
13. IWM Montgomery Papers, LMD 67/54, Montgomery to Brooke, 16 January 1945
14. IWM Montgomery Papers, LMD 67/54, Montgomery to Brooke, 17 January 1945, and LMD 67/60, M456, Montgomery to Brooke, 20 January 1945; LMD 67/68, notes on 21st Army Group conference, 23 January 1945.
15. IWM Montgomery Papers, LMD 67/61, M549, Montgomery to Brooke, 20 January 1945.
16. IWM Montgomery Papers, LMD 67/67, Montgomery to Brooke, 22 January 1945.
17. IWM Montgomery Papers, LMD 67/67, Montgomery to Brooke, 22 January 1945.
18. UK NA WO 285/11, Dempsey's Diary, February 1945; IWM Montgomery Papers, LMD 67/56, Montgomery to Eisenhower, 17 January 1945.
19. IWM Montgomery Papers, LMD 68/20, Montgomery to Brooke, 7 February 1945.
20. IWM Montgomery Papers, LMD 68/26, Montgomery to VCIGS Archie Nye, 14 February 1945.
21. UK NA WO 205/972C, *Second Army Operations*, p. 321.
22. IWM Montgomery Papers, LMD 67/65, General Situation Directive M548, 21 January 1945.
23. Brian Horrocks, *Corps Commander* (London: Sidgwick & Jackson, 1977), pp. 171–82; UK NA WO 205/972C, *Second Army Operations*, pp. 319–23.
24. Ronald Gill and John Groves, *Club Route in Europe: The Story of 30 Corps in the European Campaign* (Germany: Degener, 1946), pp. 130–2.
25. Account of 'Roadwork in the Reichswald' by Colonel F.C. Nottingham in BAOR, *Royal Engineers Battlefield Tour: The Seine to the Rhine, Vol. 1* (Germany, privately published, 1947), p. 173.
26. BAOR, *Operation VERITABLE Battlefield Tour – Directing Edition* (Germany, privately published 1947), p. 9.
27. ORS Reports, No. 31 Predicted Fire in VERITABLE, No. 29 Counterbattery Fire in VERITABLE, and No. 26 Fire Support in VERITABLE, in Terry Copp (ed.), *Montgomery's Scientists: Operational Research in Northwest Europe – The Work of No. 2 Operational Research Section with 21st Army Group, June 1944 to July 1945* (Waterloo, ON: LCMSDS, 2000); BAOR, *Operation VERITABLE*, p. 45.
28. UK NA WO 205/953, 21st Army Group, 'Report on Operation VERITABLE', March 1945, p. 46.
29. National Archives Canada, RG 24, vol. 10, 673, 'Provisional Identification of Shell Fragments', First Canadian Army, 20 April 1945.
30. UK NA WO 205/953, 21st Army Group, 'Report on Operation VERITABLE', March 1945.
31. UK NA WO 205/953, 21st Army Group, 'Report on Operation VERITABLE', March 1945, p. 47.
32. UK NA WO 171/4722, 49th Armoured Personnel Regiment War Diary, 2 February 1945, and 44th Lowland Brigade, operational order, 5 February 1945.
33. Anon., *History of the East Lancashire Regiment in the War 1939–45* (privately published, 1953), pp. 153–4.
34. C.N. Barclay, *The History of the 53rd Welsh Division in the Second World War* (London: Clowes, 1955), pp. 113–45; UK NA WO 205/953, 21st Army Group, 'Report on Operation VERITABLE', March 1945, p. 46.
35. H.G. Martin, *History of the 15th Scottish Division, 1939–1945* (London: Blackwood & sons, 1948), pp. 231–7.
36. Martin Lindsay, *So Few Got Through* (London: Arrow, 1960), p. 182.
37. UK NA WO 205/953, 21st Army Group, 'Report on Operation VERITABLE', March 1945.

38. Tom Renouf, *Black Watch: Liberating Europe and Catching Himmler – My Extraordinary World War Two with the Highland Division* (London: Little, Brown, 2011), pp. 222–3.
39. Horrocks, *Corps Commander*, pp. 186–7.
40. Brian Horrocks, quoted in BAOR, *Operation VERITABLE*, p. 65.
41. First Canadian Army Intelligence Report, February 1945, quoted in Terry Copp, *Cinderella Army: The Canadians in Northwest Europe 1944–5* (Toronto, ON: University of Toronto Press, 2006), pp. 220–1.
42. UK NA WO 205/953, First Canadian Army Intelligence Report, February 1945, in 21st Army Group, 'Report on Operation VERITABLE', March 1945.
43. UK NA WO 205/972C, *Operations of Second Army*, p. 321; Ellis, *Victory in the West, II*, p. 266; UK NA WO 205/953, 21st Army Group, 'Report on Operation VERITABLE', March 1945, p. 45.
44. UK NA WO 205/953, 21st Army Group, 'Report on Operation VERITABLE', 1945.
45. Essame, *43rd Division*, p. 213.
46. G.J.B. Watkins, *The War History of the Fourth Battalion the Dorset Regiment, June 1944–May 1945* (Eastbourne: Rowe, 1956), p. 54.
47. UK NA WO 205/953, 21st Army Group, 'Report on Operation VERITABLE', March 1945, p. 46 and appendix C.
48. D.S. Daniel, *The Royal Hampshire Regiment 1918–1954* (Aldershot: Gale & Polden, 1954), pp. 249–50; UK NA WO 205/953, 21st Army Group, 'Report on Operation VERITABLE', March 1945, pp. 29–30.
49. IWM Montgomery Papers, LMD 68/1, Montgomery's Diary, 22 February 1945.
50. IWM Montgomery Papers, LMD 68/1, Montgomery's Diary, 21 February 1945.
51. Copp, *Cinderella Army*, pp. 242–3.
52. IWM Montgomery Papers, LMD 68/31, J. Ewart GS(I) to C in C, 24 February 1945.
53. Edgar Pallamountain, *Taurus Pursuant: A History of 11th Armoured Division* (Germany: privately published, 1945), pp. 85–6.
54. Ned Thornburn, *After Antwerp: The Long Haul to Victory – The Part Played by 4th Battalion King's Shropshire Light Infantry in the Overthrow of the Third Reich, September 1944 to May 1945* (Shrewsbury: Castle Museum 1993), pp. 76–7.
55. Brian Horrocks, quoted in BAOR, *Operation VERITABLE*, p. 66.
56. UK NA WO 285/7, Second British Army Intelligence Summaries, March 1945; BAOR, *Operation PLUNDER – Battlefield Tour* (1947), p. 5.
57. Barclay, *History of the 53rd Welsh*, pp. 178–9; UK NA WO 171/357, XXX Corps Medical War Diary, March/April 1945.
58. Trevor Hart Dyke, *Normandy to Arnhem: A Story of the Infantry* (privately published, 1966), p. 70.
59. Lindsay, *So Few Got Through*, p. 214.
60. IWM Montgomery Papers, LMD 68/57, Graham to Montgomery, 22 March 1945; Max Hastings, *Armageddon: The Battle for Germany 1944–1945* (London: Macmillan, 2004), p. 212.
61. Alex Danchev and Dan Todman (eds), *War Diaries 1939–1945: Field Marshal Lord Alanbrooke* (London: Weidenfeld & Nicolson, 2001), pp. 667–8; IWM Montgomery Papers, LMD 68/1, Montgomery's Diary, 3 March 1945; Nigel Hamilton, *Monty: The Final Years of the Field-Marshal, 1944–1976* (London: Hamish Hamilton, 1986), pp. 377–82.
62. IWM Montgomery Papers, LMD 68/58, Montgomery's personal message to the troops, March 1945.
63. UK NA WO 171/4363, 34th Armoured Brigade War Diary, Report on Fighting in the Reichswald, 8–17 February 1945.
64. UK NA WO 171/3890, RAC 21st Army Group, Battle Report No. 2, April 1945; Patrick Forbes, *6th Guards Tank Brigade: The Story of Guardsmen in Churchill Tanks* (London: Sampson Low, Marston & Co., 1946), pp. 103 and 115.
65. UK NA WO 205/972C, BAOR, *Operations of Second Army in Europe, Vol. II* (Germany, privately published, 1945), pp. 335–7; BAOR, *Operation PLUNDER – Battlefield Tour*

(privately published, 1947), pp. 1–3; Montgomery of Alamein, *Normandy to the Baltic: A Personal Account of the Conquest of Germany* (London: Hutchinson, 1947), pp. 197–9.

66. UK NA WO 285/7, Second British Army Intelligence Summaries, March 1945.
67. Norman Gelb, *Ike and Monty: Generals at War* (London: Constable, 1994), pp. 403–5.
68. UK NA WO 171/4409, 153rd Brigade War Diary, March 1945, and WO 171/5159, 5th Black Watch War Diary, March 1945; Martin, *History of 15th Scottish*, pp. 278–9.
69. UK NA WO 205/972C, BAOR, *Operations of Second Army*, pp. 335–43; Ellis, *Victory in the West, II*, pp. 287 and 296; IWM Montgomery Papers, LMD 68/1, Montgomery's Diary, 13 March 1945; Norman Kirby, *1100 Miles with Monty: Security and Intelligence at TAC HQ* (Stroud: Sutton, 1989), pp. 107–9.
70. Danchev and Todman (eds), *War Diaries*, p. 673.
71. Renouf, *Black Watch*, p. 273; Lindsay, *So Few Got Through*, p. 223.
72. G.C. Hopkinson, quoted in Patrick Delaforce, *Monty's Marauders: Black Rat 4th Armoured Brigade and Red Fox 8th Armoured Brigade* (Stroud: Sutton, 1993), p. 95.
73. Ian Robertson, *From Normandy to the Baltic: The Story of the 44th Lowland Infantry Brigade of the 15th Scottish Division from D-Day to the End of the War in Europe* (Germany, privately published, 1945), p. 146.
74. BAOR, *Operation PLUNDER – Battlefield Tour*, p. 87.
75. XI Troop Carrier Command Report on Operation VARSITY, June 1945, Combined Arms Research Digital Library, http://cgsc.contentdm.oclc.org, accessed 2012.
76. Account of Lieutenant Colonel Bradley in BAOR, *Operation PLUNDER – Battlefield Tour* p. 55.
77. BAOR, *Operation VARSITY – Battlefield Tour (Directing Edition)* (Germany, privately puhlished, 1947), pp. 70–2; Terence Otway, *Airborne Forces* (London: War Office, 1951), pp. 307–11.
78. UK NA WO 205/972C, BAOR, *Operations of Second Army*, p. 358.
79. IWM LMD 69/1, Montgomery's Diary, 29 March 1945.
80. IWM Montgomery Papers, LMD 69/30, Montgomery to Frank Simpson, 2 April 1945.
81. Danchev and Todman (eds), *War Diaries*, p. 680.
82. Ellis, *Victory in the West, II*, pp. 297–304; IWM Montgomery Papers, LMD 69/28, Montgomery to Brooke, 1 April 1945.
83. Danchev and Todman (eds), *War Diaries*, pp. 680–1.
84. UK NA WO 205/1165, H.B. Wright and R.D. Harkness, 'A Survey of Casualties amongst Armoured Units in Northwest Europe', No. 2 ORS, 21st Army Group, 1945; G.P.B. Roberts, *From the Desert to the Baltic* (London: William Kimber, 1987), pp. 230–1.
85. Jary, *18 Platoon*, p. 116.
86. Geoffrey Picot, *Accidental Warrior: In the Front Line form Normandy till Victory* ([illegible]), p. [illegible]
87. William Lawrenson, *Of Straw and Stripes* (Edinburgh: Pentland, 1990), p. 190.
88. Bill Bellamy, *Troop Leader: A Tank Commander's Story* (Stroud: Sutton, 2005), p. 168.
89. IWM Montgomery Papers, LMD 69/49, VIII Corps memo on Belsen concentration camp, 13 April 1945; Ellis, *Victory in the West, II*, pp. 309–10; Roberts, *From the Desert to the Baltic*, p. 236.
90. Bill Close, *A View from the Turret* (Bredon: Dell & Bredon, 1998), p. 160.
91. Ben Shephard, *After Daybreak: The Liberation of Belsen, 1945* (London: Jonathan Cape, 2005), pp. 43–53.
92. UK NA WO 222/201, Belsen camp, 'Account given by Brigadier Hughes to Royal Society of Medicine', 1945.
93. Mark Harrison, *Medicine and Victory: British Military Medicine in the Second World War* (Oxford: Oxford University Press, 2004), pp. 266–71; UK NA WO 171/4184, 11th Armoured Division War Diary, April 1945, and WO 177/343, VIII Corps Medical War Diary, April 1945; Johannes-Dieter Steinert, 'British Relief Teams in Belsen Concentration Camp: Emergency Relief and the Perception of Survivors', and Ben Shephard, 'The Medical Relief Effort at Belsen', both in Suzanne Bardgett and

David Cesarani (eds), *Belsen 1945: New Historical Perspectives* (London: Valentine Mitchell, 2006).

94. UK NA WO 171/3985, Second Army Civil Affairs, Weekly Report to DMG 21st Army Group, 13 April 1945.
95. UK NA WO 171/3985, Weekly Report, appendix L, 'Displaced Persons' and 'Displaced Persons – Policy', Colonel C. Wood MG (Admin) to VIII, XII and XXX Corps rear areas, 12 April 1945.
96. UK NA WO 171/3985, Second Army Civil Affairs, Weekly Report to DMG 21st Army Group, 13 April 1945.
97. UK NA WO 171/3985, Second Army Civil Affairs, Weekly Report to DMG 21st Army Group, 19 April 1945.
98. UK NA WO 171/3985, XII Corps Report to DDMG Second Army, 13 April 1945.
99. UK NA WO 171/3985, Captain F. Harbord, MFA & A, appendix, Second Army Report, 13 April 1945; UK NA FO 1046/146/3, MFA & A, Policy and correspondence, 1945.
100. See Leonard Woolley, *A Record of the Work Done by the Military Authorities for the Protection of the Treasures of Art and History in War Areas* (London: HMSO, 1947), pp. 41–58; F.S.V. Donnison, *Civil Affairs and Military Government: Northwest Europe 1944–6* (London: HMSO, 1961), chapters XII and XIII.
101. Contemporary Medical Archives Collection (CCMC), Wellcome Institute for the History of Medicine Library, London: RAMC 1184/1, *21st Army Group: The Medical Services*, p. 38; UK NA WO 171/3985, XII & XXX Corps Reports to DDMG Second Army and Appendix F, 'Public Safety', Appendix I, 'Public Health', 13 April 1945; Harrison, *Medicine and Victory*, p. 266.
102. IWM Montgomery Papers, LMD 69/1, Montgomery's Diary, 16 April 1945.
103. Essame, *43rd Wessex Division at War*, p. 255.
104. Anon. *The East Lancashire Regiment 1939–45* (privately published, 1953), p. 213.
105. UK NA WO 205/972C, BAOR, *Operations of Second Army, II*, pp. 375–80.
106. Blake, *Mountain and Flood*, pp. 203–4.
107. IWM Montgomery Papers LMD 69/1, Montgomery's Diary, 27 April 1945.
108. G.S. Jackson and VIII Corps Staff, *Operations of Eighth Corps: An Account of Operations from Normandy to the River Rhine*, (London: St Clements Press, 1948), pp.138–9.
109. IWM Montgomery Papers, LMD 70/1, Montgomery's Diary, 2 May 1945.
110. IWM Montgomery Papers, LMD 70/1, Montgomery's Diary, 4 to 7 May 1945.
111. See F.S.V. Donnison, *Civil Affairs and Military Government: North-West Europe 1944–6*, and *Civil Affairs and Military Government: Central Organization and Planning* (London: HMSO, 1966).
112. Montgomery, *Memoirs*, pp. 315–16.
113. J.L.J. Meredith, *The Story of 7th Battalion, The Somerset Light Infantry – Prince Albert's* (Germany, privately published, 1946), p. 193.
114. Captain Andrew Burn, interview with author, 2002, and Andrew Burn, *May the Fathers Tell the Children: Fighting with the Desert Rats, 1942–46* (privately published, 2003), p. 284.
115. Bill Close, interview with the author, 2002; Close, *A View from the Turret*, p. 162.
116. Ellis, *Victory in the West, II*, pp. 405–7.

11 Retrospective

1. Alex Kay, 'Germany's Staatssekretäre, Mass Starvation and the Meeting of 2nd May 1941', *Journal of Contemporary History*, vol. 41, no. 4 (October 2006).
2. UK NA WO 285/29, Dempsey Papers, correspondence with Basil Liddell Hart, February 1952.

Bibliography

Archival Sources

Airborne Forces Museum Archive, Aldershot, UK.
Churchill College Archives, Cambridge, UK.
Contemporary Medical Archives Collection, Wellcome Institute for the History of Medicine Library, London.
Imperial War Museum Archives, London, UK.
King's Shropshire Light Infantry Museum, Shrewsbury, Shropshire, UK.
Laurier Centre for Military Strategic and Disarmament Studies Archive, Wilfrid Laurier University, Waterloo, Ontario, Canada.
Liddell Hart Centre for Military Archives, King's College, London, UK.
National Archives Canada.
National Army Museum, London, UK.
Royal Armoured Corps Museum Archive, Bovington, Dorset, UK.
Royal Artillery Museum Archive, Woolwich, London, UK.
Royal Engineers Museum, Gillingham, Kent, UK.
Staffordshire Regimental Museum, Lichfield, Staffordshire, UK.
UK National Archives, Kew, London, UK.
US National Archives, Maryland, USA.

Published Primary Sources

Allan Adair, *A Guards' General: The Memoirs of Major General Sir Allan Adair*, ed. O. Lindsay (London: Hamish Hamilton, 1986).
Anon. *Airborne Operations: A German Appraisal*, Office of the Chief of Military History, Department of the Army (Washington DC: Government Press, 1950).
Austin Baker, 4/7th Royal Dragoon Guards, personal account supplied to author.
BAOR, *Administration History of 21st Army Group in Europe 1944–5* (Germany: privately published, 1945).
BAOR, *Royal Engineers Battlefield Tour – Normandy to the Seine* (Germany, privately published, 1946).
BAOR, *Royal Engineers Battlefield Tour – The Seine to the Rhine*, 2 vols (Germany, privately published, 1947).
BAOR, *Operation GOODWOOD – Battlefield Tour* (Germany, privately published, 1947).
BAOR, *Operation NEPTUNE – 43rd Wessex Division's Crossing of the Seine, 25–28 August 1944 – Battlefield Tour* (Germany, privately published 1947).
BAOR, *Operation PLUNDER – Battlefield Tour* (privately published, 1947).
BAOR, *Operation TOTALIZE – Battlefield Tour (Directing Staff Edition)* (privately published, 1947).

BAOR, *Operation VARSITY – Battlefield Tour (Directing Edition)* (privately published, 1947).
BAOR, *Operation VERITABLE – Battlefield Tour (Directing Edition)* (Germany, privately published, 1947).
Robert Barer, *One Young Man and Total War – From Normandy to Concentration Camp: A Doctor's Letters Home* (Edinburgh: Pentland, 1998).
David Belchem, *All in the Day's March* (London: Collins, 1978), and *Victory in Normandy* (London: Chatto & Windus, 1981).
Noel Bell, *From the Beaches to the Baltic: The Story of G Company, 8th Rifle Brigade* (Aldershot: Gale & Polden, 1947).
Bill Bellamy, *Troop Leader: A Tank Commander's Story* (Sutton: Stroud, 2005).
George G. Blackburn, *The Guns of Normandy: A Soldier's Eye View, France 1944* (London: Constable, 1998).
Robert Boscawen, *Armoured Guardsmen: A War Diary, June 1944–April 1945* (Barnsley: Leo Cooper, 2010).
Omar Bradley, *A Soldier's Story* (New York: Holt, Rinehart and Winston, 1951).
Omar N. Bradley and Clay Blair, *A General's Life: An Autobiography by General of the Army Omar N. Bradley* (New York: Simon & Schuster, 1983).
William Steel Brownlie, *The Proud Trooper* (London: Collins, 1964); *And Came Safe Home*, unpublished personal memoir held at Bovington RAC Tank Museum Archive.
Andrew Burn, *May the Fathers Tell the Children: Fighting with the Desert Rats, 1942–46* (privately published, 2003).
Harry Butcher, *Three Years with Eisenhower* (London: Heinemann, 1946).
Kenneth Cardy, *A DCM with the REME* (privately published, n.d.).
Lord Carrington, *Reflect on Things Past: The Memoirs of Lord Carrington* (London: Collins, 1988).
Lord Carver, *Out of Step: The Memoirs of Field Marshal Lord Carver* (London: Hutchinson, 1986).
Jim Caswell, *A Cas has Nine Lives* (unpublished personal memoir).
W.S. Chalmers, *Full Cycle: The Biography of Admiral Sir Bertram Home Ramsay* (London: Hodder and Stoughton, 1959).
Bill Close, *A View from the Turret* (Bredon: Dell & Bredon, 1998).
Paul Crook, *Came the Dawn: Fifty Years an Army Officer* (London: Spellmount, 1989).
Andy Cropper, *Dad's War: A Tank Commander in Europe 1944–45 with the XXIV Lancers and Sherwood Rangers Yeomanry* (Thurlstone: Anmas, 1994).
Alex Danchev and Daniel Todman (eds), *War Diaries 1939–1945: Field Marshal Lord Alanbrooke* (London: Weidenfeld & Nicolson, 2001).
Robin Dunn, *Sword and Wig: Memoirs of a Lord Justice* (London: Universal Law, 1993).
Trevor Hart Dyke, *Normandy to Arnhem: A Story of the Infantry* (privately published, 1966).
Stephen Dyson, *Tank Twins: East End Brothers in Arms 1943–45* (London: Leo Cooper, 1994).
Dwight Eisenhower, *Crusade in Europe* (London: Heinemann, 1948).
John Frost, *A Drop Too Many* (London: Sphere edn 1984 – first published 1980).
Richard Gale, *With the 6th Airborne Division in Normandy* (London: Samson Low, 1948).
James M. Gavin, *On to Berlin* (New York: Viking, 1978 – Bantam edn 1985).
Trevor Greenwood, *D-Day to Victory: The Diaries of a British Tank Commander* (London: Simon & Schuster, 2012).
James Grigg, *Prejudice and Judgment* (London: Jonathan Cape, 1948).
Francis de Guingand, *Operation Victory* (London: Hodder & Stoughton, 1947).
Colin Hall, *Dropped In It: The Autobiography of a Cotswold Boy and Arnhem Veteran* (privately published, 2010).
Ian Hammerton, *Achtung Minen! The Making of a Flail Tank Trooper* (London: Book Guild, 1991).

Charles Hanaway, *The PBI: Memoirs of an Infantryman* (privately published, 2002).
Johnny Henderson with Jamie Douglas-Home, *Watching Monty* (Stroud: Sutton, 2005).
Patrick Hennessy, *Young Man in a Tank* (undated manuscript), held at RAC Tank Museum Archive, Bovington.
Stuart Hills, *By Tank into Normandy: A Memoir of the Campaign in Northwest Europe from D Day to VE Day* (London: Cassell, 2002).
David Holbrook, *Flesh Wounds* (London: Methuen, 1966).
Brian Horrocks, *A Full Life* (London: Collins, 1960); *Corps Commander* (London: Sidgwick & Jackson, 1977).
Lord Ismay, *The Memoirs of Lord Ismay* (London: Heinemann, 1960).
Sydney Jary, *18 Platoon* (privately published, 1987).
Keith Jones, *Sixty-Four Days of a Normandy Summer: With a Tank Unit after D-Day* (London: Robert Hale, 1990).
Lipmann Kessel, *Surgeon at Arms: Parachuting into Arnhem with the First Airborne* (London: Heinemann, 1958).
Norman Kirby, *1100 Miles with Monty: Security and Intelligence at TAC HQ* (Stroud: Sutton, 1989).
George Kitching, *Mud and Green Fields: The Memoirs of Major General George Kitching* (St Catherine's, ON: Vanwell, 1993).
William Lawrenson, *Of Straw and Stripes* (Edinburgh: Pentland, 1998).
J. Lee-Richardson, *21st Army Group Ordnance: The History of the Campaign* (Germany, privately published, 1946).
Basil Liddell Hart (ed.), *The Rommel Papers* (London: Collins, 1953).
Martin Lindsay, *So Few Got Through* (London: Arrow, 1960).
Lord Lovat, *March Past* (London: Weidenfeld & Nicolson, 1978).
Hans von Luck, *Panzer Commander: The Memoirs of Colonel Hans von Luck* (New York: Dell, 1989).
Alex McLennan, *Signals Home – 1944–46* (Salisbury: Quay, 1995).
Stanislaw Maczek, *Avec mes Blindés* (Paris: Presses de la Cité, 1967); *La Première Division Blindée Polonaise au Combat – Journal de Marche du 7 Août au 9 Septembre 1944* (privately published, contemporary document, Mont Ormel Museum).
John Mercer, *Mike Target* (London: Guild, 1990).
Kurt Meyer, *Grenadiers: The Story of Waffen SS General Kurt 'Panzer' Meyer* (Mechanicsburg, PA: Stackpole, 2005).
Montgomery of Alamein, *Normandy to the Baltic: A Personal Account of the Conquest of Germany* (London: Hutchinson, 1947), and *Memoirs* (London: Collins, 1958).
Alan Moorehead, *Montgomery: A Biography* (London: Hamish Hamilton, 1946–1967 edn).
J.L. Moulton, *Haste to the Battle* (London: Cassell, 196[illegible]).
Geoffrey Picot, *Accidental Warrior: In the Frontline from Normandy till Victory* (London: Guild, 1993).
Martin Pöppel, *Heaven and Hell: The War Diary of a German Paratrooper* (Staplehurst: Spellmount, 1996).
R.S. Price, *Just a Walk in the Sun* (privately published, 2000).
Harold Pyman, *Call to Arms* (London: Leo Cooper, 1971).
Arthur Reddish, *Normandy from the Hull of a Sherman* (London: Battlefield Associates, 1995); *Sherwood Rangers Yeomanry: The Final Advance* (York: Wilton, 1997).
Douglas Reeman, *D-Day: A Personal Reminiscence* (London: Arrow, 1984).
Tom Renouf, *Black Watch: Liberating Europe and Catching Himmler – My Extraordinary World War Two with the Highland Division* (London: Little, Brown, 2011).
Charles Richardson, *Flashback: A Soldier's Story* (London: William Kimber, 1985).
Albert Ricketts, *Memoirs* (unpublished).
Helmut Ritgen, *The Western Front 1944: Memoirs of a Panzer Lehr Officer* (Winnipeg, Manitoba: J.J. Fedorowicz, 1995).
G.P.B. Roberts, *From the Desert to the Baltic* (London: William Kimber, 1987).

James Sims, *Arnhem Spearhead: A Private Soldier's Story* (London: Sphere, 1980).
Leslie Skinner, *Sherwood Rangers Casualty Book* (privately published, n.d.).
Stanislaw Sosabowski, *Freely I Served* (London: William Kimber, 1982).
Hans Speidel, *We Defended Normandy* (London: Jenkins, 1951).
Kenneth Strong, *Intelligence at the Top* (London: Cassells, 1968).
Jack Swaab, *Field of Fire: Diary of a Gunner Officer* (Stroud: Sutton, 2005).
Lord Tedder, *With Prejudice* (London: Cassells, 1966).
John M. Thorpe, *A Soldier's Tale: To Normandy and Beyond* (unpublished memoir).
Roy Urquhart, *Arnhem* (London: Pan, 1958).
Leonard Watkins, *A Sapper's War* (London: Minerva, 1996).
S. Whitehouse and G.B. Bennett, *Fear is the Foe: A Footslogger from Normandy to the Rhine* (London: Robert Hale, 1995).
Leonard Wills, *None Had Lances: The Story of the 24th Lancers* (Old Coulsdon: 24th Lancers Old Comrades Association, 1986).
Chester Wilmot, *The Struggle for Europe* (London: Collins, 1965 edn – first published 1952).
A. Wilson, *Flamethrower* (London: privately published, 1974).

Secondary Sources: Books

John A. Adams, *The Battle for Western Europe: Fall 1944 – An Operational Assessment* (Bloomington, IN: Indiana University Press, 2010).
Paul Addison and Angus Calder (eds), *Time to Kill: The Soldier's Experience of War in the West 1939–45* (London: Pimlico, 1997).
R.H. Ahrenfeldt, *Psychiatry in the British Army in the Second World War* (London: HMSO, 1958).
Stephen Ambrose, *Supreme Commander: The War Years of General Dwight D. Eisenhower* (London: Doubleday, 1970).
Stephen Badsey, *Normandy 1944* (London: Osprey, 1990).
Jonathan Bailey, *Field Artillery and Firepower* (Oxford: Military Press, 1989).
Dominique Barbé, *Charnwood: La Bataille de Buron-Saint-Contest* (Conde: Charles Corlet, 1994).
Suzanne Bardgett and David Cesarani (eds), *Belsen 1945: New Historical Perspectives* (London: Valentine Mitchell, 2006).
Correlli Barnett, *The Desert Generals* (London: Viking, 1961); *The Audit of War: The Illusion and Reality of Britain as a Great Nation* (London: Macmillan, 1986).
Omer Bartov, *The Eastern Front 1941–45: German Troops and the Barbarisation of Warfare* (London: Palgrave, 2001).
Kevin Baverstock, *Breaking the Panzers: The Bloody Battle for Rauray, Normandy, 1 July 1944* (Stroud: Sutton, 2002).
John Baynes, *The Forgotten Victor: General Sir Richard O'Connor* (London: Brassey's, 1989); *Urquhart of Arnhem: The Life of Major General R.E. Urquhart* (London: Brassey's, 1993).
Peter Beale, *Death by Design: British Tank Development in the Second World War* (Stroud: Sutton, 1998); *The Great Mistake: The Battle for Antwerp and the Beveland Peninsula, September 1944* (Stroud: Sutton, 2004).
Antony Beevor, *D-Day* (London: Viking, 2009).
Eversley Belfield and H. Essame, *The Battle for Normandy* (London: Pan, 1967 – first published 1965).
David Bennett, *A Magnificent Disaster: The Failure of Market Garden, The Arnhem Operation, September 1944* (Newbury: Casemate, 2008).
Ralph Bennett, *Ultra in the West: The Normandy Campaign* (London: Faber and Faber, 1979).
Shelford Bidwell, *Gunners at War: A Tactical Study of the Royal Artillery in the Twentieth Century* (London: Arrow, 1972).
Shelford Bidwell and Dominick Graham, *Firepower: British Army Weapons and Theories of War 1904–1945* (London: Allen & Unwin, 1985).

Edmund Blandford, *Two Sides of the Beach: The Invasion and Defence of Europe 1944* (London: Airlife, 1999).

Martin Blumenson, *Breakout and Pursuit* (Washington, DC: Center of Military History, 1961); *The Duel for France: The Men and Battles that Changed the Fate of Europe* (New York: Da Capo, 1963); *The Battle of the Generals* (New York: Morrow, 1993).

Gunther Blumentritt, *Von Rundstedt: The Soldier and the Man* (London: Odhams, 1952).

Brian Bond, *Liddell Hart: A Study in his Military Thought* (London: Cassell, 1977).

S. Brooks (ed.), *Montgomery and the Eighth Army* (London: Bodley Head, 1991).

Gordon Brown and Terry Copp, *Look to Your Front – Regina Rifles: A Regiment at War, 1944–45* (Waterloo, ON: Laurier Centre for Military Strategic and Disarmament Studies, 2001).

Colin Bruce, *War on the Ground – 1939–45* (London: Constable, 1995).

John Buckley, *British Armour in the Normandy Campaign 1944* (London: Frank Cass, 2004); (ed.), *The Normandy Campaign 1944: Sixty Years On* (London: Routledge, 2006).

J.R.M. Butler, *Grand Strategy, Vol. II* (London: HMSO, 1971).

Angus Calder and Jeremy Crang (eds), *Time to Kill: The Soldier's Experience of War in the West 1939–45* (London: Pimlico, 1997).

Raymond Callahan, *Churchill and His Generals* (Lawrence, KS: University Press of Kansas, 2007).

James J. Carafano, *After D-Day: Operation Cobra and the Normandy Breakout* (Boulder, CO: Rienner, 2000).

Paul Carrell, *Invasion: They're Coming: The German Account of the D-Day Landings and the 80 Days' Battle for France* (Atglen, PA: Schiffer, 1995 – first published 1964).

Robert Citino, *Blitzkrieg to Desert Storm: The Evolution of Operational Warfare* (Lawrence, KS: University Press of Kansas, 2004).

Lloyd Clark, *Orne Bridgehead* (Stroud: Sutton, 2004).

Terry Copp, *Fields of Fire: The Canadians in Normandy* (Toronto, ON: University of Toronto Press, 2003), and *Cinderella Army: The Canadians in Northwest Europe 1944–5* (Toronto, ON: University of Toronto Press, 2006).

Terry Copp (ed.), *Montgomery's Scientists: Operational Research in Northwest Europe* (Waterloo, ON: LCMSDS, 2000); *1st Canadian Radar Battery*, 1944–5, (Waterloo, ON: LCMSDS, 2010).

Terry Copp and Bill McAndrew, *Battle Exhaustion: Soldiers and Psychiatrists in the Canadian Army 1939–1945* (Montreal: McGill-Queen's University Press, 1990).

Terry Copp and Robert Vogel, *Maple Leaf Route: Caen* (Alma, ON: Maple Leaf Route, 1983).

Jeremy Crang, *The British Army and the People's War 1939–1945* (Manchester: Manchester University Press, 2000).

Martin van Creveld, *Fighting Power: German and US Army Performance, 1939–45* (London: Arms and Armour Press, 1983).

Martin van Creveld, *Supplying War: Logistics from Wallenstein to Patton*, 2nd edn (Cambridge: Cambridge University Press, 2004).

F.A.E. Crew, *The Army Medical Services – Campaigns, Vol. IV: Northwest Europe* (London: HMSO, 1962).

Ian Daglish, *Operation BLUECOAT: Battleground Normandy* (Barnsley: Pen & Sword, 2003); *Operation GOODWOOD: Over the Battlefield* (Barnsley: Pen & Sword, 2005); *Operation EPSOM: Over the Battlefield* (Barnsley: Pen & Sword, 2007); *Operation BLUECOAT: Over the Battlefield* (Barnsley: Pen & Sword, 2009).

Alex Danchev, *Alchemist of War: The Life of Basil Liddell Hart* (London: Weidenfeld & Nicolson, 1998).

H. Darby and M. Cunliffe, *A Short History of 21st Army Group* (London: Gale & Polden, 1949).
Patrick Delaforce, *Invasion of the Third Reich: War & Peace – Operation Eclipse* (Stroud: Amberley, 2011).
Douglas E. Delaney, *Corps Commanders: Five British and Canadian Generals at War 1939–45* (Toronto, ON: UCB Press, 2011).
Carlo D'Este, *Decision in Normandy* (London: Collins, 1983); *Eisenhower: A Soldier's Life* (London: Weidenfeld & Nicolson, 2003).
F.S.V. Donnison, *Civil Affairs and Military Government: Northwest Europe 1944–6* (London: HMSO, 1961); *Civil Affairs and Military Government: Central Organization and Planning* (London: HMSO, 1966).
Michael Doubler, *Closing with the Enemy: How GIs Fought the War in Europe 1944–5* (Kansas: University Press of Kansas, 1994).
Paul Douglas Dickson, *A Thoroughly Canadian General: A Biography of General H.D.G. Crerar* (Toronto, ON: University of Toronto Press, 2007).
Christopher Dunphie, *Pendulum of Battle: Operation GOODWOOD July 1944* (Barnsley: Pen & Sword, 2004).
Trevor Dupuy, *A Genius for War: The German Army and General Staff, 1807–1945* (Englewood Cliffs, NJ: Prentice Hall, 1977).
John Ellis, *The Sharp End of War* (London: Compendium, 1990, first published 1983); *Brute Force: Allied Strategy and Tactics in the Second World War* (London: Andre Deutsch, 1990).
Lionel F. Ellis, *Victory in the West*, 2 vols (London: HMSO, 1962 and 1968).
John A. English, *The Canadian Army and the Normandy Campaign: A Study in the Failure of High Command* (London: Praeger, 1991).
John A. English and Bruce I. Gudmundsson, *On Infantry* (Westport, CT: Praeger, 1994).
David Fletcher, *The Great Tank Scandal: British Armour in the Second World War (Part One)* (London: HMSO, 1989), and *The Universal Tank: British Armour in the Second World War (Part Two)*, (London: HMSO, 1993), *Mr Churchill's Tank: The British Infantry Tank Mark IV* (Atglen, PA: Schiffer, 1999).
Eddy Florentin, *The Battle of the Falaise Gap* (New York: Hawthorn, 1967).
David Fraser, *And We Shall Shock Them: The British Army and the Second World War* (London: Hodder & Stoughton, 1983).
David French, *Raising Churchill's Army: The British Army and the War Against Germany 1919–1945* (Oxford: Oxford University Press, 2000).
Norman Gelb, *Ike and Monty: Generals at War* (London: Constable, 1994).
Ian Gooderson, *Air Power at the Battlefront: Allied Close Air Support in Europe, 1943–45* (London: Frank Cass, 1998).
Dominick Graham, *The Price of Command: A Biography of Guy Simonds* (Toronto, ON: Stoddart, 1993).
John Greenacre, *Churchill's Spearhead: The Development of Britain's Airborne Forces in World War Two* (Barnsley: Pen & Sword, 2010).
Bruce Gudmundsson, *On Artillery* (Westport, CT: Praeger, 1993).
Francis de Guingand, *Generals at War* (London: Hodder & Stoughton, 1964).
Nigel Hamilton, *Monty: Master of the Battlefield 1942–1944* (London: Coronet, 1985 – first published 1983); *Monty: Final Years of the Field-Marshal, 1944–1976* (London: Hamish Hamilton, 1986).
Peter Harclerode, *Arnhem: A Tragedy of Errors* (London: Caxton 2000); *Wings of War: Airborne Warfare 1918–1945* (London: Weidenfeld & Nicolson, 2005).
Richard Hargreaves, *The Germans in Normandy* (Barnsley: Pen & Sword, 2006).
Gordon Harrison, *Cross Channel Attack* (Washington, DC: Center of Military History, 1951).
Mark Harrison, *Medicine and Victory: British Military Medicine in the Second World War* (Oxford: Oxford University Press, 2004).

Timothy Harrison Place, *Military Training in the British Army, 1940–44: From Dunkirk to D-Day* (London: Frank Cass, 2000).

Russell A. Hart, *Clash of Arms: How the Allies Won in Normandy 1944* (Boulder, CO: Rienner, 2001).

Stephen Hart, *Montgomery and Colossal Cracks: 21st Army Group in Northwest Europe 1944–5* (Westport, CT: Praeger, 2000).

Max Hastings, *Overlord: D-Day and the Battle for Normandy 1944* (London: Michael Joseph, 1984), and *Armageddon: The Battle for Germany 1944–1945* (London: Macmillan, 2004).

F.H. Hinsley et al., *British Intelligence in the Second World War: Its Influence on Strategy and Operations, Vol. III (Part 2)* (London: HMSO, 1988).

Alastair Horne and David Montgomery, *The Lonely Leader: Monty 1944–45* (London: Macmillan, 1994).

J.J. How, *Normandy: The British Breakout* (London: William Kimber, 1981); *Hill 112: Cornerstone of the Normandy Campaign* (London: William Kimber, 1984).

T.E.B. Howarth (ed.), *Monty at Close Quarters: Recollections of the Man* (London: Leo Cooper, 1985).

James A. Huston, *Out of the Blue: US Army Airborne Operations in World War II* (West Lafayette, IN: Purdue, 1998).

David Irving, *The War Between the Generals* (London: Penguin, 1981).

David Isby (ed.), *Fighting in Normandy: The German Army at D-Day* (London: Greenhill, 2000); *Fighting in Normandy: The German Army from D-Day to Villers-Bocage* (London: Greenhill, 2001); *Fighting the Breakout: The German Army in Normandy from Cobra to the Falaise Gap* (London: Greenhill, 2004).

Roman Jarymowcyz, *Tank Tactics: From Normandy to Lorraine* (Boulder, CO: Rienner, 2001).

H.F. Joslen, *Orders of Battle 1939–45* (London: HMSO, 1960).

D. Kahn, *Hitler's Spies: The Extraordinary Story of German Military Intelligence* (London: Arrow, 1980).

John Keegan, *Six Armies in Normandy* (London: Viking, 1982).

Robert Kershaw, *It Never Snows in September: The German view of MARKET GARDEN and the Battle of Arnhem, September 1944* (London: Ian Allan 2004 edn, first published 1990); *D-Day: Piercing the Atlantic Wall* (London: Ian Allan, 2004 reprint).

Richard Lamb, *Montgomery in Europe 1943–5: Success or Failure?* (London: Buchan & Enright, 1983).

Eric Lefèvre, *Panzers in Normandy: Then and Now* (London: Battle of Britain International, 1983).

Ronald Lewin, *Montgomery as Military Commander* (London: Batsford, 1971).

Basil Liddell Hart, *The Other Side of the Hill* (London: Cassell, 1951); (ed.), *The Rommel Papers* (London: Collins, 1953).

John Lincoln, *Diary of a Battle: Kervenheim – An Account of the Battle Fought on 1st March 1945 by the Royal Norfolk Regiment* (privately published, 1999).

Sean Longden, *To the Victor the Spoils: D-Day to VE Day, the Reality behind the Heroism* (Moreton, Gloucs: Arris, 2004).

Paul Lund and Harry Ludlam, *The War of the Landing Craft* (London: Foulsham, 1976).

Tim Lynch, *Operation Market Garden: The Legend of the Waal Crossing* (Stroud: Spellmount, 2011).

Bill McAndrew and Terry Copp, *Battle Exhaustion: Soldiers and Psychiatrists in the Canadian Army, 1939–45* (Montreal and Kingston: McGrawHill, 1990).

Charles B. MacDonald, *The Siegfried Line Campaign* (Washington, DC: Government Press, 1947).

Evan McGilvray, *Man of Steel and Honour: General Stanislaw Maczek* (Birmingham: Helion, 2012).

Alexander McKee, *Caen: Anvil of Victory* (London: Souvenir Press, 1964).

S.P. Mackenzie, *Politics and Military Morale* (Oxford: Oxford University Press, 1992).

Henri Marie et al., *Villers-Bocage: Tigres au Combat – Le Champ de Bataille* (Bayeux: Heimdal, 1993).
S.L.A. Marshall, *Men Against Fire* (New York: Morrow, 1947).
Henry Maule, *Caen: The Brutal Battle and the Breakout from Normandy* (London: Purnell, 1976).
Richard Mead, *General 'Boy' Browning: The Life of Lieutenant General Sir Frederick Browning* (Barnsley: Pen & Sword, 2010).
John Mearsheimer, *Liddell Hart and the Weight of History* (London: Cornell University Press, 1988).
Manfred Messerschmidt, *Nazi Political Aims and German Military Law in World War Two* (Ottawa, ON: Jackson Wegren, 1981).
Russell Miller, *Nothing Less than Victory: The Oral History of D-Day* (London: Michael Joseph, 1993).
Russell Miller with Renate Miller, *VE Day: The People's Story* (London: Tempus, 1995).
J.L. Moulton, *The Battle for Antwerp*, (London: Book Club, 1978).
G.E. Patrick Murray, *Eisenhower versus Montgomery: The Continuing Debate* (Westport, CT: Praeger, 1996).
Williamson Murray and Allan R. Millett, *A War to be Won: Fighting the Second World War* (Cambridge, MA: Cambridge University Press, 2000).
Robin Neillands, *The Conquest of the Reich: D-Day to VE Day – A Soldiers' History* (New York: New York University Press, 1995); *The Battle of Normandy 1944* (London: Cassell, 2002); *The Battle for the Rhine: Arnhem and the Ardennes – The Campaign in Europe* (London: Weidenfeld & Nicolson, 2005).
John North, *NorthWest Europe 1944–45* (London: HMSO, 1953).
Vincent Orange, *Tedder: Quietly in Command* (London: Frank Cass, 2004).
Terence Otway, *Airborne Forces* (London: HMSO, 1951).
H.M.D. Parker, *Manpower: A Study in Wartime Policy and Administration* (London: HMSO, 1957).
Bryan Perrett, *Through Mud and Blood: Infantry – Tank Operations in World War Two* (London: Robert Hale, 1975); *Seize and Hold: Master Strokes on the Battlefield* (London: Arms and Armour Press, 1994).
F.W. Perry, *The Commonwealth Armies: Manpower and Organisation in Two World Wars* (Manchester: Manchester University Press, 1988).
M.M. Postan, D. Hay and J.D. Scott, *Design and Development of Weapons: Studies in Government and Industrial Organisation* (London: HMSO, 1964).
Giffard Le Quesne Martel, *East versus West* (London: Museum Press, 1952).
Richard Rapier Stokes, *Some Amazing Tank Facts* (London: Du, dale, privately published 1945).
Brian A. Reid, *No Holding Back: Operation Totalize – August 1944* (Toronto, ON: Robin Brass Studio, 2005).
Charles M. Richardson, *Send for Freddie: The Story of Monty's Chief of Staff – Major General Sir Francis de Guingand* (London: William Kimber, 1987).
F.M. Richardson, *Fighting Spirit: A Study of Psychological Factors in War* (London: Leo Cooper, 1978).
Willem Ridder, *Countdown to Freedom* (Bloomington, IN: Author House, 2007).
Tim Ripley, *The Wehrmacht: The German Army of World War Two, 1939–45 (Great Armies)* (London: Routledge, 2003).
Sebastian Ritchie, *Arnhem: Myth and Reality* (London: Robert Hale, 2010).
Duncan Rogers and Sarah Williams (eds), *On the Bloody Road to Berlin: Frontline Accounts from NorthWest Europe and the Eastern Front, 1944–45* (Solihull: Helion, 2005).
Richard Rohmer, *Patton's Gap* (London: Beaufort, 1981).
Peter Rostron, *The Military Life and Times of General Sir Miles Dempsey: Monty's Army Commander* (Barnsley: Pen & Sword, 2010).
Roland G. Ruppenthal, *Logistical Support of the Armies, Vol. 2* (Washington, DC: 1954).
Cornelius Ryan, *The Longest Day* (London: Gollancz, 1960); *A Bridge Too Far* (London: Simon & Schuster, 1974).

Rowland Ryder, *Oliver Leese* (London: Hamish Hamilton, 1987).

P.E. Schramm, *KTB des OKW Bd IV: 1.1.1944–22.5.1945* (Frankfurt am Main: Bernard & Graefe, 1961).

Ben Shephard, *After Daybreak: The Liberation of Belsen, 1945* (London: Jonathan Cape, 2005).

Gary L. Simpson, *Tiger Ace: The Life Story of Panzer Commander Michael Wittman* (Atglen, PA: Schiffer, 1994).

Nick Smart, *Biographical Dictionary of British Generals of the Second World War* (Barnsley: Pen & Sword, 2005).

Ronald Smelser and Edward J. Davies II, *The Myth of the Eastern Front: The Nazi-Soviet War in American Popular Culture* (Cambridge: Cambridge University Press, 2008).

J. Allan Snowie, *Bloody Buron: The Battle of Buron, Caen, 8 July 1944* (Erin: Boston Mills, 1984).

C.P. Stacey, *The Official History of the Canadian Army in the Second World War, Vol. III* (Ottawa, ON: Queen's Printer, 1960).

Adrian Stewart, *Six of Monty's Men* (Barnsley: Pen & Sword, 2011).

Annette Tapert, *Despatches from the Heart* (London: Hamish Hamilton, 1984).

Daniel Taylor, *Villers-Bocage Through the Lens* (London: Battle of Britain Press, 1999).

John Terraine, *The Right of the Line: The Royal Air Force in the European War 1939–1945* (London: Hodder & Stoughton, 1985).

R.W. Thompson, *Montgomery: The Field Marshal: The Campaign in North-West Europe 1944–5* (London: Allen & Unwin, 1969).

Ken Tout, *Tank! 40 Hours of Battle, August 1944* (London: Robert Hale, 1985); *A Fine Night for Tanks: The Road to Falaise* (Stroud: Sutton, 1998).

P. Warner, *The D-Day Landings* (London: William Kimber, 1990).

Philip Warner, *Horrocks: The General Who Led from the Front* (Barnsley: Pen & Sword, 2005 – first published 1984).

Russell Weigley, *Eisenhower's Lieutenants: The Campaigns of France and Germany 1944–45* (London: Sidgwick & Jackson, 1981).

Denis Whitaker and Sheila Whitaker, *Victory at Falaise: The Soldiers' Story* (Toronto, ON: Harper Collins, 2000) with Terry Copp; *Rhineland: The Battle to End the War* (London: Stoddart, 2001 – 2nd edn; Normandy: *The Real Story of How Ordinary Soldiers Defeated Hitler* (London: Presidio Press, 2004).

Willie Whitelaw, *The Whitelaw Memoirs* (London: Headline, 1990).

Theodore A. Wilson (ed.), *D-Day 1944* (Lawrence, KS: University Press of Kansas, 1994).

Leonard Woolley, *A Record of the Work Done by the Military Authorities for the Protection of the Treasures of Art and History in War Areas* (London: HMSO, 1947).

Niklas Zetterling, *Normandy 1944: German Military Organization, Combat Power and Organizational Effectiveness* (Winnipeg, Manitoba: J.J. Fedorowicz, 2000).

Secondary Sources: Articles and Chapters

After the Battle No. 139: The Capture of Le Havre (Essex: Battle of Britain International, 2008).

Stephen Badsey, 'Faction in the British Army: Its Impact on 21st Army Group Operations in Autumn 1944', *The War Studies Journal*, vol. 1, no. 1 (1995); 'Terrain as a Factor in the Battle of Normandy, 1944', in Peter Doyle and Matthew Bennett (eds), *Fields of Battle: Terrain in Military History* (London: Kluwer, 2002); 'Arnhem', in Julie Guard (ed.), *Airborne* (Oxford: Osprey, 2007).

Omer Bartov, 'Indoctrination and Motivation in the Wehrmacht: The Importance of the Unquantifiable', *Journal of Strategic Studies*, vol. 9, no. 1, (March 1986); 'Daily Life and Motivation in War: The Wehrmacht in the Soviet Union', in *Journal of Strategic Studies*, vol. 12, no. 2 (1989).

Mike Bechthold, 'The Development of an Unbeatable Combination: US Close Air Support in Normandy', *Canadian Military History*, vol. 8, no. 1 (1999).

Martin Blumenson, 'The Most Overrated General of World War Two', *Armor* (May–June 1962).

John S. Brown, 'Colonel Trevor N. Dupuy and the Mythos of Wehrmacht Superiority: A Reconsideration', *Military Affairs*, vol. 50 (1986); 'The Wehrmacht Myth Revisited: A Challenge to Colonel Trevor N. Dupuy', *Military Affairs*, vol. 51 (1987).

John Buckley, 'Tackling the Tiger: The Development of British Armoured Doctrine for Normandy 1944', *The Journal of Military History*, vol. 74, no. 4 (October 2010).

Peter Caddick Adams, 'General Sir Miles Christopher Dempsey: Not a Popular Leader', *Journal of the Royal United Services Institute* (October 2005).

Raymond A. Callahan, 'Two Armies in Normandy: Weighing British and Canadian Military Performance', in Theodore A. Wilson (ed.), *D-Day 1944* (Lawrence, KS: University Press of Kansas, 1994).

Terry Copp, ' "No Lack of Rational Speed": 1st Canadian Army Operations, September 1944', *Journal of Canadian Studies*, vol. 16, nos. 3 and 4 (1981); 'Operational Research and 21st Army Group', *Canadian Military History*, vol. 3, no. 1 (1994); 'Counter-Mortar Operational Research in 21 Army Group', *Canadian Military History*, vol. 3, no. 2 (1994); ' "If this war isn't over, and pretty damn soon, they'll be no-body left in this old platoon: First Canadian Army, February to March 1945', in Paul Addison and Angus Calder (eds), *Time to Kill: The Soldier's Experience of War in the West 1939–45* (London: Pimlico, 1997).

W.G.R. Corkhill, 'The Effectiveness of Conventional Field Branch Artillery in General War in Northwest Europe', *Journal of the Royal Artillery*, vol. 94, no. 2 (September 1967).

C.J. Dick, 'The Goodwood Concept – Situating the Appreciation', *Journal of the Royal United Services Institute*, vol. 127 (1982).

Paul D. Dickson, 'The Hand that Wields the Dagger: First Canadian Army Command and National Authority', *War and Society*, vol. 13, no. 2 (1995).

Trevor N. Dupuy, 'Mythos or Verity? The Quantified Judgement Model and German Combat Effectiveness', *Military Affairs*, vol. 50 (October 1986).

John Ferris, 'Intelligence and OVERLORD', in John Buckley (ed.), *The Normandy Campaign 1944: Sixty Years On* (London: Routledge, 2006).

Tony Foulds, 'In Support of the Canadians: A British Anti-Tank Regiment's First Five Weeks in Normandy', *Canadian Military History*, vol. 7, no. 2 (1998).

David French, 'Colonel Blimp and the British Army: British Divisional Commanders in the War Against Germany, 1939–45', *The English Historical Review*, vol. 111, no. 444 (November 1996); ' "Tommy is No Soldier": The Morale of Second British Army in Normandy, June to August 1944', in *Journal of Strategic Studies*, vol. 19, no. 4 (December 1996); 'Discipline and the Death Penalty in the British Army in the War against Germany during the Second World War', *Journal of Contemporary History*, vol. 33, no. 4 (1998).

Ian Gooderson, 'Heavy and Medium Bombers: How Successful Were They in the Close Air Support Role during World War Two?', *Journal of Strategic Studies*, vol. 15, no. 3 (September 1993).

John Grodzinski, 'Kangaroos at War', *Canadian Military History*, vol. 4, no. 3 (1995).

J. P. Harris, 'The Myth of Blitzkrieg', *War in History*, vol. 2, no. 3 (1995).

Russell A. Hart, 'Feeding Mars: The Role of Logistics in the German Defeat in Normandy 1944', *War in History*, vol. 3, no. 4 (1996).

Stephen A. Hart, ' "The Black Day Unrealised": Operation TOTALIZE and the Problems of Translating Tactical Success into a Decisive Breakout', in John Buckley (ed.), *The Normandy Campaign: Sixty Years On* (London: Routledge, 2006).

Michael Howard in 'Monty and the Price of Victory, *The Sunday Times* (16 October 1983).

Roman J. Jarymowycz, 'Der Gegenangriff vor Verrières: German Counterattacks during *Operation Spring*, 25–6 July 1944', *Canadian Military History*, vol. 2, no. 1 (1993); 'Canadian Armour in Normandy: *Operation Totalize* and the Quest for Operational Manoeuvre', *Canadian Military History*, vol. 7, no. 2 (1998).

Roman Jarymowycz, 'General Guy Simonds: The Commander as Tragic Hero', in Bernd Horn and Stephen Harris, *Warrior Chiefs: Perspectives on Senior Canadian Military Leaders* (Toronto, ON: Dundurn Press, 2001).

Alex Kay, 'Germany's Staatssekretäre, Mass Starvation and the Meeting of 2nd May 1941', *Journal of Contemporary History*, vol. 41, no. 4 (October 2006).

W. von Lossow, 'Mission Type Tactics versus Order Type Tactics', *Military Review*, vol. 57 (June 1977).

Mungo Melvin, 'The German Perspective', in John Buckley (ed.), *The Normandy Campaign 1944: Sixty Years On* (London: Routledge, 2006).

Manfred Messerschmidt, 'German Military Law in the Second World War', in W. Deist (ed.), *The German Military in the Age of Total War* (Leamington Spa: Berg, 1985).

Montgomery, Bernard L., 'Twenty-First Army Group in the Campaign in North-West Europe 1944–45', *Journal of the Royal United Services Institute*, vol. 90 (November 1945).

Williamson Murray, 'British Military Effectiveness in the Second World War', in Allan Millett and Williamson Murray (eds), *Military Effectiveness, Vol. III: The Second World War* (London: Unwin Hyman, 1988).

John Peaty, 'Myth, Reality and Carlo D'Este', *War Studies Journal*, vol. 1, no. 2 (spring 1996).

Jody Perrun, 'Best Laid Plans: Guy Simonds and Operation Totalize, 7–20 August 1944', *Journal of Military History*, vol. 67, no. 1 (January 2003).

Stephen T. Powers, 'The Battle of Normandy: The Lingering Controversy', *Journal of Military History*, vol. 56, no. 3 (July 1992).

Alfred Price, 'The Three-Inch Rocket: How Successful Was it against the German Tanks in Normandy?', *RAF Quarterly* (Summer 1975).

S.T. Rippe, 'Leadership, Firepower and Manoeuvre: The British and the Germans', *Military Review* (October 1985).

E.P.F. Rose and C. Pareyn, 'British Applications of Military Geography for *Operation Overlord* and the Battle of Normandy, France 1944', in J.R. Underwood and P.L. Guth (eds), *Military Geology in War and Peace: Reviews in Engineering Geology*, vol. XIII (Boulder, CO: Geological Society of America, 1998).

G.L. Scott, 'British and German Operational Styles in World War Two', *Military Review*, vol. 65 (October 1985).

Max Schoenfeld, 'The Navies and NEPTUNE', in Theodore A. Wilson (ed.), *D-Day 1944* (Lawrence, KS: University Press of Kansas, 1994).

Gary Sheffield, 'The Shadow of the Somme: The Influence of the First World War on British Soldiers' Perceptions and Behaviour in the Second World War', in Angus Calder and Jeremy Crang (eds), *Time to Kill: The Soldier's Experience of War in the West 1939–45* (London: Pimlico, 1997).

Ben Shephard, 'The Medical Relief Effort at Belsen', in Suzanne Bardgett and David Cesarani (eds), *Belsen 1945: New Historical Perspectives* (London: Valentine Mitchell, 2006).

Roger Spiller, 'SLA Marshall and the Ratio of Fire', in *Journal of the Royal United Services Institute*, 133/4 (winter 1988).

Johannes-Dieter Steinert, 'British Relief Teams in Belsen Concentration Camp: Emergency Relief and the Perception of Survivors', in Suzanne Bardgett and David Cesarani (eds), *Belsen 1945: New Historical Perspectives* (London: Valentine Mitchell, 2006); 'British Humanitarian Assistance: Wartime Planning and Postwar Realities', *Journal of Contemporary History*, vol. 43, no. 3 (2008).

Unit Histories

Anon., *History of the 7th Armoured Division: June 1943–July 1945* (privately published, 1945).

Anon., *The East Lancashire Regiment 1939–45* (privately published, 1953).

Anon., *The Story of the Royal Army Service Corps 1939–1945* (London: HMSO, 1955).

Anon., *The Story of the 23rd Hussars 1940–46* (privately published, Germany, 1946).

Anon., *The Story of 34th Armoured Brigade* (privately published, 1945).

Anon., *The Story of the 79th Armoured Division* (Germany, privately published, 1945).

Anon., (Captain Edgar Pallamountain), *Taurus Pursuant: A History of 11th Armoured Division* (Germany, privately published, 1945).

Anon., *The 1st and 2nd Northamptonshire Yeomanry 1939–1946* (Brunswick, Germany: Meyer, 1946).

G.N. Barclay, *The History of the 53rd Welsh Division in the Second World War* (London: Clowes, 1955).

B.S. Barnes, *The Sign of the Double T: The 50th Northumbrian Division – July 1943 to December 1944* (York: Sentinel Press, 1999).

Peter Beale, *Tank Tracks: 9th Battalion Royal Tank Regiment at War 1940–45* (Stroud: Sutton, 1995).

Raymond Bird, *XXII Dragoons 1760–1945* (London: Gale & Polden, 1950).

G.S.C. Bishop, *The Story of the 23rd Hussars* (privately published, Germany, 1946).

George Blake, *Mountain and Flood: The History of 52nd Lowland Division 1939–1946* (Glasgow: Jacksons, 1950).

Jean Brisset, *The Charge of the Bull: A History of the 11th Armoured Division in Normandy 1944* (Norwich: Bates, 1989).

G. Burden (ed.), *History of the East Lancashire Regiment in the War 1939–45* (privately published, 1953).

Michael Carver, *Second to None: The Royal Scots Greys, 1919–1945* (London: McCorquodale, 1954).

G. Courage, *The History of 15/19 The King's Royal Hussars* (Aldershot: Gale & Polden, 1949).

D.S. Daniel, *The Royal Hampshire Regiment 1918–1954* (Aldershot: Gale & Polden, 1954).

Patrick Delaforce, *The Black Bull: From Normandy to the Baltic with the 11th Armoured Division* (Stroud: Sutton, 1993); *The Polar Bears: Monty's Left Flank* (Stroud: Sutton, 1995); *Monty's Marauders: Black Rat 4th Armoured Brigade and Red Fox 8th Armoured Brigade* (Stroud: Sutton, 1993); *The Fighting Wessex Wyverns: From Normandy to Bremerhaven with 43rd Division* (Stroud: Sutton, 1994); *Churchill's Desert Rats: From Normandy to Berlin with the 7th Armoured Division* (Stroud: Sutton, 1994).

J.C.J. Elson, *The 7th Battalion South Staffordshire Regiment 1939–44* (privately published, 1990–2007 edn).

D. Erskine, *The Scots Guards 1919–1945* (Edinburgh: W. Clowes, 1956).

H. Essame, *The 43rd Wessex Division at War, 1944–5* (London: Clowes, 1952).

D.J.L. Fitzgerald, *History of the Irish Guards in the Second World War* (Aldershot: Gale & Polden, 1952).

Patrick Forbes, *6th Guards Tank Brigade: The Story of Guardsmen in Churchill Tanks* (London: Sampson Low, Marston & Co., 1946).

Ronald Gill and John Groves, *Club Route in Europe: The Story of 30 Corps in the European Campaign* (Germany: Degener, 1946).

G.R. Hartwell and M.A. Edwards, *The Story of 5th Battalion, the Dorsetshire Regiment in Northwest Europe* (privately published, 1945).

Andrew Holborn, *The 56th Infantry Brigade and D-Day: An Independent Infantry Brigade and the Campaign in North West Europe 1944–45* (London: Continuum, 2010).

G.S. Jackson and VIII Corps Staff, *Operations of Eight Corps: An Account of Operations from Normandy to the River Rhine* (London: St Clements Press, 1948)

N.C.E. Kenrick, *The Wiltshire Regiment in the Second World War: 4th/5th Battalions*, 2nd edn (Salisbury: RGBW, 2006); *The Wiltshire Regiment in the Second World War, 5th Battalion* (Salisbury: Rifles Wardrobe and Museum Trust, 2006).

Peter Knight, *The 59th Division: Its War Story* (London: Muller, 1954).

Jean-Luc Leleu, *10th SS Panzer Division 'Frundsberg'* (Bayeux: Heimdal, 2001).

P.J. Lewis and I.R. English, *8th Battalion The Durham Light Infantry 1939–1945* (privately published, 1949).

John Lincoln, *Thank God and the Infantry: From D-Day to VE Day with the 1st Battalion Royal Norfolk Regiment* (Stroud: Sutton, 1994).

T.M. Lindsay, *Sherwood Rangers 1939–45* (London: Burrup, Mathieson & Co., 1952).

H.G. Martin, *History of the 15th Scottish Infantry Division, 1939–1945* (London: Blackwood & Sons, 1948).

Robin McNish, *Iron Division* (HQ, 3rd Division, 2000 – 3rd edn).

J.L.J. Meredith, *The Story of 7th Battalion Somerset Light Infantry – Prince Albert's* (privately published, 1946).

Hubert Meyer, *The History of the 12th SS Panzer Division Hitlerjugend* (Winnipeg, Manitoba: J.J. Fedorowicz, 1994).

C.H. Miller, *History of 13/18 Hussars, 1922–1947* (London: Bradshaw, 1949).

William Moore, *Panzer Bait: With the 3rd Royal Tank Regiment 1940–1944* (London: Leo Cooper, 1991).

Robin Neillands, *The Desert Rats: 7th Armoured Division 1940–45* (London: Weidenfeld & Nicolson, 1991).

David Orr and David Truesdale, *The Rifles are There: 1st and 2nd Battalions The Royal Ulster Rifles in the Second World War* (Barnsley: Pen & Sword, 2005).

Michael Reynolds, *Steel Inferno: I SS Panzer Corps in Normandy* (London: Spellmount, 1997); *Sons of the Reich: II SS Panzer Corps* (London: Spellmount, 2002); *Eagles and Bulldogs in Normandy 1944* (Staplehurst: Spellmount, 2003).

David Rissik, *The DLI at War: The History of the Durham Light Infantry, 1939–1945* (Uckfield: Naval and Military Press, 2004).

Ian Robertson, *From Normandy to the Baltic: The Story of the 44th Lowland Infantry Brigade of the 15th Scottish Division from D-Day to the End of the War in Europe* (Germany, privately published, 1945).

Earl of Rosse and E.R.H. Hill, *The Story of the Guards Armoured Division 1941–45* (London: Geoffrey Bles, 1956).

J.B. Salmond, *The History of the 51st Highland Division* (London: Blackwood, 1953).

Norman Scarfe, *Assault Division: A History of 3rd Division from the Invasion of Normandy to the Surrender of Germany* (London: Collins, 1947).

Frederick Steinhardt, *Panzer Lehr Division 1944–45* (Solihull: Helion, 2008).

Ned Thornburn, *The 4th KSLI in Normandy: June to August 1944* (Shrewsbury: Castle Museum, 1990); *After Antwerp: The Long Haul to Victory – The Part Played by 4th Battalion King's Shropshire Light Infantry in the Overthrow of the Third Reich, September 1944 to May 1945* (Shrewsbury: Castle Museum, 1993).

Gerald Verney, *The Desert Rats: The 7th Armoured Division in World War Two* (London: Greenhill, 1996 edn – first published 1954).

A.A. Vince, *The Pompadours: 2nd Battalion Essex Regiment – D-Day to VE Day in Northwest Europe* (originally late 1940s – reprinted 1987).

[illegible] *the Dorset Regiment, June 1944 to May 1945* (Eastbourne: Rowe, [illegible]; regimental museum reprint).

Edward Wilson, *Press on Regardless: The Story of the Fifth Royal Tank Regiment in World War Two* (Staplehurst, Kent: Spellmount, 2003).

Robert Woollcombe, *Lion Rampant* (London: Chatto & Windus, 1955).

Interviews

Harry Askew, 2012.
Dennis Avey, 2012.
Austin Baker, 2003.
Andrew Burn, 2002.
Jim Caswell, 2004.
Bill Close, 2002.
Dickie Cox, 2012.
Roy Dixon, 2002.
Frank Duckett, 2012.

Joe Ekins, 2012.
Ray Gordon, 2011.
Vic Gregg, 2011.
Ian Hamerton, 2011.
Ted Hunt, 2011.
Mike Hutchinson, 2012.
Trevor Jenks, 2011.
Stan Jones, 1997.
Johnny Langdon, 2002.
Dennis Laws, 2011.
Robin Lemon, 2002.
Bill Partridge, 2011.
Stan Proctor, 2012.
Reg Spittles, 2012.
Ken Tout, 2011.
Peter Walker, 2012.

Royal Military Academy Sandhurst, Camberley

Hans von Luck, interview 1979.
Freimark von Rosen, interview 1979.
David Stileman, interview 1979.

Merville Battery Museum, Normandy

Terence Otway, video interview.

Media Sources

Films: *The Longest Day* (1962); *A Bridge Too Far* (1977); *Saving Private Ryan* (1998).
Television: BBC TV documentary, *Weekend Nazis* (2007); *Band of Brothers* (2001).
DVD & Video: *The Fighting Wessex Wyverns: Their Legacy* (2008); Hill 112 documentary, Albert Figg; Peter Duckers, *The History of the King's Shropshire Light Infantry* (1998).

Internet Sources

Corporal G.B. Bland quoted at http://daimlerfightingvehicles.co.uk/DFVFile%20Part%20D001aHoushold%20Cavalry%2019391945.pdf.
Martin Blumenson, 'General Bradley's Decision at Argentan (13 August 1944)', in *Command Decisions*, online edn, Center of Military History, Department of the Army, Washington, DC, 2000 (originally published in 1959).
Combined Arms Research Digital Library, http://cgsc.contentdm.oclc.org.
Memoir of Roy Young, 72nd Field Company, RE, contributed to BBC People's War online programme, June 2005 – http://www.bbc.co.uk/history/ww2peopleswar/stories/72/a4281572.shtml.

Theses

C. Bielecki, 'Mail and Morale in the British Army in World War Two', University College London, MA (1997).
Sam E.J. Cates, 'Why was General Richard O'Connor's Command in Northwest Europe Less Effective than Expected?', US Army Command and General Staff College, Fort Leavenworth, Kansas, MA (2011).
Charles Forrester, ' "Montgomery and His Legions": A Study of Operational Development, Innovation and Command in 21st Army Group, Northwest Europe 1944–45', University of Leeds, PhD (2010).

Joel J. Jefferson, 'Operation Market Garden: Ultra Intelligence Ignored', US Army Command and General Staff College, Fort Leavenworth, Kansas, MA (1998).

John Peaty, 'British Army Manpower Crisis 1944', King's College, London, PhD (2000).

Andrew Robinson, 'The British Sixth Airborne Division in Normandy 6 June–27 August 1944', University of Birmingham, MPhil (2008).

Ethan Rawls Williams, '50th Division in Normandy: A Critical Analysis of the British 50th (Northumbrian) Division on D-Day and in the Battle of Normandy', US Army Command and General Staff College, Fort Leavenworth, Kansas (1997).

INDEX